Shojo Beat

BABY & Me

Vol. 17

Story & Art by **Marimo Ragawa**

Baby & Me

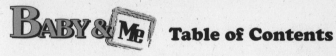

Table of Contents

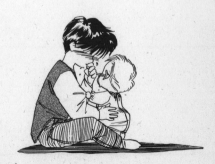

BABY & ME, Vol. 17
Shojo Beat Manga Edition

Story & Art by
MARIMO RAGAWA

English Adaptation/Lance Caselman
Translation/JN Productions
Touch-up Art & Lettering/HudsonYards
Design/Yuki Ameda
Editor/Shaenon K. Garrity

VP, Production/Alvin Lu
VP, Publishing Licensing/Rika Inouye
VP, Sales & Product Marketing/Gonzalo Ferreyra
VP, Creative/Linda Espinosa
Publisher/Hyoe Narita

Akachan to Boku by Marimo Ragawa © Marimo Ragawa
1997. All rights reserved. First published in Japan in 1997 by
HAKUSENSHA, Inc., Tokyo. English language translation
rights arranged with HAKUSENSHA, Inc., Tokyo.

The stories, characters and incidents mentioned in this
publication are entirely fictional.

Printed in Canada

Published by VIZ Media, LLC
P.O. Box 77010
San Francisco, CA 94107

10 9 8 7 6 5 4 3 2 1
First printing, December 2009

www.viz.com

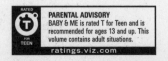

PARENTAL ADVISORY
BABY & ME is rated T for Teen and is
recommended for ages 13 and up. This
volume contains adult situations.
ratings.viz.com

www.shojobeat.com

BABY & ME

Creator: Marimo Ragawa

SBM Title: *Baby & Me*

Date of Birth: September 21

Blood Type: B

Major Works: *Time Limit, Baby & Me, N.Y. N.Y.,* and *Shanimuni—Go* (Desperately—Go)

Marimo Ragawa first started submitting manga to a comic magazine when she was 12 years old. She kept up her submissions for four years, but to no avail. She decided to submit her work to the magazine *Hana to Yume*, where she received Top Prize in the Monthly Manga Contest as well as an honorable mention (Kasaku) in the magazine's Big Challenge contest. Her first manga was titled *Time Limit*. *Baby & Me* was honored with a Shogakukan Manga Award in 1995 and was spun off into an anime.

Ragawa's work showcases some very cute and expressive line work along with an incredible ability to depict complex emotions and relationships. Some of her other works include *N.Y. N.Y.* and the tennis manga *Shanimuni—Go*.

Ragawa has two brothers and two sisters.

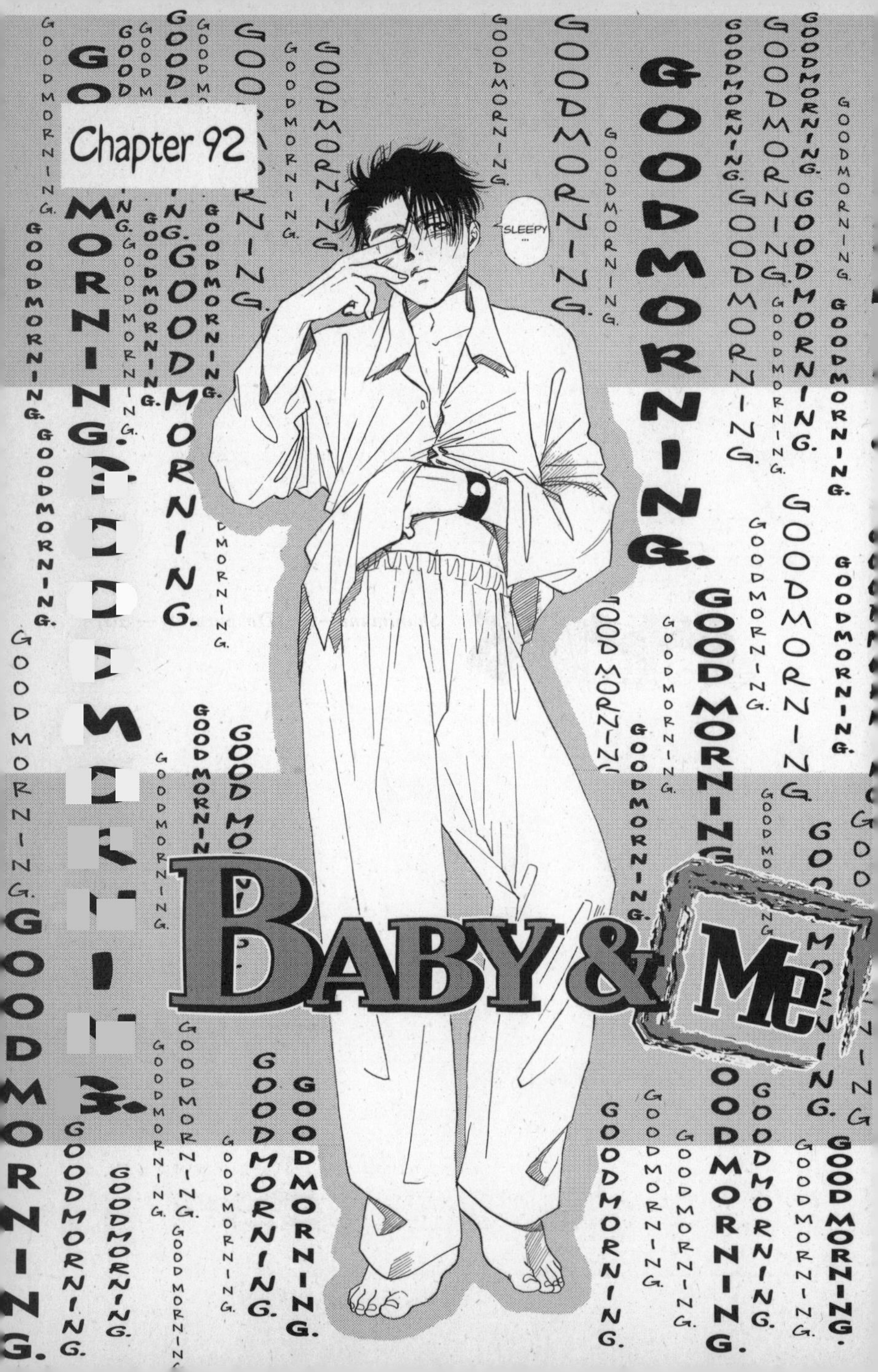
Chapter 92
SLEEPY ...
GOODMORNING.
BABY & Me

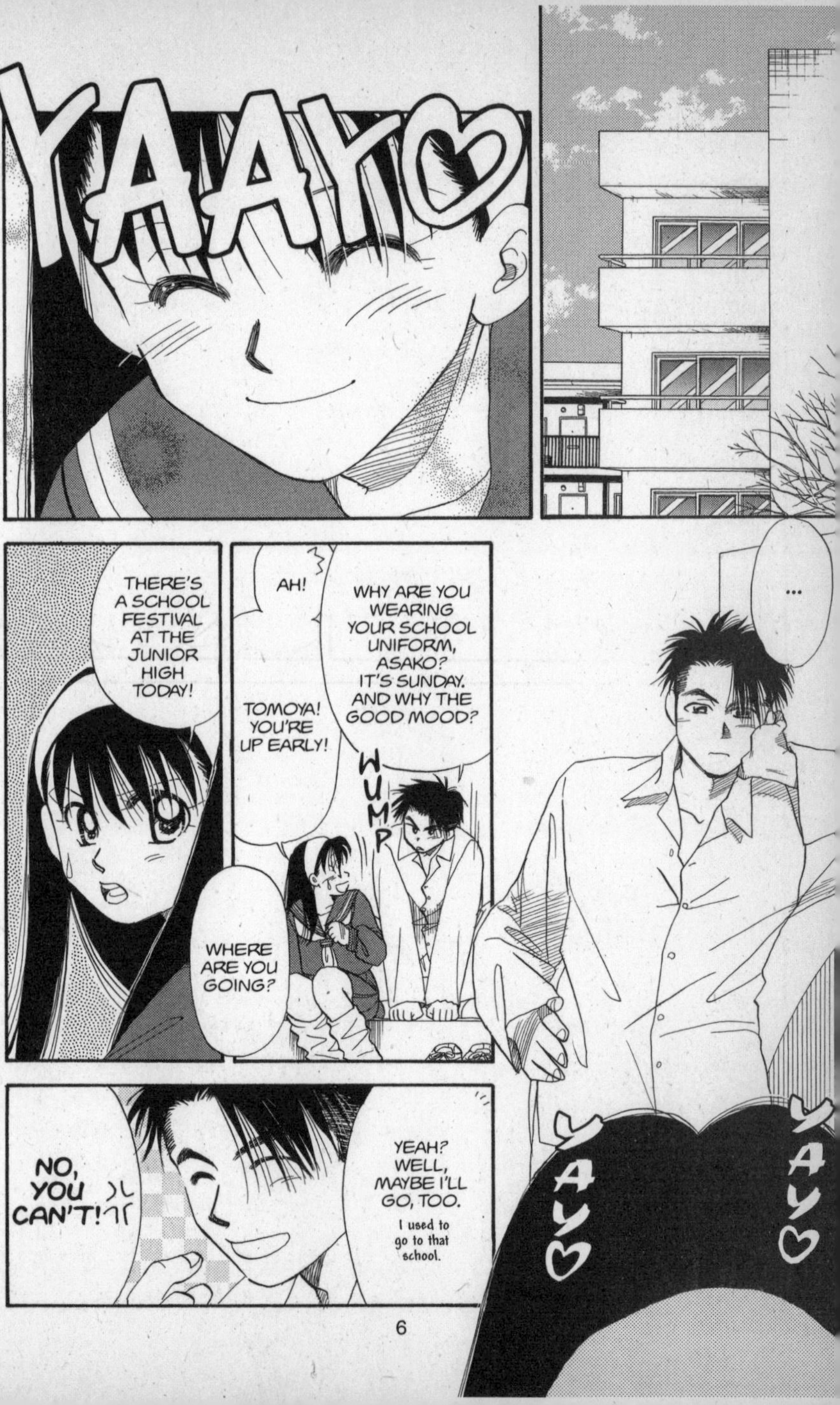
YAAY♡
...
YAY♡ YAY♡
WHY ARE YOU WEARING YOUR SCHOOL UNIFORM, ASAKO? IT'S SUNDAY. AND WHY THE GOOD MOOD?
AH!
TOMOYA! YOU'RE UP EARLY!
WUMP
WHERE ARE YOU GOING?
THERE'S A SCHOOL FESTIVAL AT THE JUNIOR HIGH TODAY!
YEAH? WELL, MAYBE I'LL GO, TOO.
I used to go to that school.
NO, YOU CAN'T!

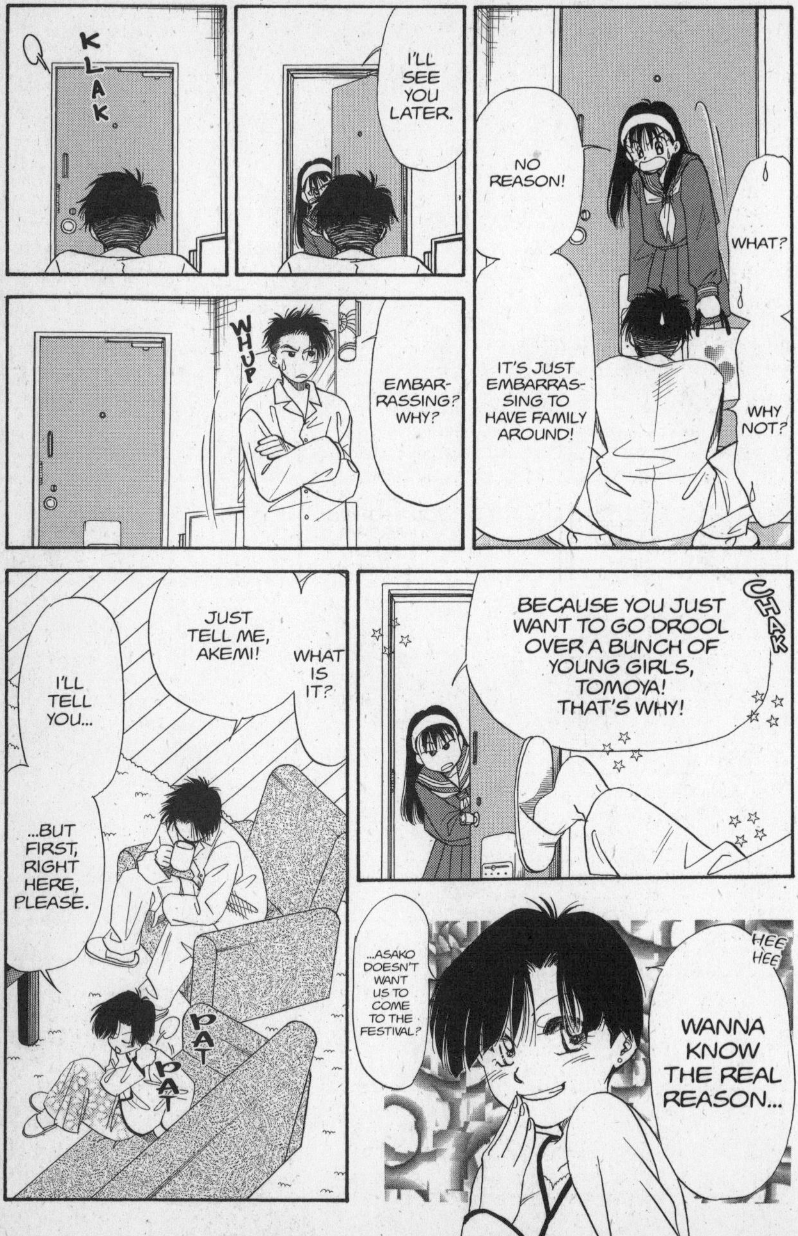
WHAT?
NO REASON!
WHY NOT?
IT'S JUST EMBARRAS-SING TO HAVE FAMILY AROUND!
I'LL SEE YOU LATER.
KLAK
EMBAR-RASSING? WHY?
WHUP
CHAK
BECAUSE YOU JUST WANT TO GO DROOL OVER A BUNCH OF YOUNG GIRLS, TOMOYA! THAT'S WHY!
HEE HEE
WANNA KNOW THE REAL REASON...
...ASAKO DOESN'T WANT US TO COME TO THE FESTIVAL?
WHAT IS IT?
JUST TELL ME, AKEMI!
I'LL TELL YOU...
...BUT FIRST, RIGHT HERE, PLEASE.
PAT
PAT

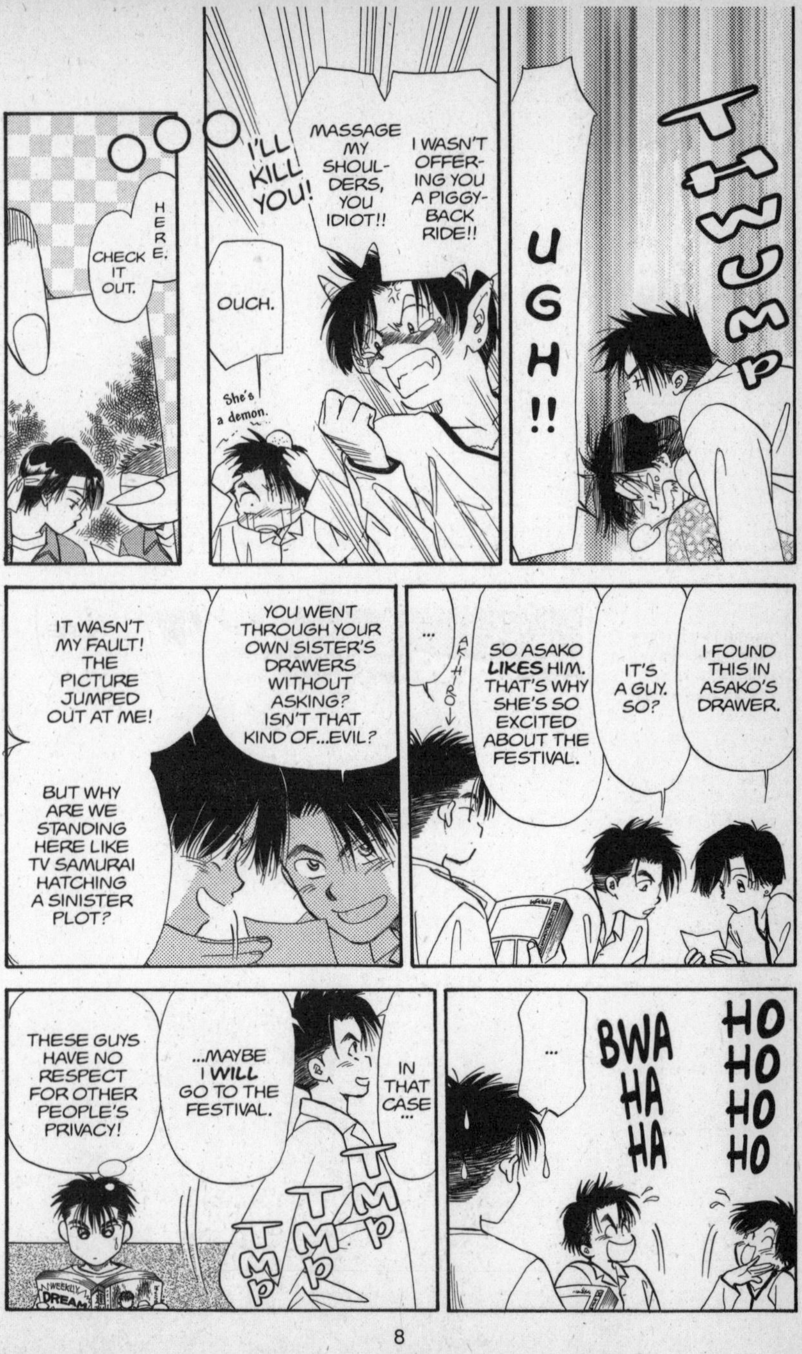
THWUMP
UGH!!
I WASN'T OFFERING YOU A PIGGY-BACK RIDE!!
MASSAGE MY SHOULDERS, YOU IDIOT!!
I'LL KILL YOU!
OUCH.
She's a demon.
HERE.
CHECK IT OUT.
I FOUND THIS IN ASAKO'S DRAWER.
IT'S A GUY. SO?
SO ASAKO **LIKES** HIM. THAT'S WHY SHE'S SO EXCITED ABOUT THE FESTIVAL.
AKIHIRO
...
YOU WENT THROUGH YOUR OWN SISTER'S DRAWERS WITHOUT ASKING? ISN'T THAT KIND OF...EVIL?
IT WASN'T MY FAULT! THE PICTURE JUMPED OUT AT ME!
BUT WHY ARE WE STANDING HERE LIKE TV SAMURAI HATCHING A SINISTER PLOT?
HO HO HO HO HO
BWA HA HA HA
...
IN THAT CASE...
...MAYBE I **WILL** GO TO THE FESTIVAL.
TMP TMP TMP
THESE GUYS HAVE NO RESPECT FOR OTHER PEOPLE'S PRIVACY!
WEEKLY DREAM

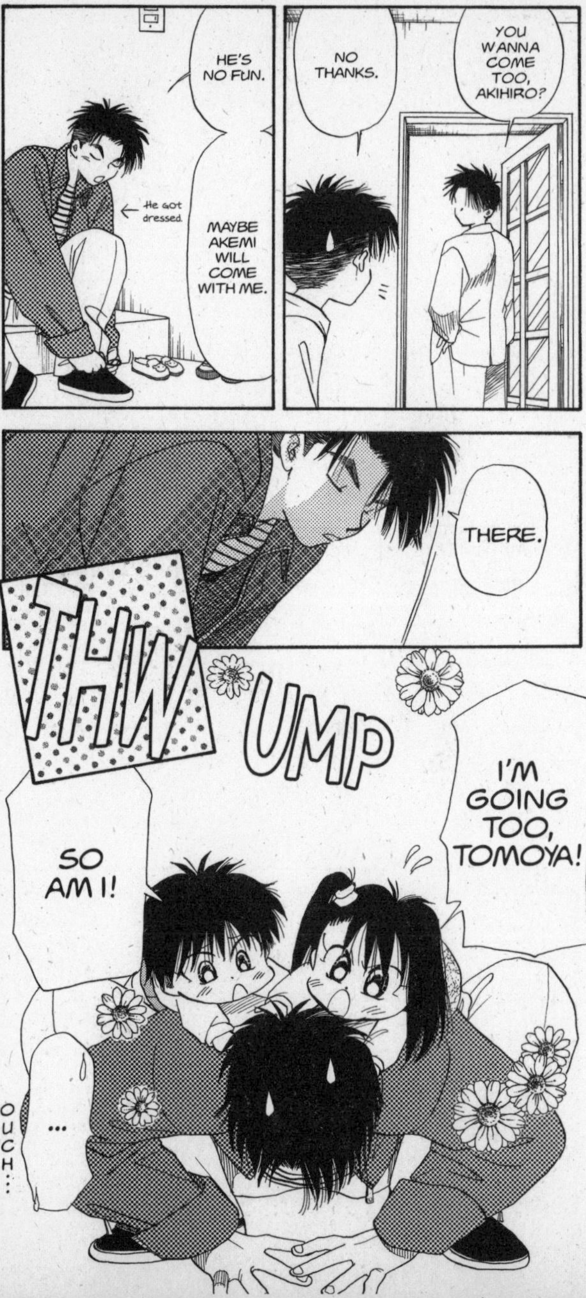
YOU WANNA COME TOO, AKIHIRO?
NO THANKS.
HE'S NO FUN.
He got dressed.
MAYBE AKEMI WILL COME WITH ME.
THERE.
THWUMP
I'M GOING TOO, TOMOYA!
SO AM I!
...
OUCH...

Author's Note Part 1

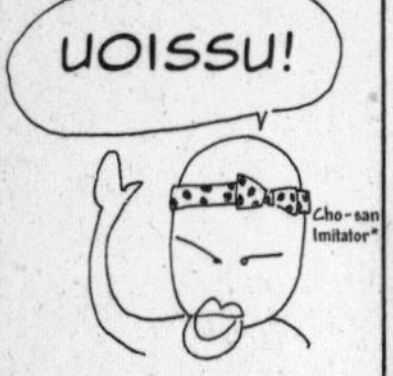
UOISSU!
Cho-san Imitator*

This is Marimo Ragawa. I just finished coloring some covers, so I'm exhausted. I don't mind coloring one or two covers at a time, but three is too much.

Anyway, here's volume 17. After I finished coloring the cover, I noticed that the faces were too much in close-up. If you compare this cover to all the previous volumes, you'll see the difference right away. Oh well, never mind.

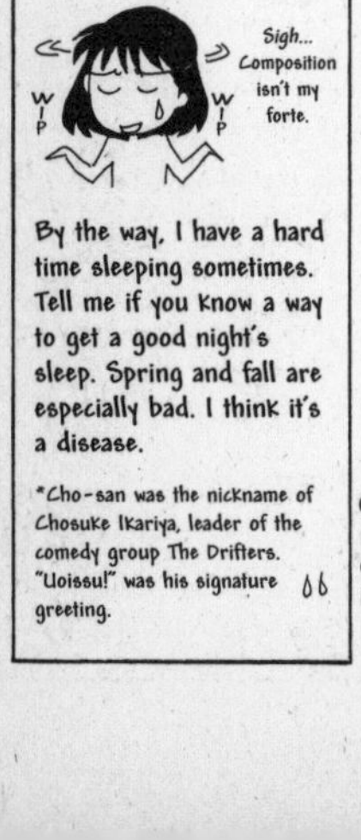
WIP
WIP
Sigh... Composition isn't my forte.

By the way, I have a hard time sleeping sometimes. Tell me if you know a way to get a good night's sleep. Spring and fall are especially bad. I think it's a disease.

*Cho-san was the nickname of Chosuke Ikariya, leader of the comedy group The Drifters. "Uoissu!" was his signature greeting.

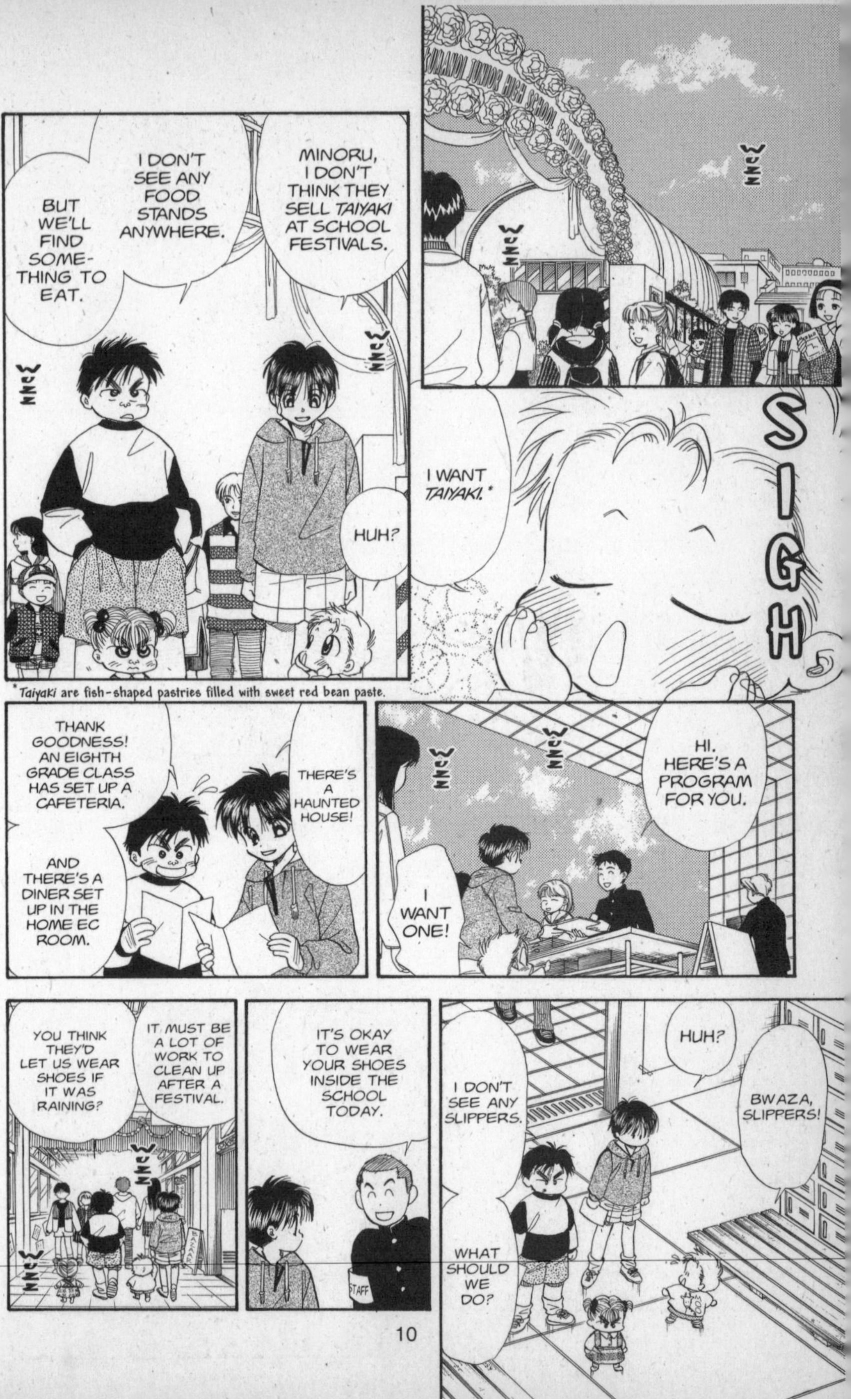
JUNIOR HIGH SCHOOL FESTIVAL
WUNN
WUNN
SIGH
I WANT TAIYAKI.*
HUH?
MINORU, I DON'T THINK THEY SELL TAIYAKI AT SCHOOL FESTIVALS.
I DON'T SEE ANY FOOD STANDS ANYWHERE.
BUT WE'LL FIND SOME-THING TO EAT.
WUNN
WUNN
HI. HERE'S A PROGRAM FOR YOU.
WUNN
I WANT ONE!
WUNN
THERE'S A HAUNTED HOUSE!
THANK GOODNESS! AN EIGHTH GRADE CLASS HAS SET UP A CAFETERIA.
AND THERE'S A DINER SET UP IN THE HOME EC ROOM.
BWAZA, SLIPPERS!
HUH?
I DON'T SEE ANY SLIPPERS.
WHAT SHOULD WE DO?
IT'S OKAY TO WEAR YOUR SHOES INSIDE THE SCHOOL TODAY.
STAFF
IT MUST BE A LOT OF WORK TO CLEAN UP AFTER A FESTIVAL.
YOU THINK THEY'D LET US WEAR SHOES IF IT WAS RAINING?
WUNN
WUNN

*Taiyaki are fish-shaped pastries filled with sweet red bean paste.

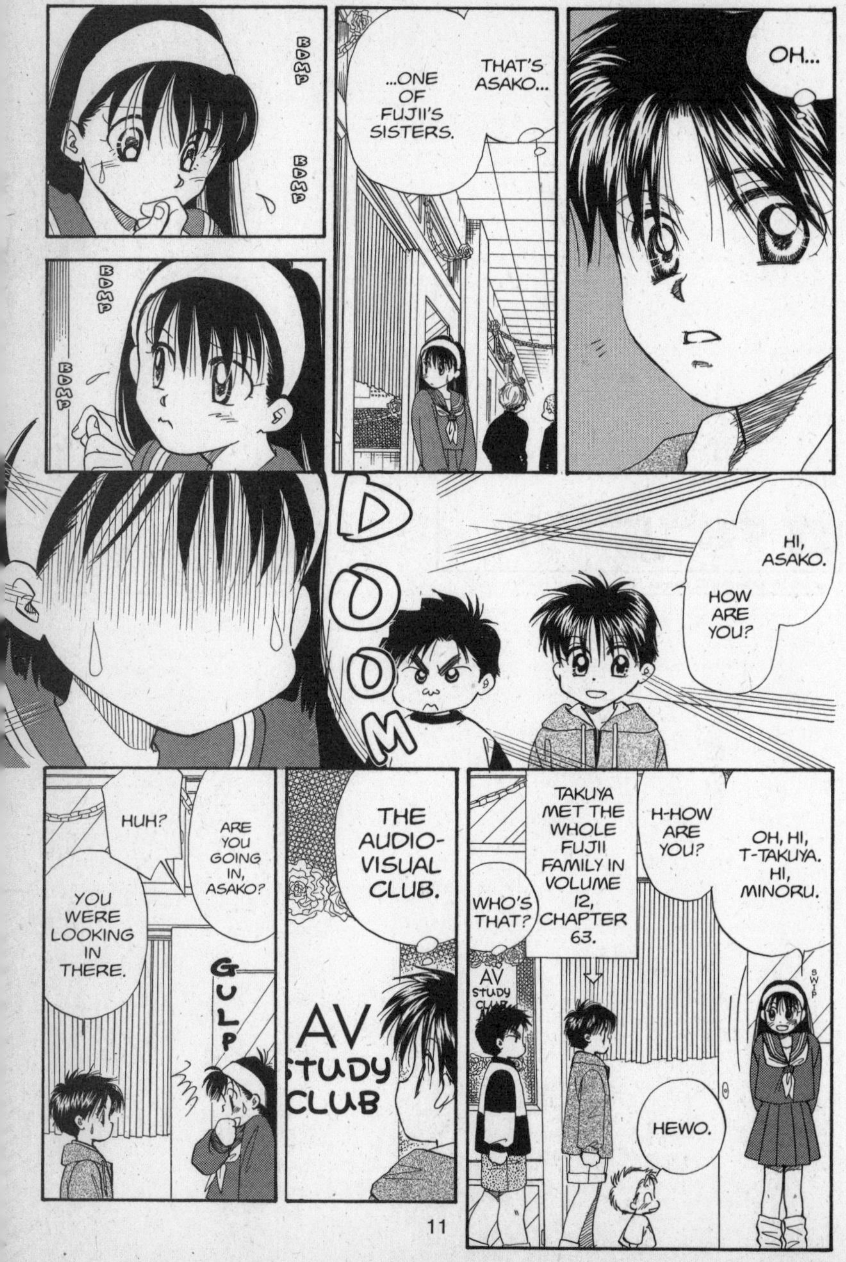
OH...
THAT'S ASAKO...
...ONE OF FUJII'S SISTERS.
BDMP BDMP
BDMP BDMP
HI, ASAKO.
HOW ARE YOU?
DOOM
OH, HI, T-TAKUYA. HI, MINORU.
SWIP
H-HOW ARE YOU?
TAKUYA MET THE WHOLE FUJII FAMILY IN VOLUME 12, CHAPTER 63.
WHO'S THAT?
AV STUDY CLUB
HEWO.
THE AUDIO-VISUAL CLUB.
AV STUDY CLUB
ARE YOU GOING IN, ASAKO?
HUH?
YOU WERE LOOKING IN THERE.
GULP

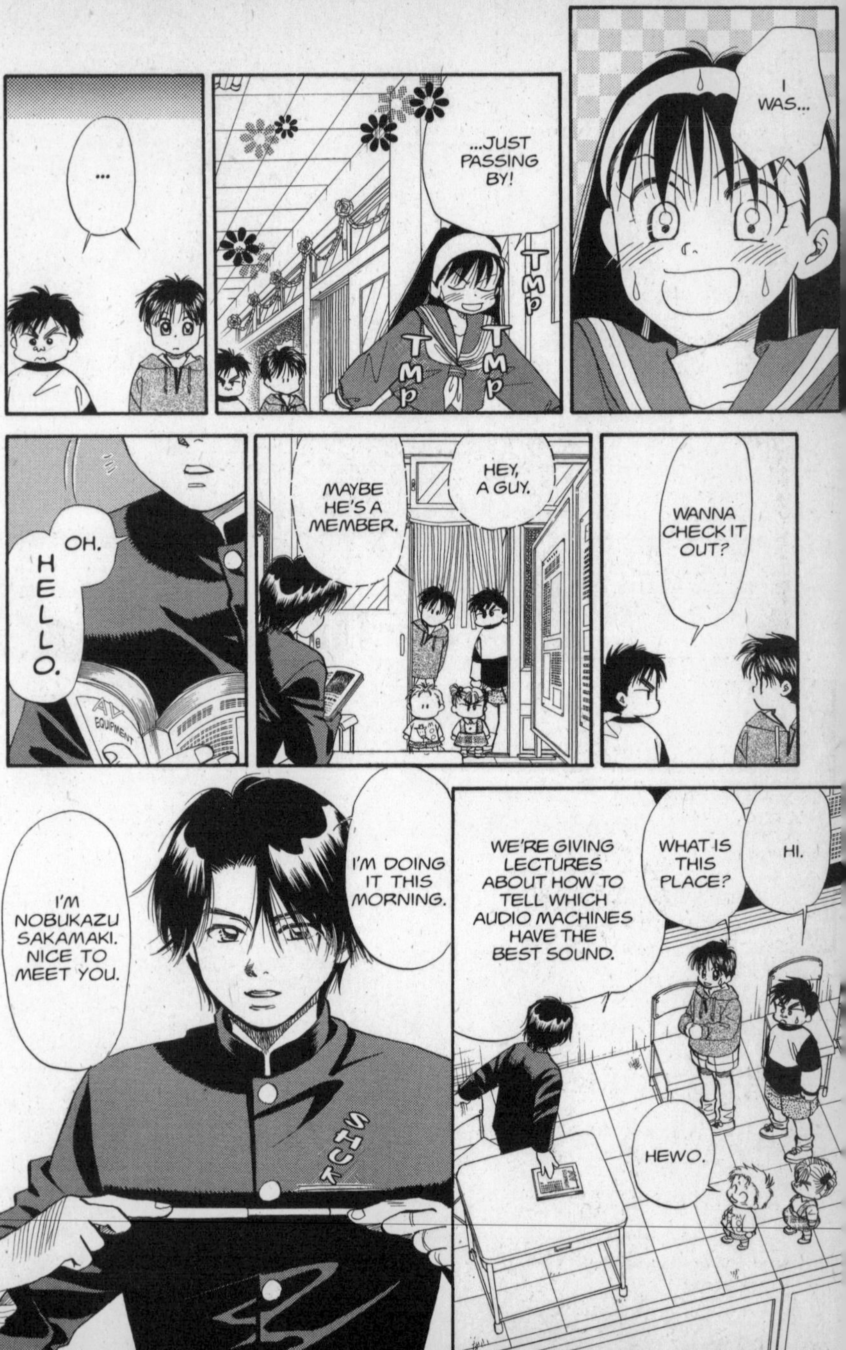
I WAS...
...JUST PASSING BY!
TMP
TMP
TMP
...
WANNA CHECK IT OUT?
HEY, A GUY.
MAYBE HE'S A MEMBER.
OH.
HELLO.
AV EQUIPMENT
HI.
WHAT IS THIS PLACE?
WE'RE GIVING LECTURES ABOUT HOW TO TELL WHICH AUDIO MACHINES HAVE THE BEST SOUND.
HEWO.
I'M DOING IT THIS MORNING.
I'M NOBUKAZU SAKAMAKI. NICE TO MEET YOU.
SHUK

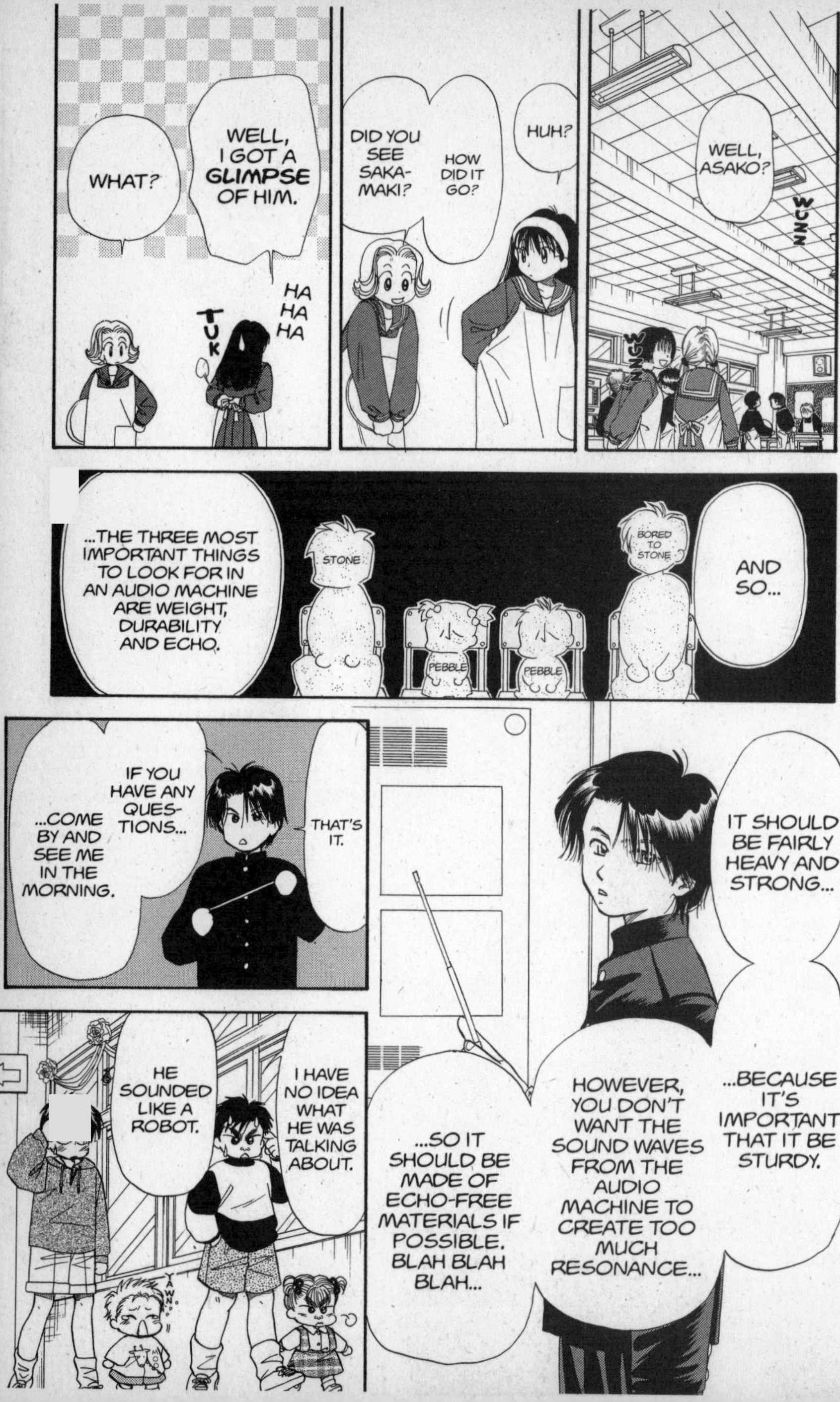
WELL, ASAKO?
WUZZ
WUZZ
HUH?
HOW DID IT GO?
DID YOU SEE SAKA-MAKI?
WELL, I GOT A GLIMPSE OF HIM.
HA HA HA
TUK
WHAT?
AND SO...
BORED TO STONE
PEBBLE
PEBBLE
STONE
...THE THREE MOST IMPORTANT THINGS TO LOOK FOR IN AN AUDIO MACHINE ARE WEIGHT, DURABILITY AND ECHO.
IT SHOULD BE FAIRLY HEAVY AND STRONG...
...BECAUSE IT'S IMPORTANT THAT IT BE STURDY.
HOWEVER, YOU DON'T WANT THE SOUND WAVES FROM THE AUDIO MACHINE TO CREATE TOO MUCH RESONANCE...
...SO IT SHOULD BE MADE OF ECHO-FREE MATERIALS IF POSSIBLE. BLAH BLAH BLAH...
THAT'S IT.
IF YOU HAVE ANY QUES-TIONS...
...COME BY AND SEE ME IN THE MORNING.
I HAVE NO IDEA WHAT HE WAS TALKING ABOUT.
HE SOUNDED LIKE A ROBOT.
YAWN

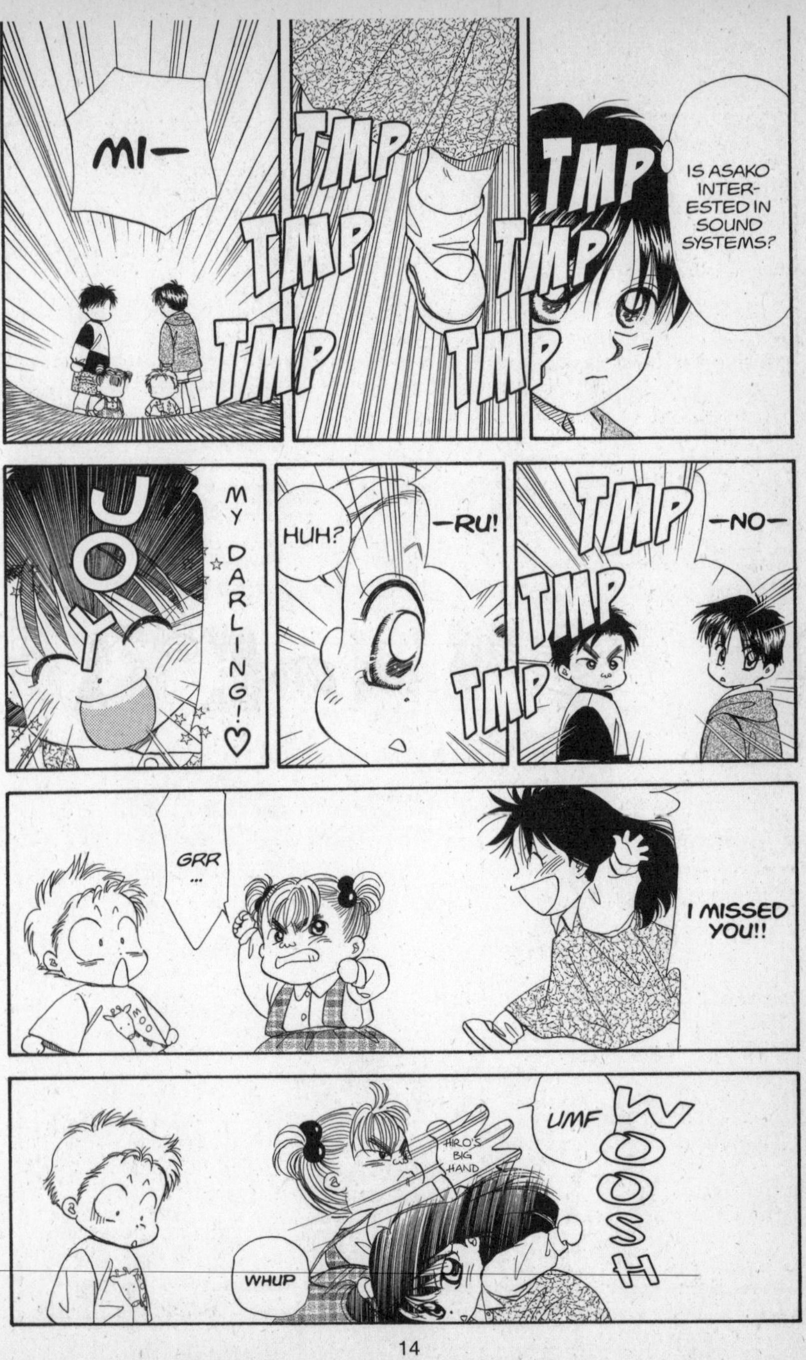
IS ASAKO INTER-ESTED IN SOUND SYSTEMS?
TMP
TMP
TMP
TMP
TMP
TMP
MI—
-NO-
TMP
TMP
TMP
-RU!
HUH?
MY DARLING! ♥
JOY
I MISSED YOU!!
GRR ...
MOO
WOOSH
UMF
HIRO'S BIG HAND
WHUP

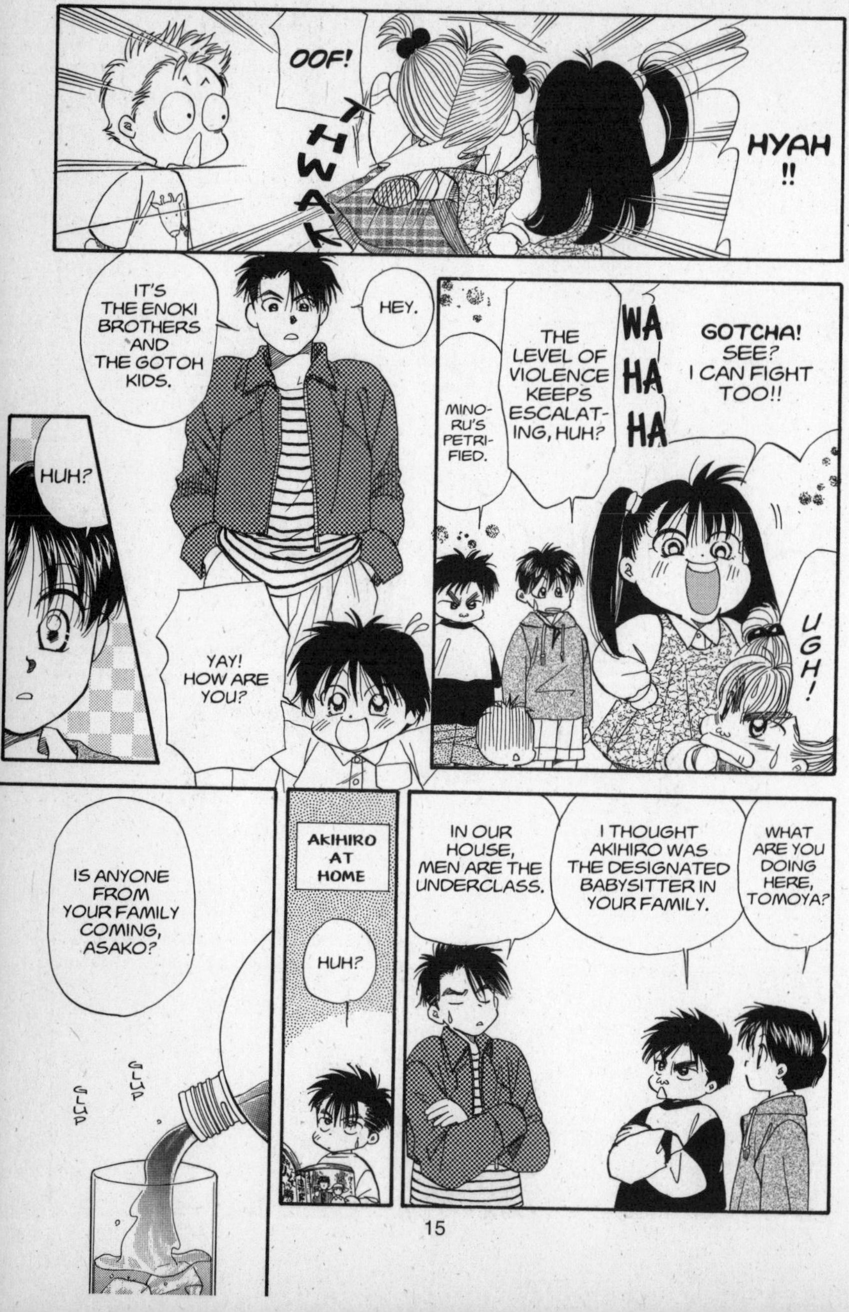
HYAH!!
OOF!
THWAK
GOTCHA! SEE? I CAN FIGHT TOO!!
WA HA HA
THE LEVEL OF VIOLENCE KEEPS ESCALATING, HUH?
MINORU'S PETRIFIED.
UGH!
HEY.
IT'S THE ENOKI BROTHERS AND THE GOTOH KIDS.
YAY! HOW ARE YOU?
HUH?
WHAT ARE YOU DOING HERE, TOMOYA?
I THOUGHT AKIHIRO WAS THE DESIGNATED BABYSITTER IN YOUR FAMILY.
IN OUR HOUSE, MEN ARE THE UNDERCLASS.
AKIHIRO AT HOME
HUH?
IS ANYONE FROM YOUR FAMILY COMING, ASAKO?
GLUP
GLUP

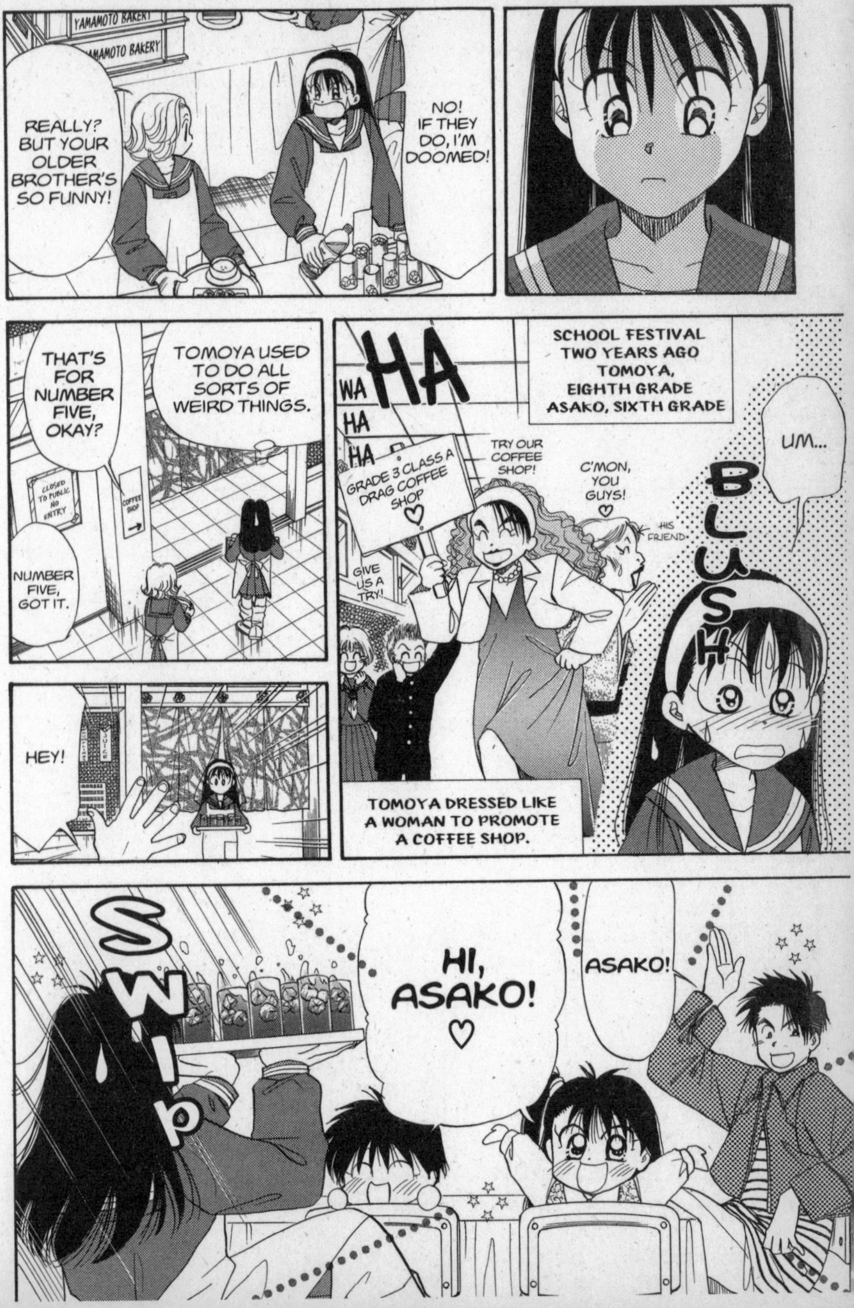
YAMAMOTO BAKERY
YAMAMOTO BAKERY
NO! IF THEY DO, I'M DOOMED!
REALLY? BUT YOUR OLDER BROTHER'S SO FUNNY!
SCHOOL FESTIVAL TWO YEARS AGO TOMOYA, EIGHTH GRADE ASAKO, SIXTH GRADE
UM...
BLUSH
WA HA HA HA
GRADE 3 CLASS A DRAG COFFEE SHOP ♡
TRY OUR COFFEE SHOP!
C'MON, YOU GUYS! ♡
HIS FRIEND
GIVE US A TRY!
TOMOYA DRESSED LIKE A WOMAN TO PROMOTE A COFFEE SHOP.
TOMOYA USED TO DO ALL SORTS OF WEIRD THINGS.
THAT'S FOR NUMBER FIVE, OKAY?
CLOSED TO PUBLIC NO ENTRY
COFFEE SHOP
NUMBER FIVE, GOT IT.
HEY!
JUICE
ASAKO!
HI, ASAKO! ♡
SWIP

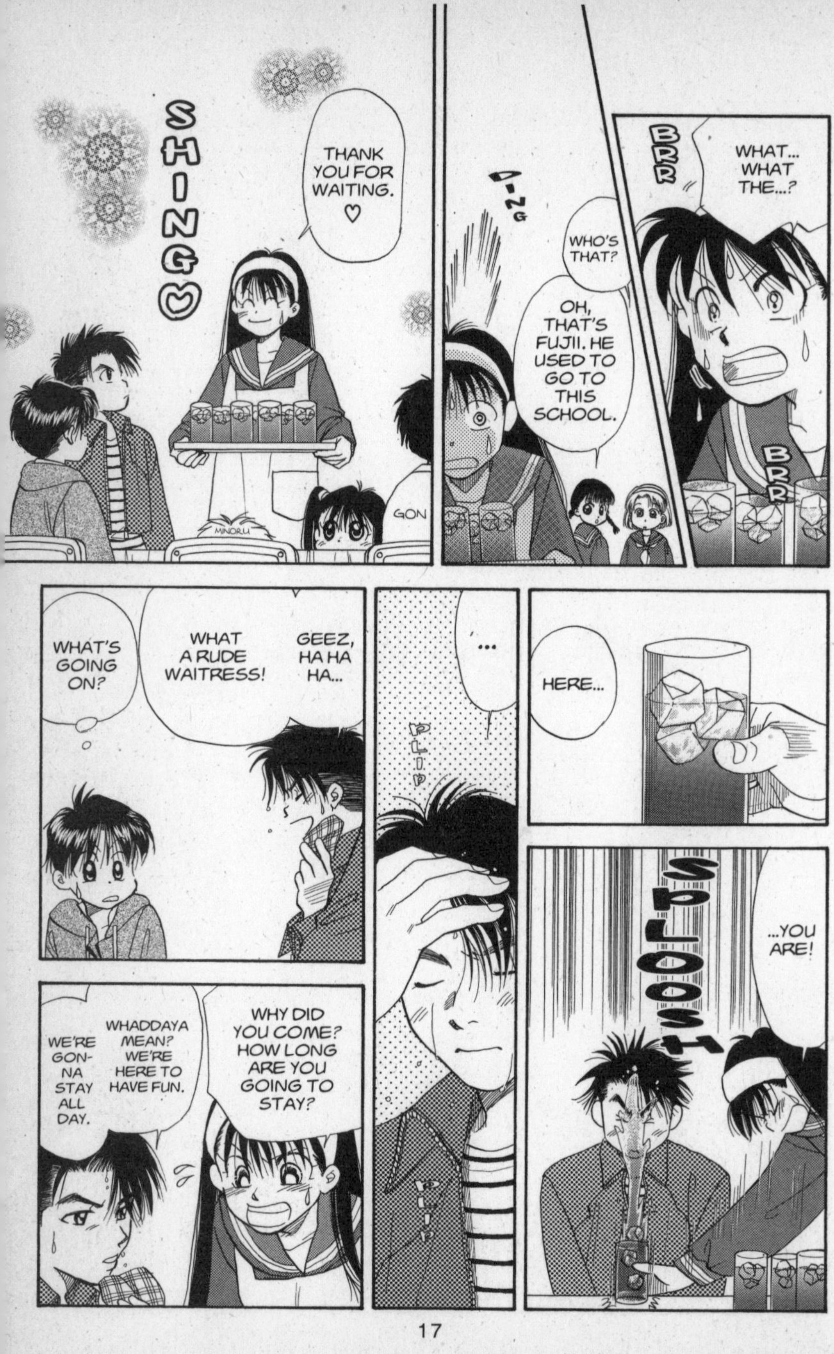
BRR
WHAT... WHAT THE...?
BRR
DING
WHO'S THAT?
OH, THAT'S FUJII. HE USED TO GO TO THIS SCHOOL.
SHINGO♡
THANK YOU FOR WAITING. ♡
MINORU
GON
HERE...
...YOU ARE!
SPLOOSH
...
PLIP
PLIP
GEEZ, HA HA HA...
WHAT A RUDE WAITRESS!
WHAT'S GOING ON?
WHY DID YOU COME? HOW LONG ARE YOU GOING TO STAY?
WHADDAYA MEAN? WE'RE HERE TO HAVE FUN.
WE'RE GON-NA STAY ALL DAY.

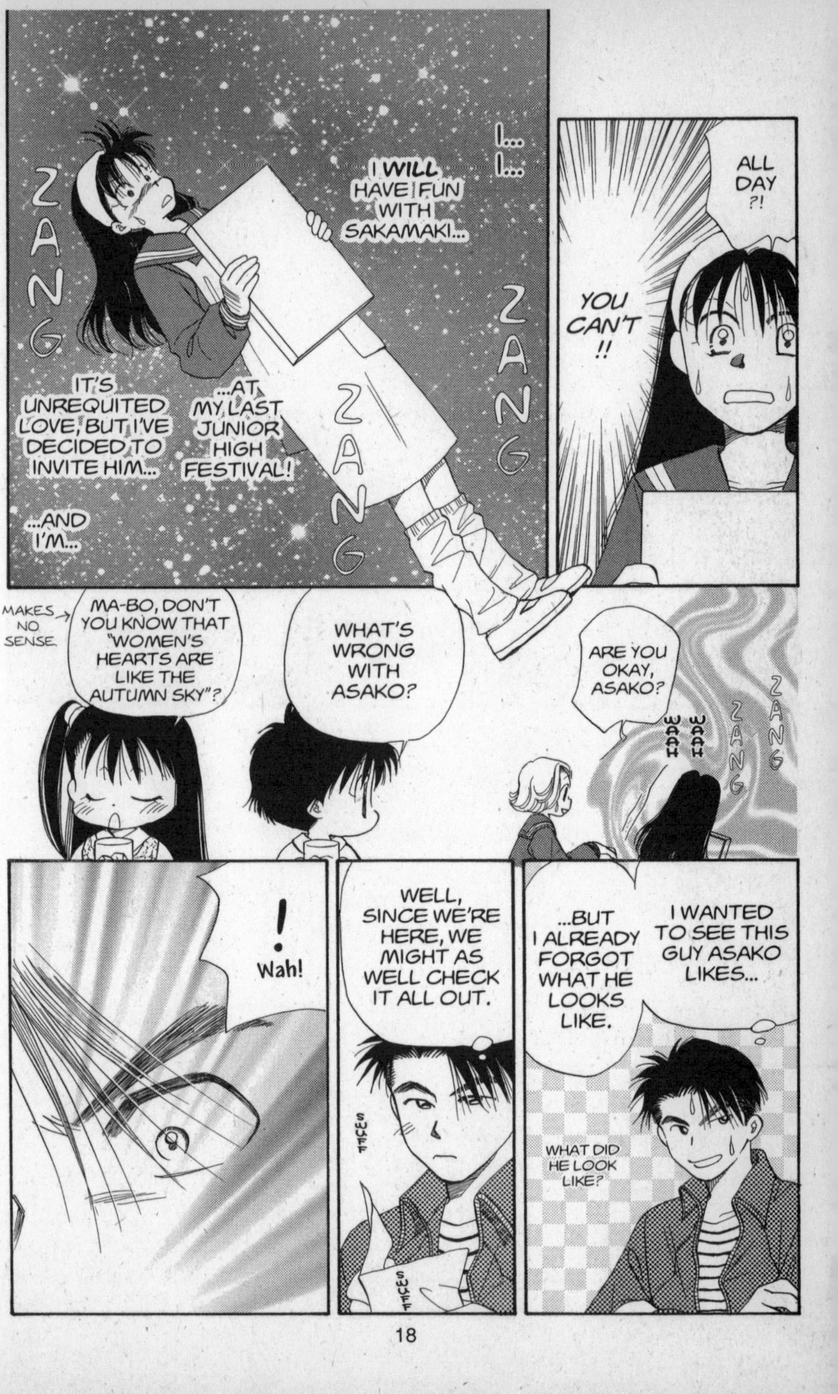
ALL DAY ?!
YOU CAN'T !!
I... I...
I WILL HAVE FUN WITH SAKAMAKI...
...AT MY LAST JUNIOR HIGH FESTIVAL!
IT'S UNREQUITED LOVE, BUT I'VE DECIDED TO INVITE HIM...
...AND I'M...
ZANG
ZANG
ZANG
ARE YOU OKAY, ASAKO?
ZANG
ZANG
WAAH WAAH
WHAT'S WRONG WITH ASAKO?
MA-BO, DON'T YOU KNOW THAT "WOMEN'S HEARTS ARE LIKE THE AUTUMN SKY"?
MAKES NO SENSE.
I WANTED TO SEE THIS GUY ASAKO LIKES...
...BUT I ALREADY FORGOT WHAT HE LOOKS LIKE.
WHAT DID HE LOOK LIKE?
WELL, SINCE WE'RE HERE, WE MIGHT AS WELL CHECK IT ALL OUT.
SWUFF
SWUFF
!
Wah!

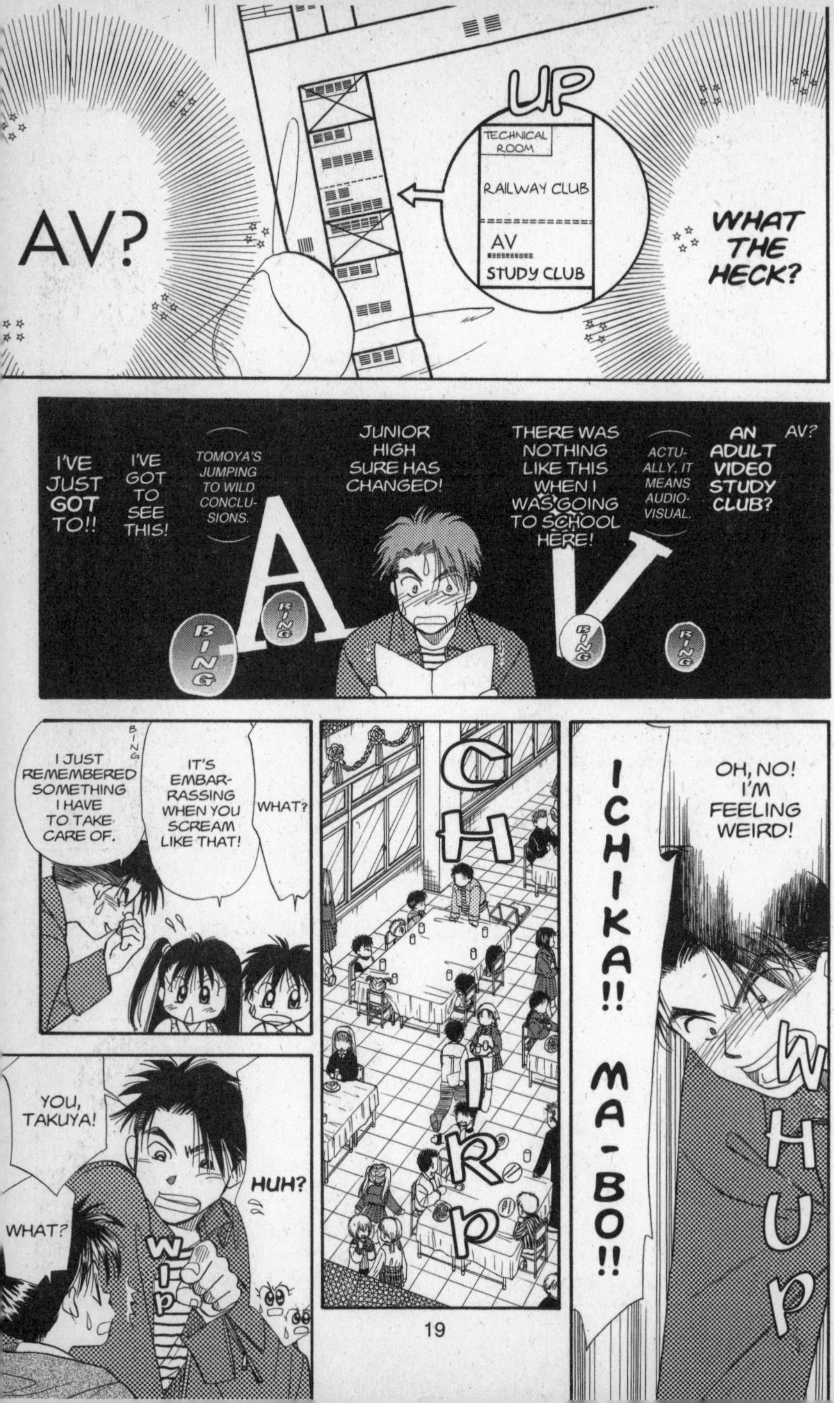
WHAT THE HECK?
UP
TECHNICAL ROOM
RAILWAY CLUB
AV
STUDY CLUB
AV?
AV?
AN ADULT VIDEO STUDY CLUB?
ACTUALLY, IT MEANS AUDIO-VISUAL.
THERE WAS NOTHING LIKE THIS WHEN I WAS GOING TO SCHOOL HERE!
JUNIOR HIGH SURE HAS CHANGED!
TOMOYA'S JUMPING TO WILD CONCLUSIONS.
I'VE GOT TO SEE THIS!
I'VE JUST GOT TO!!
A
V
BING
BING
BING
BING
OH, NO! I'M FEELING WEIRD!
WHUP
ICHIKA!! MA-BO!!
CHIRP
WHAT?
IT'S EMBARRASSING WHEN YOU SCREAM LIKE THAT!
BING
I JUST REMEMBERED SOMETHING I HAVE TO TAKE CARE OF.
YOU, TAKUYA!
HUH?
WHAT?
WIP

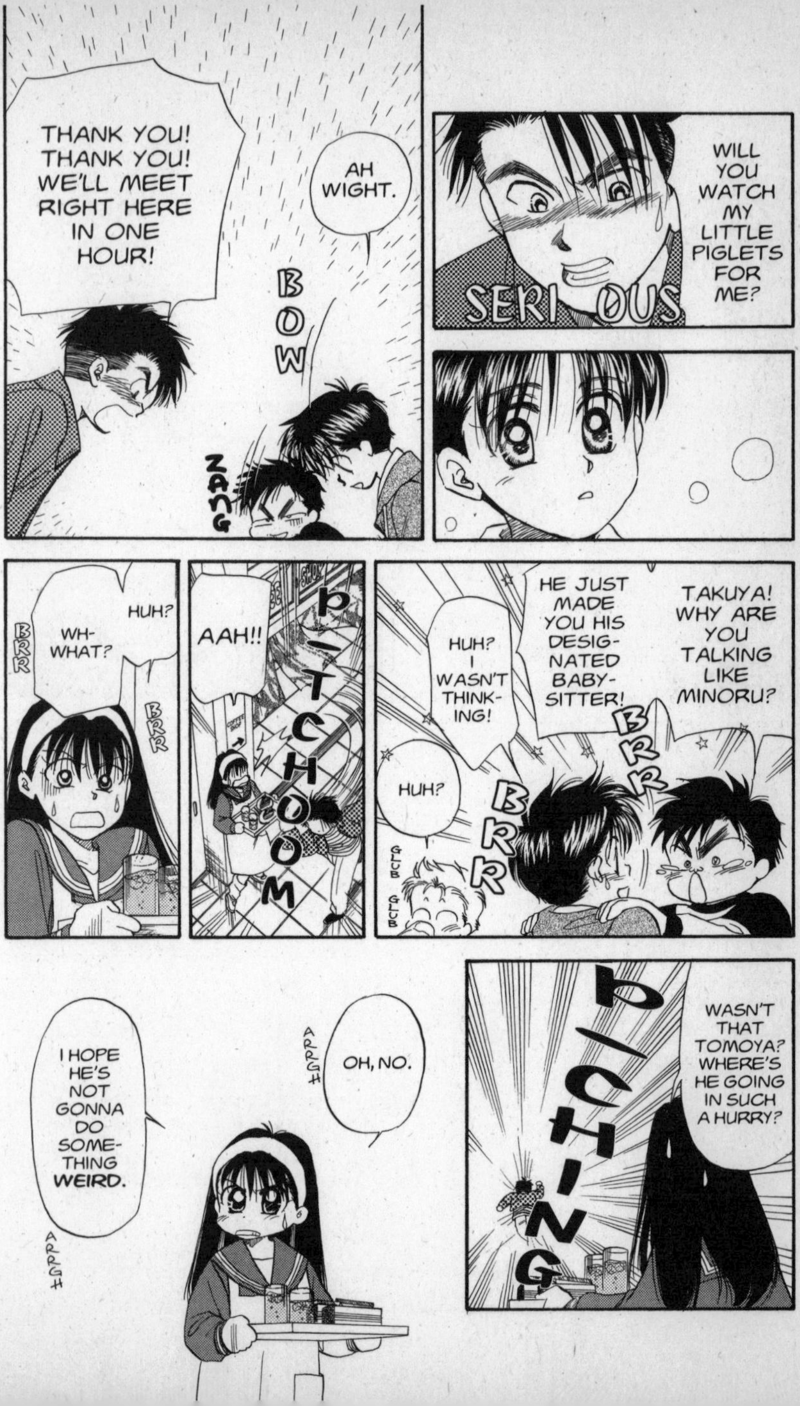
WILL YOU WATCH MY LITTLE PIGLETS FOR ME?
SERI OUS
AH WIGHT.
BOW
THANK YOU! THANK YOU! WE'LL MEET RIGHT HERE IN ONE HOUR!
ZANG
TAKUYA! WHY ARE YOU TALKING LIKE MINORU?
HE JUST MADE YOU HIS DESIGNATED BABY-SITTER!
HUH? I WASN'T THINKING!
BRR
BRR
HUH?
GLUB GLUB
P-TCHOOM
AAH!!
HUH?
WH-WHAT?
BRR
BRR
WASN'T THAT TOMOYA? WHERE'S HE GOING IN SUCH A HURRY?
P/CHING
OH, NO.
ARRGH
I HOPE HE'S NOT GONNA DO SOMETHING **WEIRD**.
ARRGH

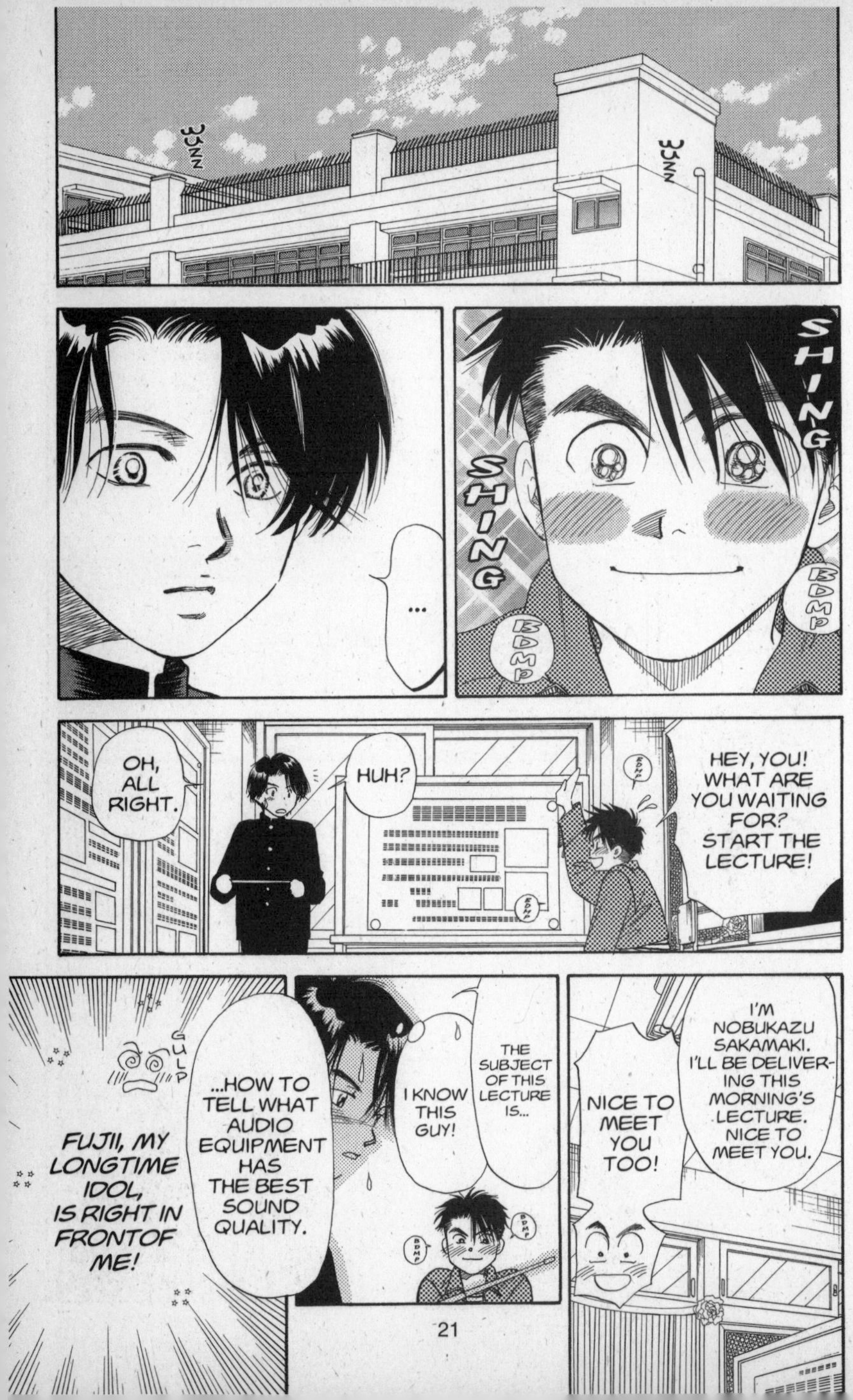
SHING
SHING
BDMP
BDMP
...
HEY, YOU! WHAT ARE YOU WAITING FOR? START THE LECTURE!
HUH?
OH, ALL RIGHT.
I'M NOBUKAZU SAKAMAKI. I'LL BE DELIVERING THIS MORNING'S LECTURE. NICE TO MEET YOU.
NICE TO MEET YOU TOO!
THE SUBJECT OF THIS LECTURE IS...
I KNOW THIS GUY!
...HOW TO TELL WHAT AUDIO EQUIPMENT HAS THE BEST SOUND QUALITY.
GULP
FUJII, MY LONGTIME IDOL, IS RIGHT IN FRONTOF ME!

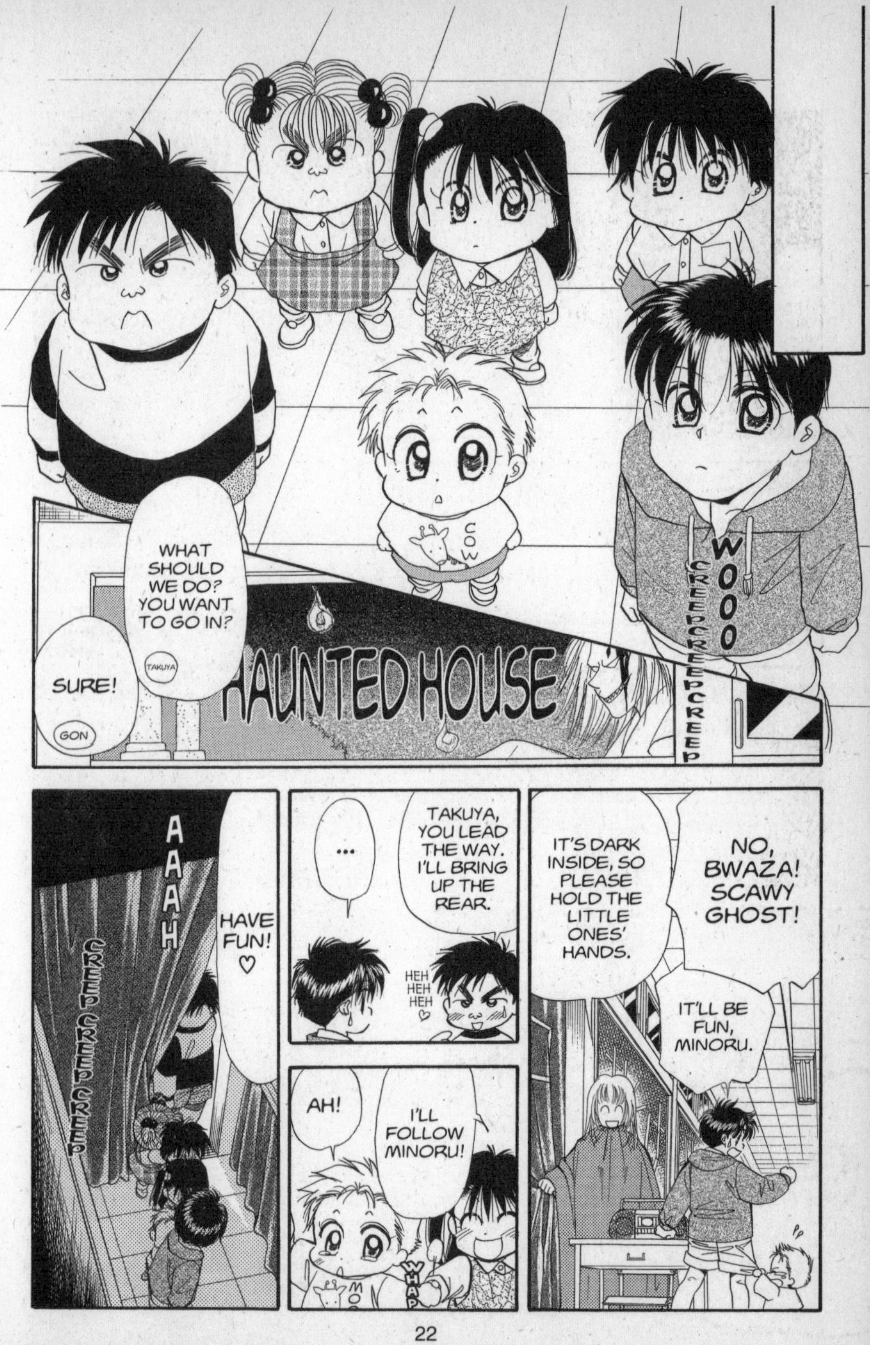
WOOO
CREEP CREEP CREEP CREEP
WHAT SHOULD WE DO? YOU WANT TO GO IN?
TAKUYA
HAUNTED HOUSE
SURE!
GON
NO, BWAZA! SCAWY GHOST!
IT'S DARK INSIDE, SO PLEASE HOLD THE LITTLE ONES' HANDS.
IT'LL BE FUN, MINORU.
TAKUYA, YOU LEAD THE WAY. I'LL BRING UP THE REAR.
...
HEH HEH HEH ♡
I'LL FOLLOW MINORU!
AH!
WHAP
MO
HAVE FUN! ♡
AAAH
CREEP CREEP CREEP

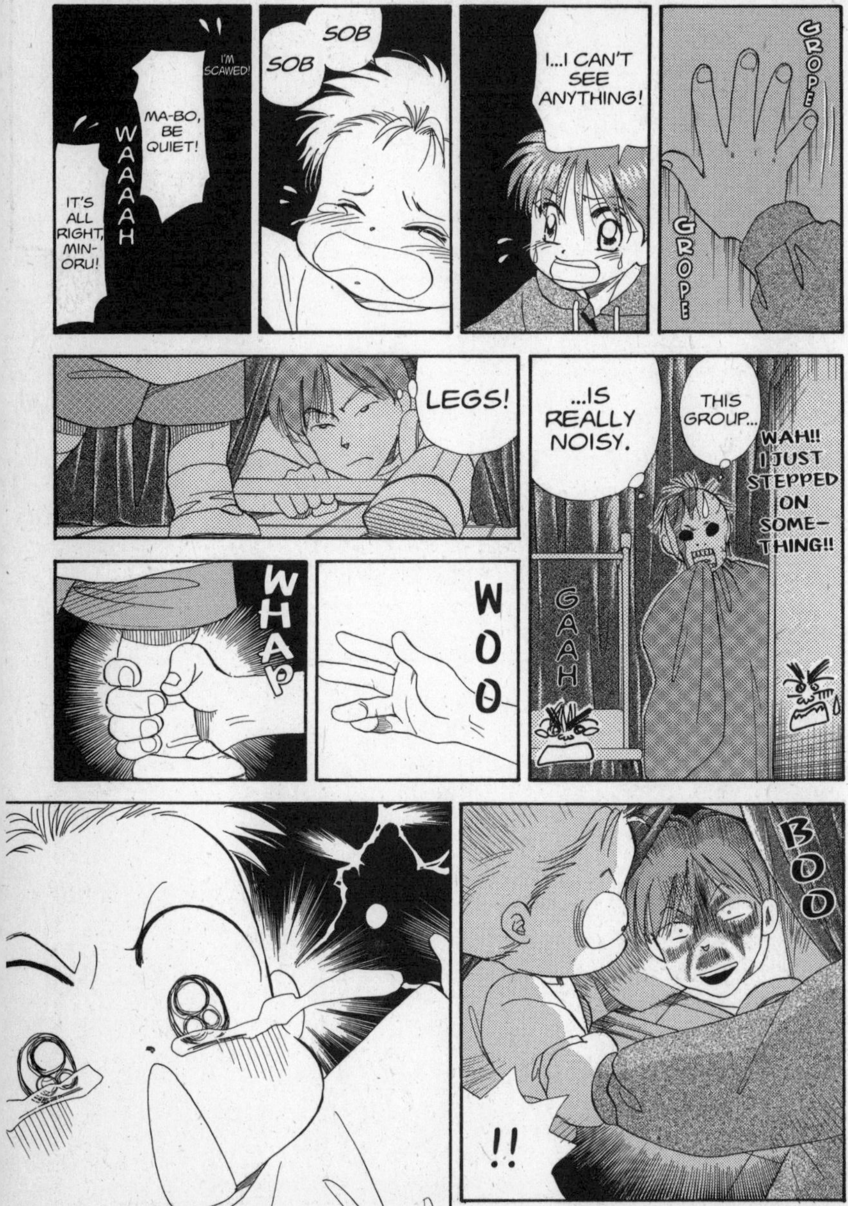
GROPE
GROPE
I...I CAN'T SEE ANYTHING!
SOB
SOB
I'M SCAWED!
MA-BO, BE QUIET!
WAAAAAH
IT'S ALL RIGHT, MIN-ORU!
THIS GROUP...
...IS REALLY NOISY.
WAH!! I JUST STEPPED ON SOME-THING!!
GAAAH
LEGS!
WOO
WHAP
BOO
!!

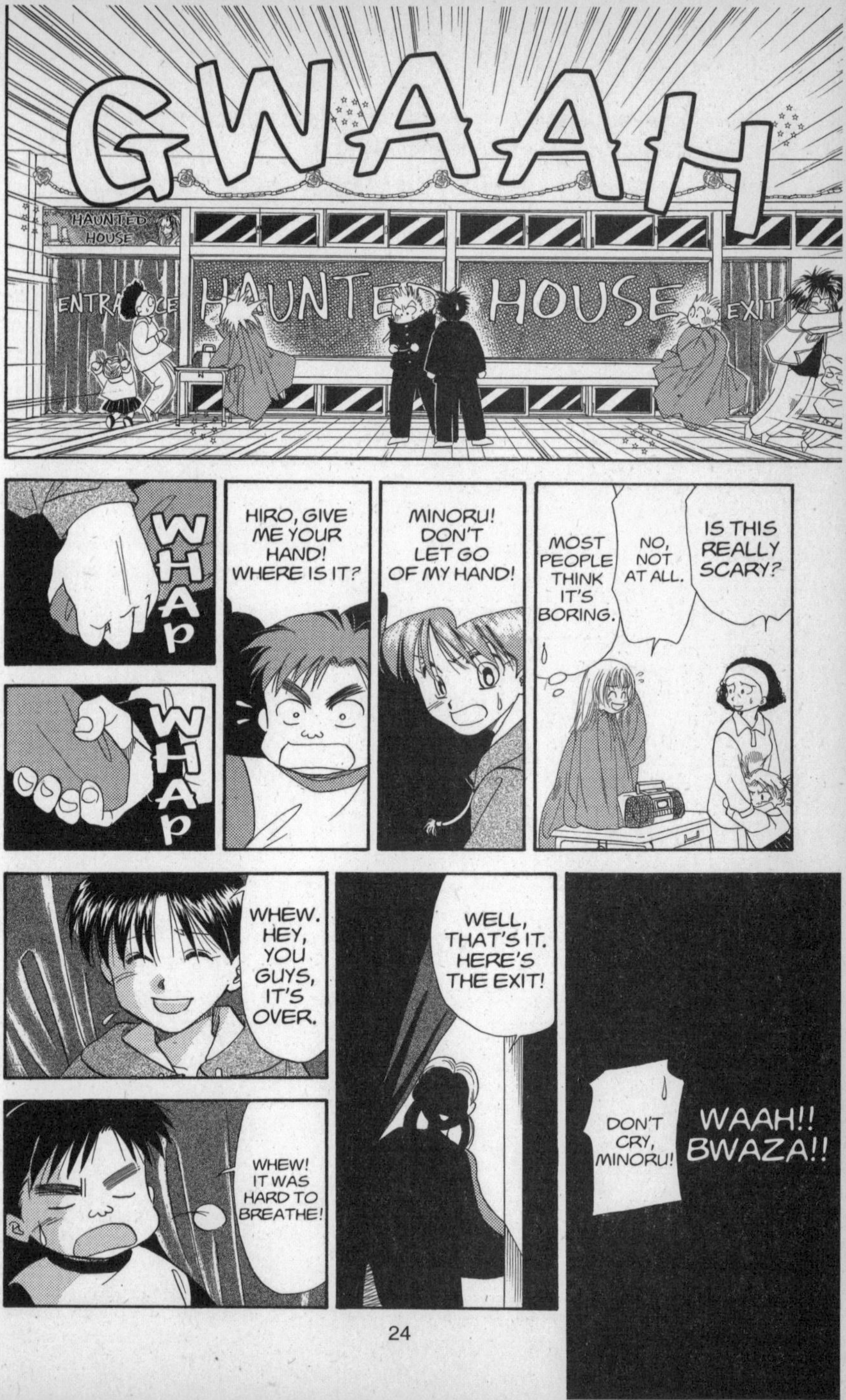
GWAAH
HAUNTED HOUSE
ENTRANCE
HAUNTED HOUSE
EXIT
IS THIS REALLY SCARY?
NO, NOT AT ALL.
MOST PEOPLE THINK IT'S BORING.
MINORU! DON'T LET GO OF MY HAND!
HIRO, GIVE ME YOUR HAND! WHERE IS IT?
WHAp
WHAp
WAAH!! BWAZA!!
DON'T CRY, MINORU!
WELL, THAT'S IT. HERE'S THE EXIT!
WHEW. HEY, YOU GUYS, IT'S OVER.
WHEW! IT WAS HARD TO BREATHE!

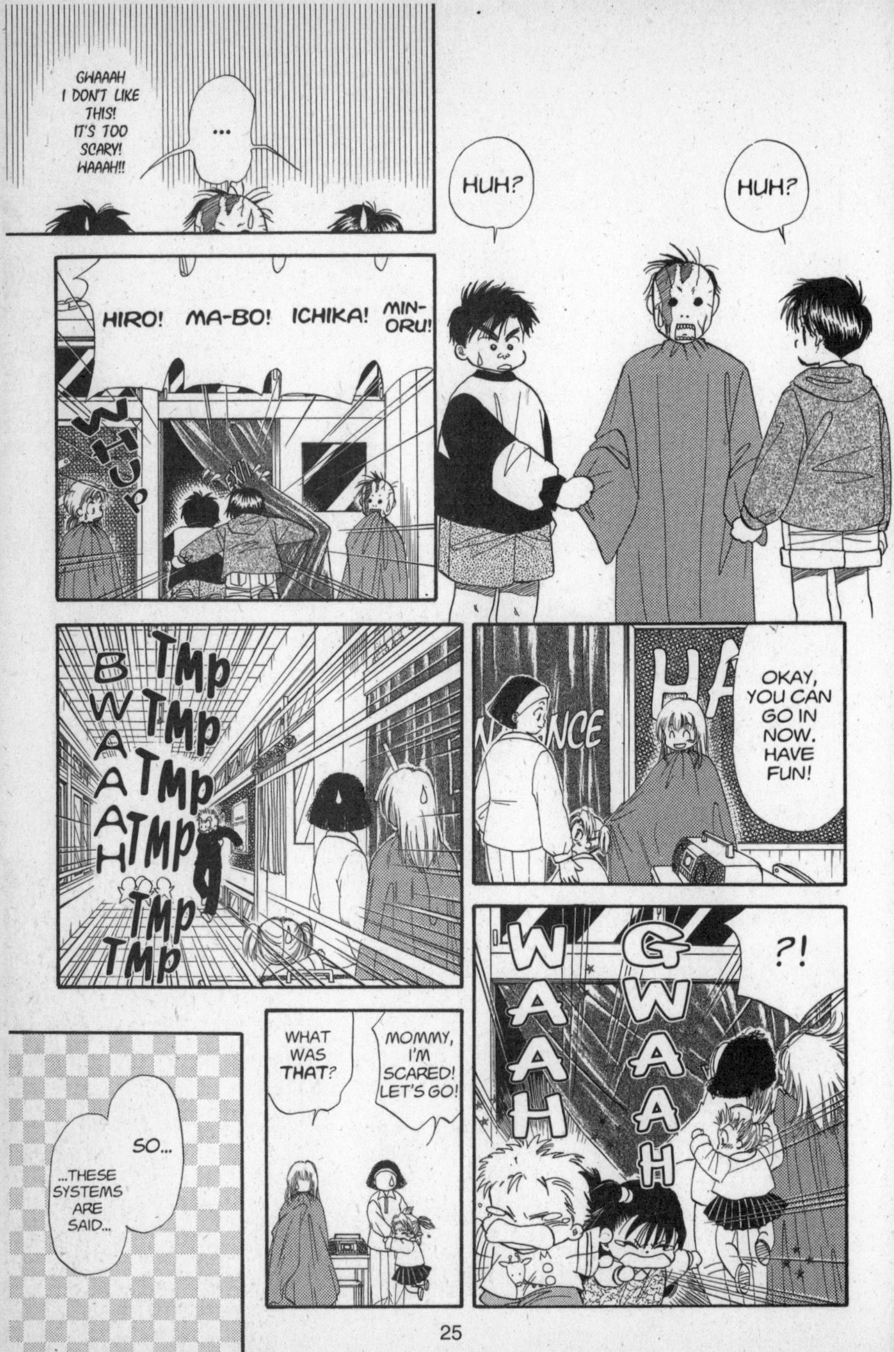
HUH?
HUH?
GWAAAH I DON'T LIKE THIS! IT'S TOO SCARY! WAAAH!!
...
HIRO! MA-BO! ICHIKA! MIN-ORU!
WHUP
OKAY, YOU CAN GO IN NOW. HAVE FUN!
TMP TMP TMP TMP TMP TMP
BWAAAAH
?!
GWAAH
WAAAH
MOMMY, I'M SCARED! LET'S GO!
WHAT WAS THAT?
SO...
...THESE SYSTEMS ARE SAID...

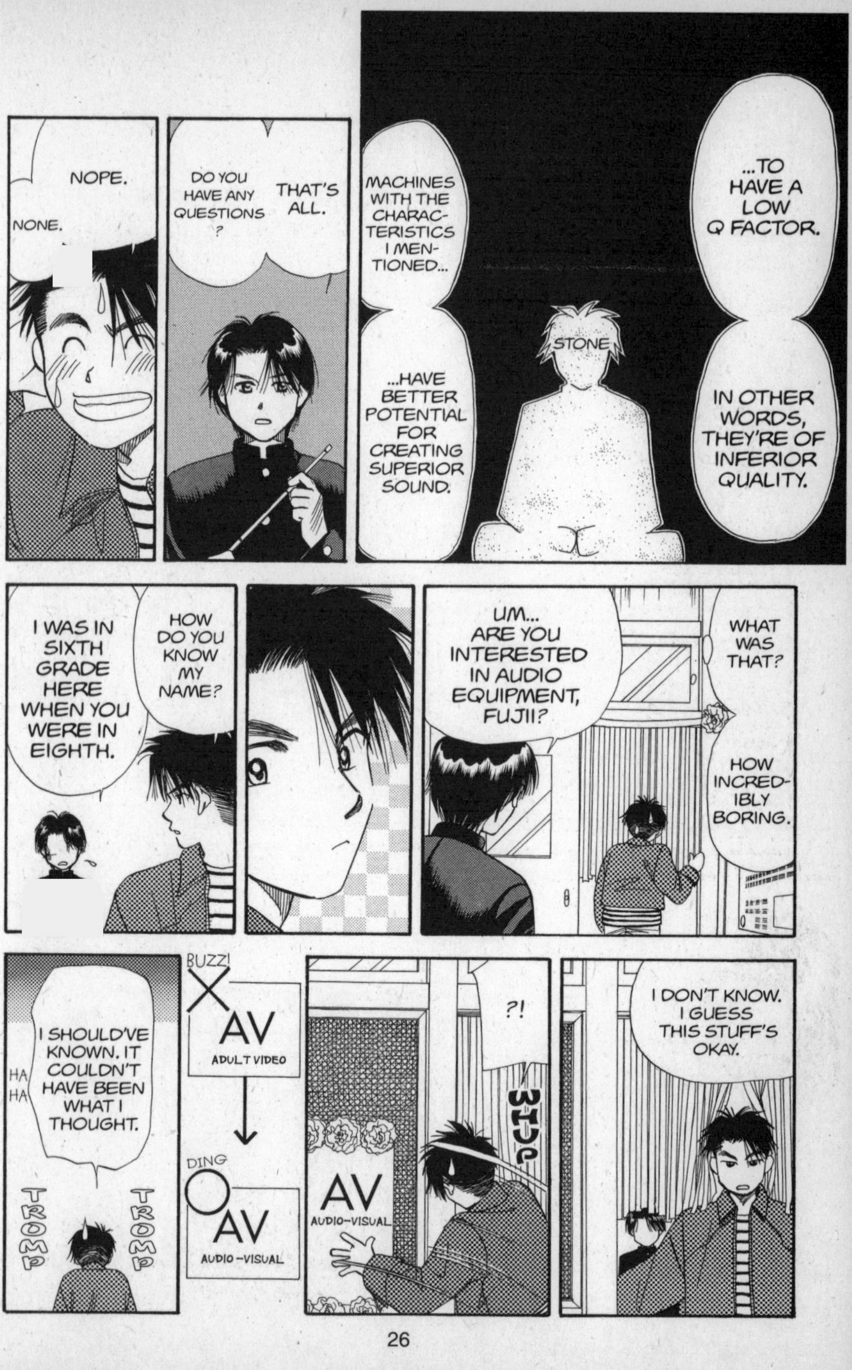
...TO HAVE A LOW Q FACTOR.
IN OTHER WORDS, THEY'RE OF INFERIOR QUALITY.
MACHINES WITH THE CHARACTERISTICS I MENTIONED...
...HAVE BETTER POTENTIAL FOR CREATING SUPERIOR SOUND.
STONE
THAT'S ALL.
DO YOU HAVE ANY QUESTIONS?
NOPE.
NONE.
WHAT WAS THAT?
HOW INCREDIBLY BORING.
UM... ARE YOU INTERESTED IN AUDIO EQUIPMENT, FUJII?
HOW DO YOU KNOW MY NAME?
I WAS IN SIXTH GRADE HERE WHEN YOU WERE IN EIGHTH.
I DON'T KNOW. I GUESS THIS STUFF'S OKAY.
?!
WHUP
AV
AUDIO-VISUAL
BUZZ!
AV
ADULT VIDEO
DING
AV
AUDIO-VISUAL
I SHOULD'VE KNOWN. IT COULDN'T HAVE BEEN WHAT I THOUGHT.
HA HA
TROMP TROMP

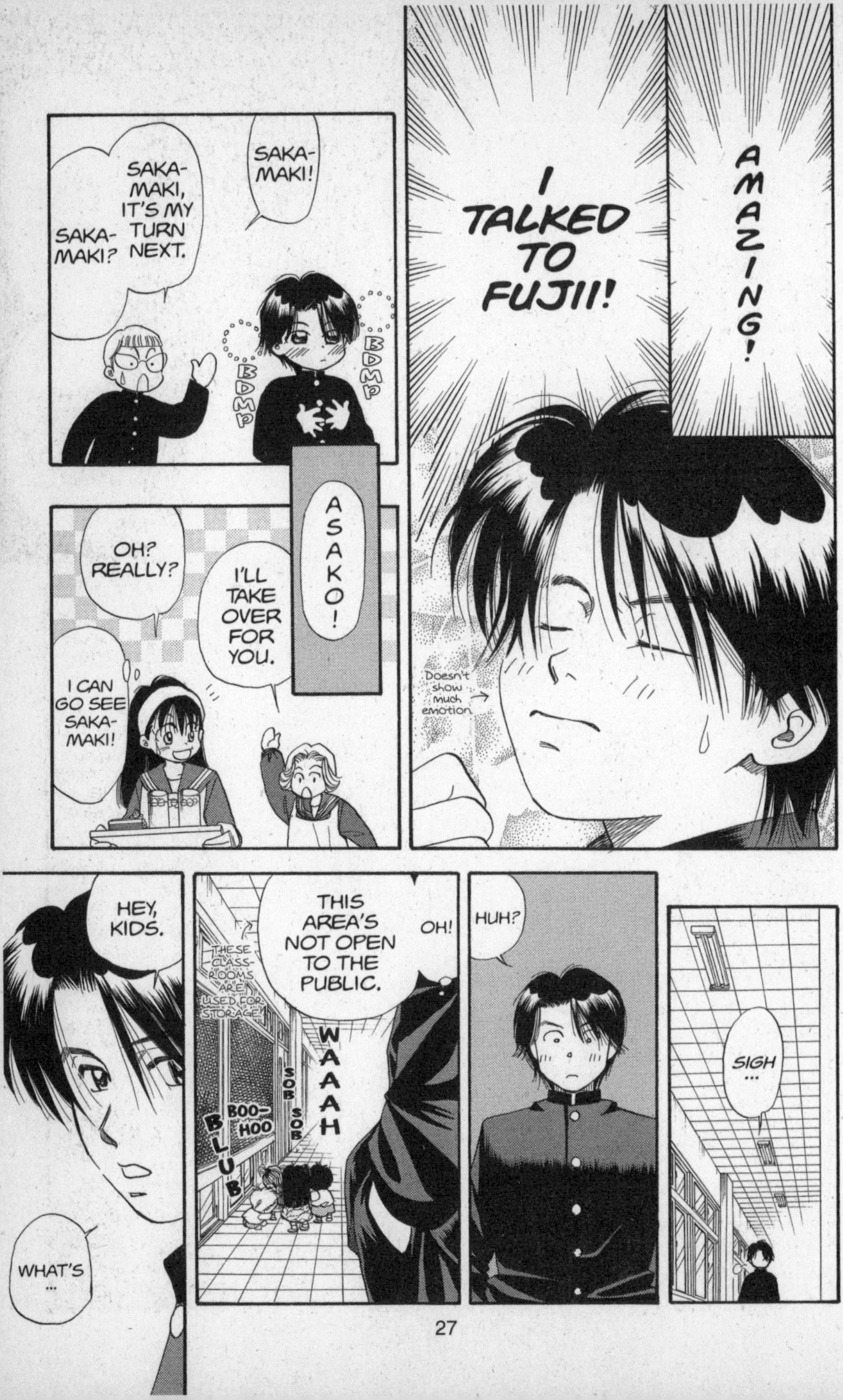
AMAZING!
I TALKED TO FUJII!
Doesn't show much emotion
SAKA-MAKI!
SAKA-MAKI, IT'S MY TURN NEXT.
SAKA-MAKI?
BDMP
BDMP
ASAKO!
I'LL TAKE OVER FOR YOU.
OH? REALLY?
I CAN GO SEE SAKA-MAKI!
SIGH...
HUH?
OH!
THIS AREA'S NOT OPEN TO THE PUBLIC.
THESE CLASS-ROOMS ARE USED FOR STORAGE!
WAAAAH
SOB SOB
BOO-HOO
BLUB
HEY, KIDS.
WHAT'S...

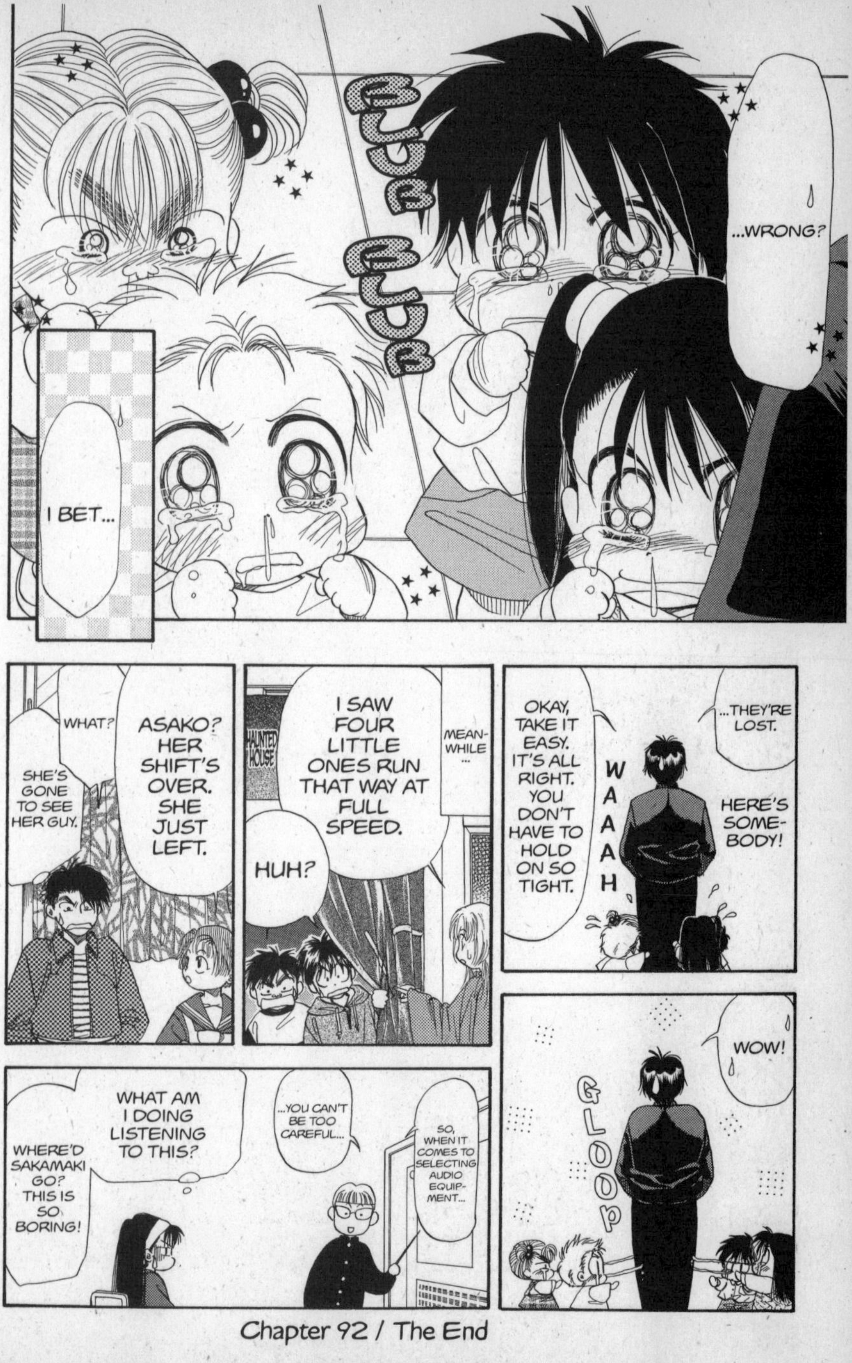
...WRONG?
BLUB BLUB
I BET...
...THEY'RE LOST.
HERE'S SOMEBODY!
OKAY, TAKE IT EASY. IT'S ALL RIGHT. YOU DON'T HAVE TO HOLD ON SO TIGHT.
WAAAH
WOW!
GLOOP
MEANWHILE...
I SAW FOUR LITTLE ONES RUN THAT WAY AT FULL SPEED.
HUH?
HAUNTED HOUSE
ASAKO? HER SHIFT'S OVER. SHE JUST LEFT.
WHAT?
SHE'S GONE TO SEE HER GUY.
SO, WHEN IT COMES TO SELECTING AUDIO EQUIPMENT...
...YOU CAN'T BE TOO CAREFUL...
WHAT AM I DOING LISTENING TO THIS?
WHERE'D SAKAMAKI GO? THIS IS SO BORING!

Chapter 92 / The End

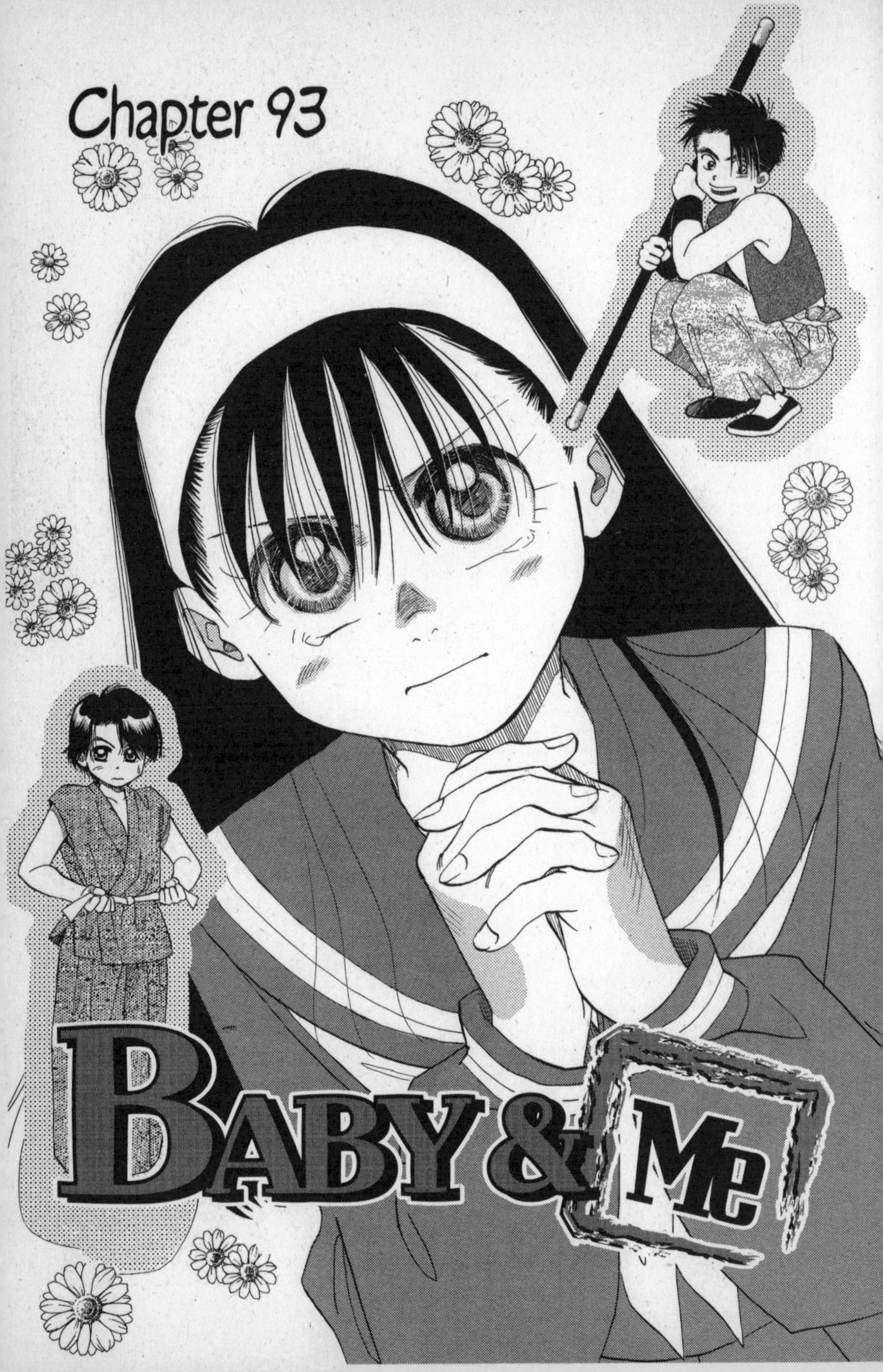
Chapter 93
BABY & Me

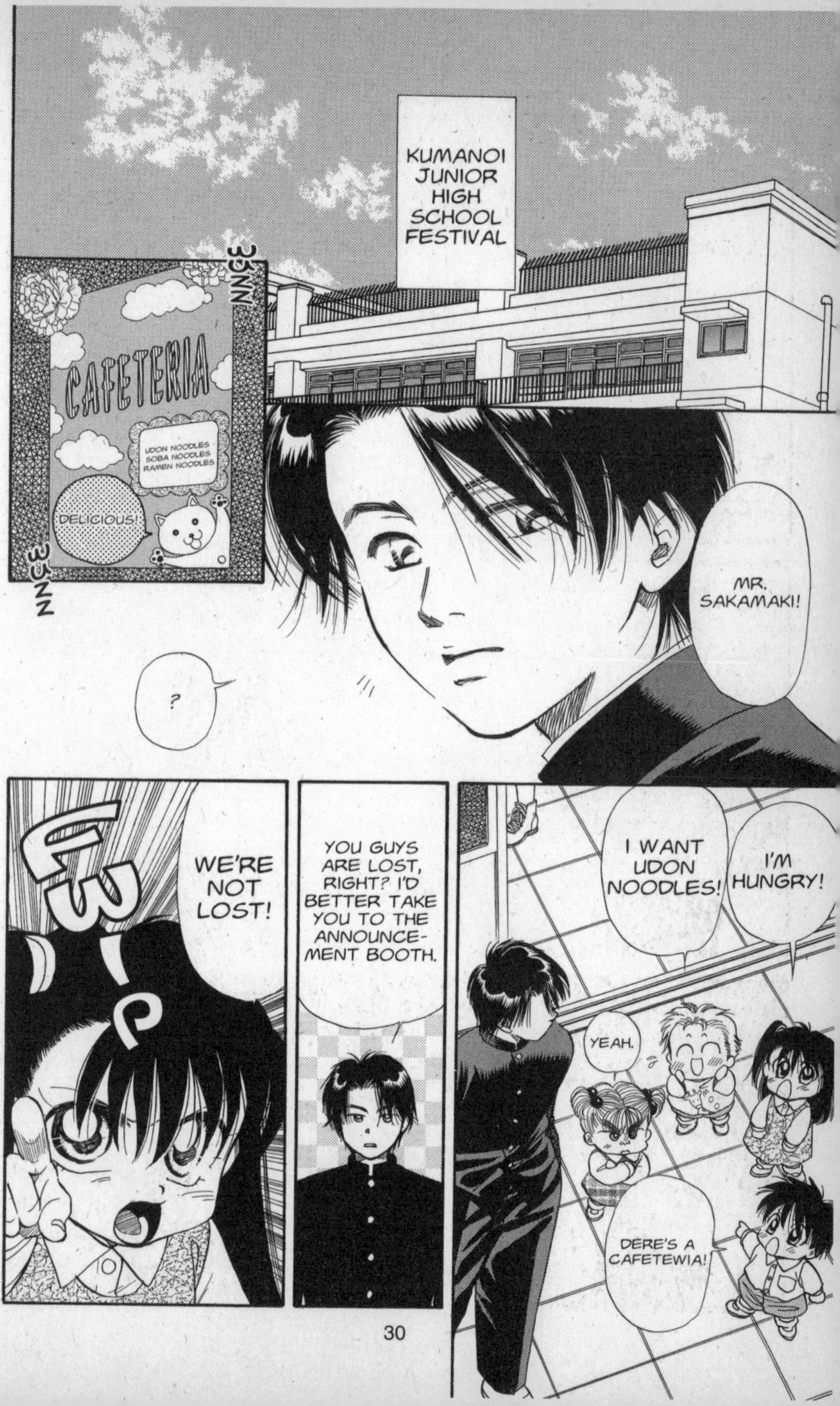
KUMANOI JUNIOR HIGH SCHOOL FESTIVAL
CAFETERIA
UDON NOODLES SOBA NOODLES RAMEN NOODLES
DELICIOUS!
MR. SAKAMAKI!
?
I'M HUNGRY!
I WANT UDON NOODLES!
YEAH.
DERE'S A CAFETEWIA!
YOU GUYS ARE LOST, RIGHT? I'D BETTER TAKE YOU TO THE ANNOUNCEMENT BOOTH.
WE'RE NOT LOST!

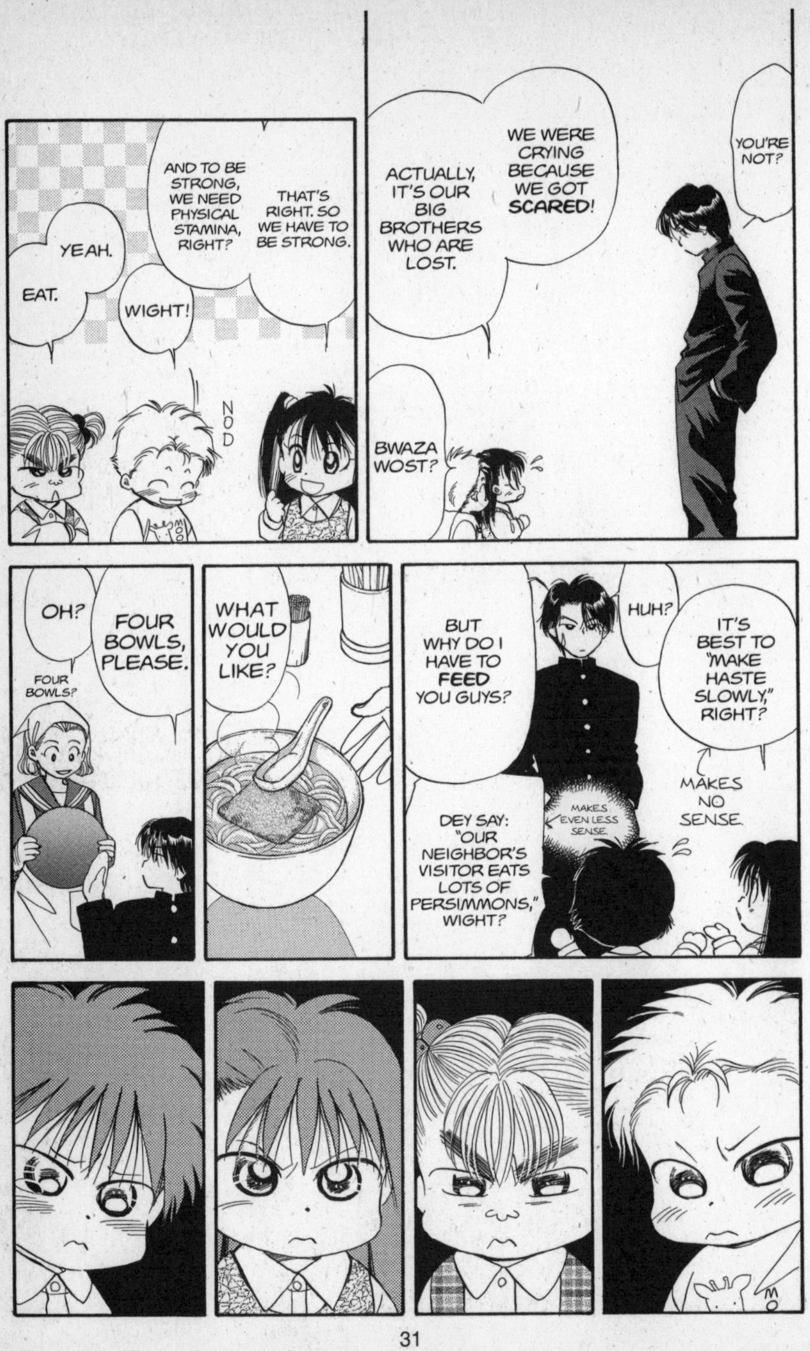
YOU'RE NOT?
WE WERE CRYING BECAUSE WE GOT **SCARED**!
ACTUALLY, IT'S OUR BIG BROTHERS WHO ARE LOST.
BWAZA WOST?
THAT'S RIGHT. SO WE HAVE TO BE STRONG.
AND TO BE STRONG, WE NEED PHYSICAL STAMINA, RIGHT?
WIGHT!
NOD
YEAH.
EAT.
IT'S BEST TO "MAKE HASTE SLOWLY," RIGHT?
HUH?
BUT WHY DO I HAVE TO **FEED** YOU GUYS?
MAKES NO SENSE.
DEY SAY: "OUR NEIGHBOR'S VISITOR EATS LOTS OF PERSIMMONS," WIGHT?
MAKES EVEN LESS SENSE.
WHAT WOULD YOU LIKE?
FOUR BOWLS, PLEASE.
OH?
FOUR BOWLS?

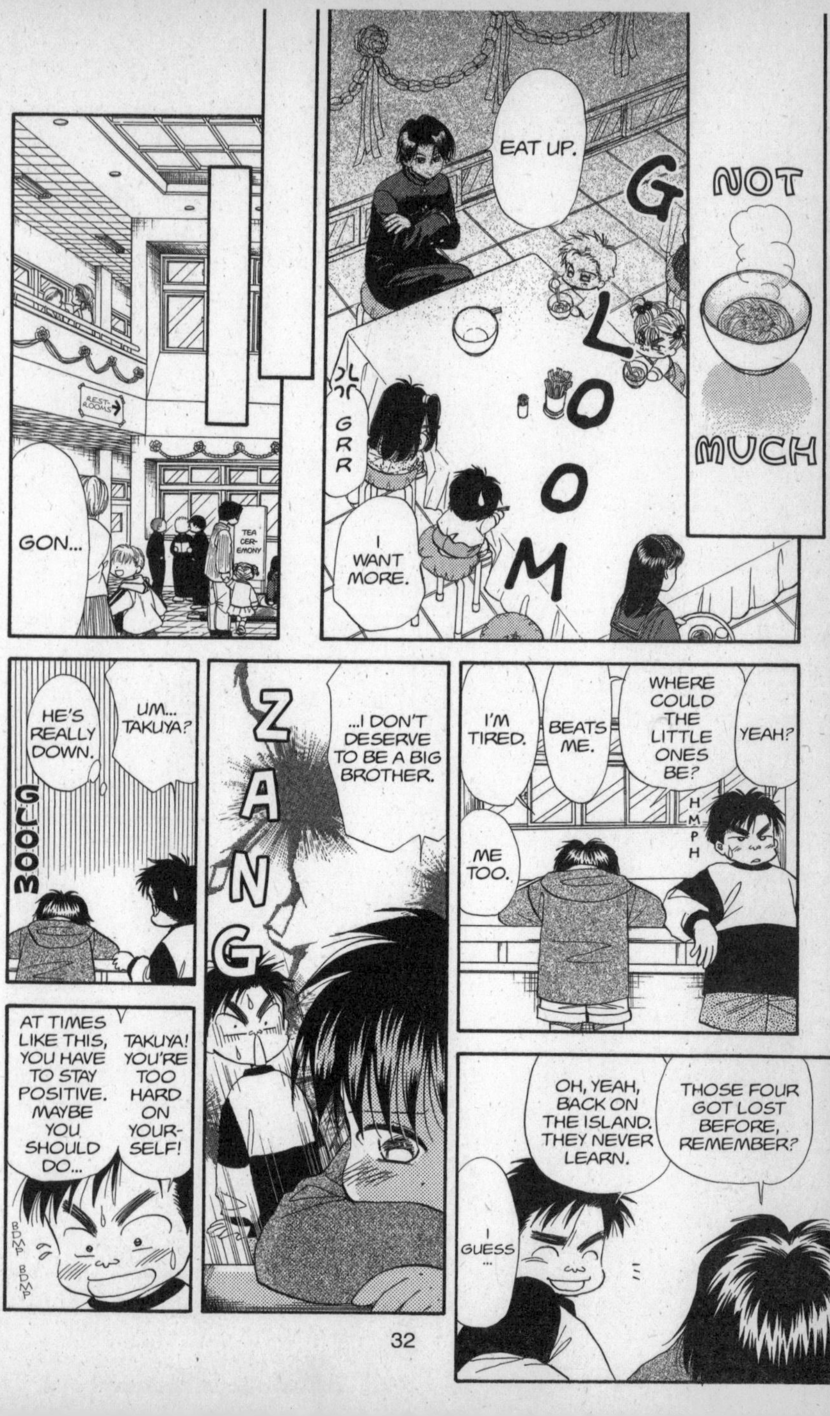
NOT MUCH
EAT UP.
GLOOM
GRR
I WANT MORE.
GON...
YEAH?
WHERE COULD THE LITTLE ONES BE?
HMPH
BEATS ME.
I'M TIRED.
ME TOO.
THOSE FOUR GOT LOST BEFORE, REMEMBER?
OH, YEAH, BACK ON THE ISLAND. THEY NEVER LEARN.
I GUESS...
ZANG
...I DON'T DESERVE TO BE A BIG BROTHER.
UM... TAKUYA?
HE'S REALLY DOWN.
GLOOM
TAKUYA! YOU'RE TOO HARD ON YOURSELF!
AT TIMES LIKE THIS, YOU HAVE TO STAY POSITIVE. MAYBE YOU SHOULD DO...
BDMP BDMP

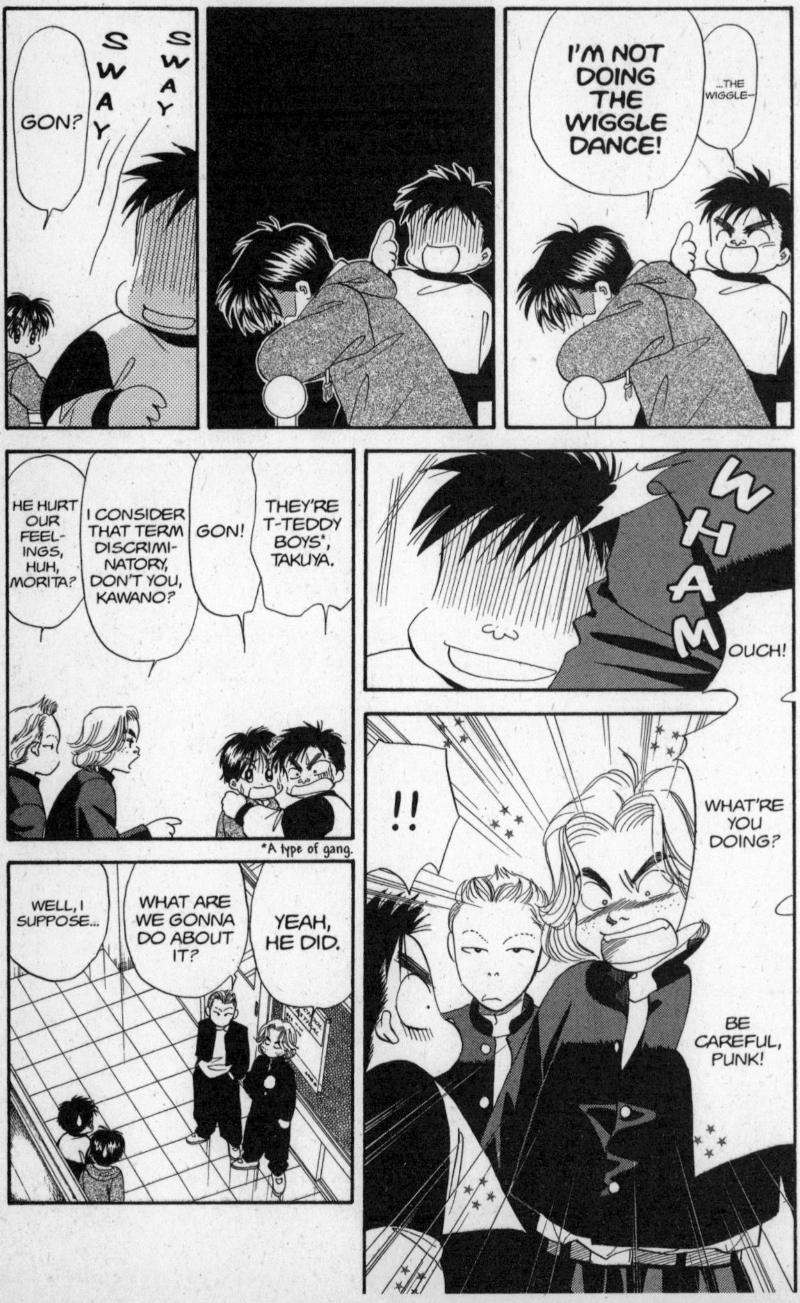
...THE WIGGLE—
I'M NOT DOING THE WIGGLE DANCE!
SWAY
SWAY
GON?
WHAM
OUCH!
WHAT'RE YOU DOING?
!!
BE CAREFUL, PUNK!
THEY'RE T-TEDDY BOYS*, TAKUYA.
GON!
I CONSIDER THAT TERM DISCRIMINATORY, DON'T YOU, KAWANO?
HE HURT OUR FEELINGS, HUH, MORITA?
YEAH, HE DID.
WHAT ARE WE GONNA DO ABOUT IT?
WELL, I SUPPOSE...

*A type of gang.

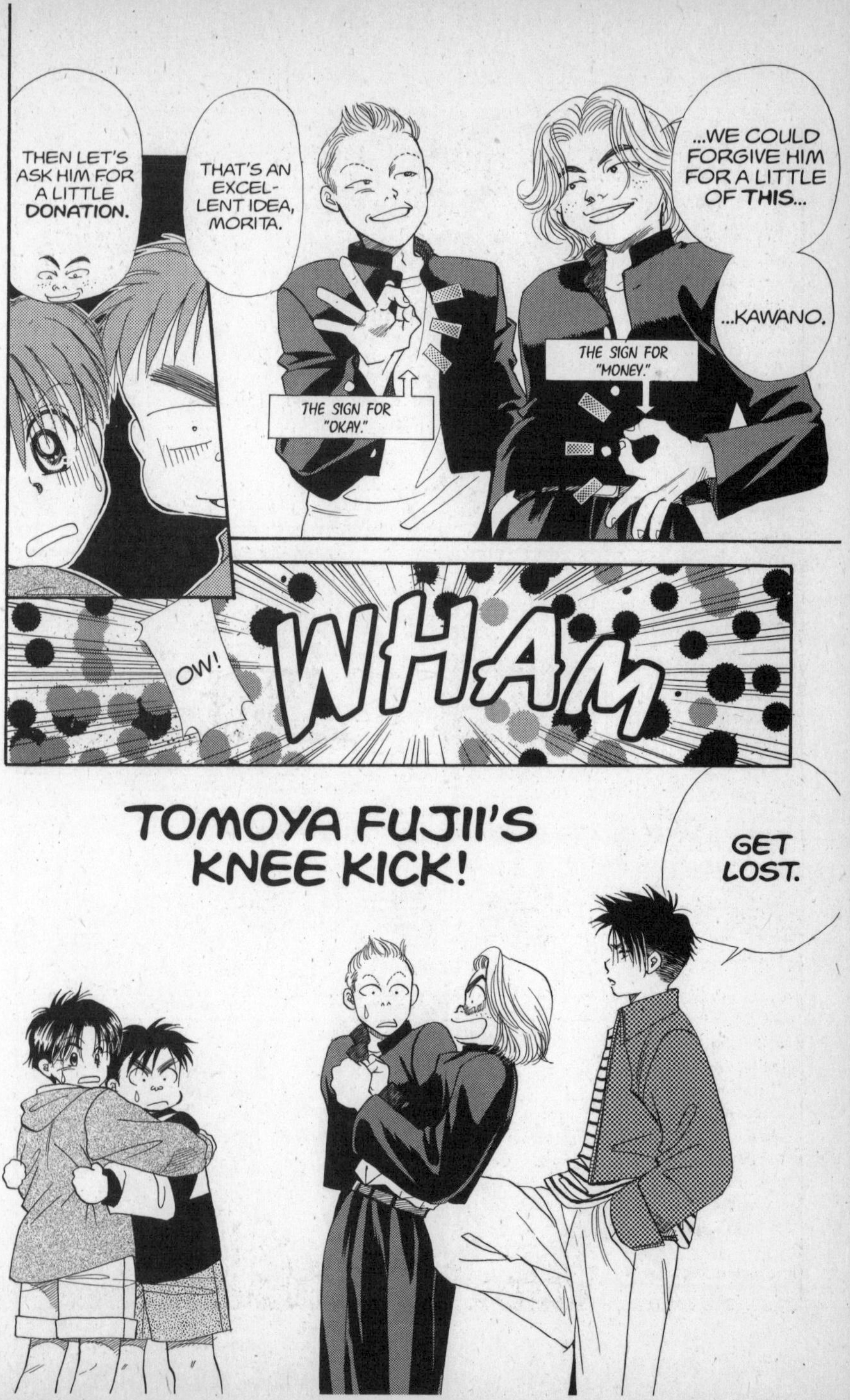
...WE COULD FORGIVE HIM FOR A LITTLE OF THIS...
...KAWANO.
THE SIGN FOR "MONEY."
THAT'S AN EXCEL-LENT IDEA, MORITA.
THE SIGN FOR "OKAY."
THEN LET'S ASK HIM FOR A LITTLE DONATION.
WHAM
OW!
GET LOST.
TOMOYA FUJII'S KNEE KICK!

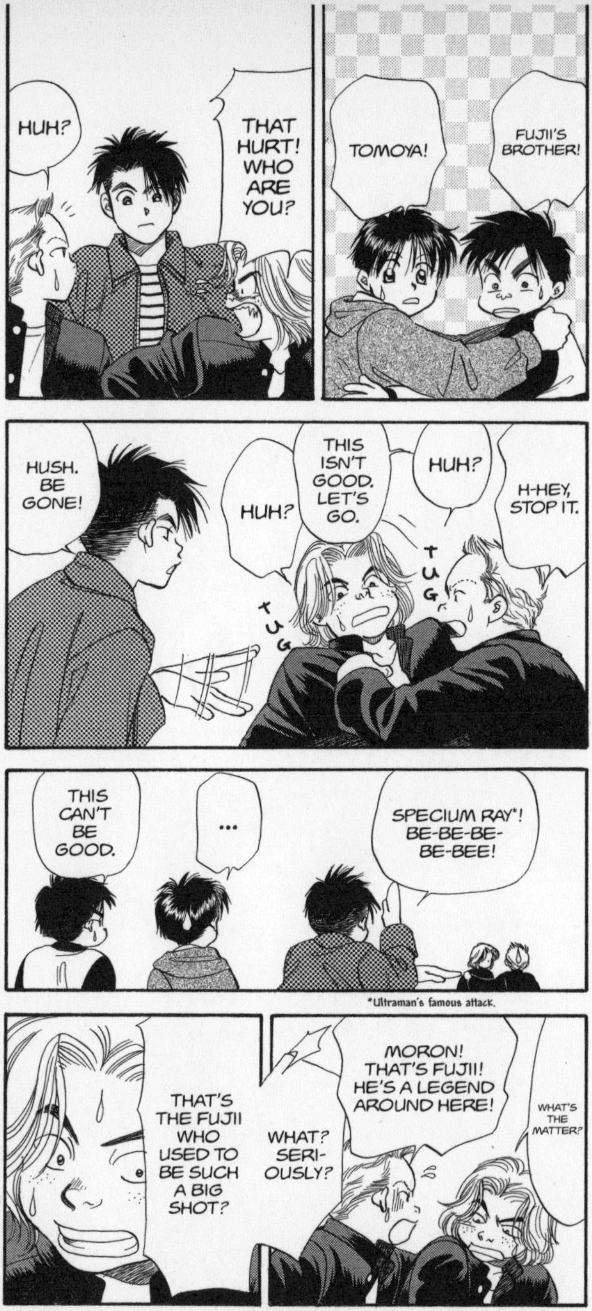
FUJII'S BROTHER!
TOMOYA!
THAT HURT! WHO ARE YOU?
HUH?
H-HEY, STOP IT.
HUH?
THIS ISN'T GOOD. LET'S GO.
HUH?
TUG
TUG
HUSH. BE GONE!
SPECIUM RAY*! BE-BE-BE-BE-BEE!
...
THIS CAN'T BE GOOD.
MORON! THAT'S FUJII! HE'S A LEGEND AROUND HERE!
WHAT'S THE MATTER?
WHAT? SERIOUSLY?
THAT'S THE FUJII WHO USED TO BE SUCH A BIG SHOT?

*Ultraman's famous attack.

Author's Note Part 2

This column is always hard for me because I can never think of anything good to write about. One day, my brother wanted to drink a soda I had in the refrigerator, and I was furious. He said, "Be nice and let me have half of it." I said, "No. I don't feel like drinking it right now and the fizz will be gone if you drink half of it." He frowned for awhile and drank half my soda anyway. And here was his solution to the problem.

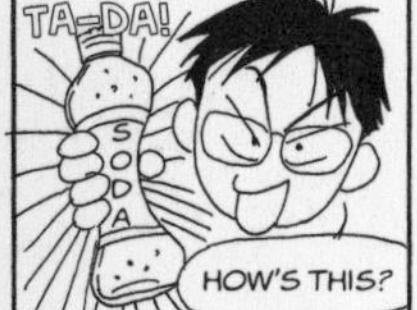
TA-DA!
SODA
HOW'S THIS?

He squeezed all the air out of the soda bottle and screwed the top back on. (The soda still wasn't carbonated enough when I had it later.) I thought the episode was funny, so I wrote it down to use in one of these columns.

Continued in Part 3

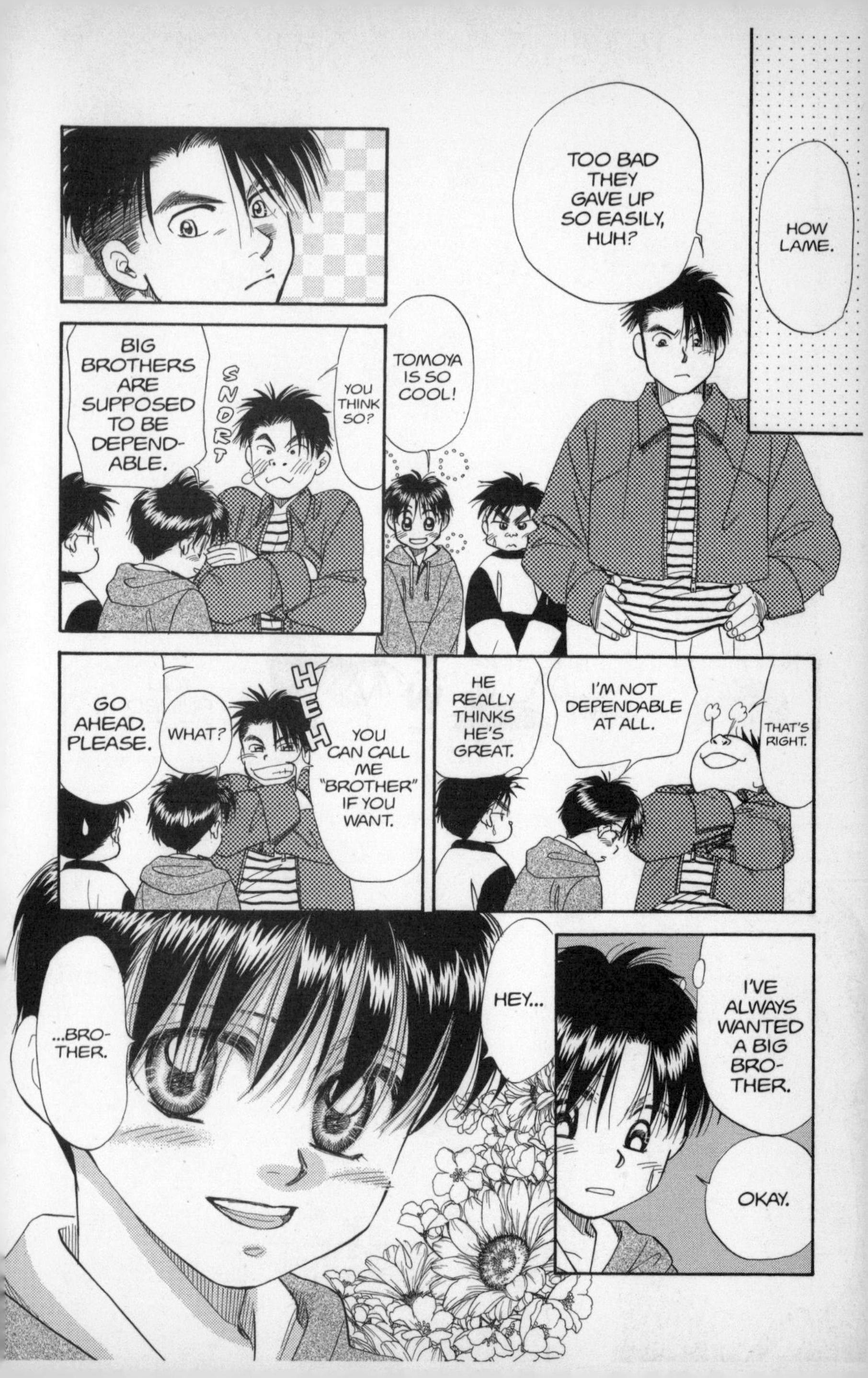
HOW LAME.
TOO BAD THEY GAVE UP SO EASILY, HUH?
TOMOYA IS SO COOL!
YOU THINK SO?
BIG BROTHERS ARE SUPPOSED TO BE DEPENDABLE.
SNORT
THAT'S RIGHT.
I'M NOT DEPENDABLE AT ALL.
HE REALLY THINKS HE'S GREAT.
HEH
YOU CAN CALL ME "BROTHER" IF YOU WANT.
WHAT?
GO AHEAD. PLEASE.
I'VE ALWAYS WANTED A BIG BROTHER.
OKAY.
HEY...
...BROTHER.

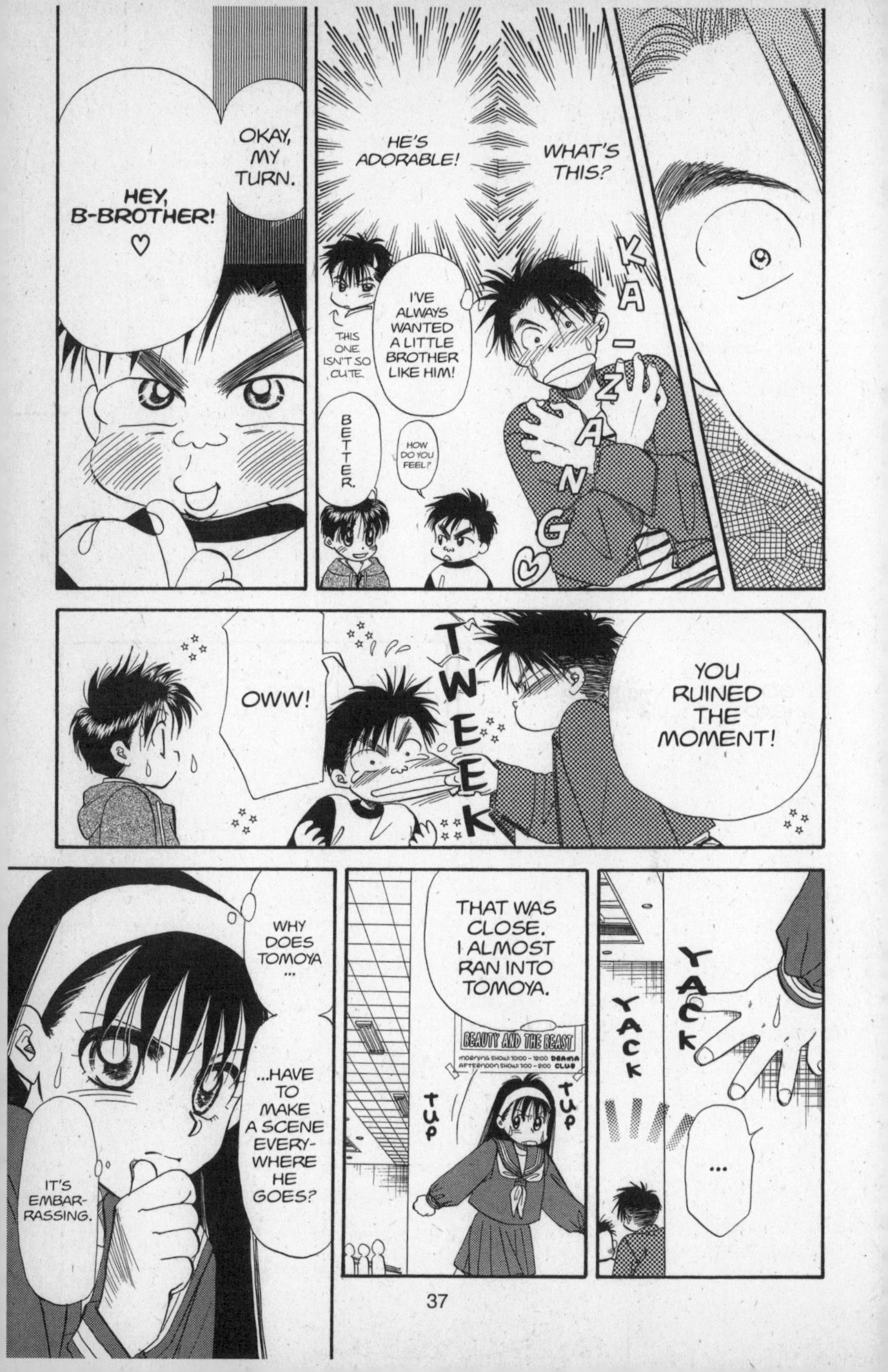
WHAT'S THIS?
HE'S ADORABLE!
I'VE ALWAYS WANTED A LITTLE BROTHER LIKE HIM!
THIS ONE ISN'T SO CUTE.
KA-ZANG
HOW DO YOU FEEL?
BETTER.
OKAY, MY TURN.
HEY, B-BROTHER! ♡
YOU RUINED THE MOMENT!
TWEEK
OWW!
YACK YACK
...
THAT WAS CLOSE. I ALMOST RAN INTO TOMOYA.
BEAUTY AND THE BEAST
TUP TUP
WHY DOES TOMOYA ...
...HAVE TO MAKE A SCENE EVERYWHERE HE GOES?
IT'S EMBARRASSING.

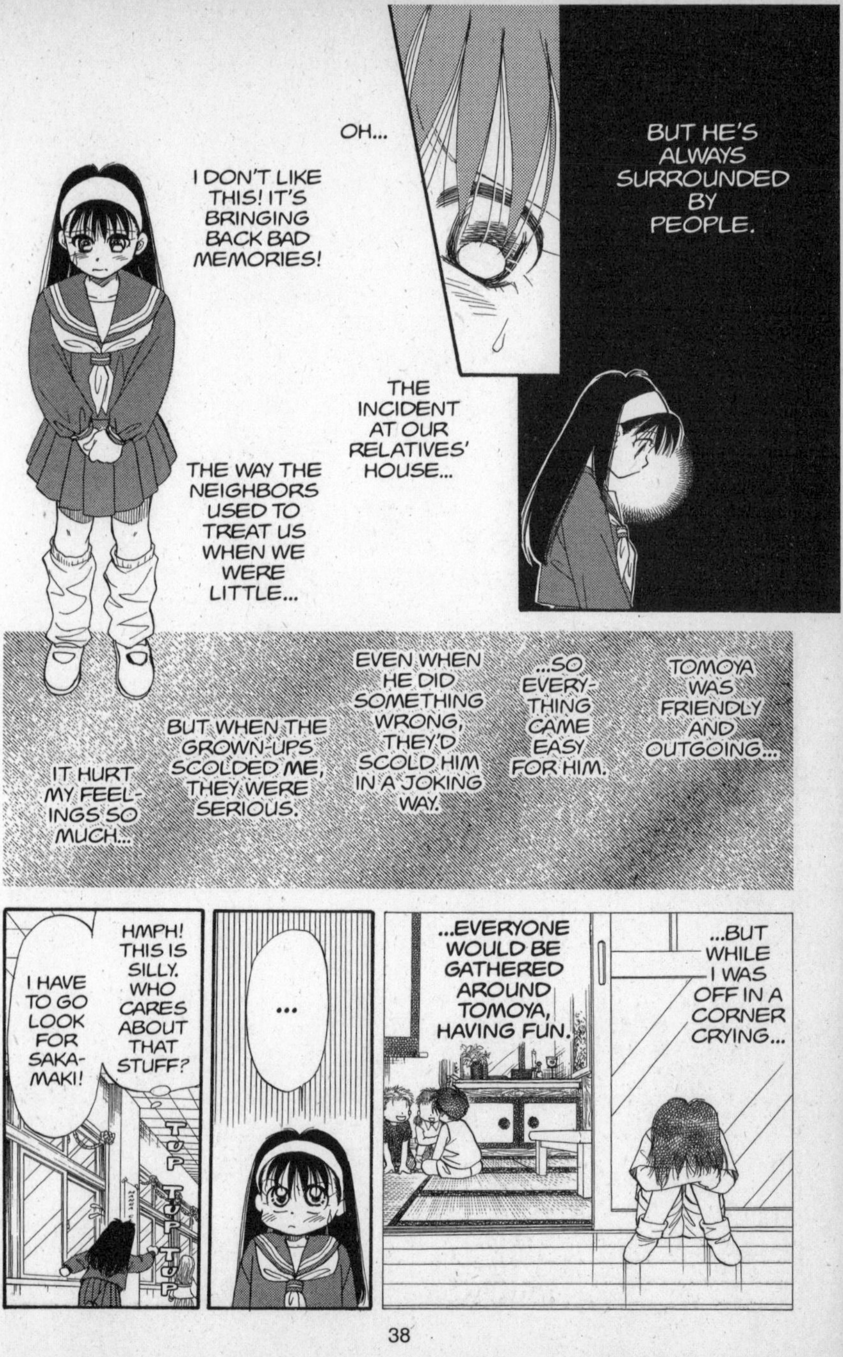
BUT HE'S ALWAYS SURROUNDED BY PEOPLE.
OH...
I DON'T LIKE THIS! IT'S BRINGING BACK BAD MEMORIES!
THE INCIDENT AT OUR RELATIVES' HOUSE...
THE WAY THE NEIGHBORS USED TO TREAT US WHEN WE WERE LITTLE...
TOMOYA WAS FRIENDLY AND OUTGOING...
...SO EVERY-THING CAME EASY FOR HIM.
EVEN WHEN HE DID SOMETHING WRONG, THEY'D SCOLD HIM IN A JOKING WAY.
BUT WHEN THE GROWN-UPS SCOLDED ME, THEY WERE SERIOUS.
IT HURT MY FEEL-INGS SO MUCH...
...BUT WHILE I WAS OFF IN A CORNER CRYING...
...EVERYONE WOULD BE GATHERED AROUND TOMOYA, HAVING FUN.
...
HMPH! THIS IS SILLY. WHO CARES ABOUT THAT STUFF?
I HAVE TO GO LOOK FOR SAKA-MAKI!
TUP TUP TUP TUP

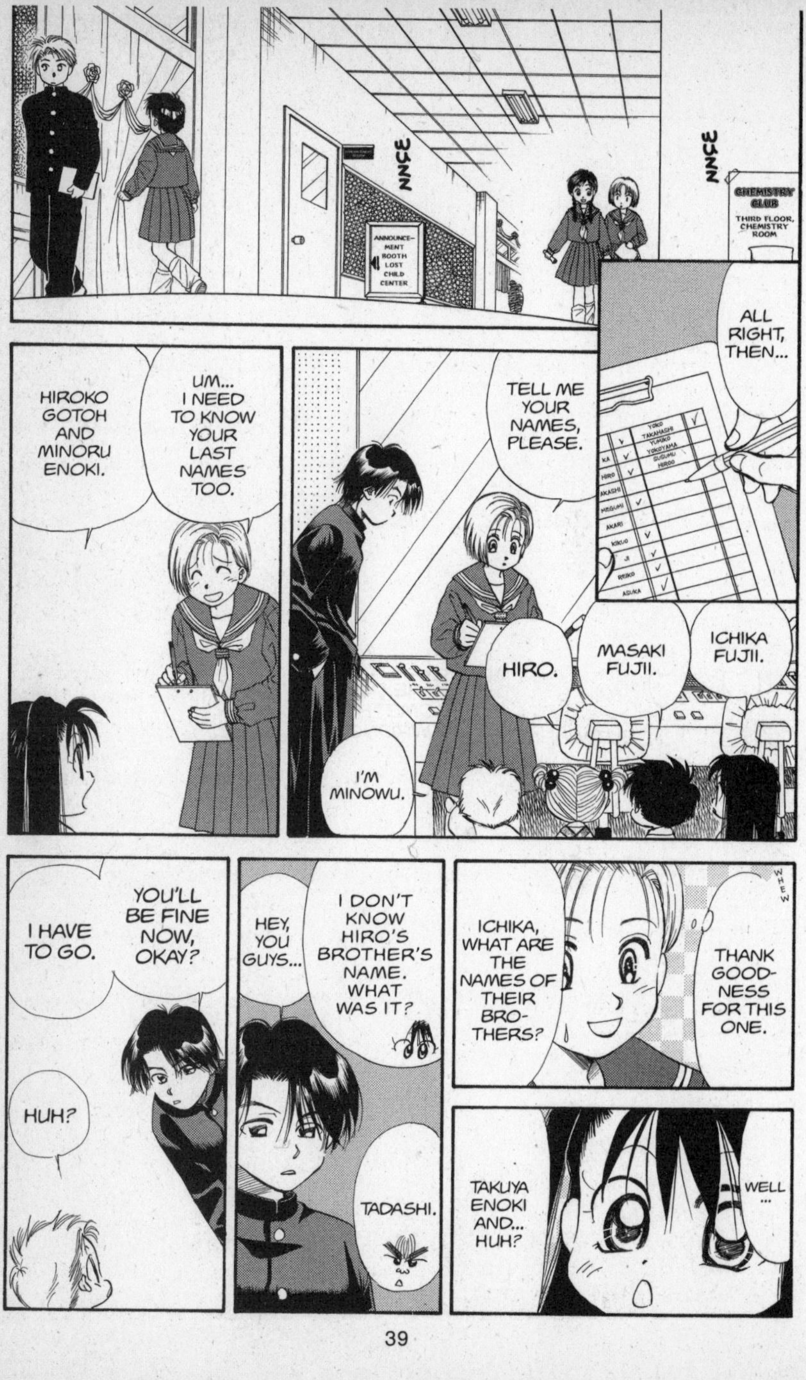
ZUNN
CHEMISTRY CLUB
THIRD FLOOR, CHEMISTRY ROOM
ZUNN
ANNOUNCE-MENT BOOTH
LOST CHILD CENTER
ALL RIGHT, THEN...
YOKO TAKAHASHI
YUMIKO YOKOYAMA
SUSUMU HIROO
KA
HIRO
AKASHI
MEGUMI
AKARI
KIKUO
JI
REIKO
ASUKA
TELL ME YOUR NAMES, PLEASE.
ICHIKA FUJII.
MASAKI FUJII.
HIRO.
I'M MINOWU.
UM... I NEED TO KNOW YOUR LAST NAMES TOO.
HIROKO GOTOH AND MINORU ENOKI.
WHEW
THANK GOODNESS FOR THIS ONE.
ICHIKA, WHAT ARE THE NAMES OF THEIR BROTHERS?
WELL ...
TAKUYA ENOKI AND... HUH?
I DON'T KNOW HIRO'S BROTHER'S NAME. WHAT WAS IT?
HEY, YOU GUYS...
TADASHI.
YOU'LL BE FINE NOW, OKAY?
I HAVE TO GO.
HUH?

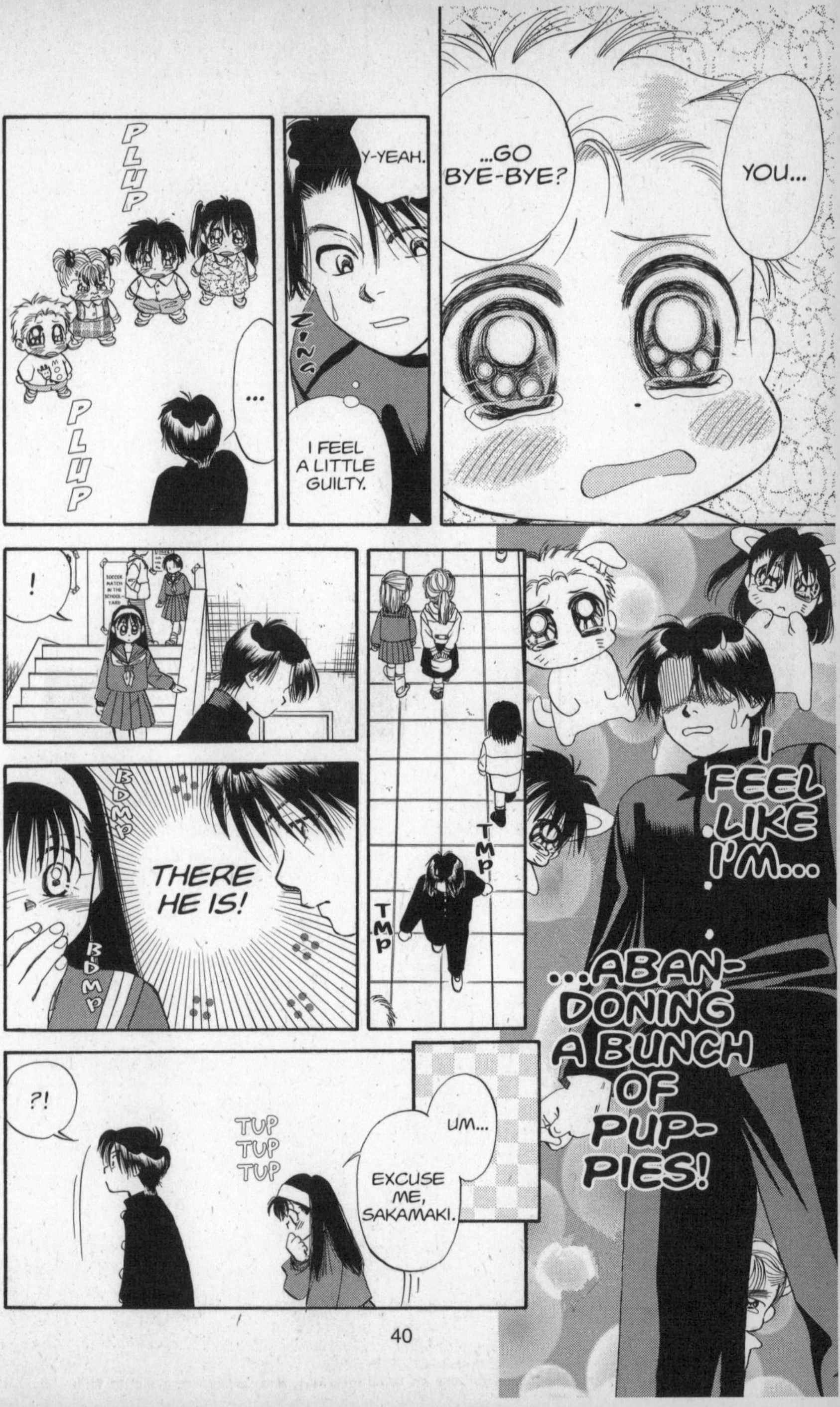
YOU...
...GO BYE-BYE?
Y-YEAH.
ZING
I FEEL A LITTLE GUILTY.
...
PLUP
PLUP
I FEEL LIKE I'M...
...ABAN-DONING A BUNCH OF PUP-PIES!
TMP
TMP
SOCCER MATCH IN THE SCHOOL-YARD
!
BDMP
THERE HE IS!
BDMP
UM...
EXCUSE ME, SAKAMAKI.
TUP TUP TUP
?!

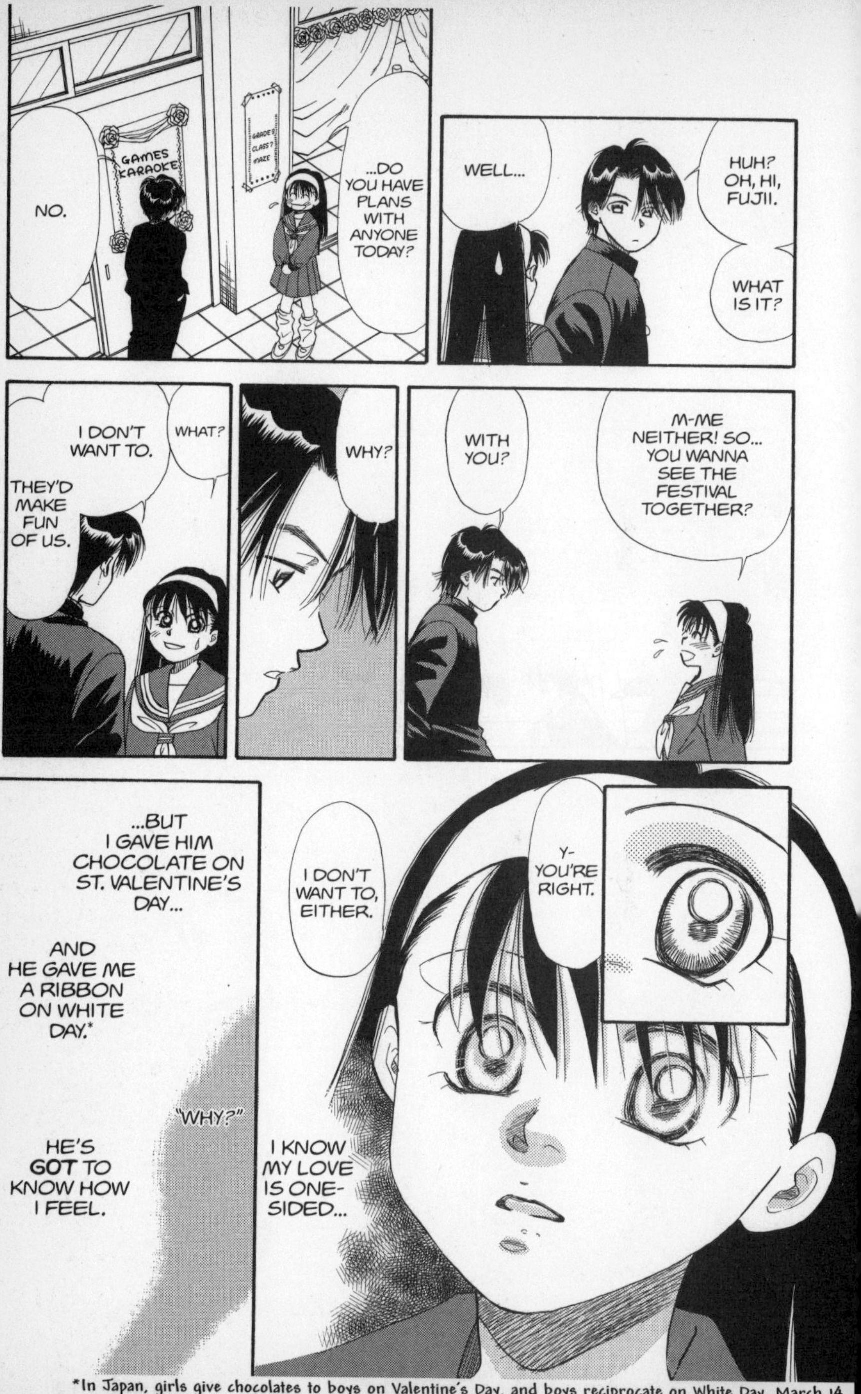
HUH? OH, HI, FUJII.
WHAT IS IT?
WELL...
...DO YOU HAVE PLANS WITH ANYONE TODAY?
GAMES KARAOKE
NO.
M-ME NEITHER! SO... YOU WANNA SEE THE FESTIVAL TOGETHER?
WITH YOU?
WHY?
WHAT?
I DON'T WANT TO.
THEY'D MAKE FUN OF US.
Y- YOU'RE RIGHT.
I DON'T WANT TO, EITHER.
I KNOW MY LOVE IS ONE-SIDED...
...BUT I GAVE HIM CHOCOLATE ON ST. VALENTINE'S DAY...
AND HE GAVE ME A RIBBON ON WHITE DAY.*
"WHY?"
HE'S **GOT** TO KNOW HOW I FEEL.

*In Japan, girls give chocolates to boys on Valentine's Day, and boys reciprocate on White Day, March 14.

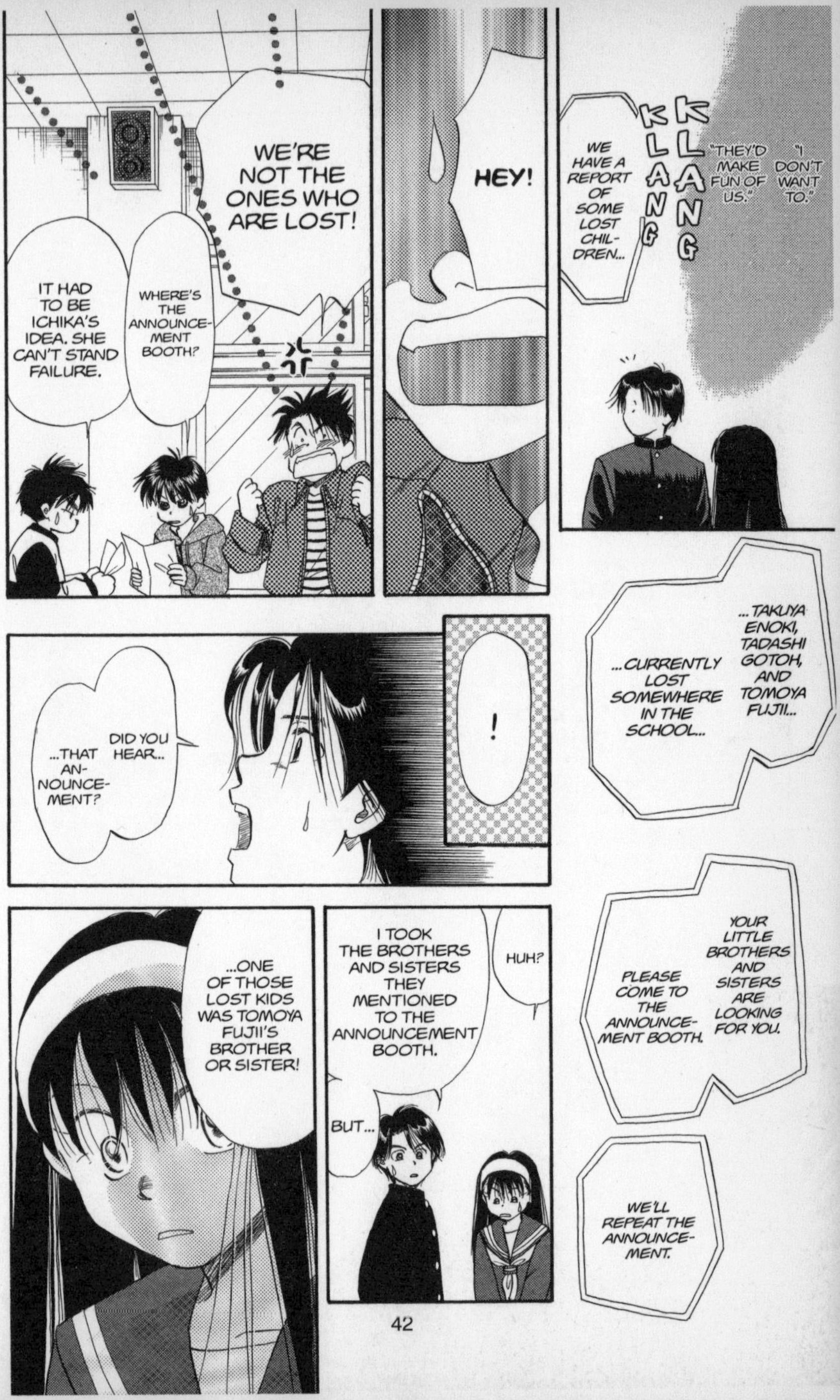
WE HAVE A REPORT OF SOME LOST CHILDREN...
KLANG
KLANG
"I DON'T WANT TO."
"THEY'D MAKE FUN OF US."
HEY!
WE'RE NOT THE ONES WHO ARE LOST!
WHERE'S THE ANNOUNCEMENT BOOTH?
IT HAD TO BE ICHIKA'S IDEA. SHE CAN'T STAND FAILURE.
...TAKUYA ENOKI, TADASHI GOTOH, AND TOMOYA FUJII...
...CURRENTLY LOST SOMEWHERE IN THE SCHOOL...
!
DID YOU HEAR...
...THAT ANNOUNCEMENT?
YOUR LITTLE BROTHERS AND SISTERS ARE LOOKING FOR YOU.
PLEASE COME TO THE ANNOUNCEMENT BOOTH.
HUH?
I TOOK THE BROTHERS AND SISTERS THEY MENTIONED TO THE ANNOUNCEMENT BOOTH.
BUT...
...ONE OF THOSE LOST KIDS WAS TOMOYA FUJII'S BROTHER OR SISTER!
WE'LL REPEAT THE ANNOUNCEMENT.

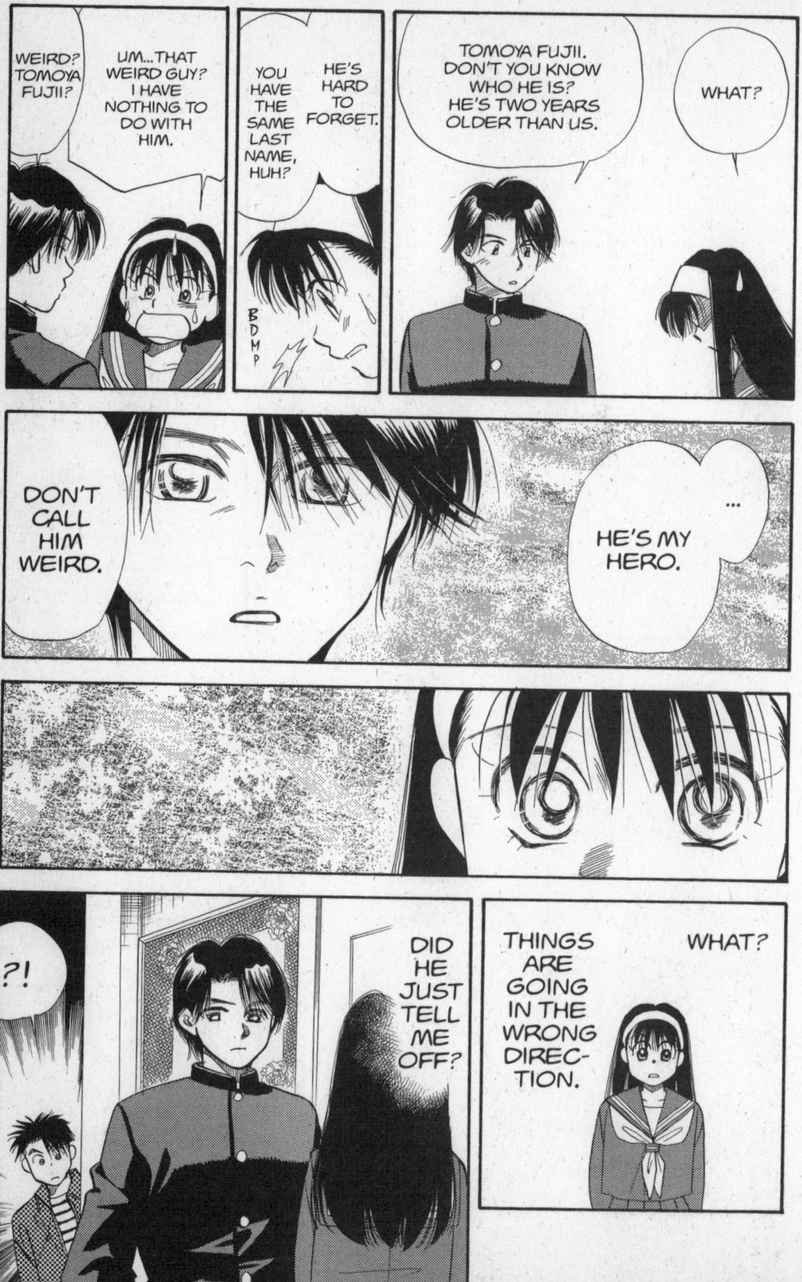
WHAT?
TOMOYA FUJII. DON'T YOU KNOW WHO HE IS? HE'S TWO YEARS OLDER THAN US.
HE'S HARD TO FORGET.
YOU HAVE THE SAME LAST NAME, HUH?
BDMP
UM...THAT WEIRD GUY? I HAVE NOTHING TO DO WITH HIM.
WEIRD? TOMOYA FUJII?
... HE'S MY HERO.
DON'T CALL HIM WEIRD.
WHAT?
THINGS ARE GOING IN THE WRONG DIREC-TION.
DID HE JUST TELL ME OFF?
?!

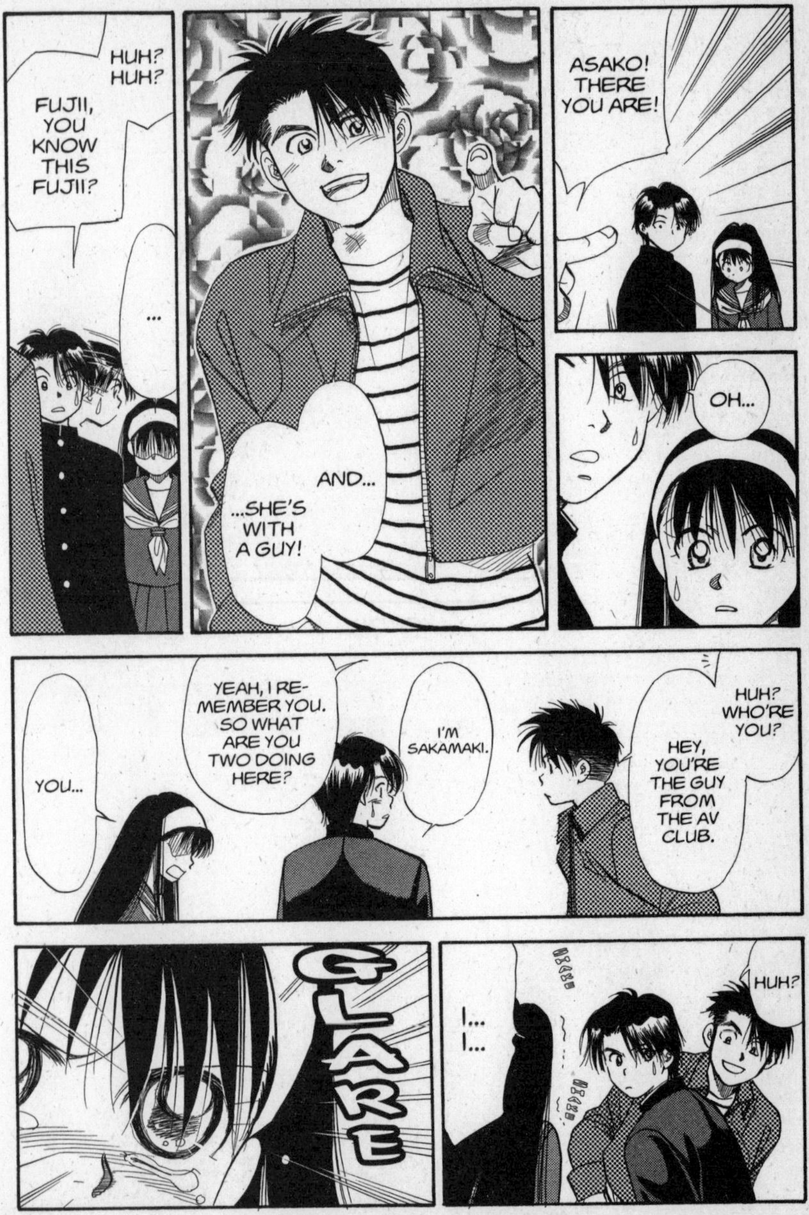
ASAKO! THERE YOU ARE!
OH...
AND...
...SHE'S WITH A GUY!
HUH? HUH?
FUJII, YOU KNOW THIS FUJII?
...
HUH? WHO'RE YOU?
HEY, YOU'RE THE GUY FROM THE AV CLUB.
I'M SAKAMAKI.
YEAH, I REMEMBER YOU. SO WHAT ARE YOU TWO DOING HERE?
YOU...
HUH?
I... I...
GLARE

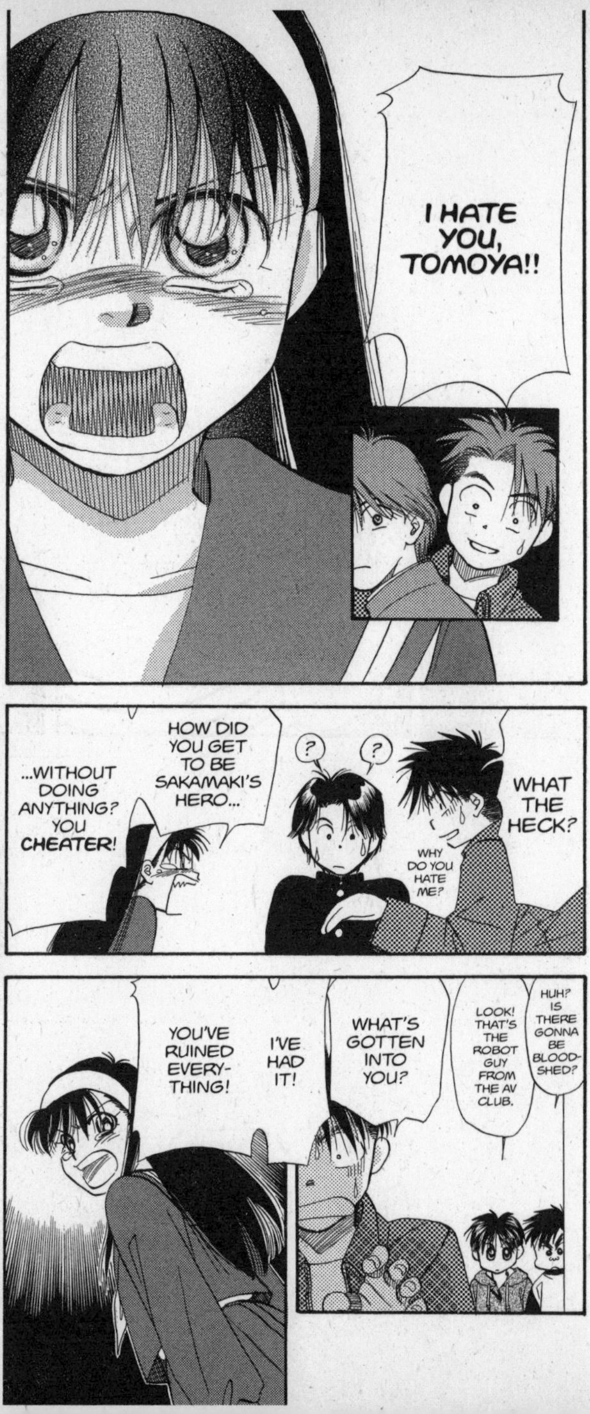
I HATE YOU, TOMOYA!!
WHAT THE HECK?
WHY DO YOU HATE ME?
HOW DID YOU GET TO BE SAKAMAKI'S HERO...
...WITHOUT DOING ANYTHING? YOU CHEATER!
HUH? IS THERE GONNA BE BLOOD-SHED?
LOOK! THAT'S THE ROBOT GUY FROM THE AV CLUB.
WHAT'S GOTTEN INTO YOU?
I'VE HAD IT!
YOU'VE RUINED EVERY-THING!

Author's Note Part 3

Continued from Part 2

To remind myself of the incident, I jotted down "carbonated," *tan-san* in Japanese, on a memo pad. But that created a problem. I have a habit of writing down everything sloppily, including important phone calls and the like. A few days later, I found a memo pad with "tan-san" written on it in hiragana. (Hiragana only tells you the pronunciation of a word, not its meaning.) I had no idea what it meant.

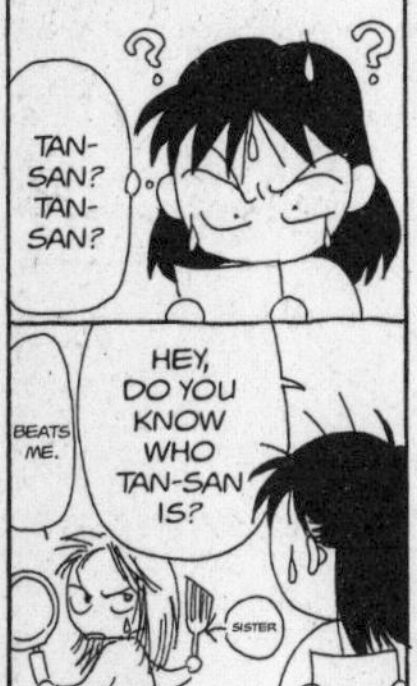
TAN-SAN? TAN-SAN?
HEY, DO YOU KNOW WHO TAN-SAN IS?
BEATS ME.
SISTER

I was stumped for a long time. I assumed it was somebody named Tan. Finally I remembered the incident with the soda bottle and had a good laugh. Have you ever done something like that?
Bye for now.

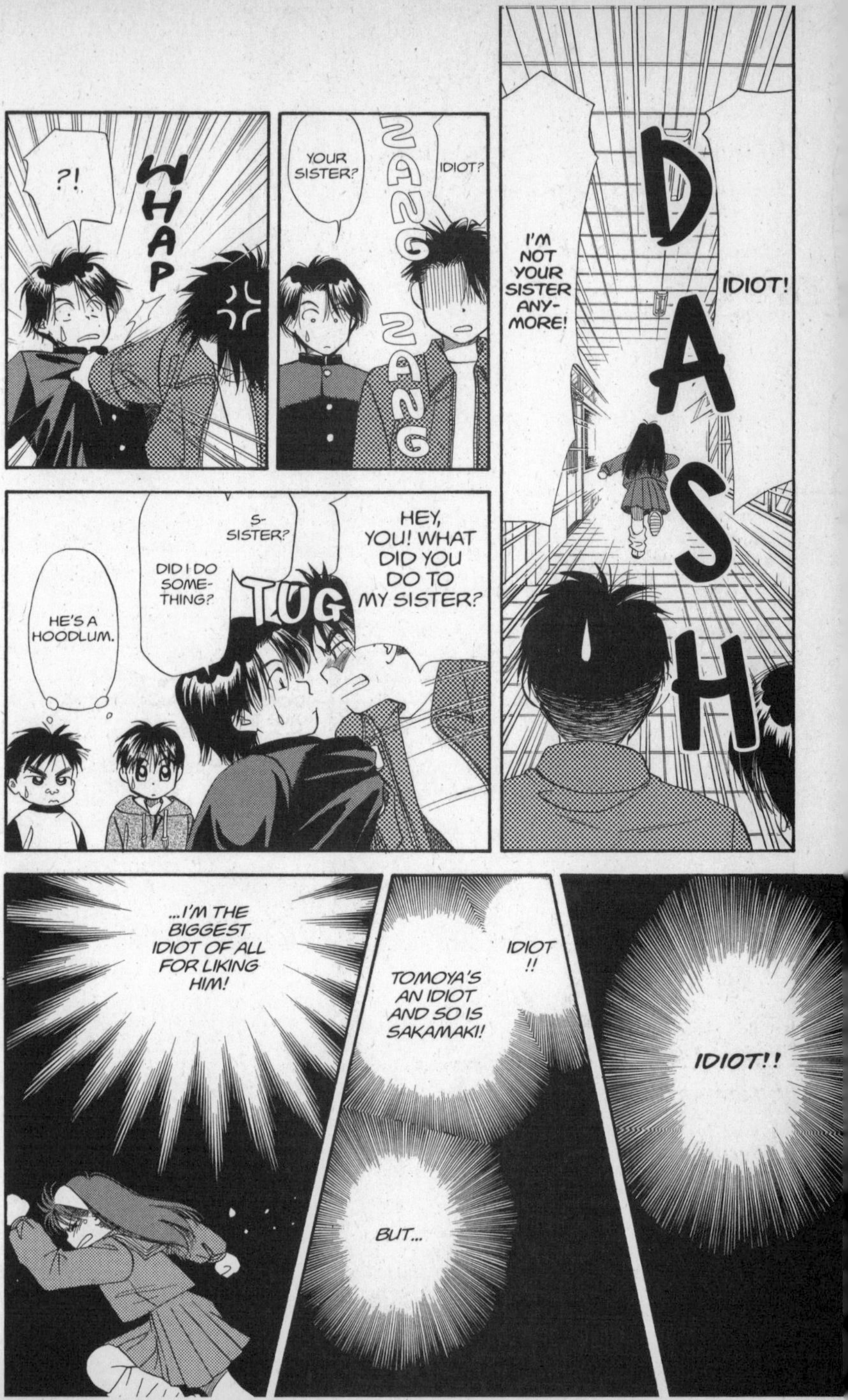
I'M NOT YOUR SISTER ANY-MORE!
IDIOT!
DASH
IDIOT?
YOUR SISTER?
ZANG ZANG
WHAP
?!
HEY, YOU! WHAT DID YOU DO TO MY SISTER?
S-SISTER?
DID I DO SOME-THING?
TUG
HE'S A HOODLUM.
IDIOT!!
IDIOT !!
TOMOYA'S AN IDIOT AND SO IS SAKAMAKI!
BUT...
...I'M THE BIGGEST IDIOT OF ALL FOR LIKING HIM!

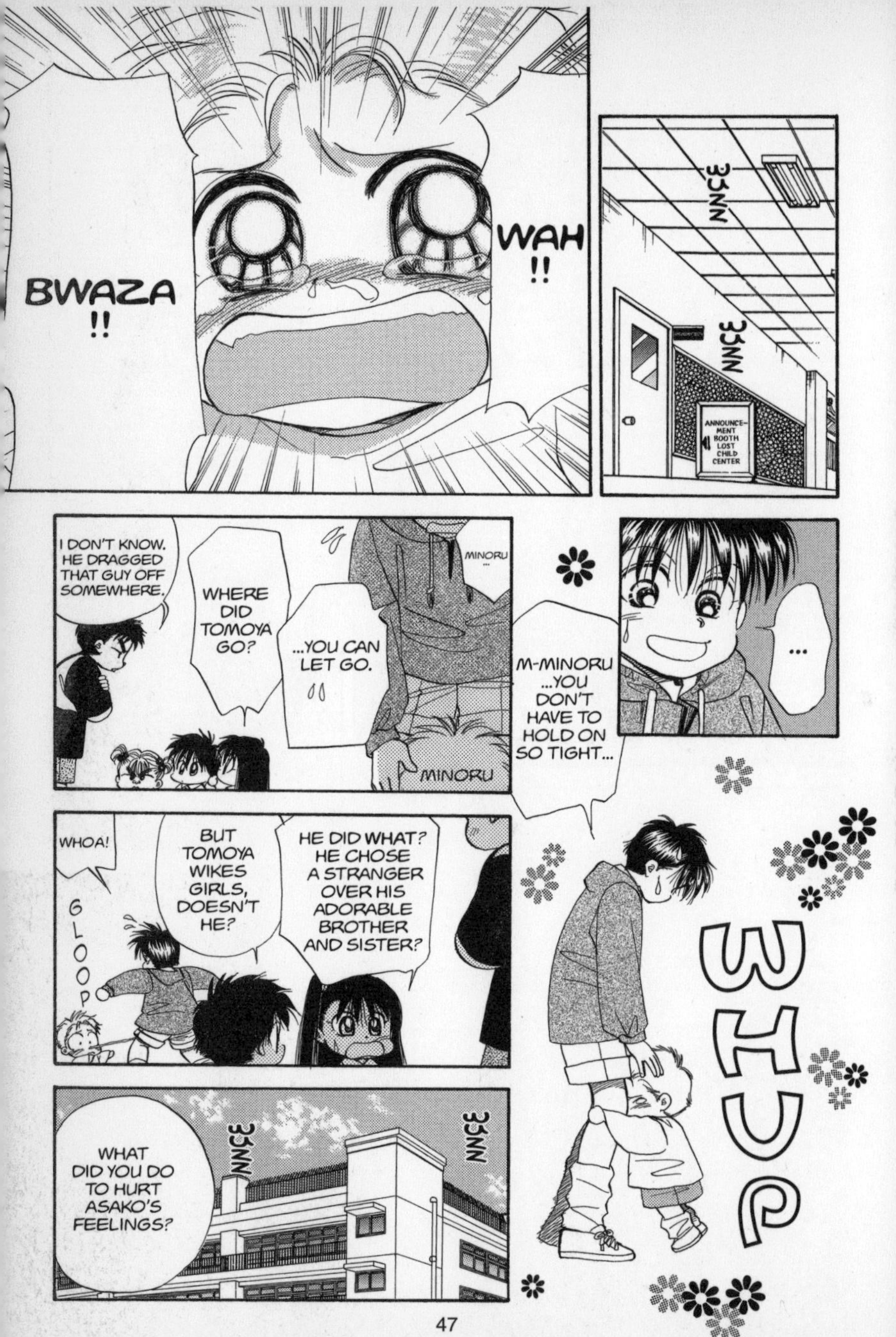
ANNOUNCEMENT BOOTH LOST CHILD CENTER
WAH!!
BWAZA!!
...
M-MINORU ...YOU DON'T HAVE TO HOLD ON SO TIGHT...
MINORU ...
...YOU CAN LET GO.
MINORU
WHERE DID TOMOYA GO?
I DON'T KNOW. HE DRAGGED THAT GUY OFF SOMEWHERE.
HE DID WHAT? HE CHOSE A STRANGER OVER HIS ADORABLE BROTHER AND SISTER?
BUT TOMOYA WIKES GIRLS, DOESN'T HE?
WHOA!
GLOOP
WHAT DID YOU DO TO HURT ASAKO'S FEELINGS?

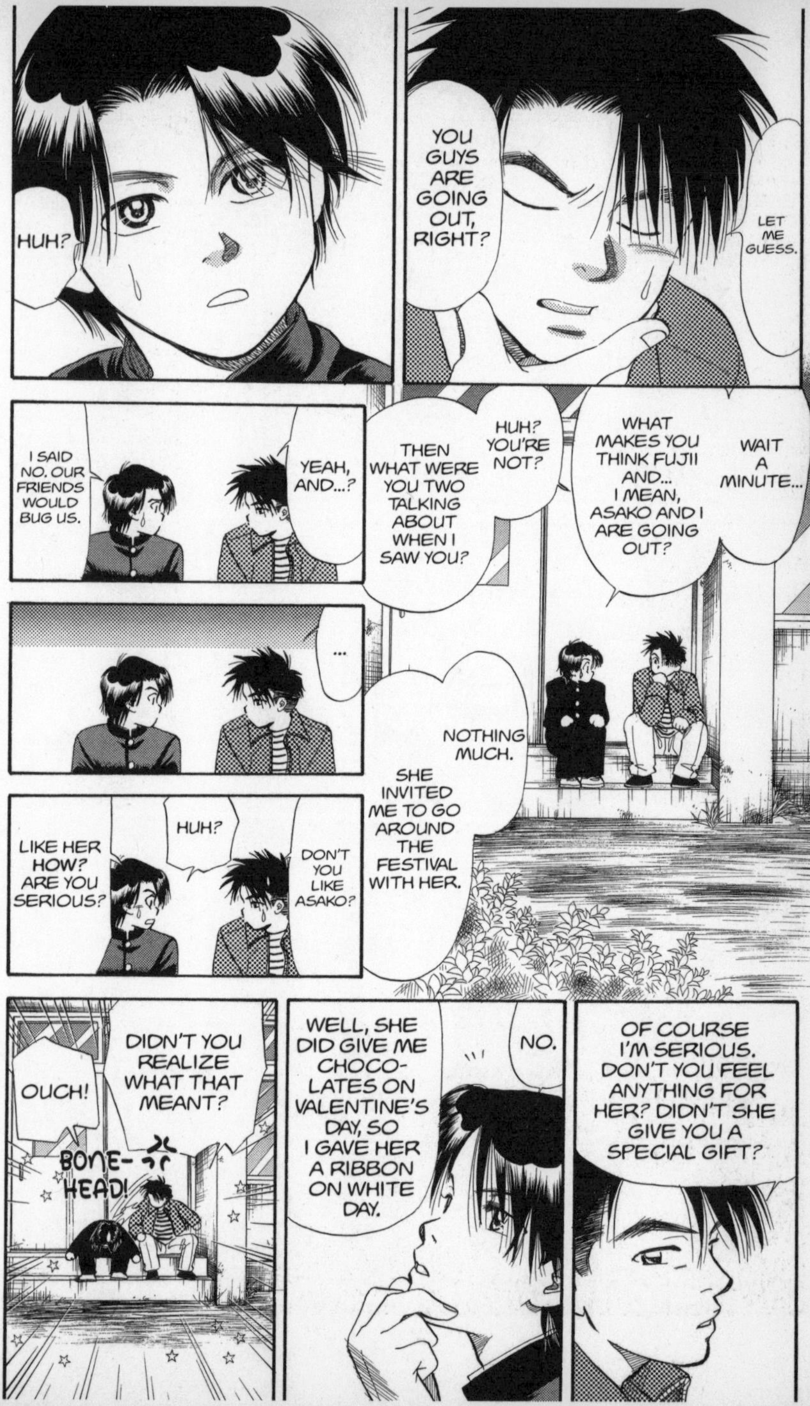
LET ME GUESS.
YOU GUYS ARE GOING OUT, RIGHT?
HUH?
WAIT A MINUTE...
WHAT MAKES YOU THINK FUJII AND... I MEAN, ASAKO AND I ARE GOING OUT?
HUH? YOU'RE NOT?
THEN WHAT WERE YOU TWO TALKING ABOUT WHEN I SAW YOU?
NOTHING MUCH.
SHE INVITED ME TO GO AROUND THE FESTIVAL WITH HER.
YEAH, AND...?
I SAID NO. OUR FRIENDS WOULD BUG US.
...
DON'T YOU LIKE ASAKO?
HUH?
LIKE HER HOW? ARE YOU SERIOUS?
OF COURSE I'M SERIOUS. DON'T YOU FEEL ANYTHING FOR HER? DIDN'T SHE GIVE YOU A SPECIAL GIFT?
NO.
WELL, SHE DID GIVE ME CHOCO-LATES ON VALENTINE'S DAY, SO I GAVE HER A RIBBON ON WHITE DAY.
DIDN'T YOU REALIZE WHAT THAT MEANT?
BONE-HEAD!
OUCH!

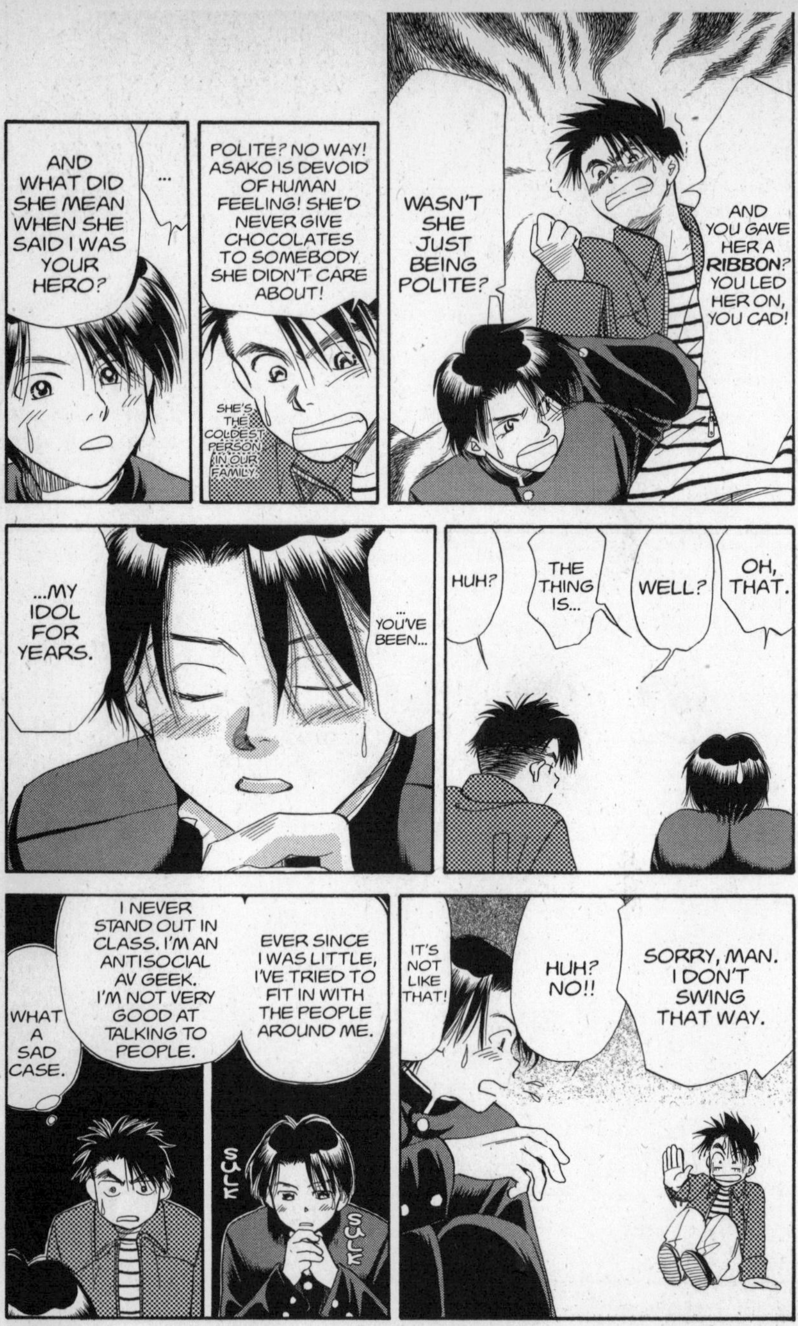
AND YOU GAVE HER A RIBBON? YOU LED HER ON, YOU CAD!
WASN'T SHE JUST BEING POLITE?
POLITE? NO WAY! ASAKO IS DEVOID OF HUMAN FEELING! SHE'D NEVER GIVE CHOCOLATES TO SOMEBODY SHE DIDN'T CARE ABOUT!
SHE'S THE COLDEST PERSON IN OUR FAMILY.
...
AND WHAT DID SHE MEAN WHEN SHE SAID I WAS YOUR HERO?
OH, THAT.
WELL?
THE THING IS...
HUH?
...YOU'VE BEEN...
...MY IDOL FOR YEARS.
SORRY, MAN. I DON'T SWING THAT WAY.
HUH? NO!!
IT'S NOT LIKE THAT!
EVER SINCE I WAS LITTLE, I'VE TRIED TO FIT IN WITH THE PEOPLE AROUND ME.
I NEVER STAND OUT IN CLASS. I'M AN ANTISOCIAL AV GEEK. I'M NOT VERY GOOD AT TALKING TO PEOPLE.
WHAT A SAD CASE.
SULK
SULK

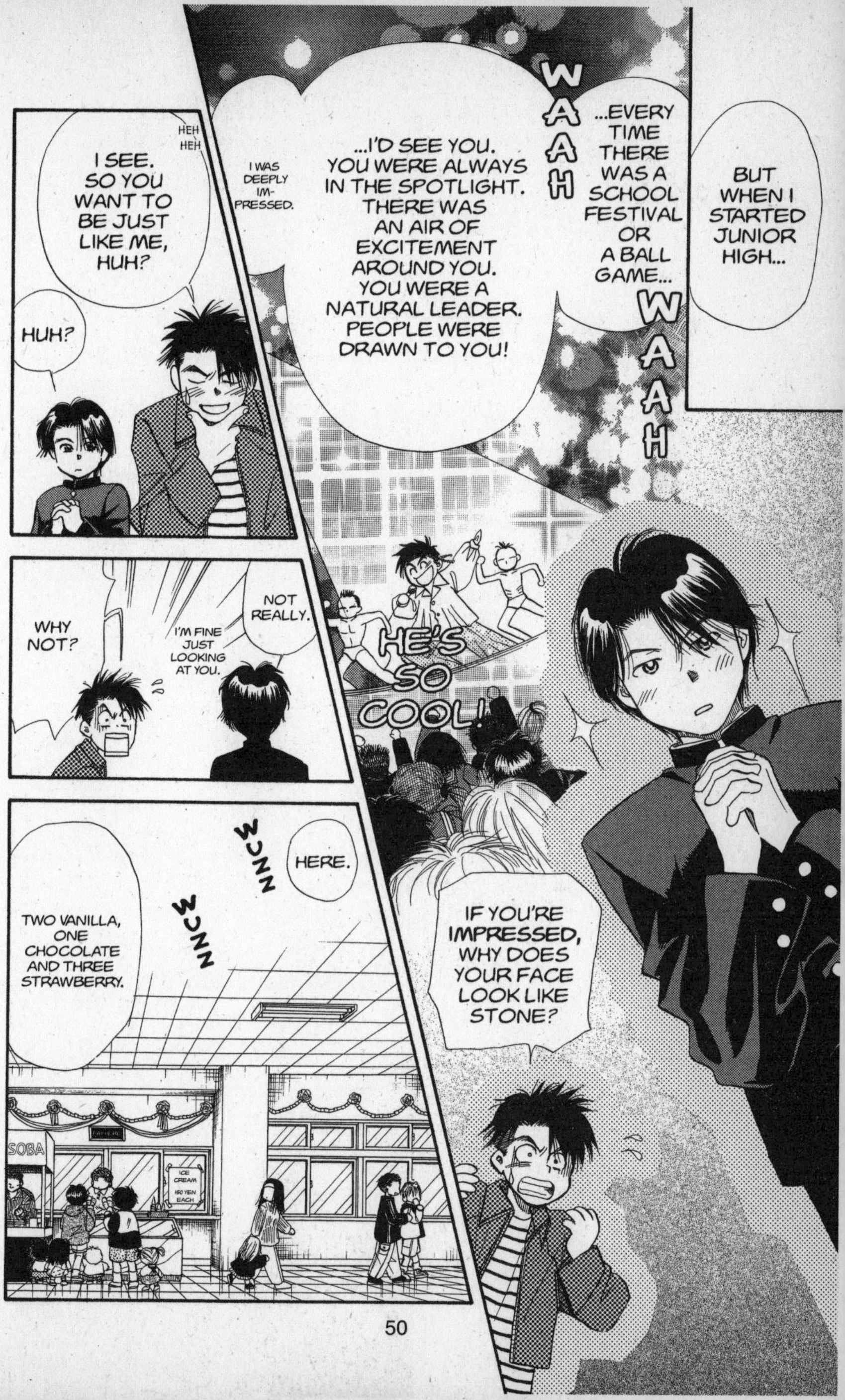
BUT WHEN I STARTED JUNIOR HIGH...
...EVERY TIME THERE WAS A SCHOOL FESTIVAL OR A BALL GAME...
WAAH
WAAH
...I'D SEE YOU. YOU WERE ALWAYS IN THE SPOTLIGHT. THERE WAS AN AIR OF EXCITEMENT AROUND YOU. YOU WERE A NATURAL LEADER. PEOPLE WERE DRAWN TO YOU!
I WAS DEEPLY IM-PRESSED.
HE'S SO COOL!
IF YOU'RE IMPRESSED, WHY DOES YOUR FACE LOOK LIKE STONE?
HEH HEH
I SEE. SO YOU WANT TO BE JUST LIKE ME, HUH?
HUH?
NOT REALLY.
I'M FINE JUST LOOKING AT YOU.
WHY NOT?
HERE.
WUNN
WUNN
TWO VANILLA, ONE CHOCOLATE AND THREE STRAWBERRY.
SOBA
ICE CREAM 150 YEN EACH

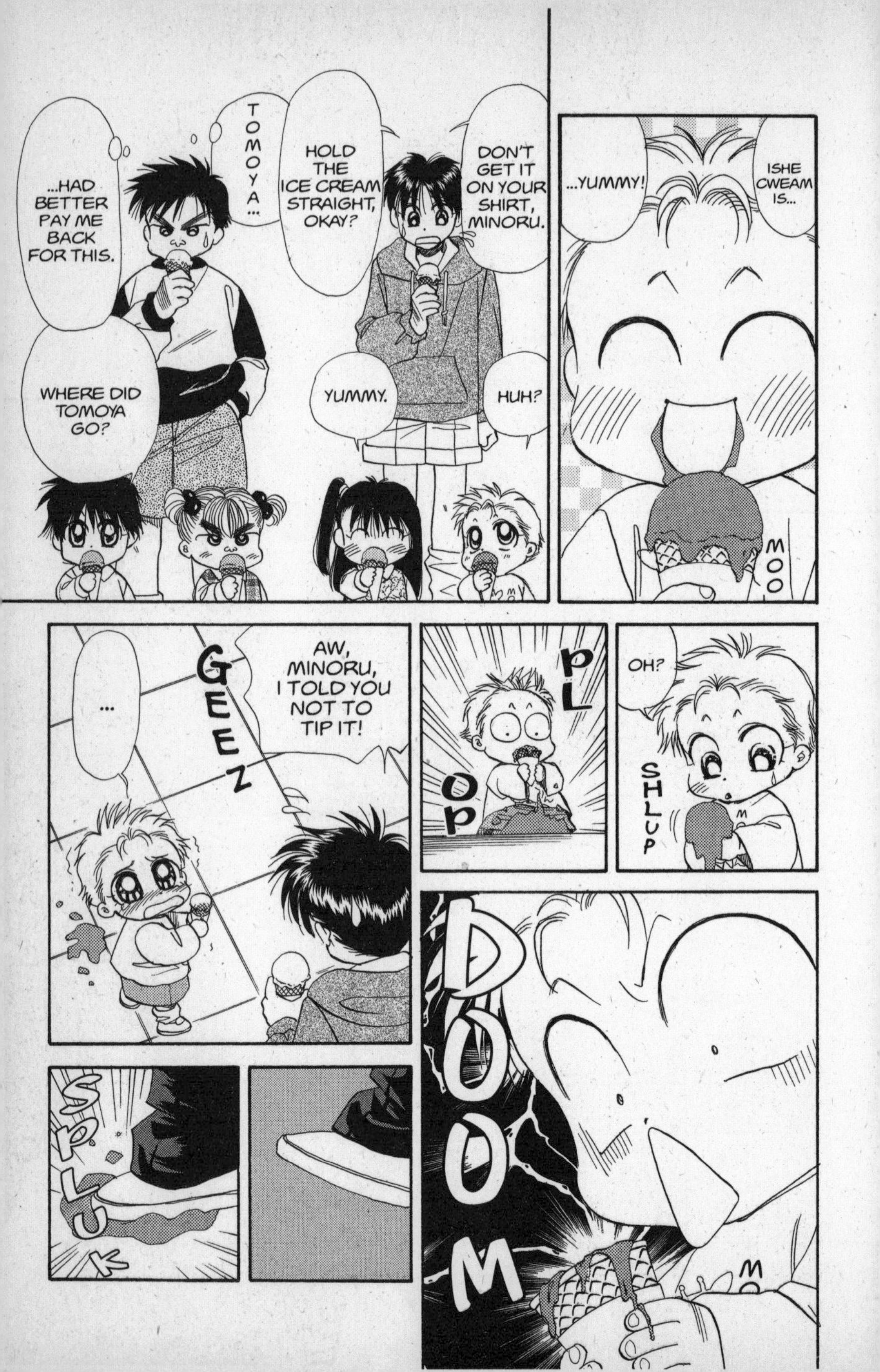
ISHE CWEAM IS...
...YUMMY!
MOO
DON'T GET IT ON YOUR SHIRT, MINORU.
HOLD THE ICE CREAM STRAIGHT, OKAY?
TOMOYA...
...HAD BETTER PAY ME BACK FOR THIS.
HUH?
YUMMY.
WHERE DID TOMOYA GO?
OH?
SHLUP
PL
OP
AW, MINORU, I TOLD YOU NOT TO TIP IT!
GEEZ
...
DOOM
MO
SPLUK

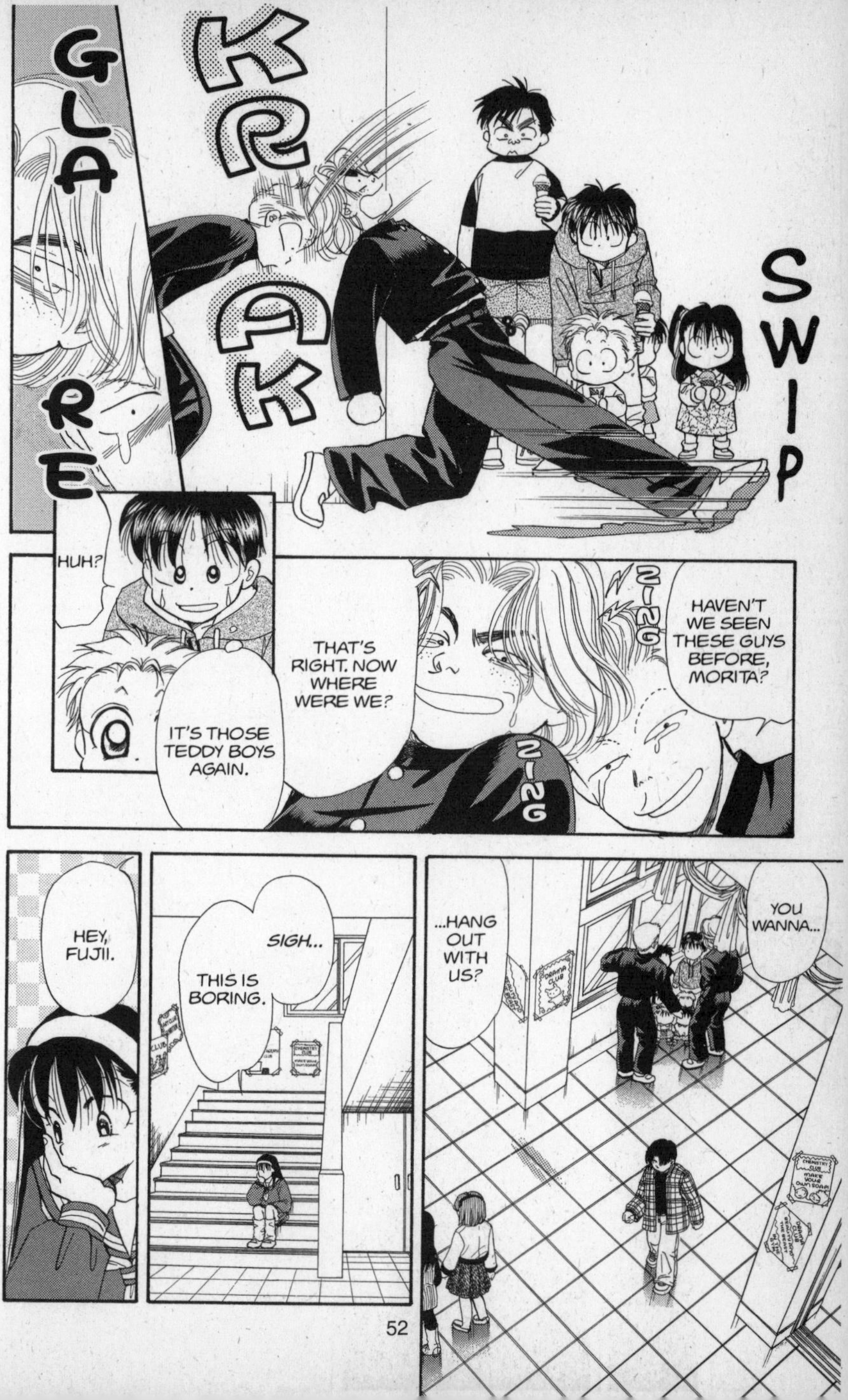
SWIP
KRAK
GLARE
HAVEN'T WE SEEN THESE GUYS BEFORE, MORITA?
ZING
ZING
THAT'S RIGHT. NOW WHERE WERE WE?
HUH?
IT'S THOSE TEDDY BOYS AGAIN.
YOU WANNA...
...HANG OUT WITH US?
SIGH...
THIS IS BORING.
HEY, FUJII.

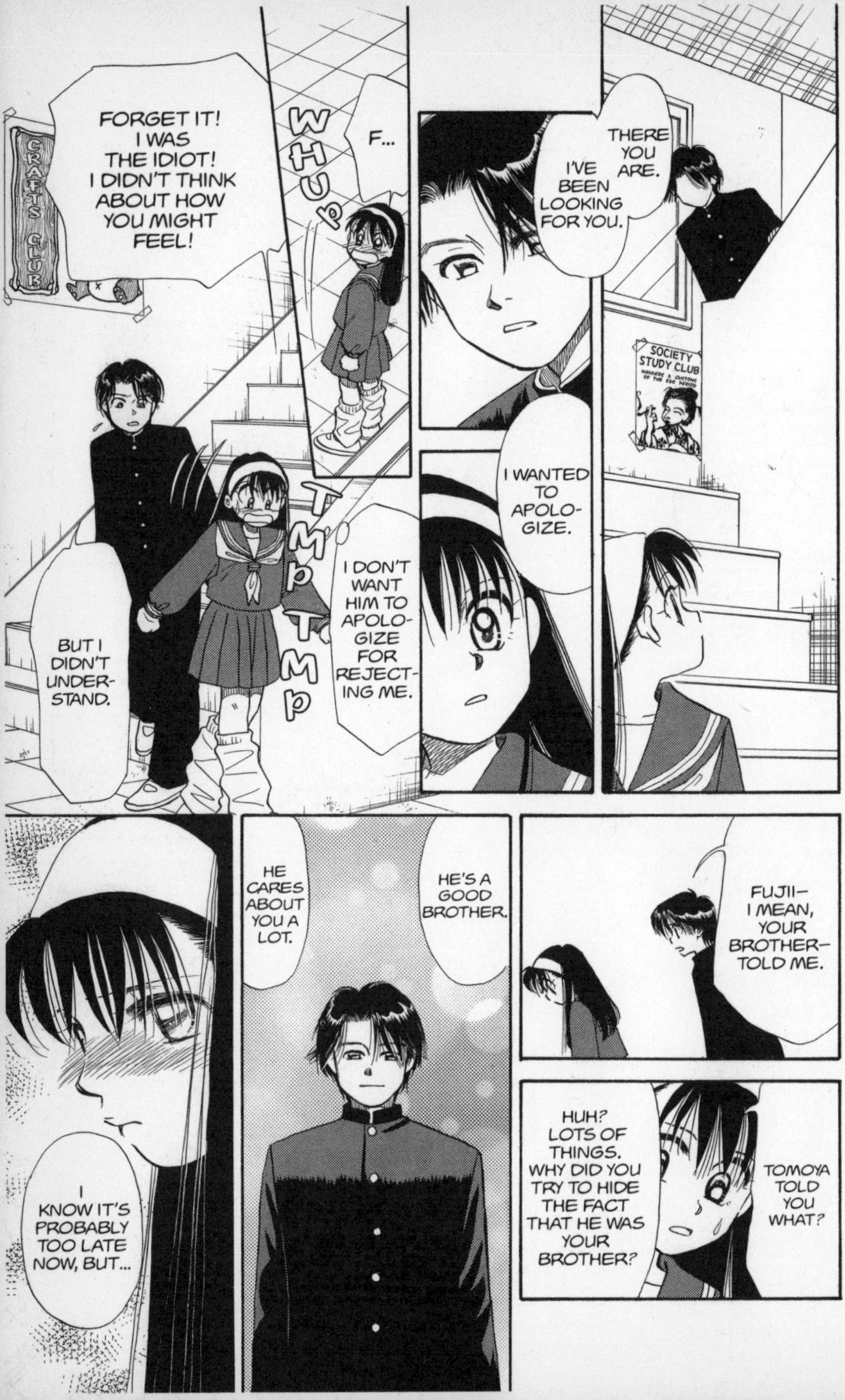
THERE YOU ARE.
I'VE BEEN LOOKING FOR YOU.
SOCIETY STUDY CLUB
MANNERS & CUSTOMS OF THE EDO PERIOD
I WANTED TO APOLOGIZE.
F...
WHUP
CRAFTS CLUB
FORGET IT! I WAS THE IDIOT! I DIDN'T THINK ABOUT HOW YOU MIGHT FEEL!
TMP TMP
I DON'T WANT HIM TO APOLOGIZE FOR REJECTING ME.
BUT I DIDN'T UNDERSTAND.
FUJII- I MEAN, YOUR BROTHER- TOLD ME.
TOMOYA TOLD YOU WHAT?
HUH? LOTS OF THINGS. WHY DID YOU TRY TO HIDE THE FACT THAT HE WAS YOUR BROTHER?
HE'S A GOOD BROTHER.
HE CARES ABOUT YOU A LOT.
I KNOW IT'S PROBABLY TOO LATE NOW, BUT...

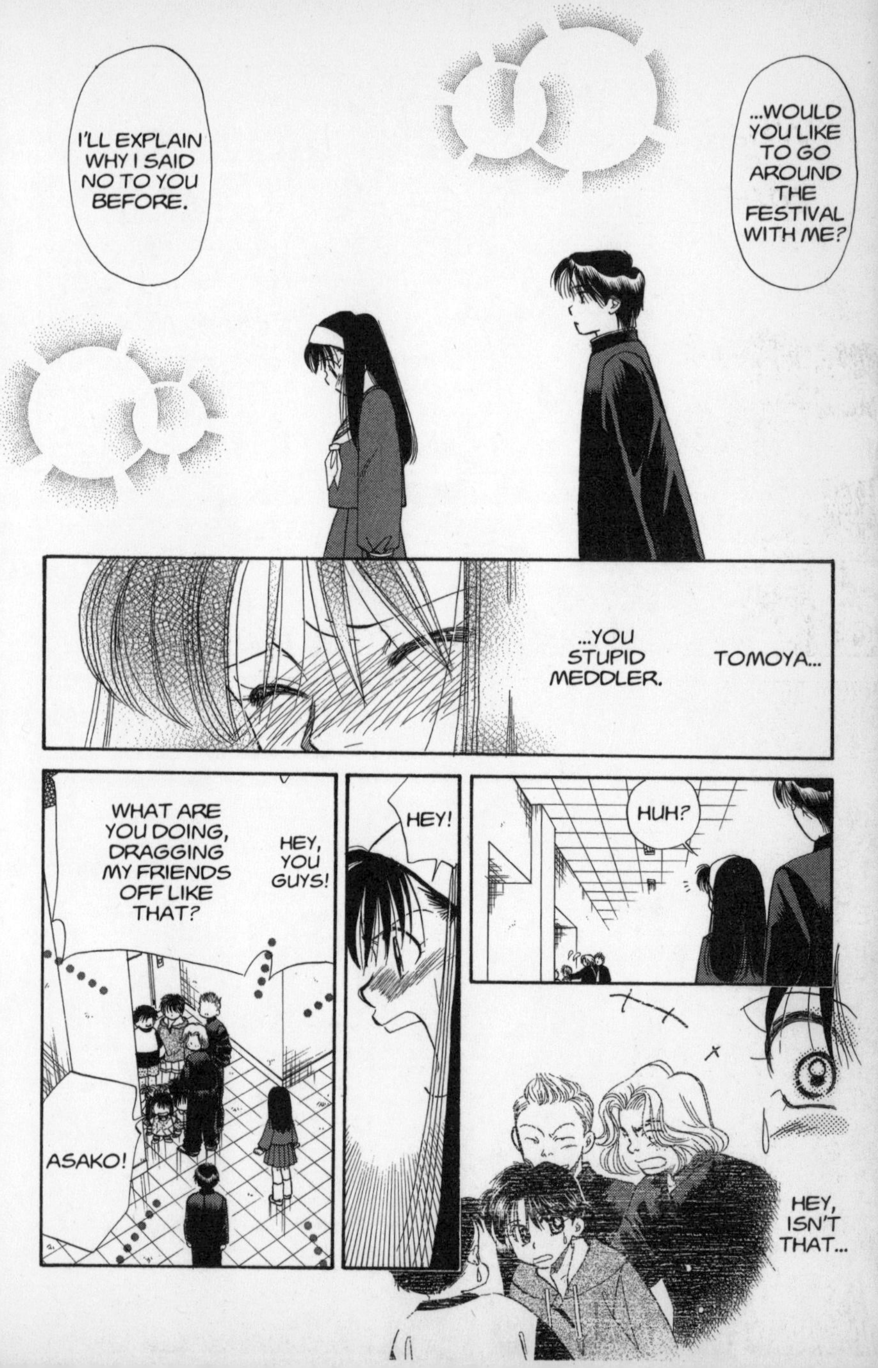
...WOULD YOU LIKE TO GO AROUND THE FESTIVAL WITH ME?
I'LL EXPLAIN WHY I SAID NO TO YOU BEFORE.
TOMOYA...
...YOU STUPID MEDDLER.
HUH?
HEY, ISN'T THAT...
HEY!
HEY, YOU GUYS!
WHAT ARE YOU DOING, DRAGGING MY FRIENDS OFF LIKE THAT?
ASAKO!

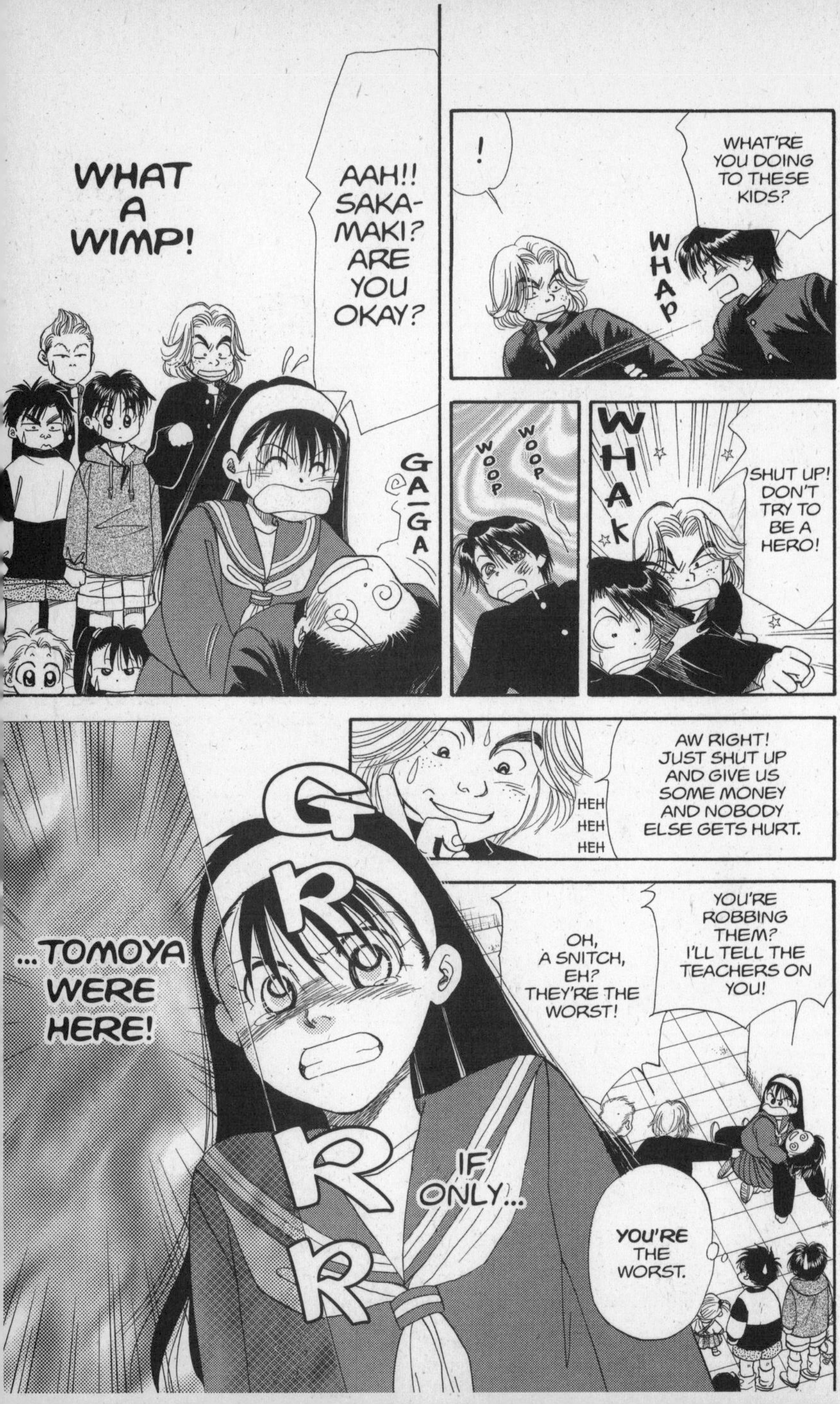
WHAT'RE YOU DOING TO THESE KIDS?
!
WHAP
WHAK
SHUT UP! DON'T TRY TO BE A HERO!
WOOP WOOP
AAH!! SAKA-MAKI? ARE YOU OKAY?
WHAT A WIMP!
GA-GA
AW RIGHT! JUST SHUT UP AND GIVE US SOME MONEY AND NOBODY ELSE GETS HURT.
HEH HEH HEH
YOU'RE ROBBING THEM? I'LL TELL THE TEACHERS ON YOU!
OH, A SNITCH, EH? THEY'RE THE WORST!
YOU'RE THE WORST.
GRRR
IF ONLY...
...TOMOYA WERE HERE!

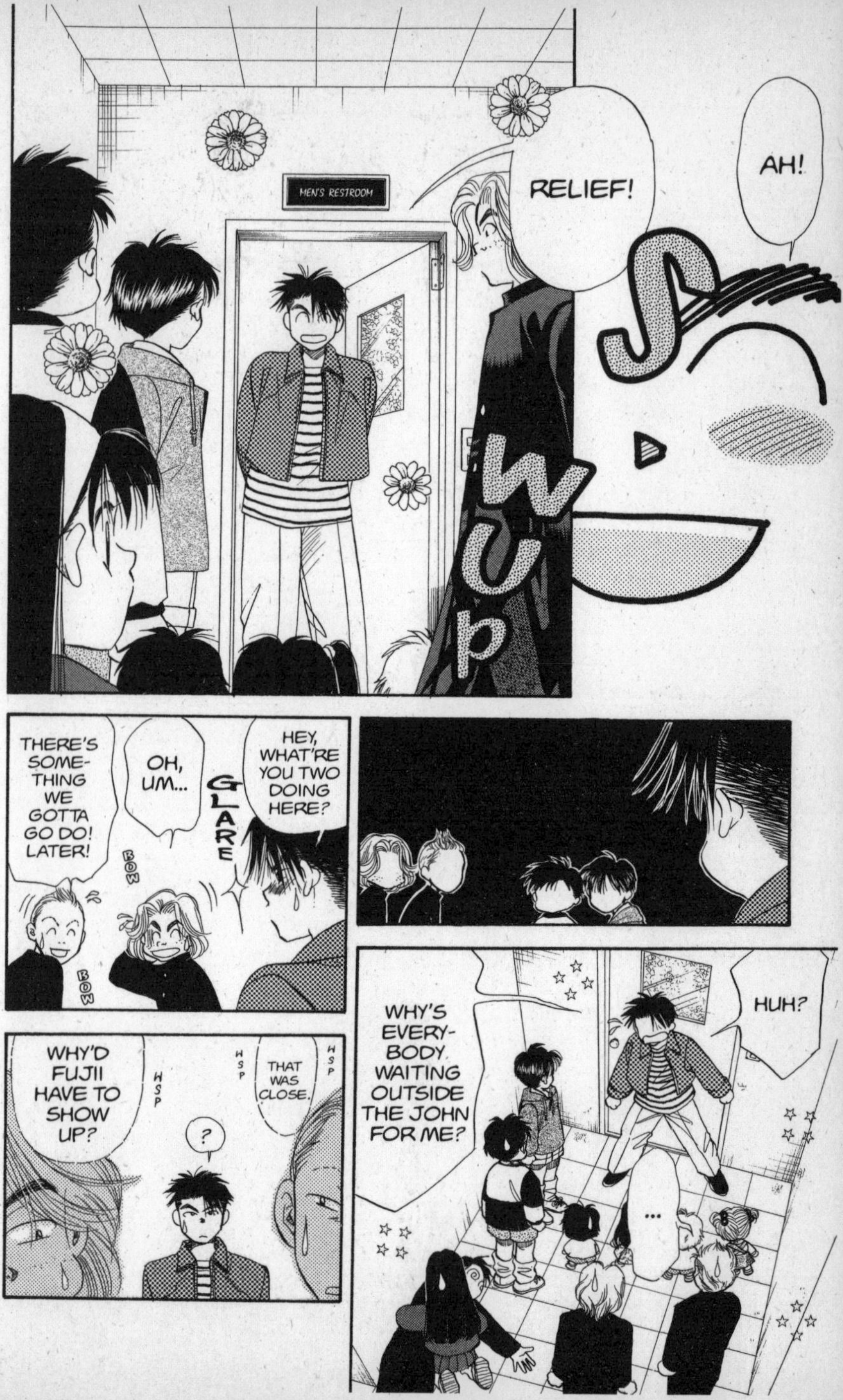
AH!
RELIEF!
SWUP
MEN'S RESTROOM
HEY, WHAT'RE YOU TWO DOING HERE?
GLARE
OH, UM...
THERE'S SOME-THING WE GOTTA GO DO! LATER!
BOW
BOW
HUH?
WHY'S EVERY-BODY WAITING OUTSIDE THE JOHN FOR ME?
...
HSP
THAT WAS CLOSE.
HSP
?
HSP
WHY'D FUJII HAVE TO SHOW UP?

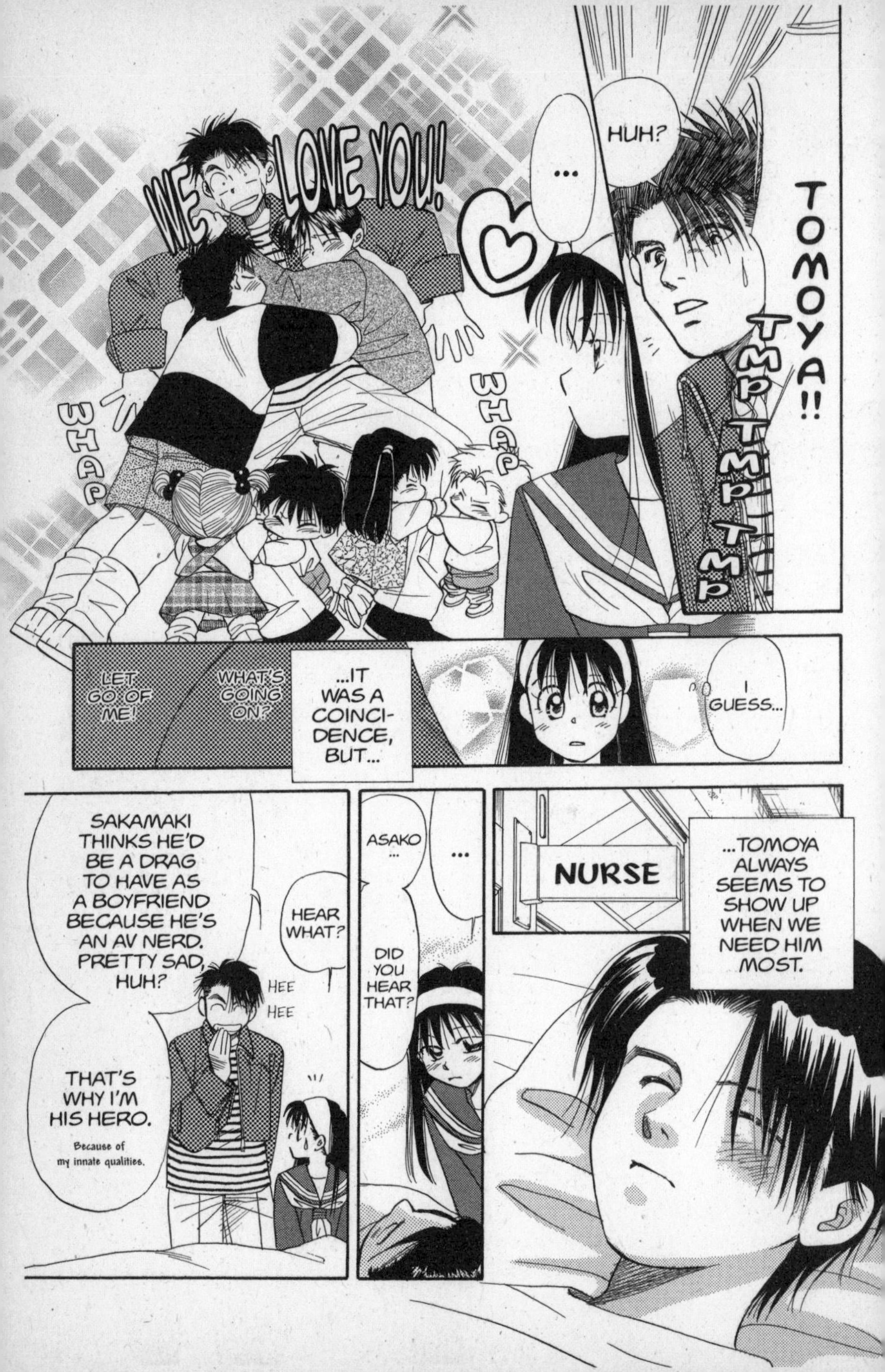
TOMOYA!!
HUH?
...
TMP TMP TMP TMP
WE LOVE YOU!
WHAP
WHAP
I GUESS...
...IT WAS A COINCIDENCE, BUT...
WHAT'S GOING ON?
LET GO OF ME!
NURSE
...TOMOYA ALWAYS SEEMS TO SHOW UP WHEN WE NEED HIM MOST.
...
ASAKO...
HEAR WHAT?
DID YOU HEAR THAT?
SAKAMAKI THINKS HE'D BE A DRAG TO HAVE AS A BOYFRIEND BECAUSE HE'S AN AV NERD. PRETTY SAD, HUH?
HEE HEE
THAT'S WHY I'M HIS HERO.
Because of my innate qualities.

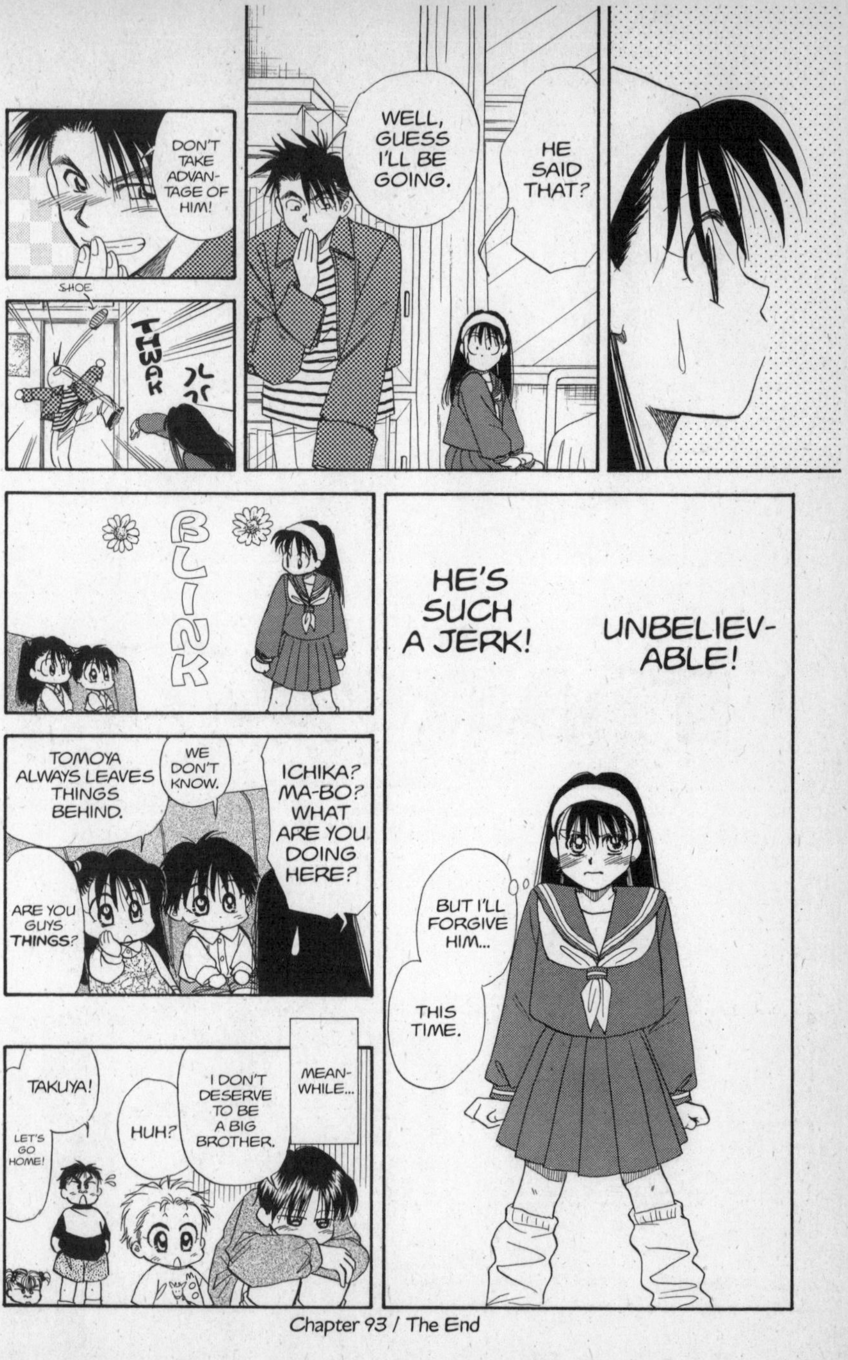
HE SAID THAT?
WELL, GUESS I'LL BE GOING.
DON'T TAKE ADVAN-TAGE OF HIM!
SHOE
THWAK
UNBELIEV-ABLE!
HE'S SUCH A JERK!
BUT I'LL FORGIVE HIM...
THIS TIME.
BLINK
ICHIKA? MA-BO? WHAT ARE YOU DOING HERE?
WE DON'T KNOW.
TOMOYA ALWAYS LEAVES THINGS BEHIND.
ARE YOU GUYS THINGS?
MEAN-WHILE...
I DON'T DESERVE TO BE A BIG BROTHER.
HUH?
TAKUYA!
LET'S GO HOME!

Chapter 93 / The End

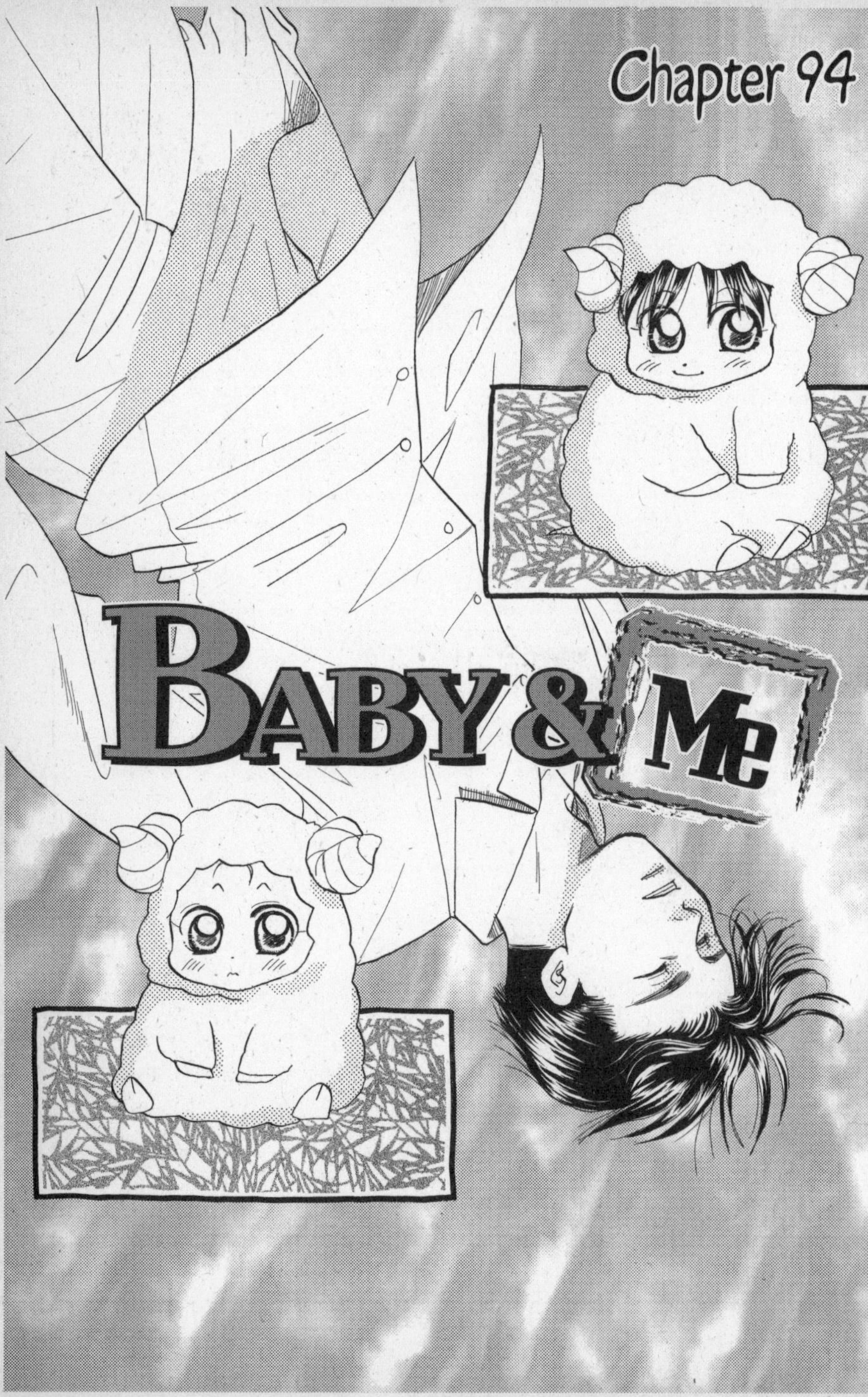
Chapter 94
BABY & Me

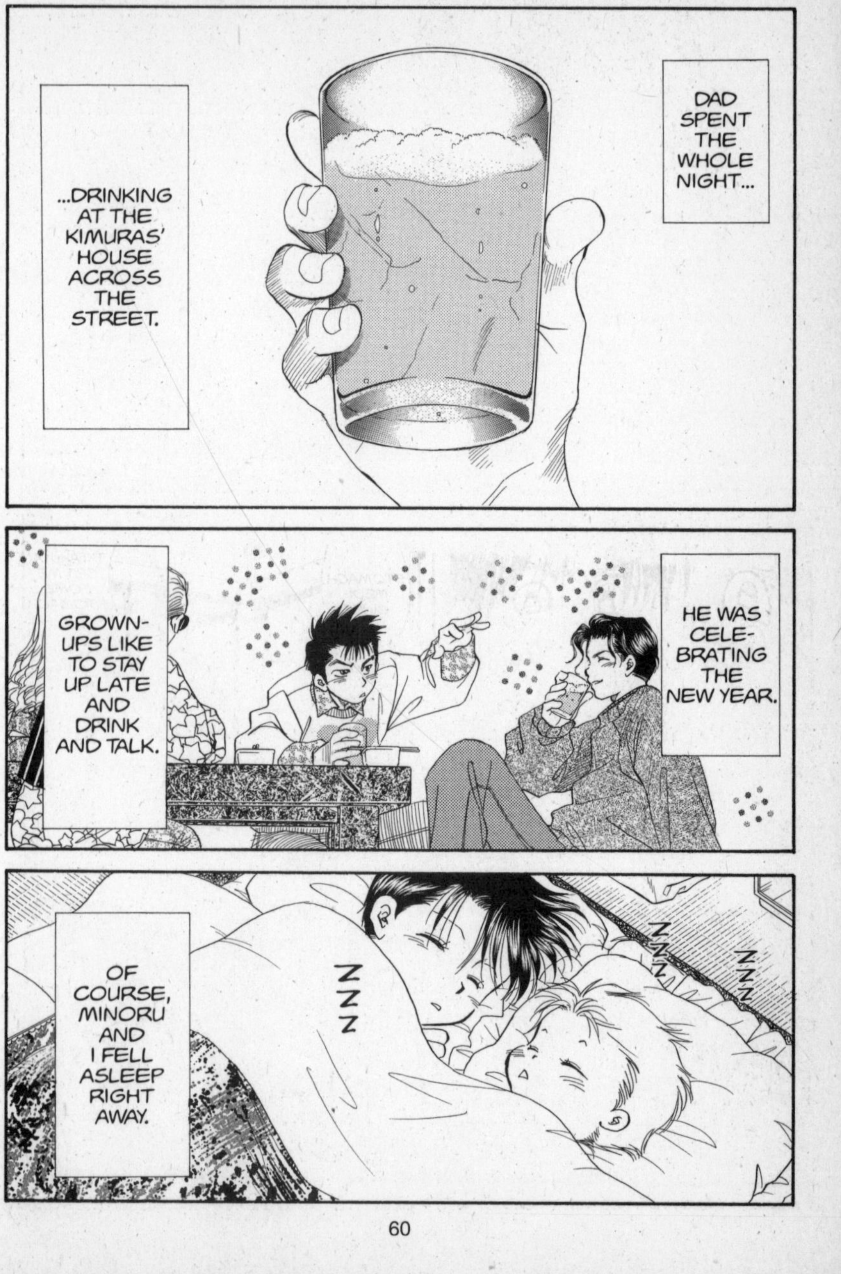
DAD SPENT THE WHOLE NIGHT...
...DRINKING AT THE KIMURAS' HOUSE ACROSS THE STREET.
HE WAS CELE-BRATING THE NEW YEAR.
GROWN-UPS LIKE TO STAY UP LATE AND DRINK AND TALK.
ZZZ
ZZZ
ZZZ
OF COURSE, MINORU AND I FELL ASLEEP RIGHT AWAY.

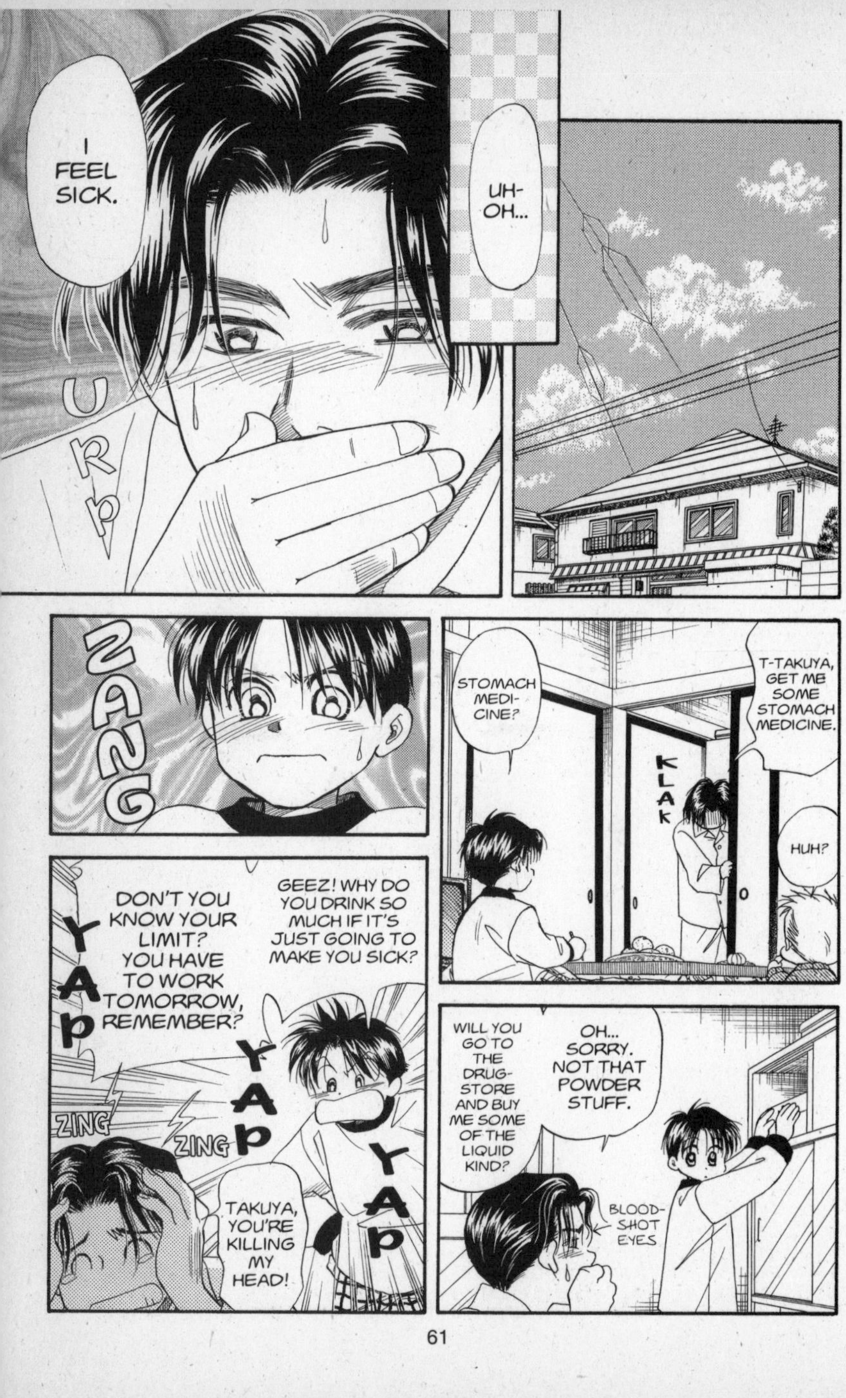
UH-OH...
I FEEL SICK.
URP
T-TAKUYA, GET ME SOME STOMACH MEDICINE.
STOMACH MEDICINE?
KLAK
HUH?
ZANG
OH... SORRY. NOT THAT POWDER STUFF.
WILL YOU GO TO THE DRUG-STORE AND BUY ME SOME OF THE LIQUID KIND?
BLOOD-SHOT EYES
GEEZ! WHY DO YOU DRINK SO MUCH IF IT'S JUST GOING TO MAKE YOU SICK?
DON'T YOU KNOW YOUR LIMIT? YOU HAVE TO WORK TOMORROW, REMEMBER?
YAP
YAP
YAP
YAP
ZING
ZING
TAKUYA, YOU'RE KILLING MY HEAD!

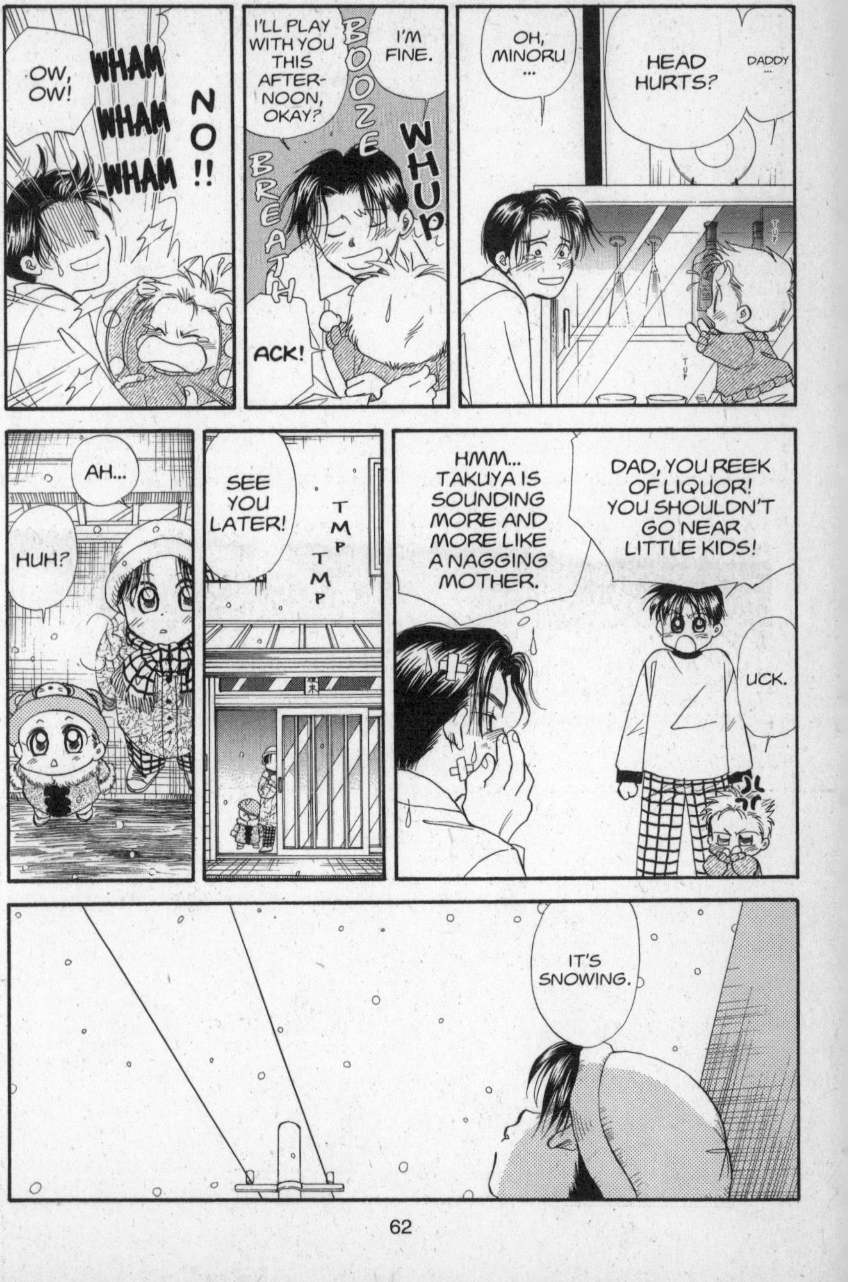
DADDY ...
HEAD HURTS?
OH, MINORU ...
TUP
TUP
I'M FINE.
WHUP
I'LL PLAY WITH YOU THIS AFTER-NOON, OKAY?
BOOZE BREATH
ACK!
NO!!
WHAM WHAM WHAM
OW, OW!
DAD, YOU REEK OF LIQUOR! YOU SHOULDN'T GO NEAR LITTLE KIDS!
UCK.
HMM... TAKUYA IS SOUNDING MORE AND MORE LIKE A NAGGING MOTHER.
TMP TMP
SEE YOU LATER!
AH...
HUH?
IT'S SNOWING.

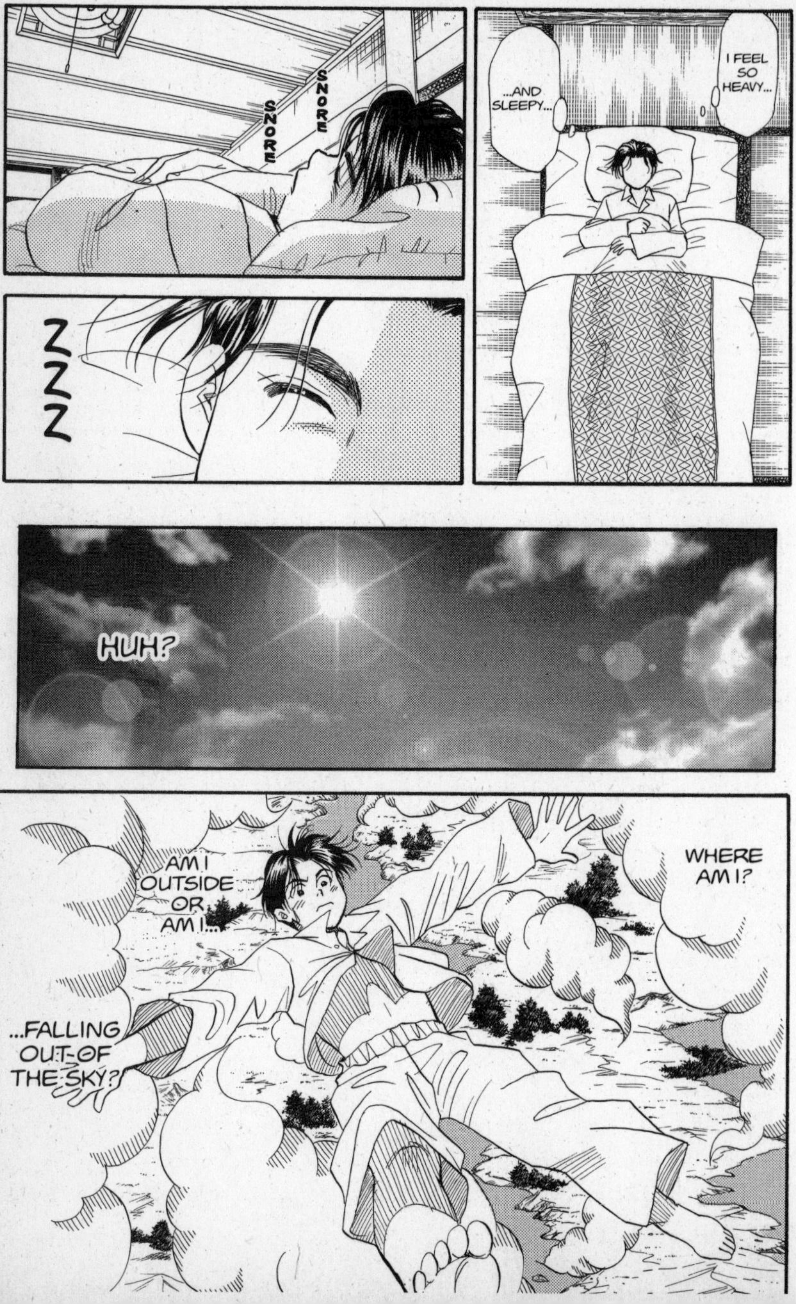
I FEEL SO HEAVY...
...AND SLEEPY...
SNORE
SNORE
ZZZ
HUH?
WHERE AM I?
AM I OUTSIDE OR AM I...
...FALLING OUT OF THE SKY?

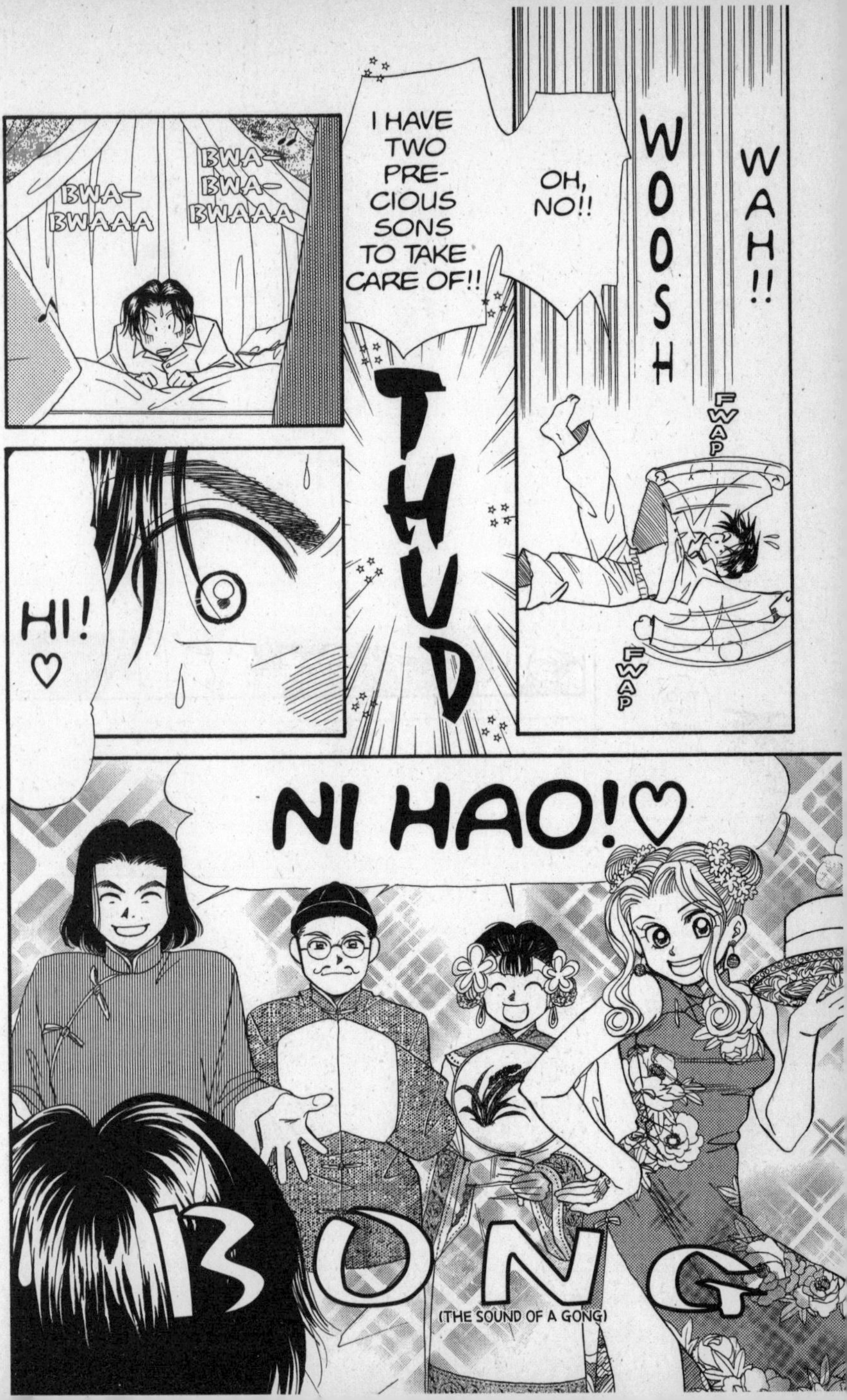
WAH!!
WOOSH
OH, NO!!
I HAVE TWO PRE-CIOUS SONS TO TAKE CARE OF!!
FWAP
FWAP
THUD
BWA-BWA-BWAAA
BWA-BWAAA
HI! ♥
NI HAO! ♥
BONG
(THE SOUND OF A GONG)

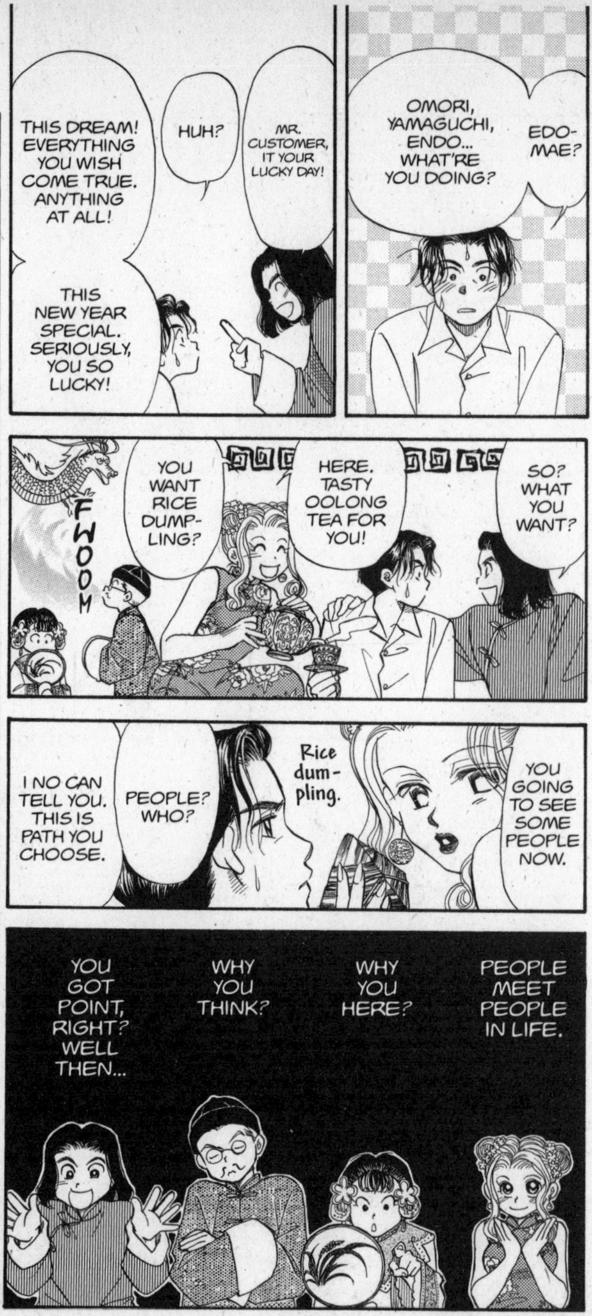
EDO-MAE?
OMORI, YAMAGUCHI, ENDO... WHAT'RE YOU DOING?
MR. CUSTOMER, IT YOUR LUCKY DAY!
HUH?
THIS DREAM! EVERYTHING YOU WISH COME TRUE. ANYTHING AT ALL!
THIS NEW YEAR SPECIAL. SERIOUSLY, YOU SO LUCKY!
SO? WHAT YOU WANT?
HERE. TASTY OOLONG TEA FOR YOU!
YOU WANT RICE DUMPLING?
FWOOOM
YOU GOING TO SEE SOME PEOPLE NOW.
Rice dumpling.
PEOPLE? WHO?
I NO CAN TELL YOU. THIS IS PATH YOU CHOOSE.
PEOPLE MEET PEOPLE IN LIFE.
WHY YOU HERE?
WHY YOU THINK?
YOU GOT POINT, RIGHT? WELL THEN...

Author's Note Part 4

We've got a bigger workroom now.

It's so much more spacious that I feel lost when I'm in there by myself, so I made a rule not to go in there unless I have work to do.

But I have to go in the workroom when I work on colored illustrations.

So I work quietly all by myself, but everything — the TV, the stereo, the speakers — is far away. I feel so lonely!

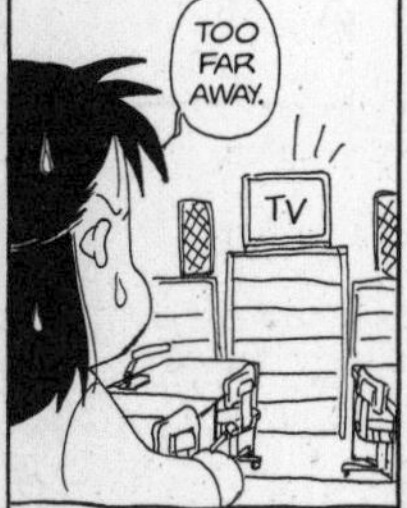
TOO FAR AWAY.
TV

If you want to know how I feel, here's a good analogy. It's like I'm all by myself in a classroom after school practicing kanji, one hundred times each. That's the feeling.

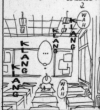

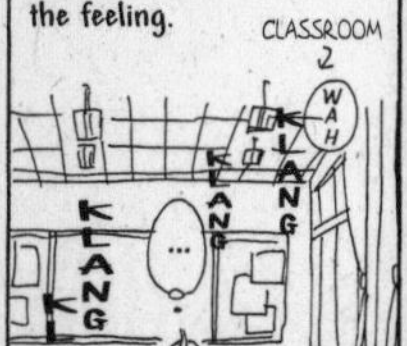
CLASSROOM
WAH
KLANG
KLANG
KLANG
KLANG
KLANG
...
WAH

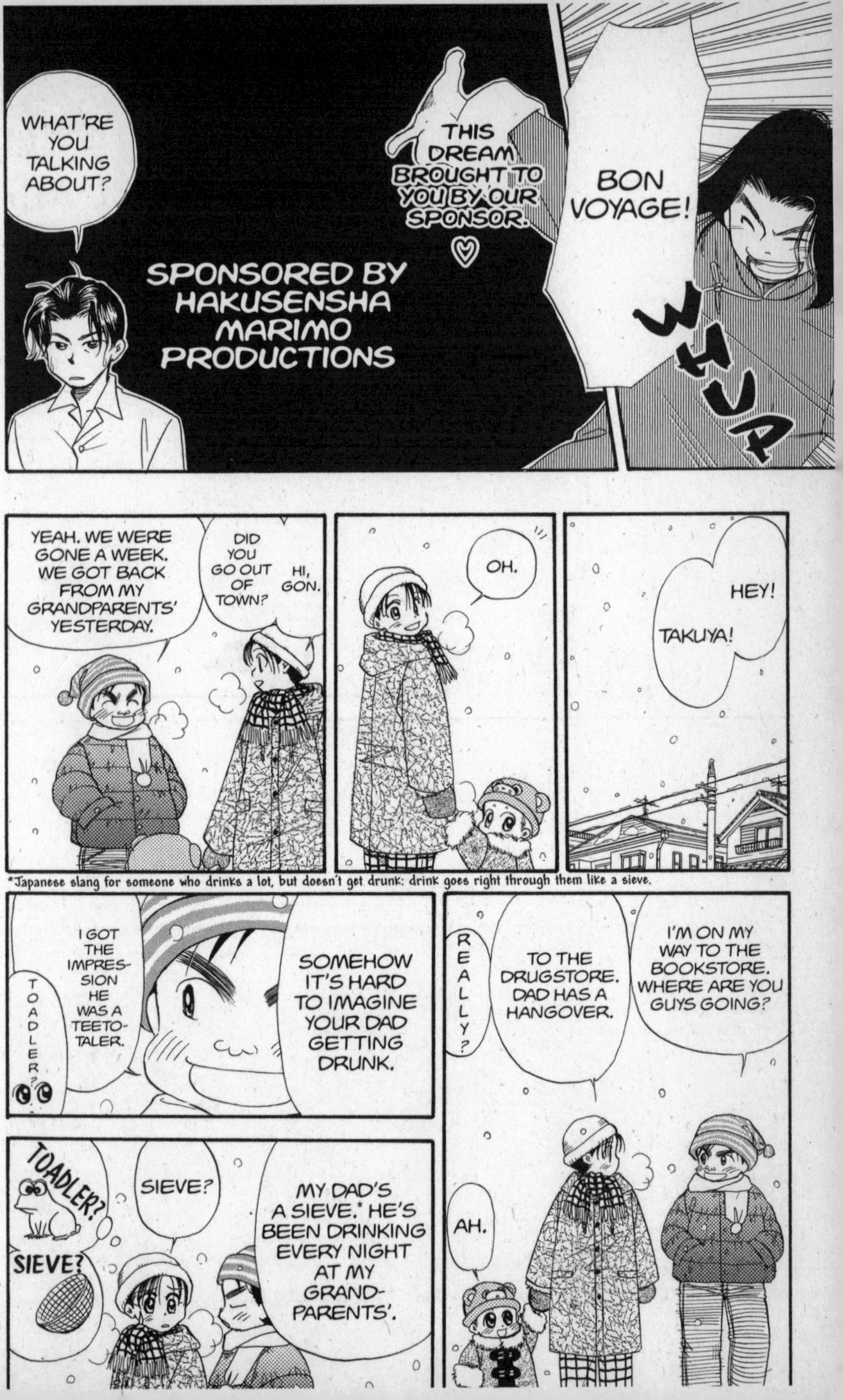
BON VOYAGE!
THIS DREAM BROUGHT TO YOU BY OUR SPONSOR. ♡
WHUP
WHAT'RE YOU TALKING ABOUT?
SPONSORED BY HAKUSENSHA MARIMO PRODUCTIONS
HEY!
TAKUYA!
OH.
HI, GON.
DID YOU GO OUT OF TOWN?
YEAH. WE WERE GONE A WEEK. WE GOT BACK FROM MY GRANDPARENTS' YESTERDAY.
I'M ON MY WAY TO THE BOOKSTORE. WHERE ARE YOU GUYS GOING?
TO THE DRUGSTORE. DAD HAS A HANGOVER.
REALLY?
AH.
SOMEHOW IT'S HARD TO IMAGINE YOUR DAD GETTING DRUNK.
I GOT THE IMPRESSION HE WAS A TEETOTALER.
TOADLER?
MY DAD'S A SIEVE.* HE'S BEEN DRINKING EVERY NIGHT AT MY GRANDPARENTS'.
SIEVE?
TOADLER?
SIEVE?

*Japanese slang for someone who drinks a lot, but doesn't get drunk: drink goes right through them like a sieve.

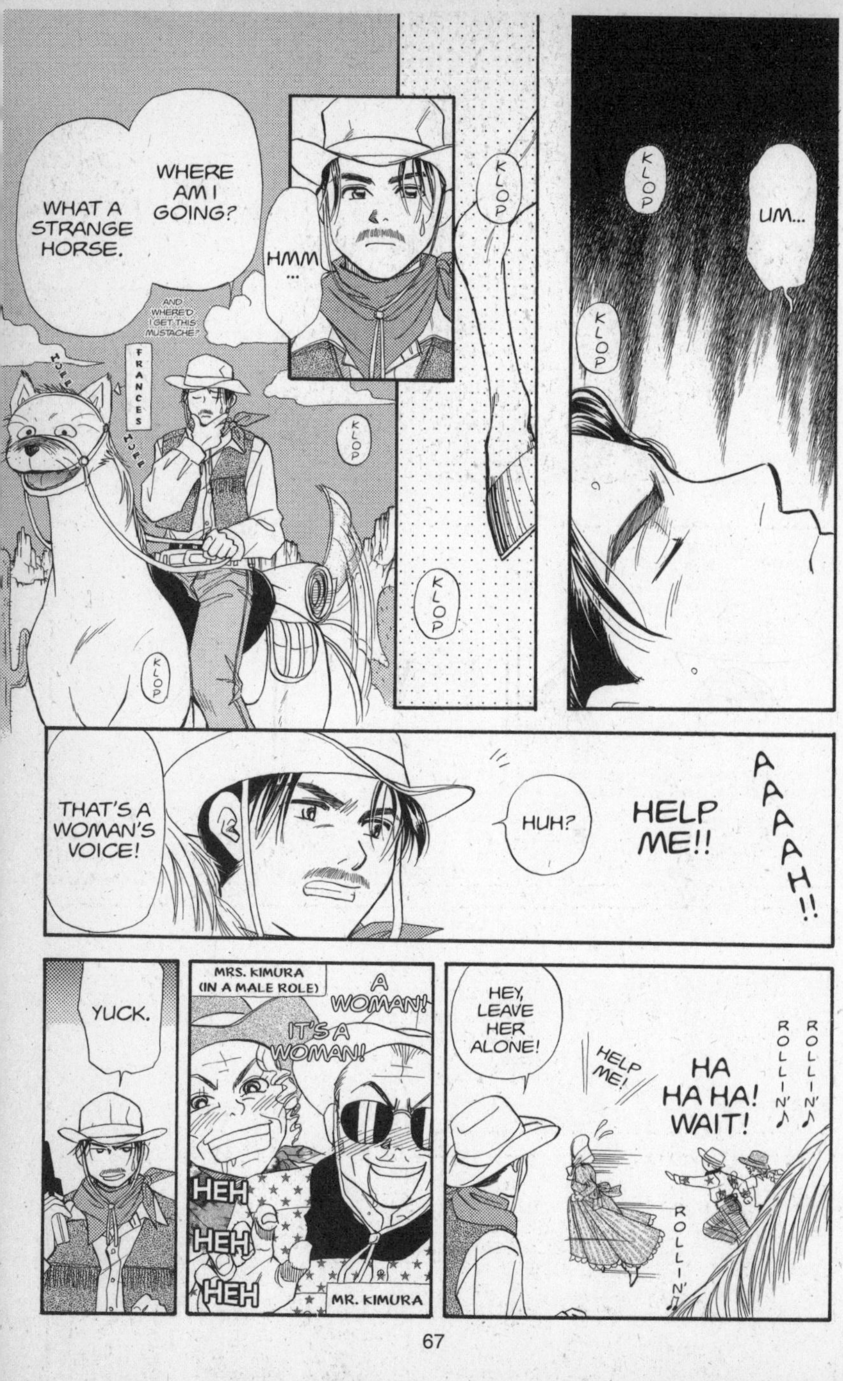
KLOP
UM...
KLOP
KLOP
KLOP
HMM ...
WHERE AM I GOING?
WHAT A STRANGE HORSE.
AND WHERE'D I GET THIS MUSTACHE?
FRANCES
KLOP
KLOP
AAAAH!!
HELP ME!!
HUH?
THAT'S A WOMAN'S VOICE!
ROLLIN'♪
ROLLIN'♪
HA HA HA! WAIT!
HELP ME!
ROLLIN'
HEY, LEAVE HER ALONE!
A WOMAN!
IT'S A WOMAN!
MRS. KIMURA (IN A MALE ROLE)
HEH
HEH
HEH
MR. KIMURA
YUCK.

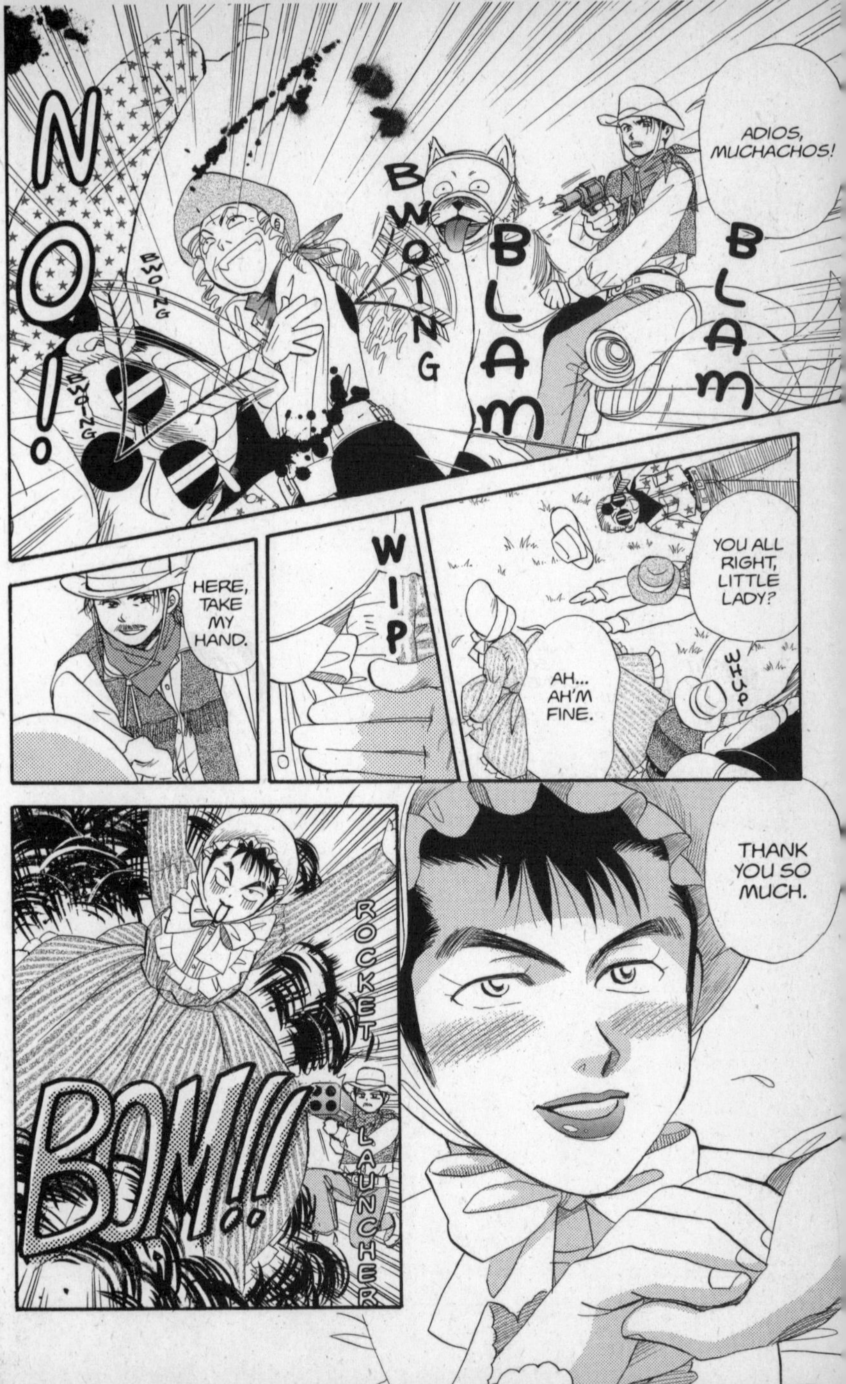
ADIOS, MUCHACHOS!
BLAM
BLAM
BWOING
BWOING
BWOING
NO!!
YOU ALL RIGHT, LITTLE LADY?
WHUP
AH... AH'M FINE.
WIP
HERE, TAKE MY HAND.
THANK YOU SO MUCH.
ROCKET LAUNCHER
BOM!!

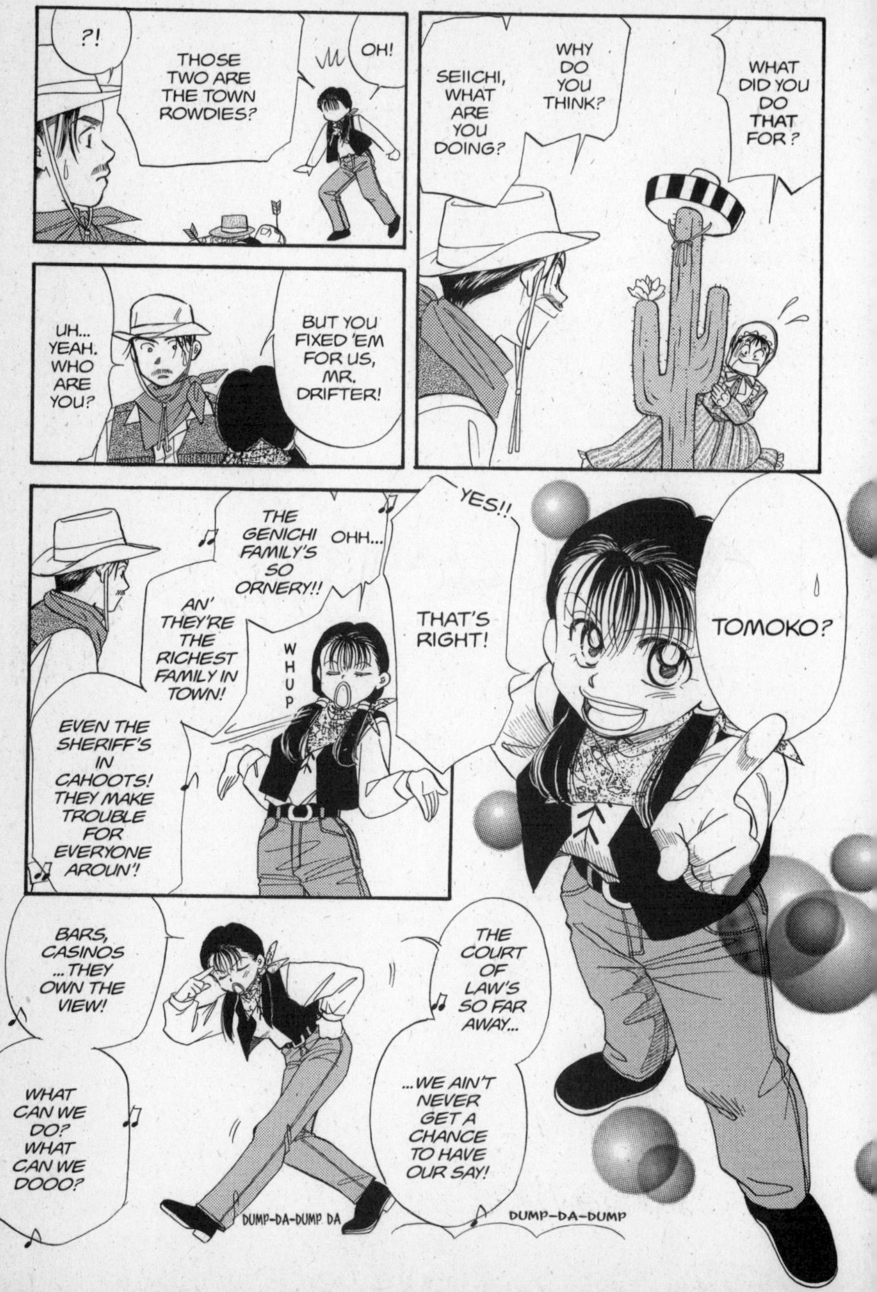
WHAT DID YOU DO THAT FOR?
WHY DO YOU THINK?
SEIICHI, WHAT ARE YOU DOING?
OH!
THOSE TWO ARE THE TOWN ROWDIES?
?!
BUT YOU FIXED 'EM FOR US, MR. DRIFTER!
UH... YEAH. WHO ARE YOU?
TOMOKO?
YES!!
THAT'S RIGHT!
OHH...
THE GENICHI FAMILY'S SO ORNERY!!
AN' THEY'RE THE RICHEST FAMILY IN TOWN!
WHUP
EVEN THE SHERIFF'S IN CAHOOTS! THEY MAKE TROUBLE FOR EVERYONE AROUN'!
THE COURT OF LAW'S SO FAR AWAY...
...WE AIN'T NEVER GET A CHANCE TO HAVE OUR SAY!
DUMP-DA-DUMP
BARS, CASINOS ...THEY OWN THE VIEW!
WHAT CAN WE DO? WHAT CAN WE DOOO?
DUMP-DA-DUMP DA

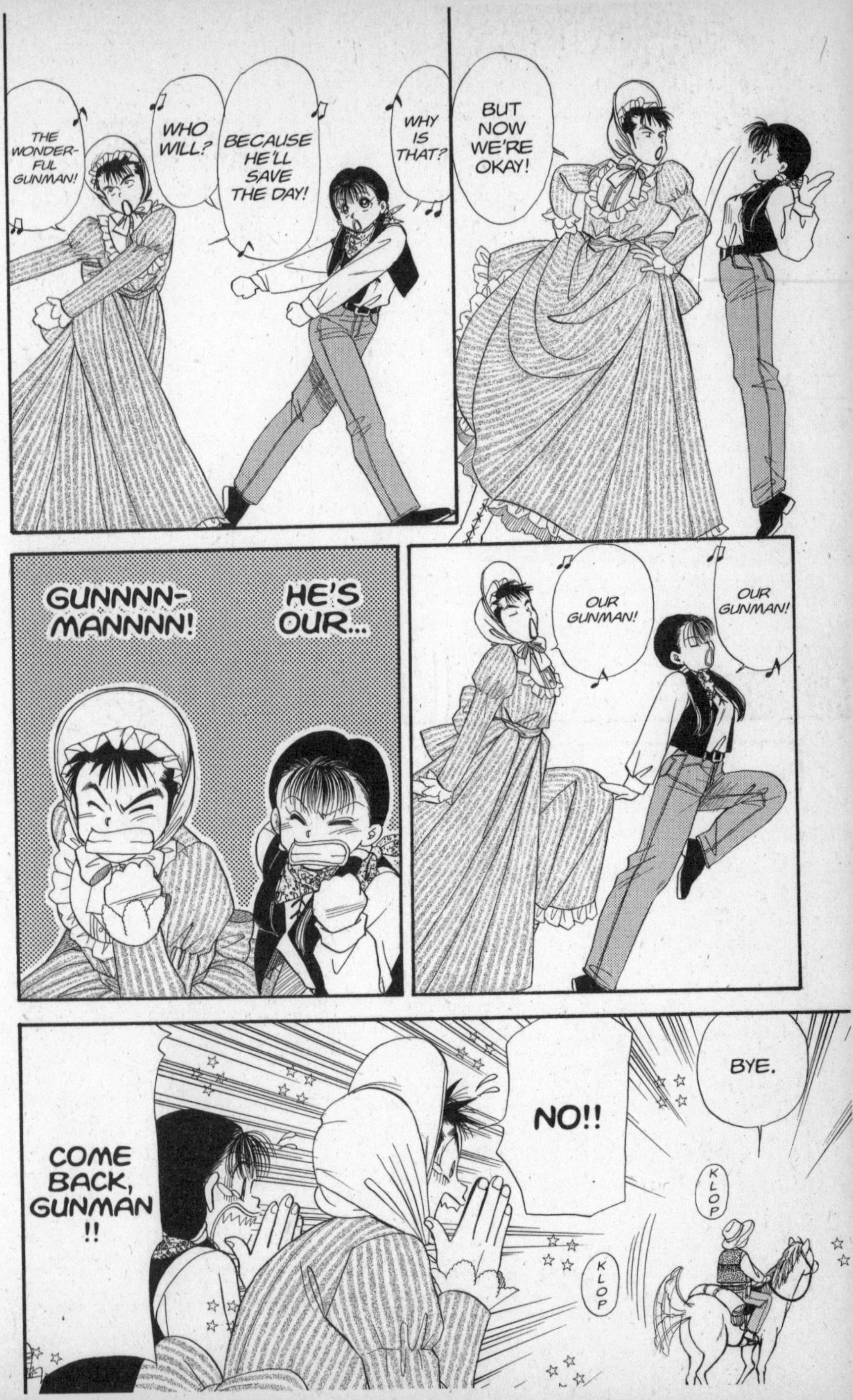
BUT NOW WE'RE OKAY!
WHY IS THAT?
BECAUSE HE'LL SAVE THE DAY!
WHO WILL?
THE WONDERFUL GUNMAN!
OUR GUNMAN!
OUR GUNMAN!
HE'S OUR...
GUNNNN-MANNNN!
BYE.
KLOP
KLOP
NO!!
COME BACK, GUNMAN!!

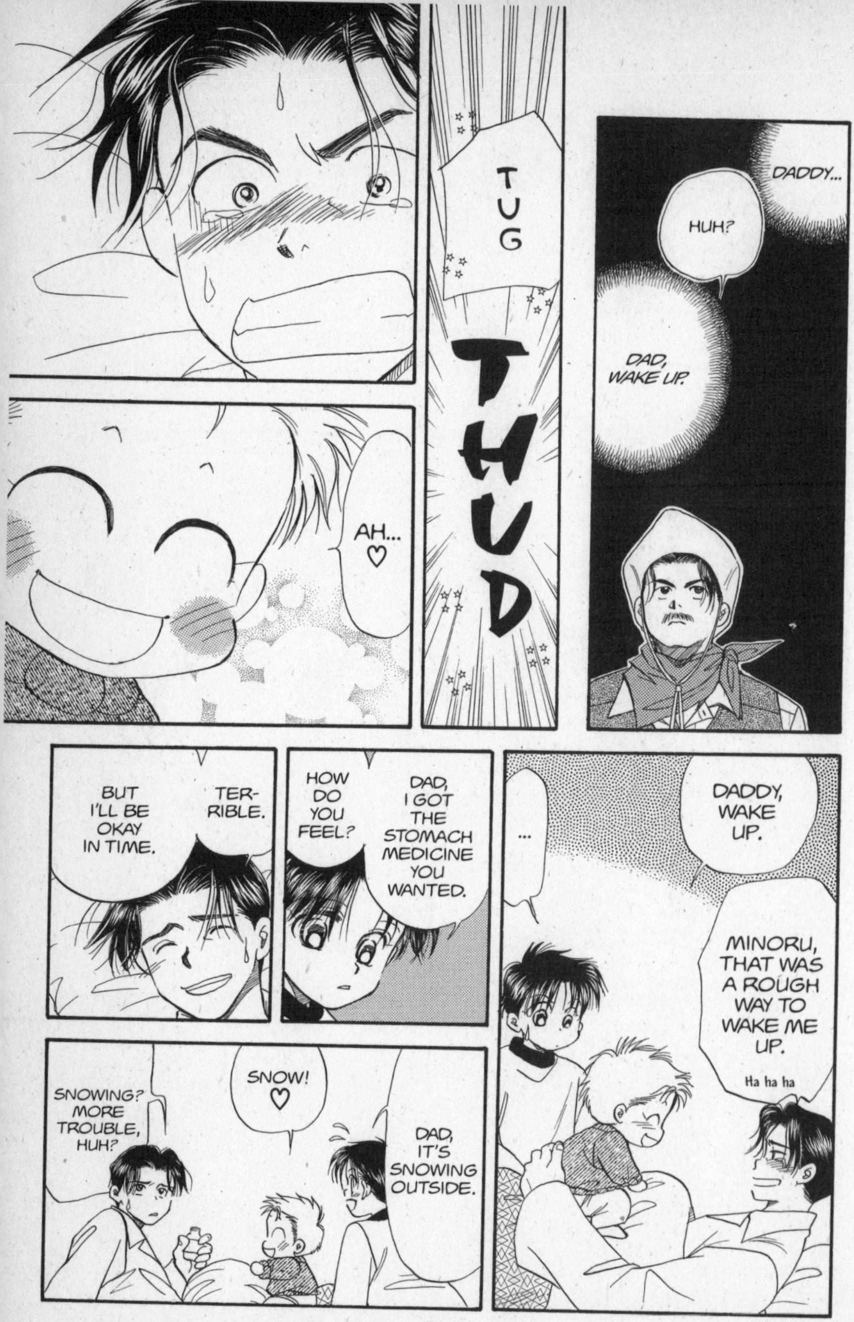
DADDY...
HUH?
DAD, WAKE UP.
TUG
THUD
AH... ♡
DADDY, WAKE UP.
...
MINORU, THAT WAS A ROUGH WAY TO WAKE ME UP.
Ha ha ha
DAD, I GOT THE STOMACH MEDICINE YOU WANTED.
HOW DO YOU FEEL?
TER-RIBLE.
BUT I'LL BE OKAY IN TIME.
DAD, IT'S SNOWING OUTSIDE.
SNOW! ♡
SNOWING? MORE TROUBLE, HUH?

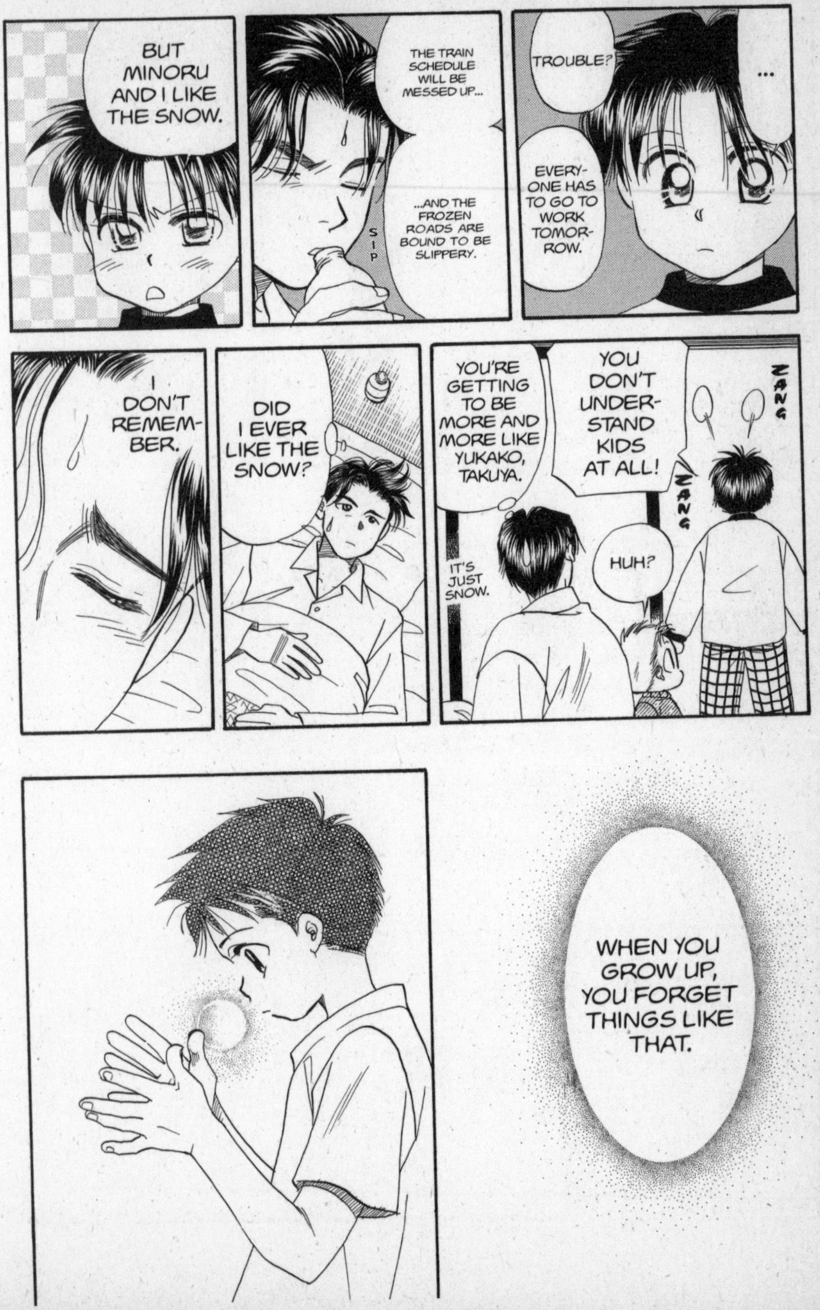
TROUBLE?
...
EVERY-ONE HAS TO GO TO WORK TOMOR-ROW.
THE TRAIN SCHEDULE WILL BE MESSED UP...
...AND THE FROZEN ROADS ARE BOUND TO BE SLIPPERY.
SIP
BUT MINORU AND I LIKE THE SNOW.
ZANG
YOU DON'T UNDER-STAND KIDS AT ALL!
ZANG
YOU'RE GETTING TO BE MORE AND MORE LIKE YUKAKO, TAKUYA.
HUH?
IT'S JUST SNOW.
DID I EVER LIKE THE SNOW?
I DON'T REMEM-BER.
WHEN YOU GROW UP, YOU FORGET THINGS LIKE THAT.

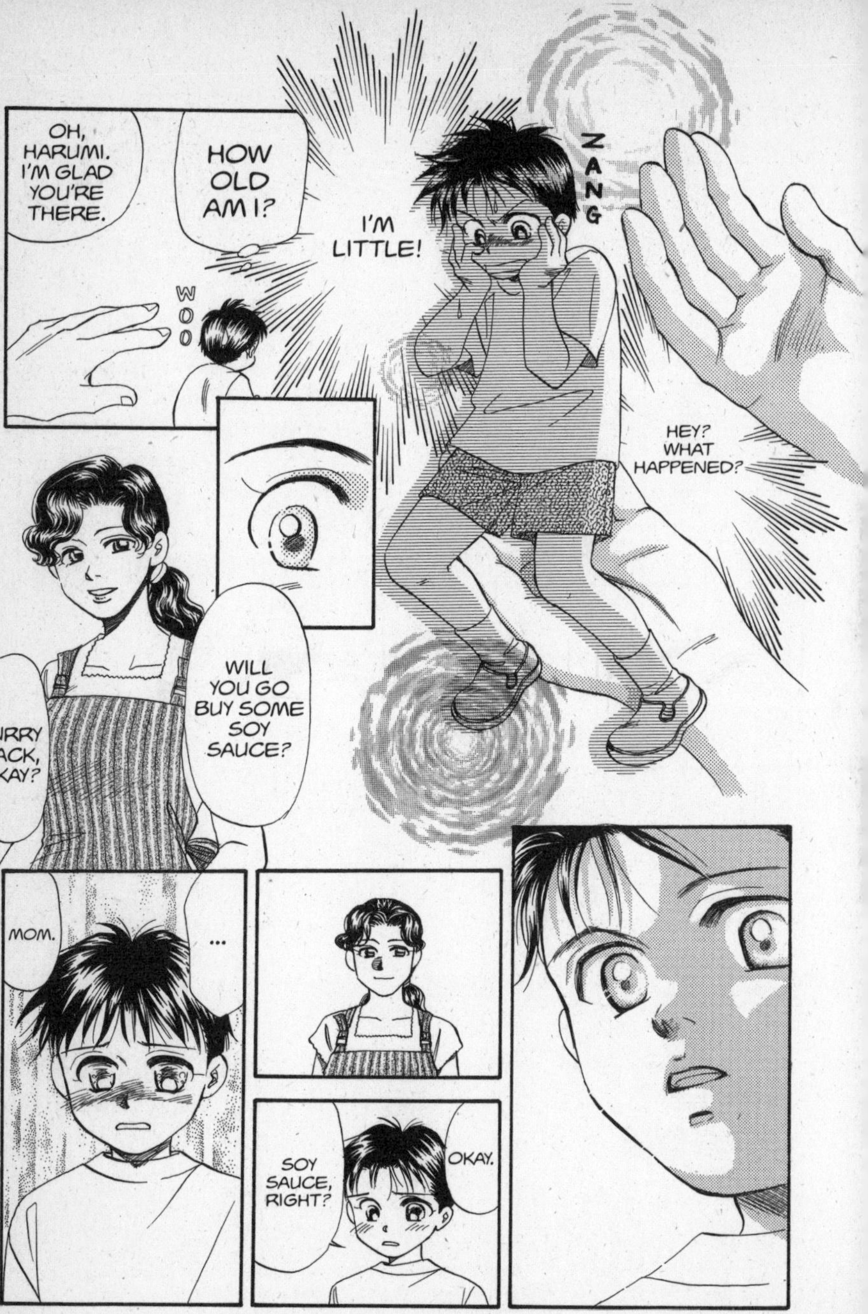
ZANG
I'M LITTLE!
HEY? WHAT HAPPENED?
HOW OLD AM I?
OH, HARUMI. I'M GLAD YOU'RE THERE.
WOO
WILL YOU GO BUY SOME SOY SAUCE?
HURRY BACK, OKAY?
OKAY.
SOY SAUCE, RIGHT?
...
MOM.

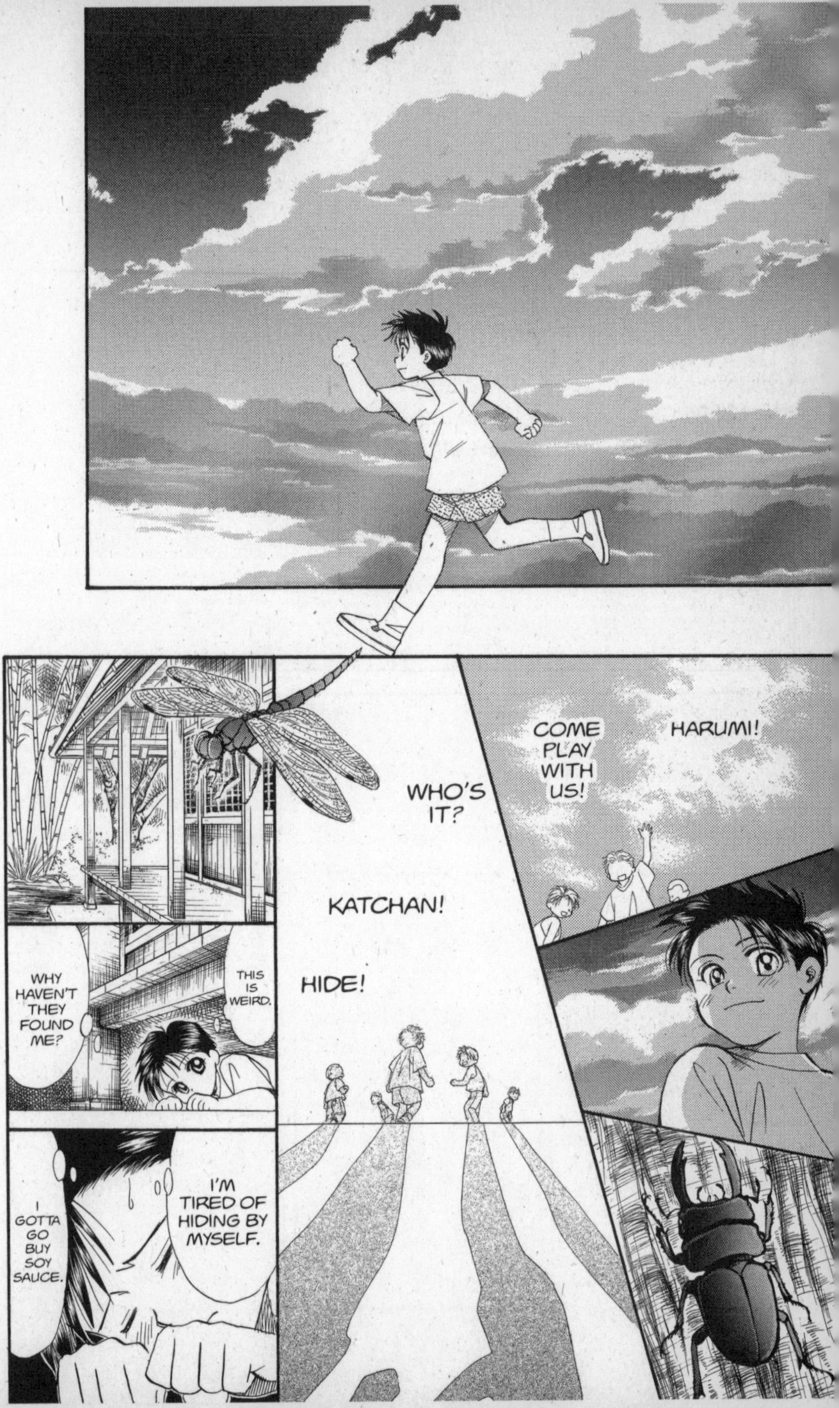
HARUMI!
COME PLAY WITH US!
WHO'S IT?
KATCHAN!
HIDE!
THIS IS WEIRD.
WHY HAVEN'T THEY FOUND ME?
I'M TIRED OF HIDING BY MYSELF.
I GOTTA GO BUY SOY SAUCE.

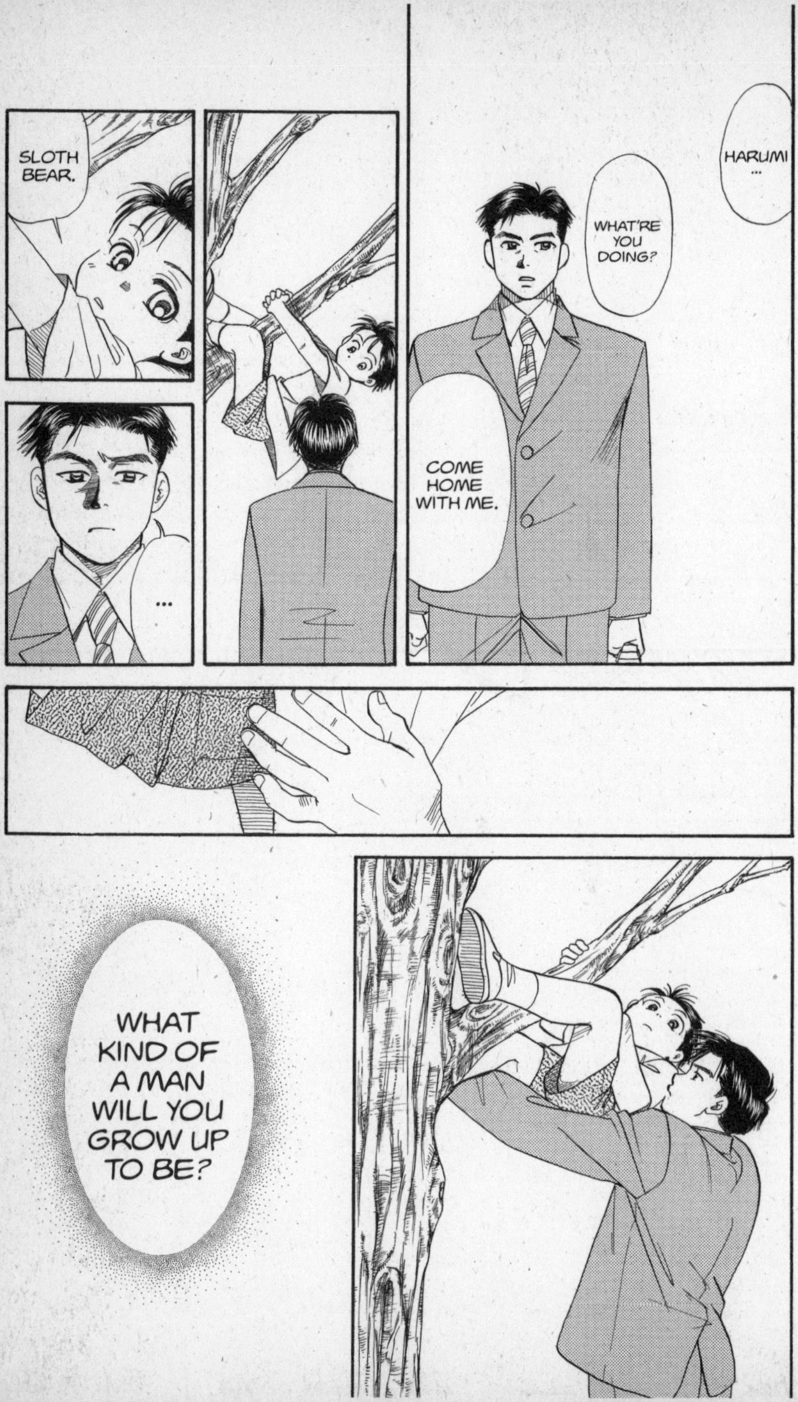
HARUMI ...
WHAT'RE YOU DOING?
COME HOME WITH ME.
SLOTH BEAR.
...
WHAT KIND OF A MAN WILL YOU GROW UP TO BE?

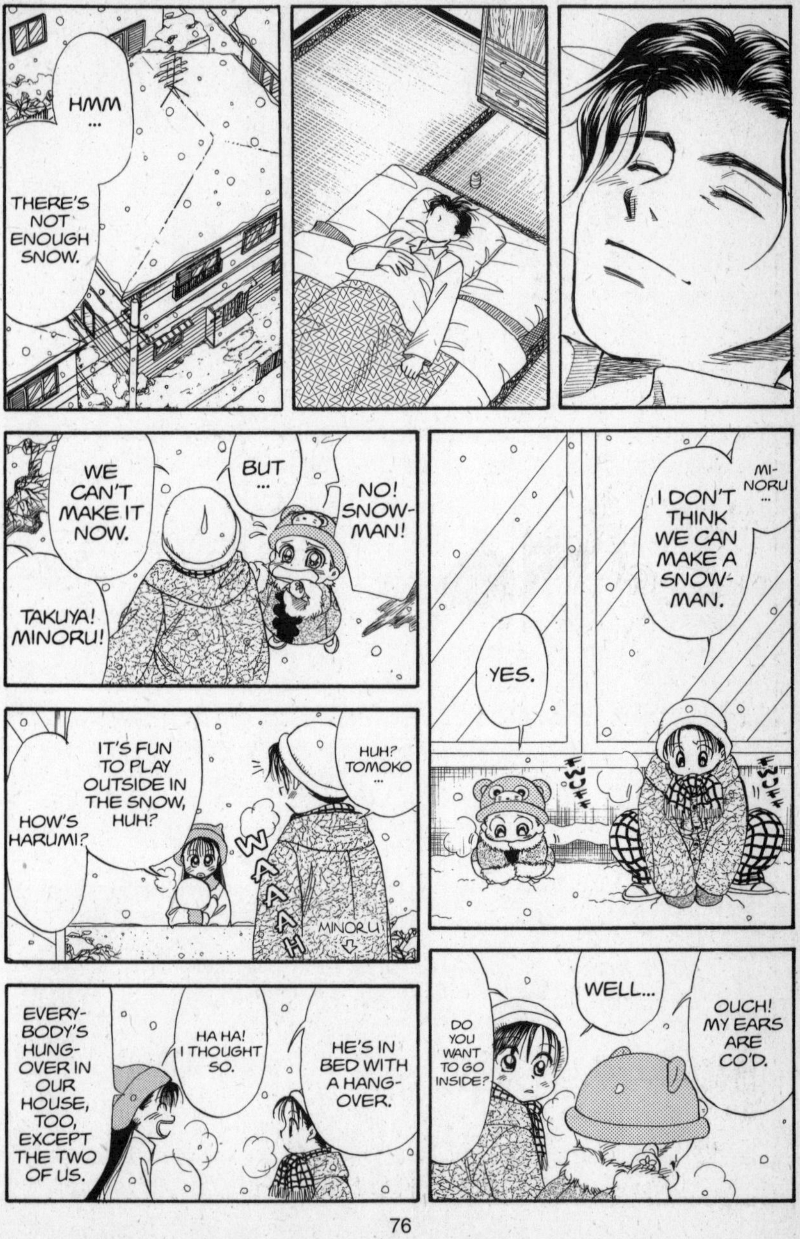
HMM ...
THERE'S NOT ENOUGH SNOW.
MI-NORU ...
I DON'T THINK WE CAN MAKE A SNOW-MAN.
YES.
FWUFF
FWUFF
NO! SNOW-MAN!
BUT ...
WE CAN'T MAKE IT NOW.
TAKUYA! MINORU!
HUH? TOMOKO ...
IT'S FUN TO PLAY OUTSIDE IN THE SNOW, HUH?
HOW'S HARUMI?
WAAAAH
MINORU
OUCH! MY EARS ARE CO'D.
WELL...
DO YOU WANT TO GO INSIDE?
HE'S IN BED WITH A HANG-OVER.
HA HA! I THOUGHT SO.
EVERY-BODY'S HUNG-OVER IN OUR HOUSE, TOO, EXCEPT THE TWO OF US.

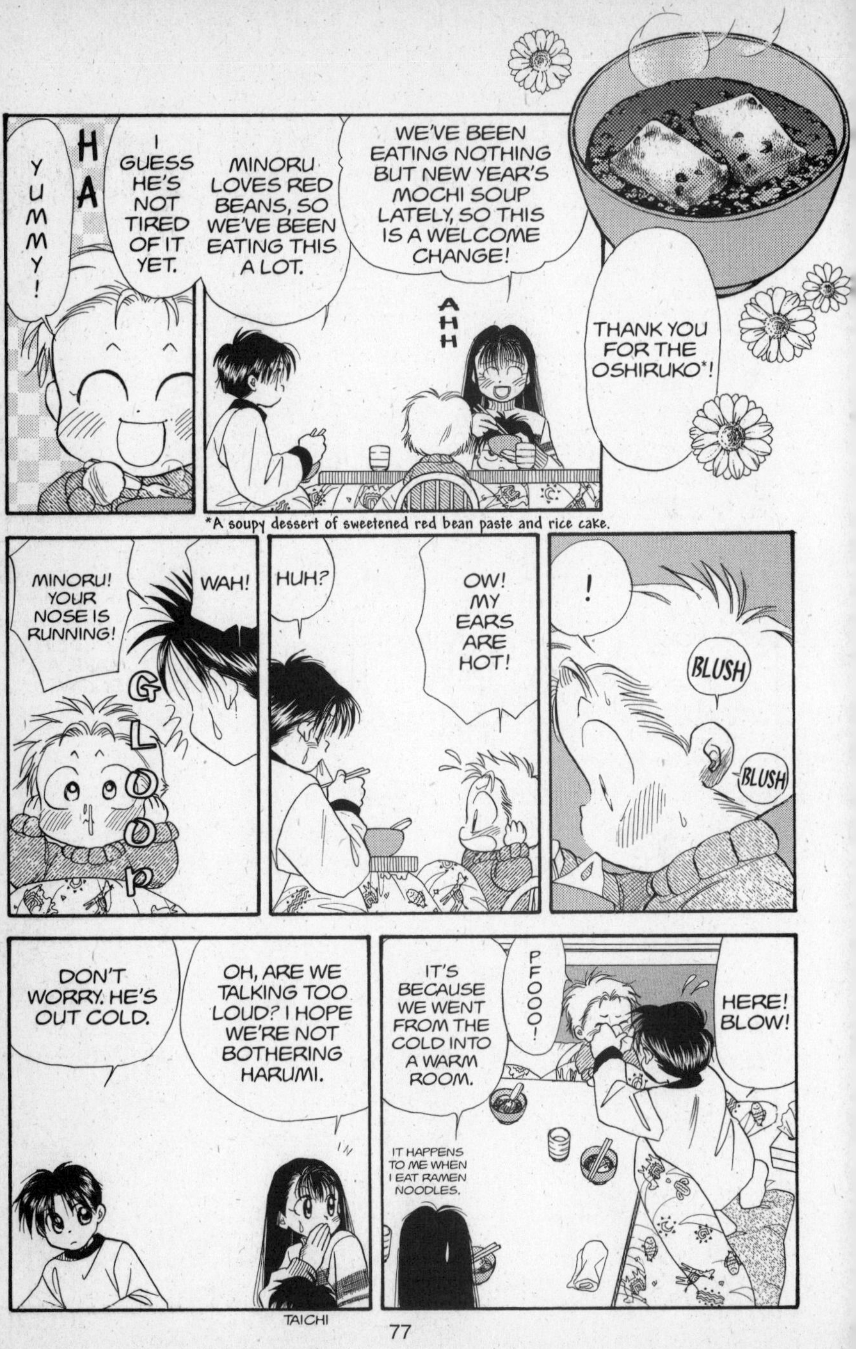
THANK YOU FOR THE OSHIRUKO*!
WE'VE BEEN EATING NOTHING BUT NEW YEAR'S MOCHI SOUP LATELY, SO THIS IS A WELCOME CHANGE!
AHH
MINORU LOVES RED BEANS, SO WE'VE BEEN EATING THIS A LOT.
I GUESS HE'S NOT TIRED OF IT YET.
HA
YUMMY!
!
BLUSH
BLUSH
OW! MY EARS ARE HOT!
HUH?
WAH!
MINORU! YOUR NOSE IS RUNNING!
GLOOP
HERE! BLOW!
PFOOO!
IT'S BECAUSE WE WENT FROM THE COLD INTO A WARM ROOM.
IT HAPPENS TO ME WHEN I EAT RAMEN NOODLES.
OH, ARE WE TALKING TOO LOUD? I HOPE WE'RE NOT BOTHERING HARUMI.
DON'T WORRY. HE'S OUT COLD.
TAICHI

*A soupy dessert of sweetened red bean paste and rice cake.

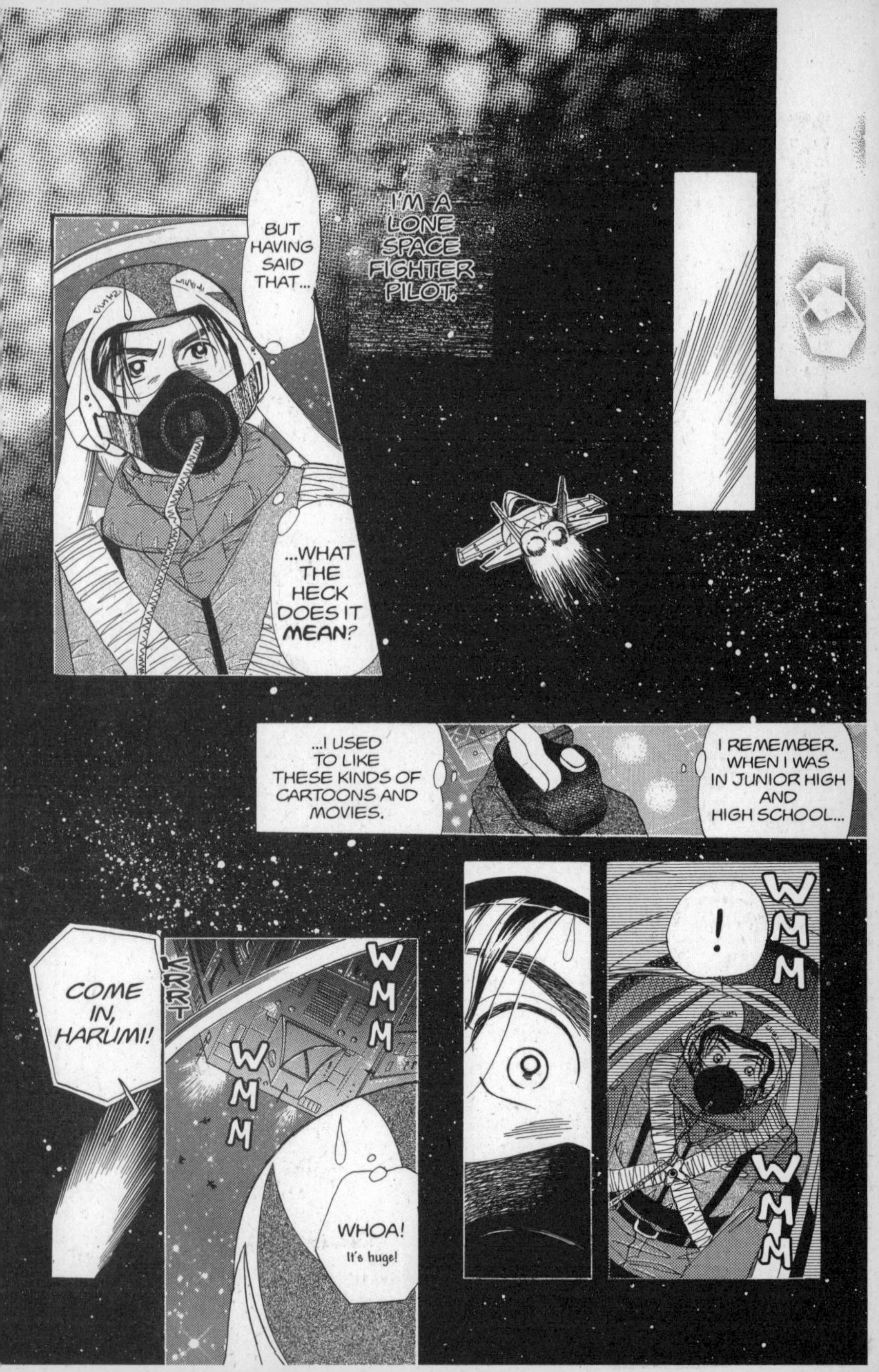
I'M A LONE SPACE FIGHTER PILOT.
BUT HAVING SAID THAT...
...WHAT THE HECK DOES IT MEAN?
I REMEMBER. WHEN I WAS IN JUNIOR HIGH AND HIGH SCHOOL...
...I USED TO LIKE THESE KINDS OF CARTOONS AND MOVIES.
WMM
!
WMM
WMM
KRRT
WMM
COME IN, HARUMI!
WHOA!
It's huge!

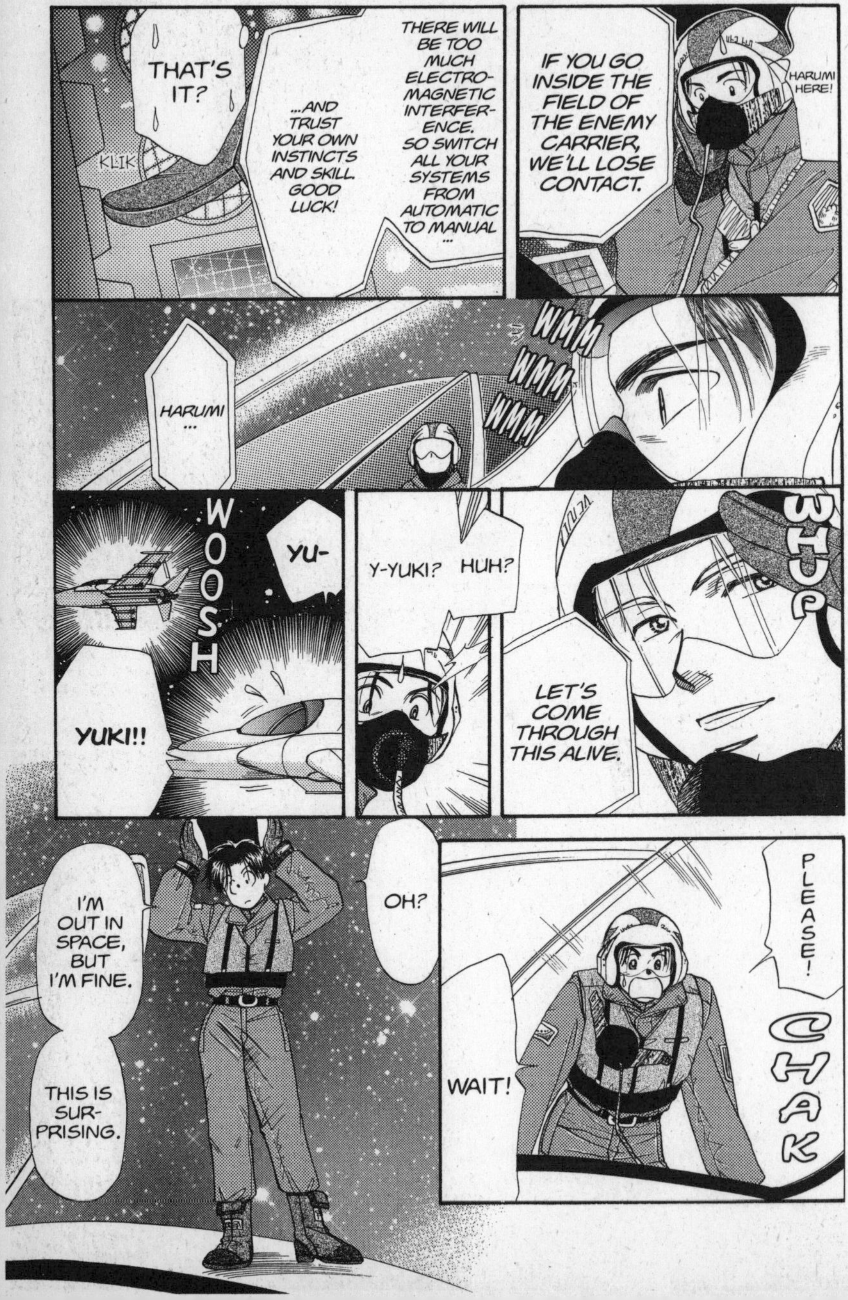
HARUMI HERE!
IF YOU GO INSIDE THE FIELD OF THE ENEMY CARRIER, WE'LL LOSE CONTACT.
THERE WILL BE TOO MUCH ELECTRO-MAGNETIC INTERFER-ENCE. SO SWITCH ALL YOUR SYSTEMS FROM AUTOMATIC TO MANUAL ...
...AND TRUST YOUR OWN INSTINCTS AND SKILL. GOOD LUCK!
THAT'S IT?
KLIK
WMM WMM WMM
HARUMI ...
WHUP
LET'S COME THROUGH THIS ALIVE.
HUH?
Y-YUKI?
YU-
WOOSH
YUKI!!
PLEASE!
CHAK
WAIT!
OH?
I'M OUT IN SPACE, BUT I'M FINE.
THIS IS SUR-PRISING.

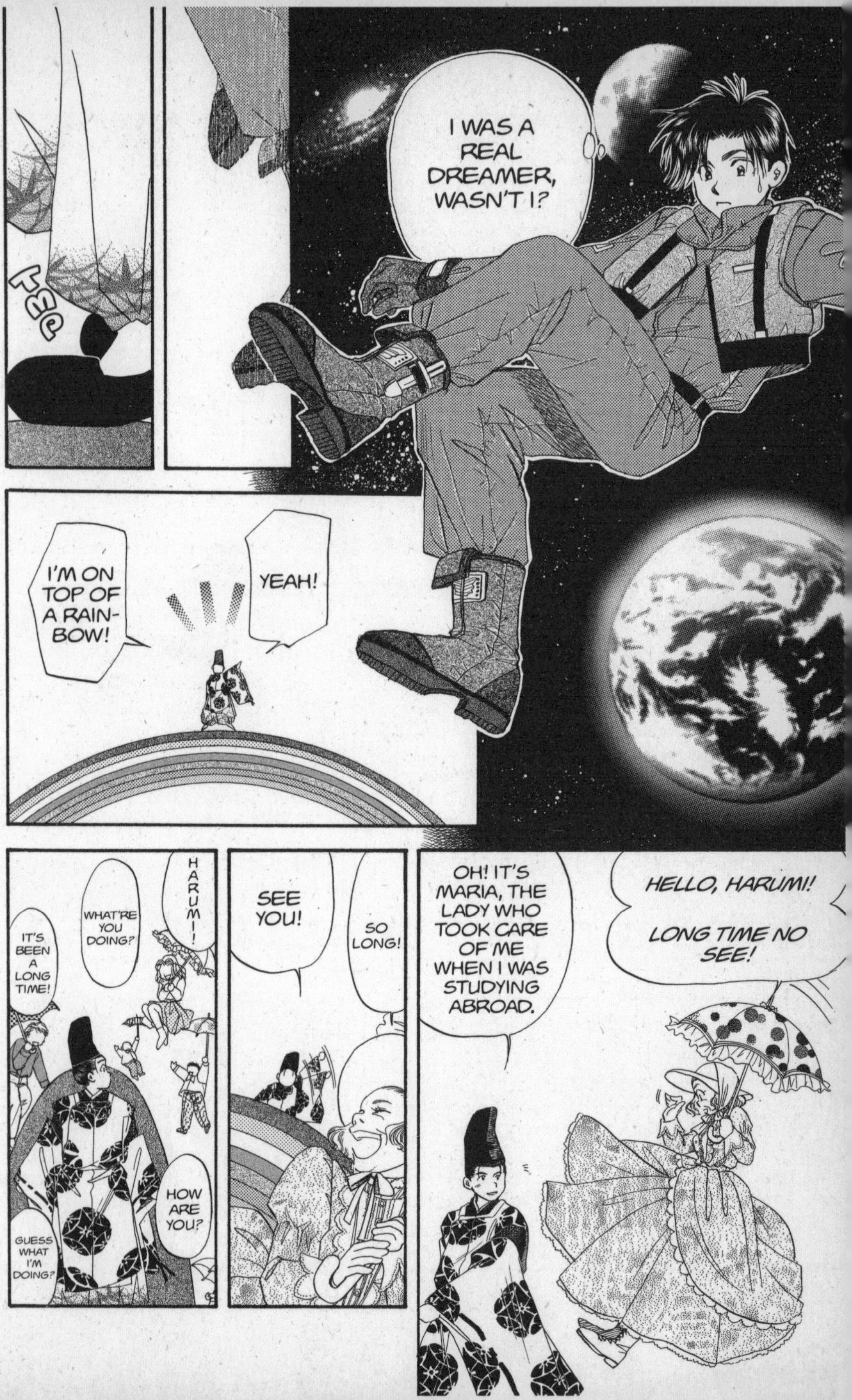
I WAS A REAL DREAMER, WASN'T I?
TMP
YEAH!
I'M ON TOP OF A RAIN-BOW!
HELLO, HARUMI!
LONG TIME NO SEE!
OH! IT'S MARIA, THE LADY WHO TOOK CARE OF ME WHEN I WAS STUDYING ABROAD.
SO LONG!
SEE YOU!
HARUMI!
WHAT'RE YOU DOING?
IT'S BEEN A LONG TIME!
HOW ARE YOU?
GUESS WHAT I'M DOING?

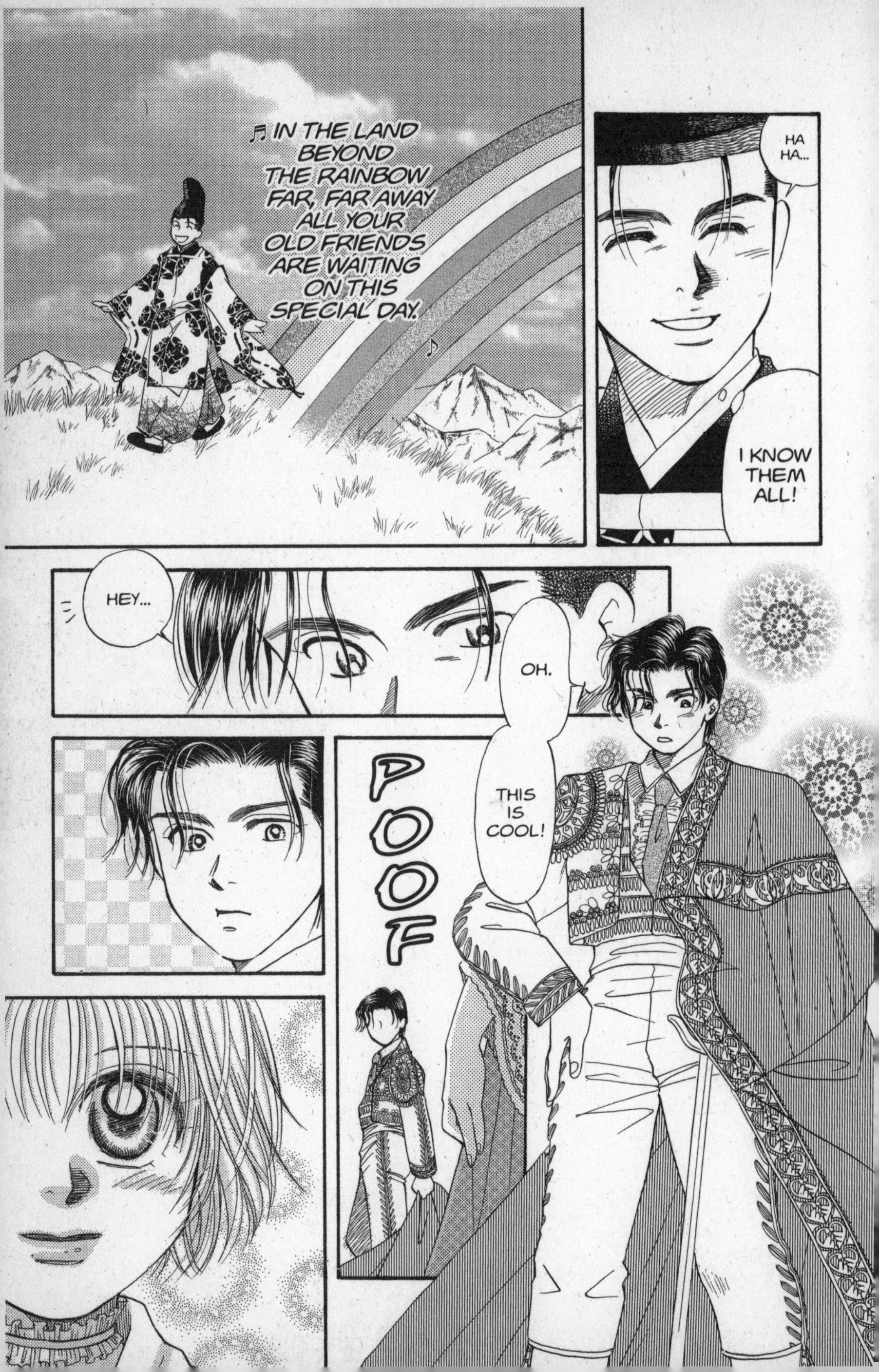
HA HA...
I KNOW THEM ALL!
♬ IN THE LAND BEYOND THE RAINBOW FAR, FAR AWAY ALL YOUR OLD FRIENDS ARE WAITING ON THIS SPECIAL DAY. ♪
HEY...
OH.
THIS IS COOL!
POOF

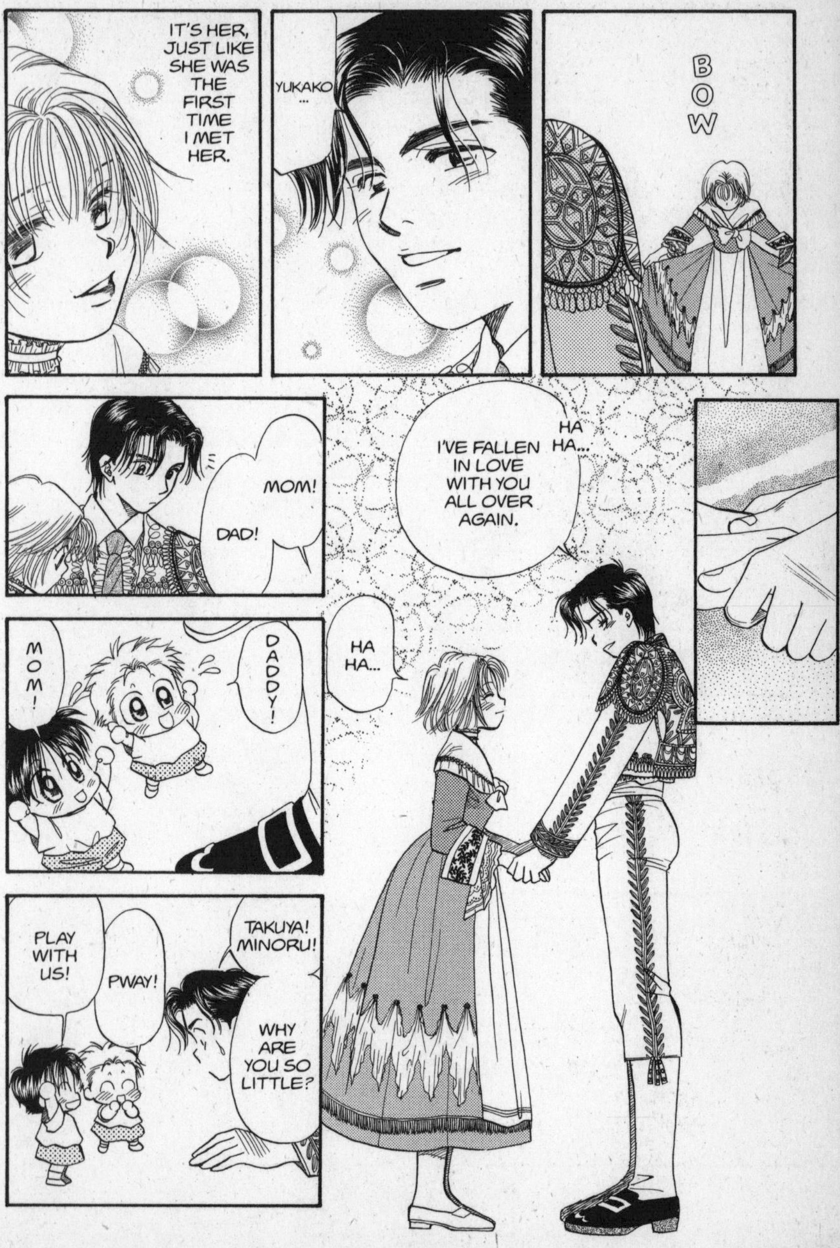
BOW
YUKAKO...
IT'S HER, JUST LIKE SHE WAS THE FIRST TIME I MET HER.
HA HA... I'VE FALLEN IN LOVE WITH YOU ALL OVER AGAIN.
HA HA...
MOM!
DAD!
DADDY!
MOM!
TAKUYA! MINORU!
WHY ARE YOU SO LITTLE?
PWAY!
PLAY WITH US!

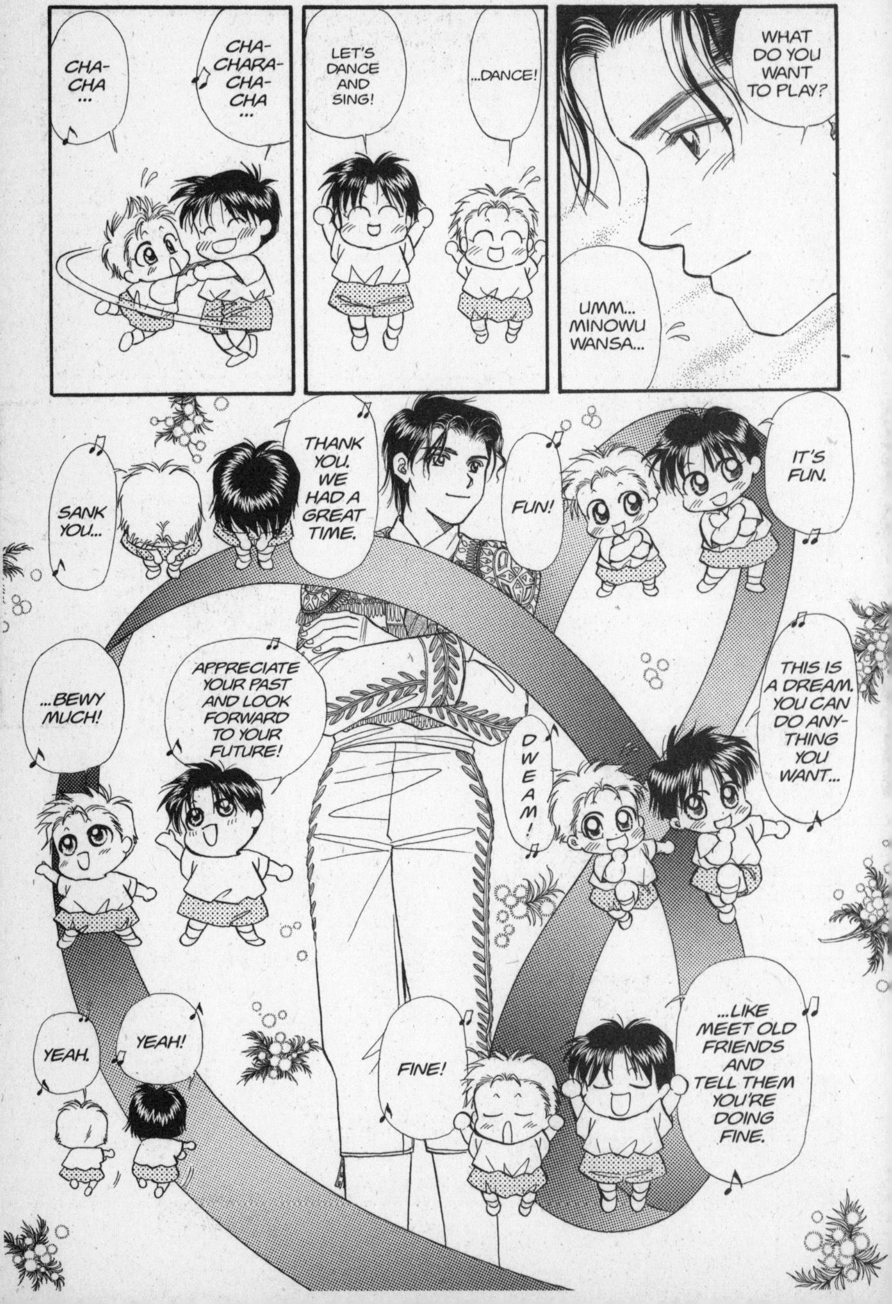
WHAT DO YOU WANT TO PLAY?
UMM... MINOWU WANSA...
LET'S DANCE AND SING!
...DANCE!
CHA-CHARA-CHA-CHA...
CHA-CHA...
IT'S FUN.
FUN!
THANK YOU. WE HAD A GREAT TIME.
SANK YOU...
THIS IS A DREAM. YOU CAN DO ANY-THING YOU WANT...
DWEAM!
APPRECIATE YOUR PAST AND LOOK FORWARD TO YOUR FUTURE!
...BEWY MUCH!
...LIKE MEET OLD FRIENDS AND TELL THEM YOU'RE DOING FINE.
FINE!
YEAH!
YEAH.

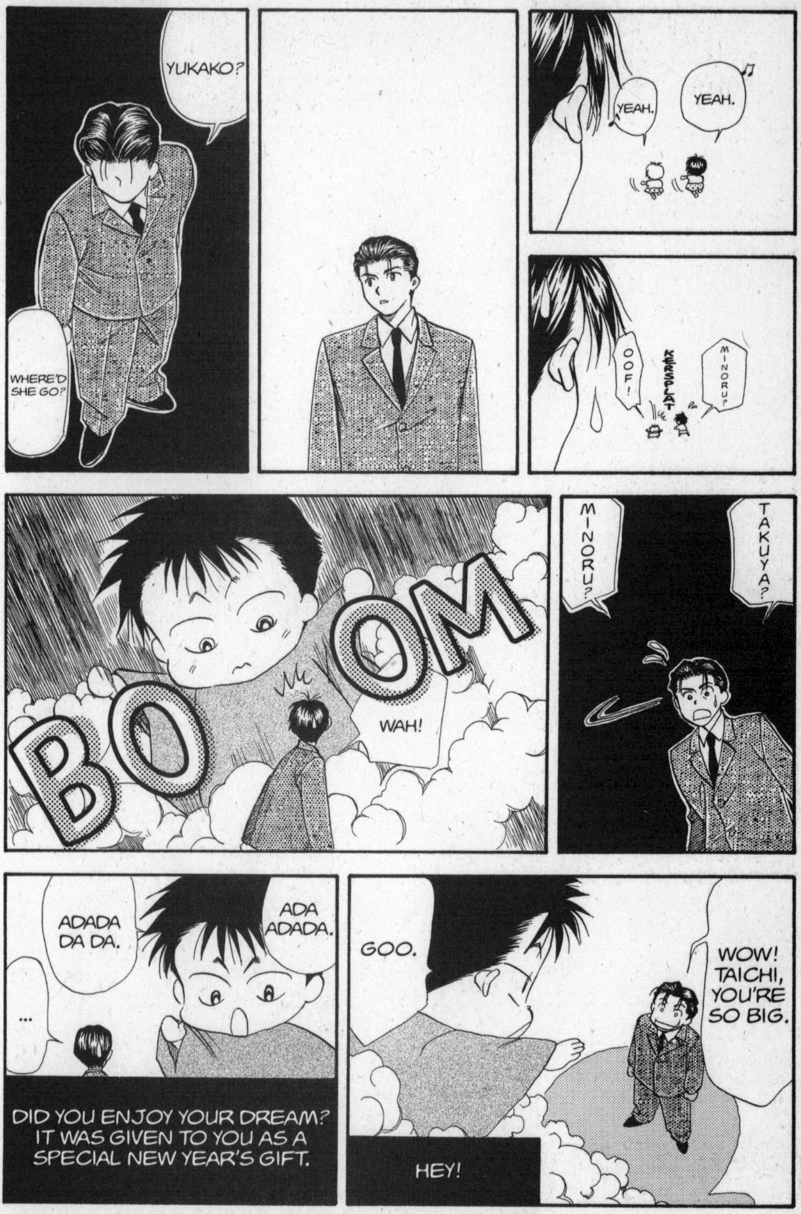
YEAH.
YEAH.
MINORU?
KERSPLAT
OOF!
YUKAKO?
WHERE'D SHE GO?
TAKUYA?
MINORU?
BOOM
WAH!
WOW! TAICHI, YOU'RE SO BIG.
GOO.
HEY!
ADA ADADA.
ADADA DA DA.
...
DID YOU ENJOY YOUR DREAM? IT WAS GIVEN TO YOU AS A SPECIAL NEW YEAR'S GIFT.

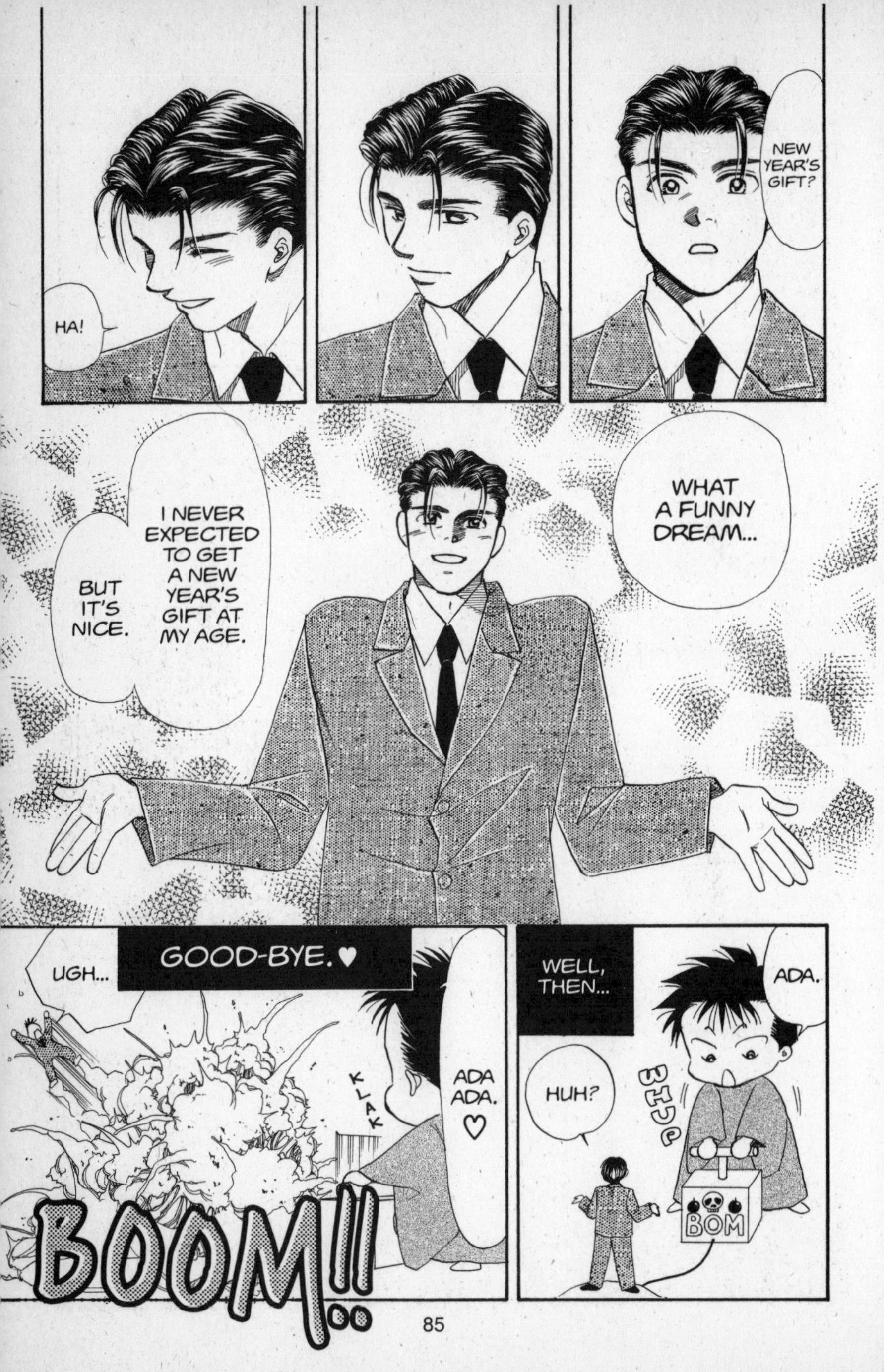
NEW YEAR'S GIFT?
HA!
WHAT A FUNNY DREAM...
I NEVER EXPECTED TO GET A NEW YEAR'S GIFT AT MY AGE.
BUT IT'S NICE.
ADA.
WELL, THEN...
WHUP
HUH?
BOM
ADA ADA. ♥
KLAK
GOOD-BYE. ♥
UGH...
BOOM!!

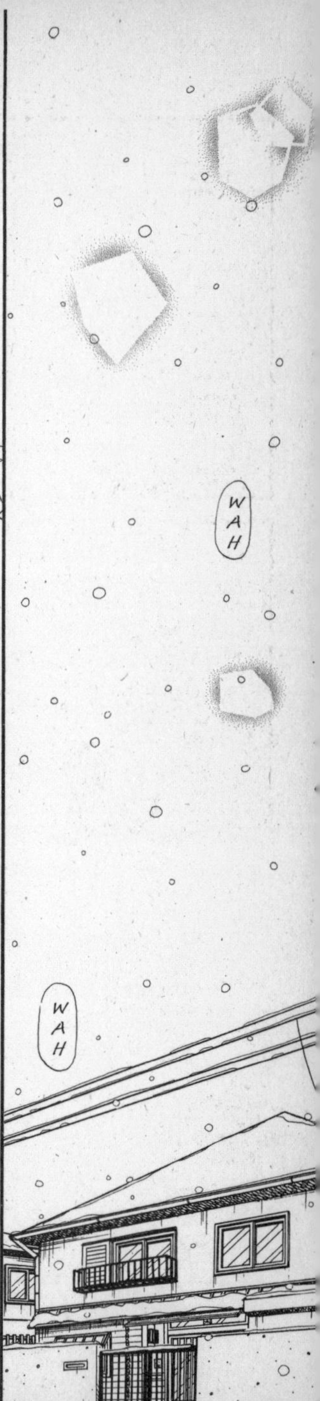
WAH
WAH

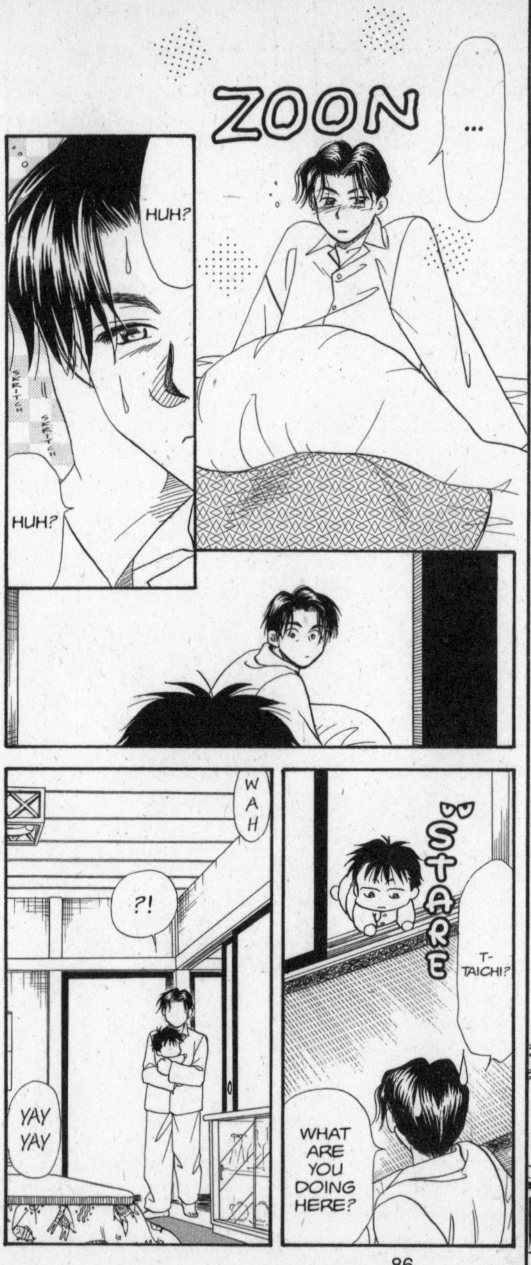
ZOON
...
HUH?
SKRITCH
SKRITCH
HUH?
STARE
T-TAICHI?
WHAT ARE YOU DOING HERE?
WAH
?!
YAY YAY

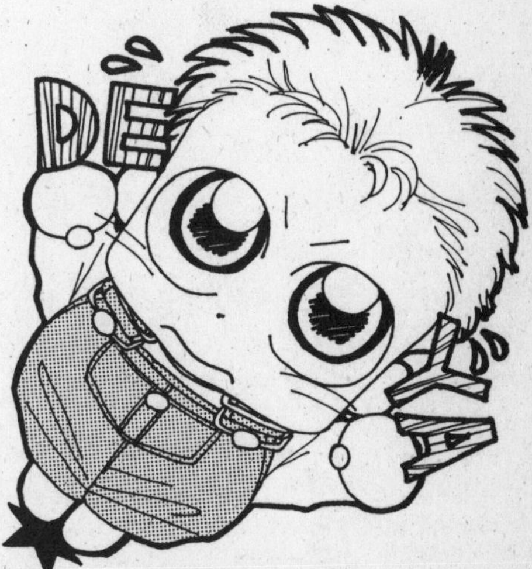
DE
YA
*Ultraman's battle cry.

Chapter 95

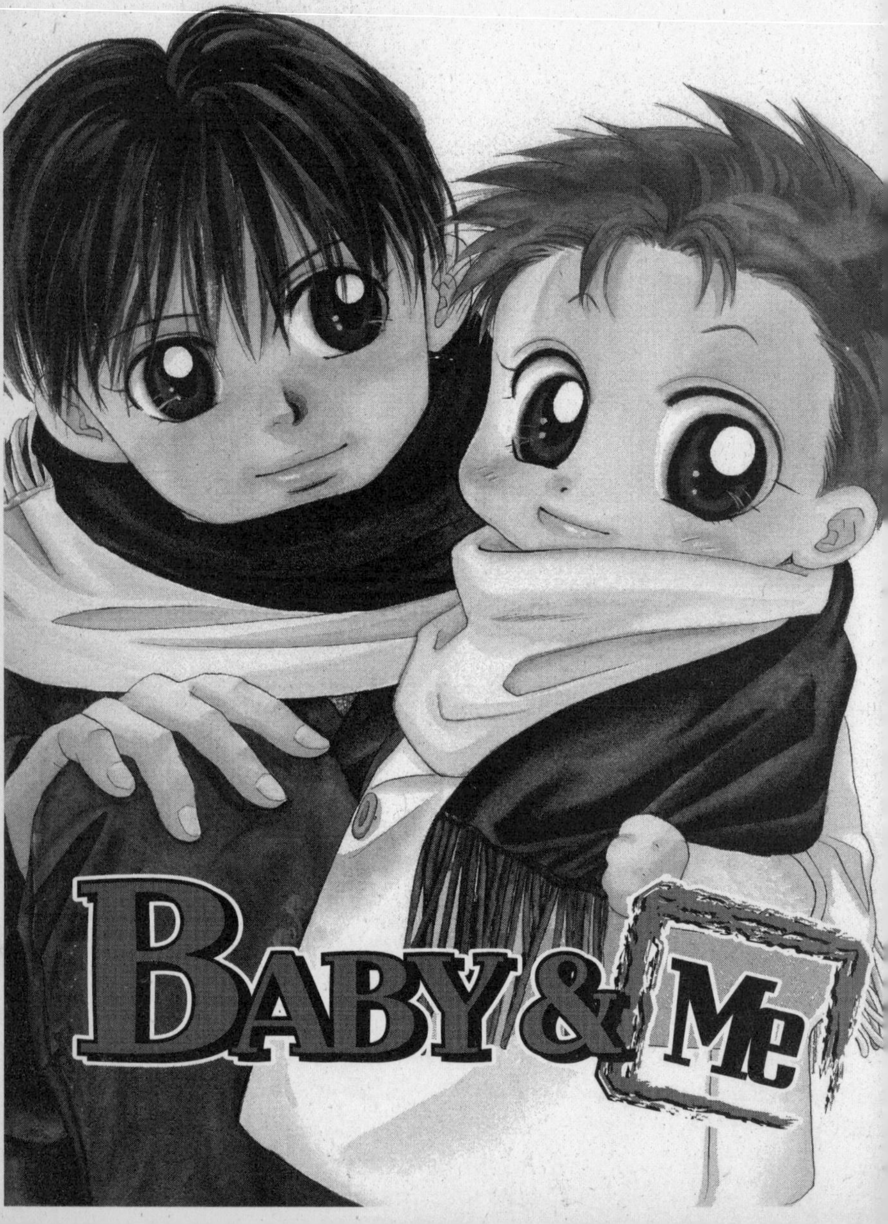
BABY & Me

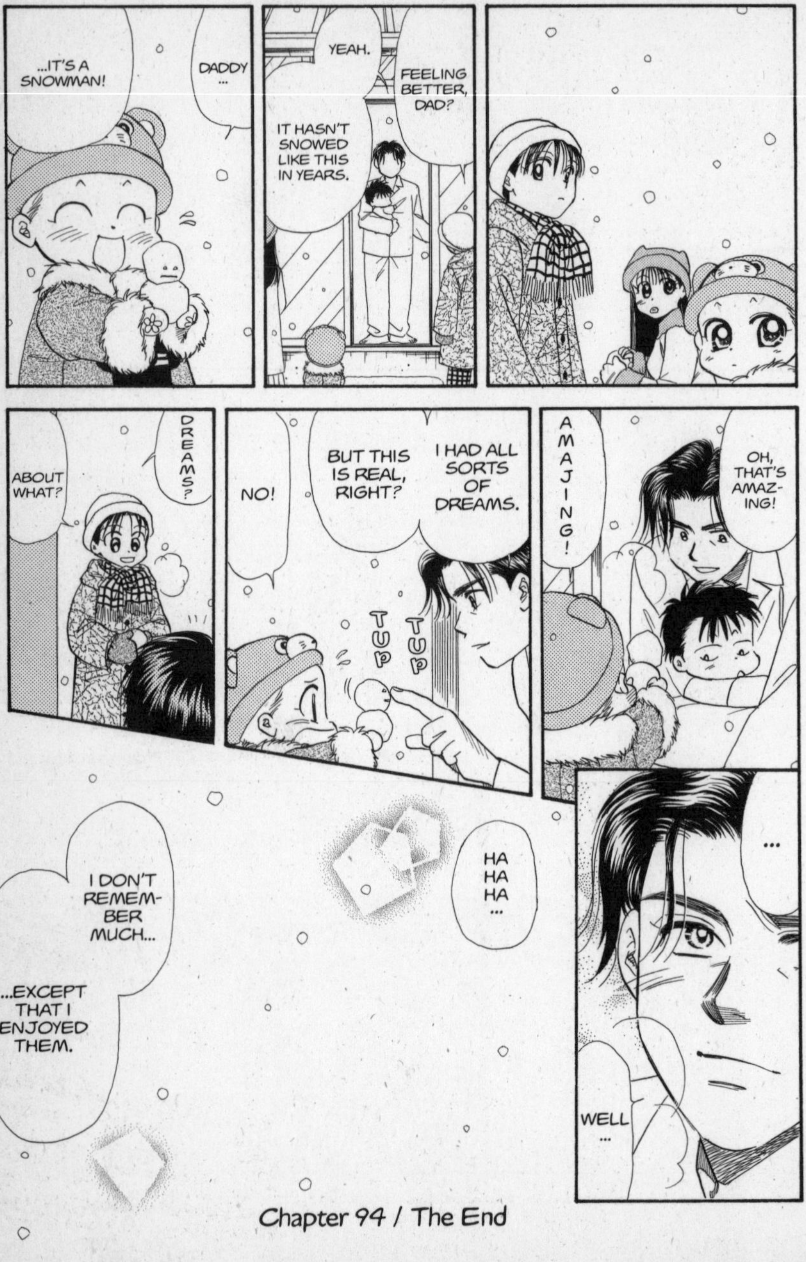
FEELING BETTER, DAD?
YEAH.
IT HASN'T SNOWED LIKE THIS IN YEARS.
DADDY ...
...IT'S A SNOWMAN!
OH, THAT'S AMAZ-ING!
AMAJING!
I HAD ALL SORTS OF DREAMS.
BUT THIS IS REAL, RIGHT?
NO!
TUP TUP
DREAMS?
ABOUT WHAT?
...
WELL ...
HA HA HA ...
I DON'T REMEM-BER MUCH...
...EXCEPT THAT I ENJOYED THEM.

Chapter 94 / The End

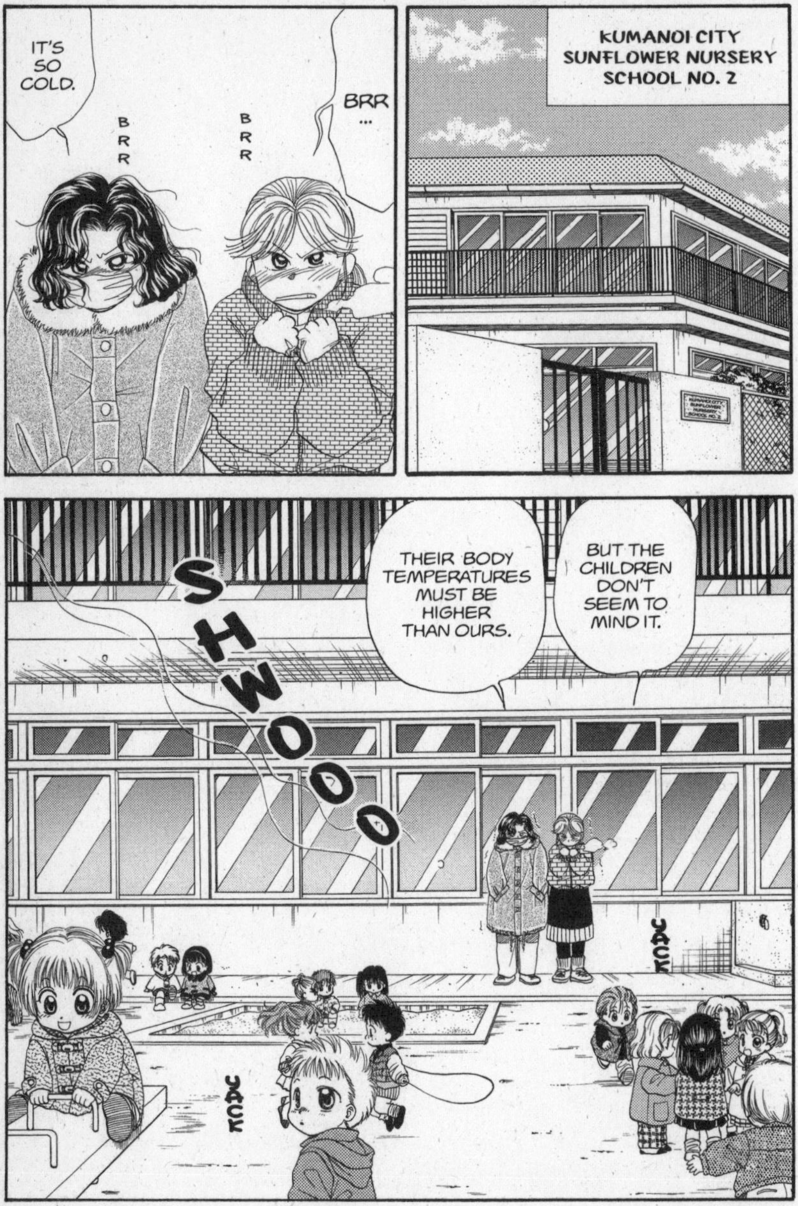
KUMANOI CITY SUNFLOWER NURSERY SCHOOL NO. 2
BRR ...
BRR
BRR
IT'S SO COLD.
BUT THE CHILDREN DON'T SEEM TO MIND IT.
THEIR BODY TEMPERATURES MUST BE HIGHER THAN OURS.
SHWOOO
YACK
YACK

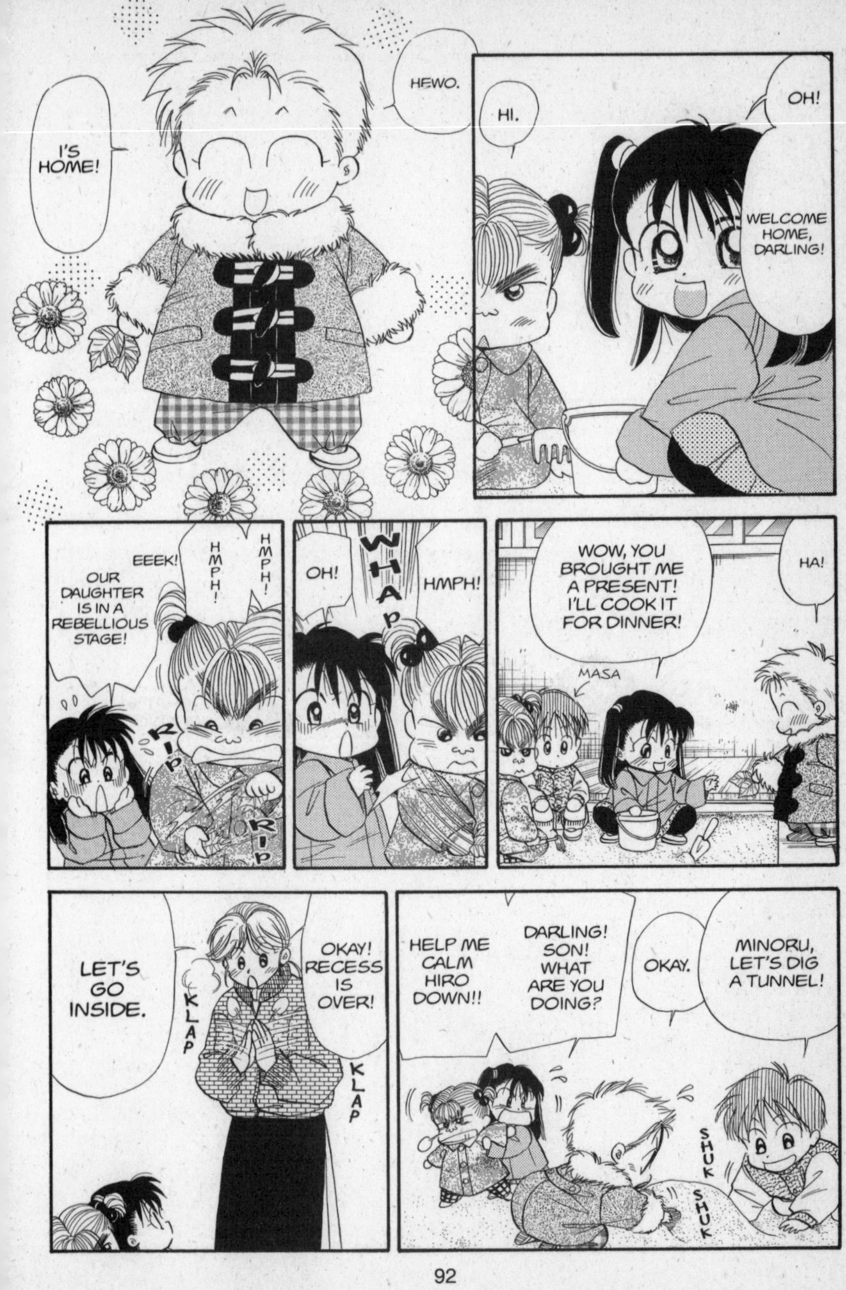
OH!
WELCOME HOME, DARLING!
HI.
HEWO.
I'S HOME!
HA!
WOW, YOU BROUGHT ME A PRESENT! I'LL COOK IT FOR DINNER!
MASA
WHAP
HMPH!
OH!
HMPH!
HMPH!
EEEK! OUR DAUGHTER IS IN A REBELLIOUS STAGE!
RIP
RIP
MINORU, LET'S DIG A TUNNEL!
OKAY.
DARLING! SON! WHAT ARE YOU DOING?
HELP ME CALM HIRO DOWN!!
SHUK
SHUK
OKAY! RECESS IS OVER!
KLAP
KLAP
LET'S GO INSIDE.

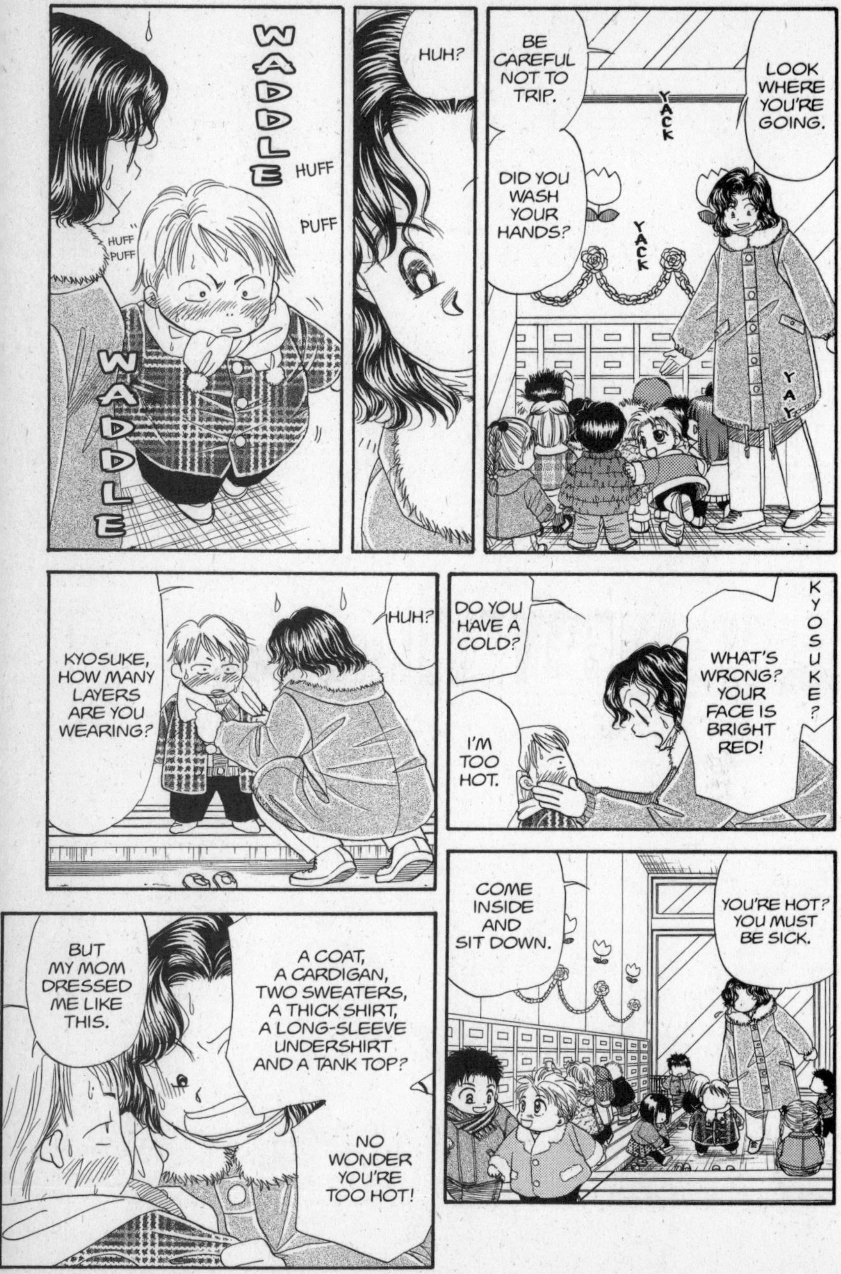
LOOK WHERE YOU'RE GOING.
BE CAREFUL NOT TO TRIP.
YACK
DID YOU WASH YOUR HANDS?
YACK
YAY
HUH?
WADDLE
HUFF
PUFF
HUFF PUFF
WADDLE
KYOSUKE?
WHAT'S WRONG? YOUR FACE IS BRIGHT RED!
DO YOU HAVE A COLD?
I'M TOO HOT.
HUH?
KYOSUKE, HOW MANY LAYERS ARE YOU WEARING?
YOU'RE HOT? YOU MUST BE SICK.
COME INSIDE AND SIT DOWN.
A COAT, A CARDIGAN, TWO SWEATERS, A THICK SHIRT, A LONG-SLEEVE UNDERSHIRT AND A TANK TOP?
BUT MY MOM DRESSED ME LIKE THIS.
NO WONDER YOU'RE TOO HOT!

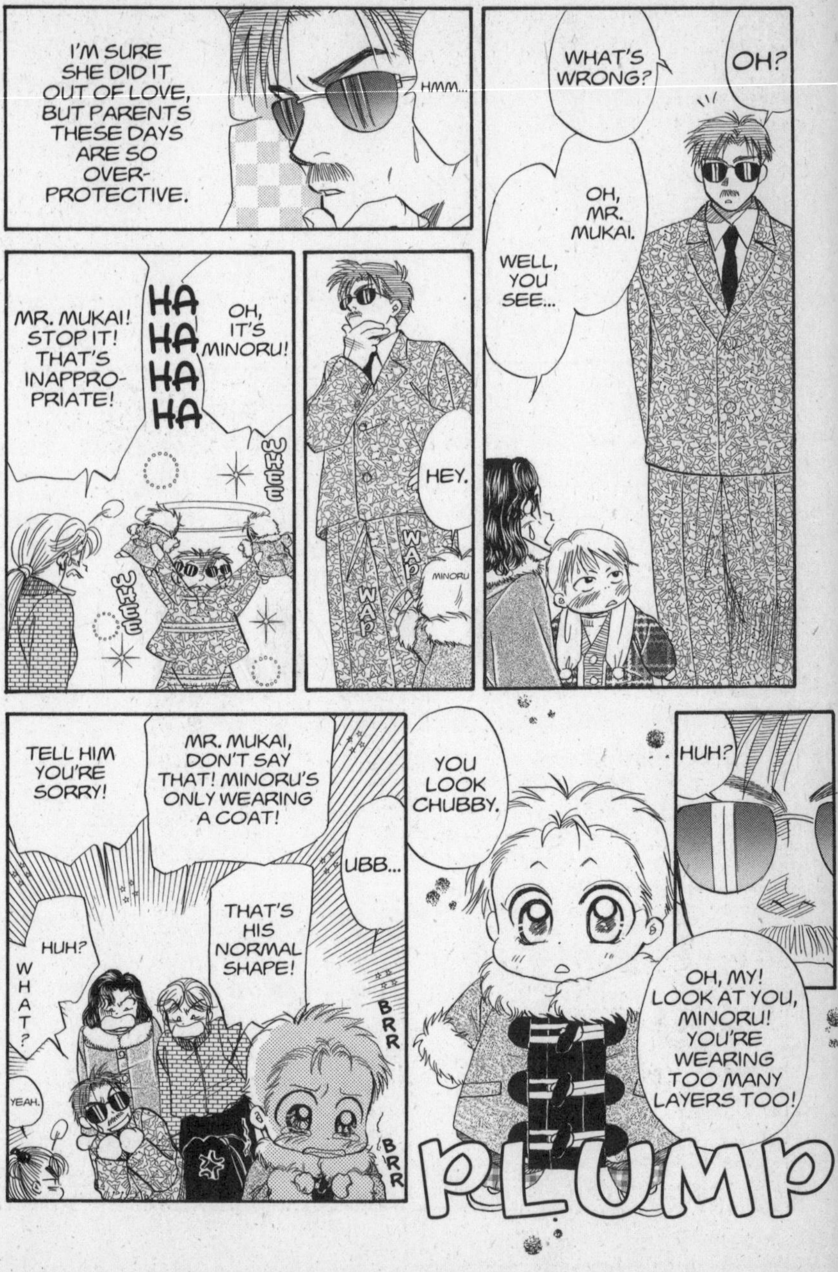
OH?
WHAT'S WRONG?
OH, MR. MUKAI.
WELL, YOU SEE...
HMM...
I'M SURE SHE DID IT OUT OF LOVE, BUT PARENTS THESE DAYS ARE SO OVER-PROTECTIVE.
HEY.
WAP WAP
MINORU
OH, IT'S MINORU!
HA HA HA HA HA
MR. MUKAI! STOP IT! THAT'S INAPPROPRIATE!
WHEE
WHEE
HUH?
OH, MY! LOOK AT YOU, MINORU! YOU'RE WEARING TOO MANY LAYERS TOO!
YOU LOOK CHUBBY.
PLUMP
UBB...
MR. MUKAI, DON'T SAY THAT! MINORU'S ONLY WEARING A COAT!
TELL HIM YOU'RE SORRY!
THAT'S HIS NORMAL SHAPE!
BRR
BRR
HUH?
WHAT?
YEAH.

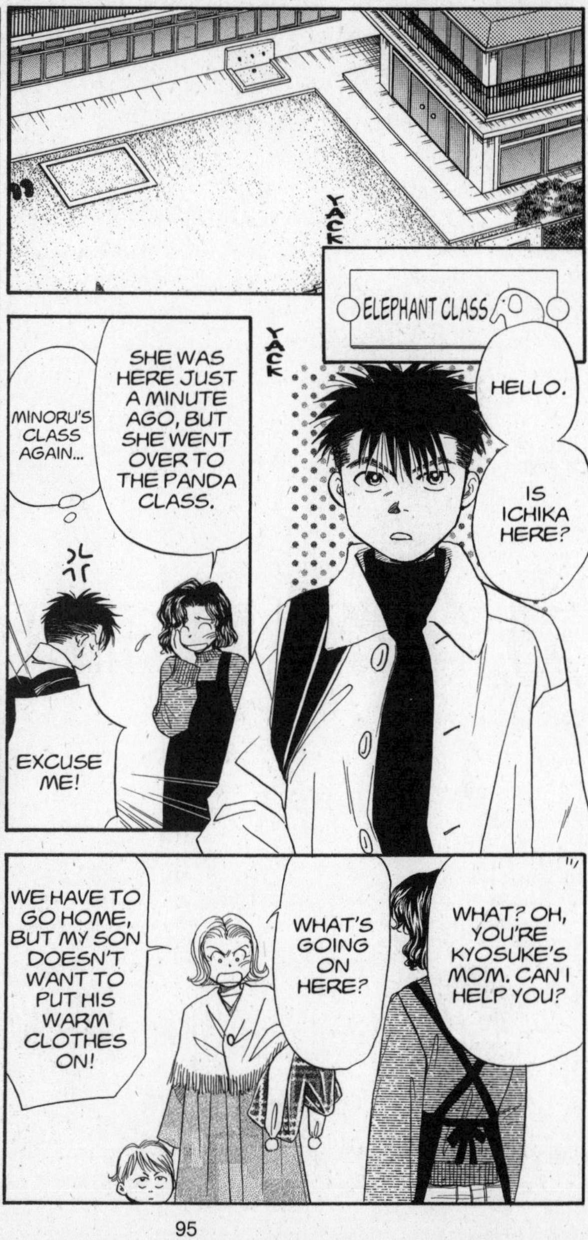
YACK
ELEPHANT CLASS
YACK
HELLO.
IS ICHIKA HERE?
SHE WAS HERE JUST A MINUTE AGO, BUT SHE WENT OVER TO THE PANDA CLASS.
MINORU'S CLASS AGAIN...
EXCUSE ME!
WHAT? OH, YOU'RE KYOSUKE'S MOM. CAN I HELP YOU?
WHAT'S GOING ON HERE?
WE HAVE TO GO HOME, BUT MY SON DOESN'T WANT TO PUT HIS WARM CLOTHES ON!

Author's Note Part 5

About three months ago, in March of 1997, I got to observe the post-recording of the final episode of the *Baby & Me* anime. It was wonderful! In fact, I wanted to go see it a lot sooner, but I couldn't because I'm so terrible at adjusting my work schedule. The post-recording process was amazing. The timing of the voice actors and the people doing the recording (are they called sound engineers?) was perfect! They showed me what professionalism really means!

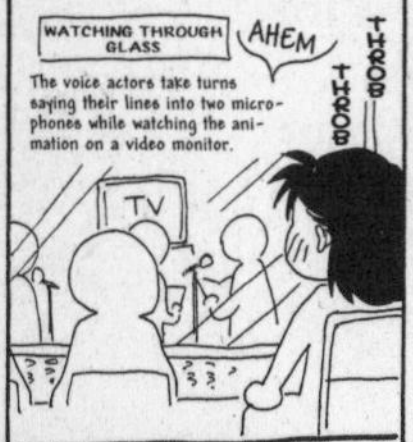
WATCHING THROUGH GLASS
AHEM
THROB
THROB
The voice actors take turns saying their lines into two microphones while watching the animation on a video monitor.
TV

I had my picture taken with all of them and got them to autograph it. It's hanging on my wall now.

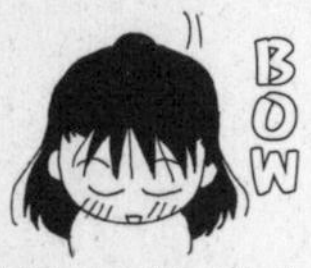
BOW

I'd like to thank all the staff and voice actors! I appreciate all your hard work! ♡
Director Omori, thank you for the illustration of Snufkin!

(Snufkin is a character from the *Moomin* books by Finnish author Tove Jansson.)

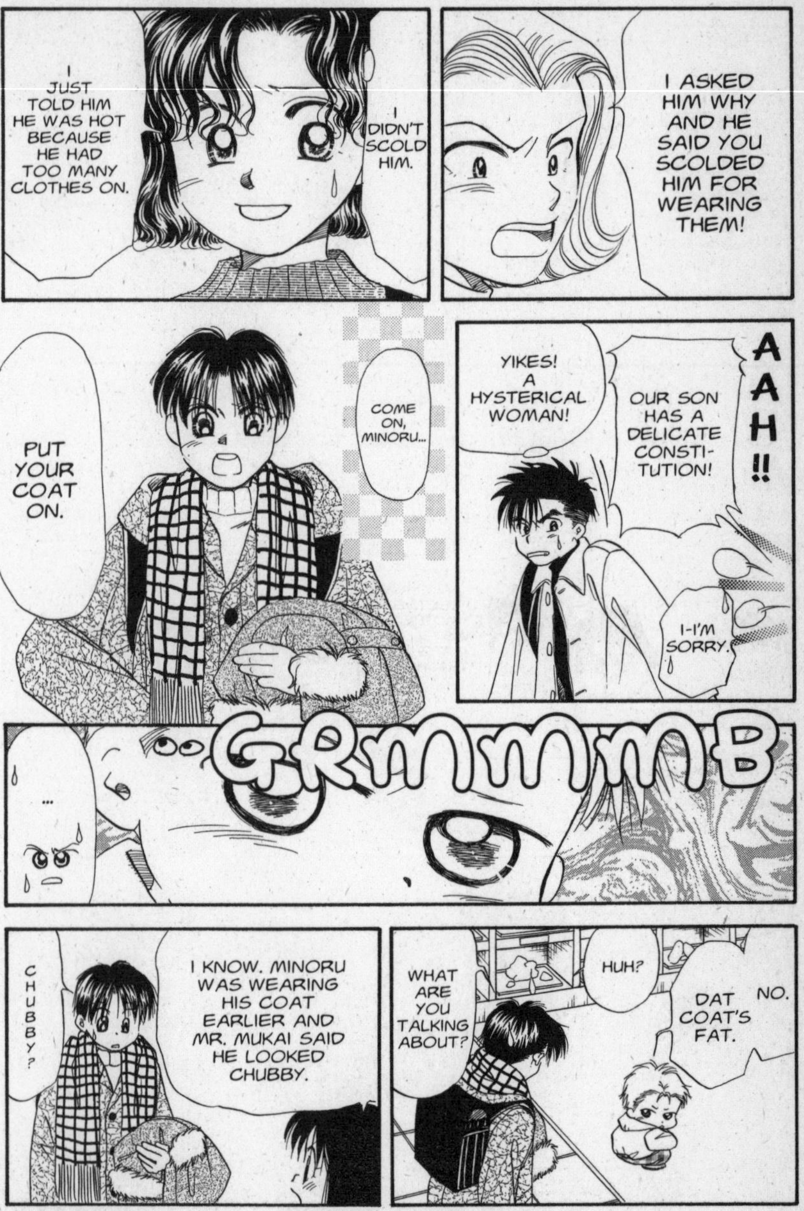
I ASKED HIM WHY AND HE SAID YOU SCOLDED HIM FOR WEARING THEM!
I DIDN'T SCOLD HIM.
I JUST TOLD HIM HE WAS HOT BECAUSE HE HAD TOO MANY CLOTHES ON.
AAH!!
OUR SON HAS A DELICATE CONSTI-TUTION!
YIKES! A HYSTERICAL WOMAN!
I-I'M SORRY.
COME ON, MINORU...
PUT YOUR COAT ON.
GRMMMB
...
NO.
DAT COAT'S FAT.
HUH?
WHAT ARE YOU TALKING ABOUT?
I KNOW. MINORU WAS WEARING HIS COAT EARLIER AND MR. MUKAI SAID HE LOOKED CHUBBY.
CHUBBY?

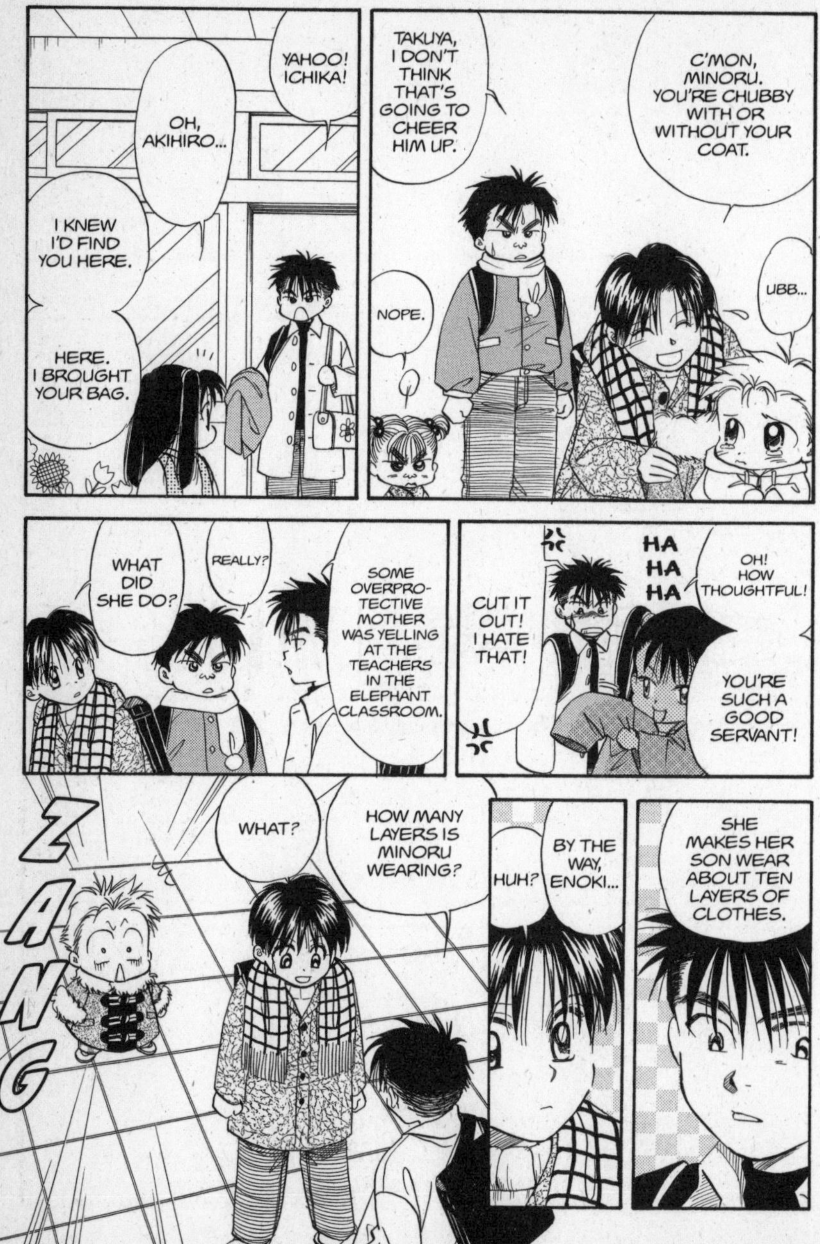
C'MON, MINORU. YOU'RE CHUBBY WITH OR WITHOUT YOUR COAT.
UBB...
TAKUYA, I DON'T THINK THAT'S GOING TO CHEER HIM UP.
NOPE.
YAHOO! ICHIKA!
OH, AKIHIRO...
I KNEW I'D FIND YOU HERE.
HERE. I BROUGHT YOUR BAG.
OH! HOW THOUGHTFUL!
HA HA HA
YOU'RE SUCH A GOOD SERVANT!
CUT IT OUT! I HATE THAT!
SOME OVERPRO-TECTIVE MOTHER WAS YELLING AT THE TEACHERS IN THE ELEPHANT CLASSROOM.
REALLY?
WHAT DID SHE DO?
SHE MAKES HER SON WEAR ABOUT TEN LAYERS OF CLOTHES.
BY THE WAY, ENOKI...
HUH?
HOW MANY LAYERS IS MINORU WEARING?
WHAT?
ZANG

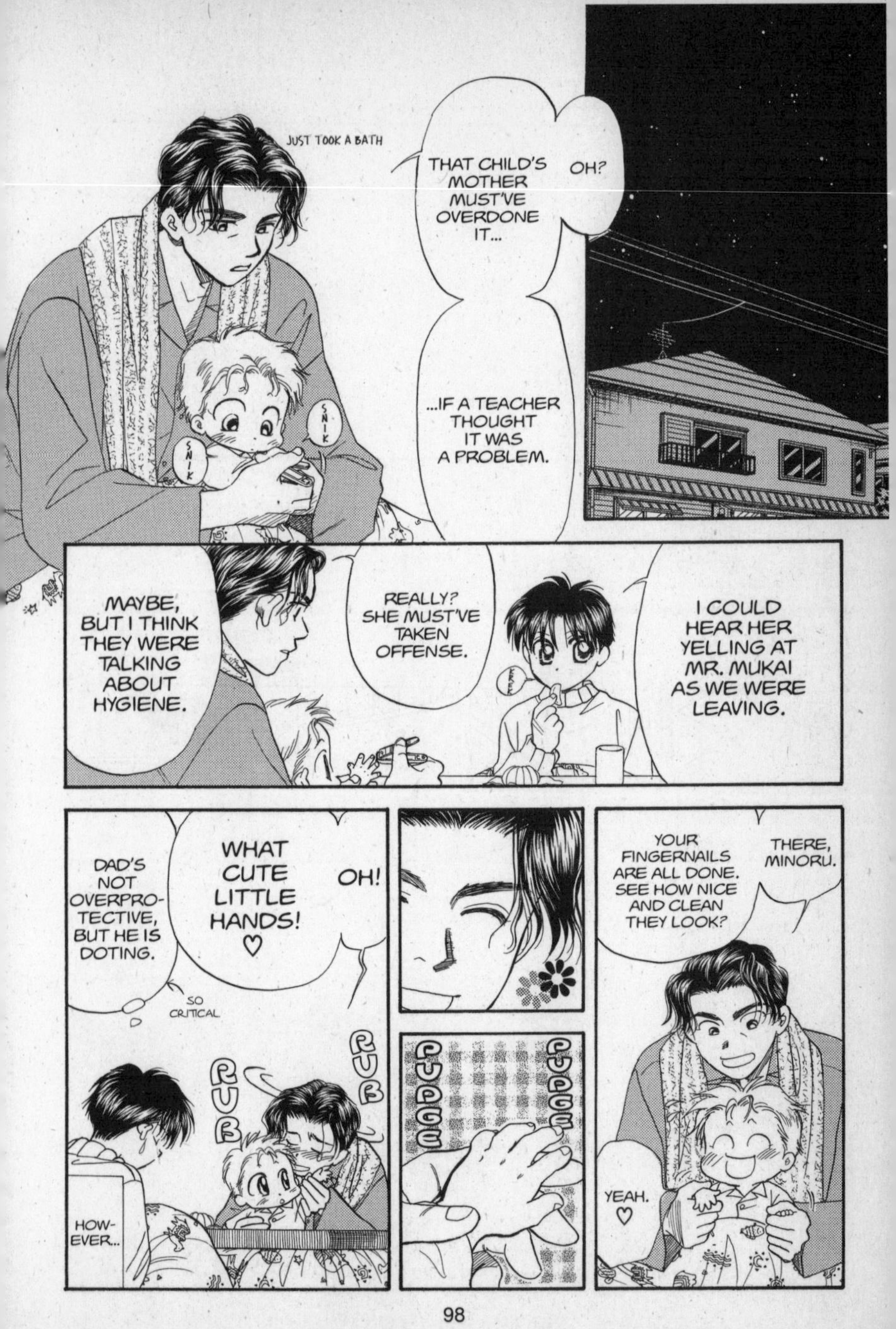
OH?
THAT CHILD'S MOTHER MUST'VE OVERDONE IT...
...IF A TEACHER THOUGHT IT WAS A PROBLEM.
JUST TOOK A BATH
SNIK
SNIK
I COULD HEAR HER YELLING AT MR. MUKAI AS WE WERE LEAVING.
REALLY? SHE MUST'VE TAKEN OFFENSE.
MAYBE, BUT I THINK THEY WERE TALKING ABOUT HYGIENE.
THERE, MINORU.
YOUR FINGERNAILS ARE ALL DONE. SEE HOW NICE AND CLEAN THEY LOOK?
YEAH. ♡
PUDGE
PUDGE
OH!
WHAT CUTE LITTLE HANDS! ♡
DAD'S NOT OVERPROTECTIVE, BUT HE IS DOTING.
SO CRITICAL
RUB
RUB
HOW-EVER...

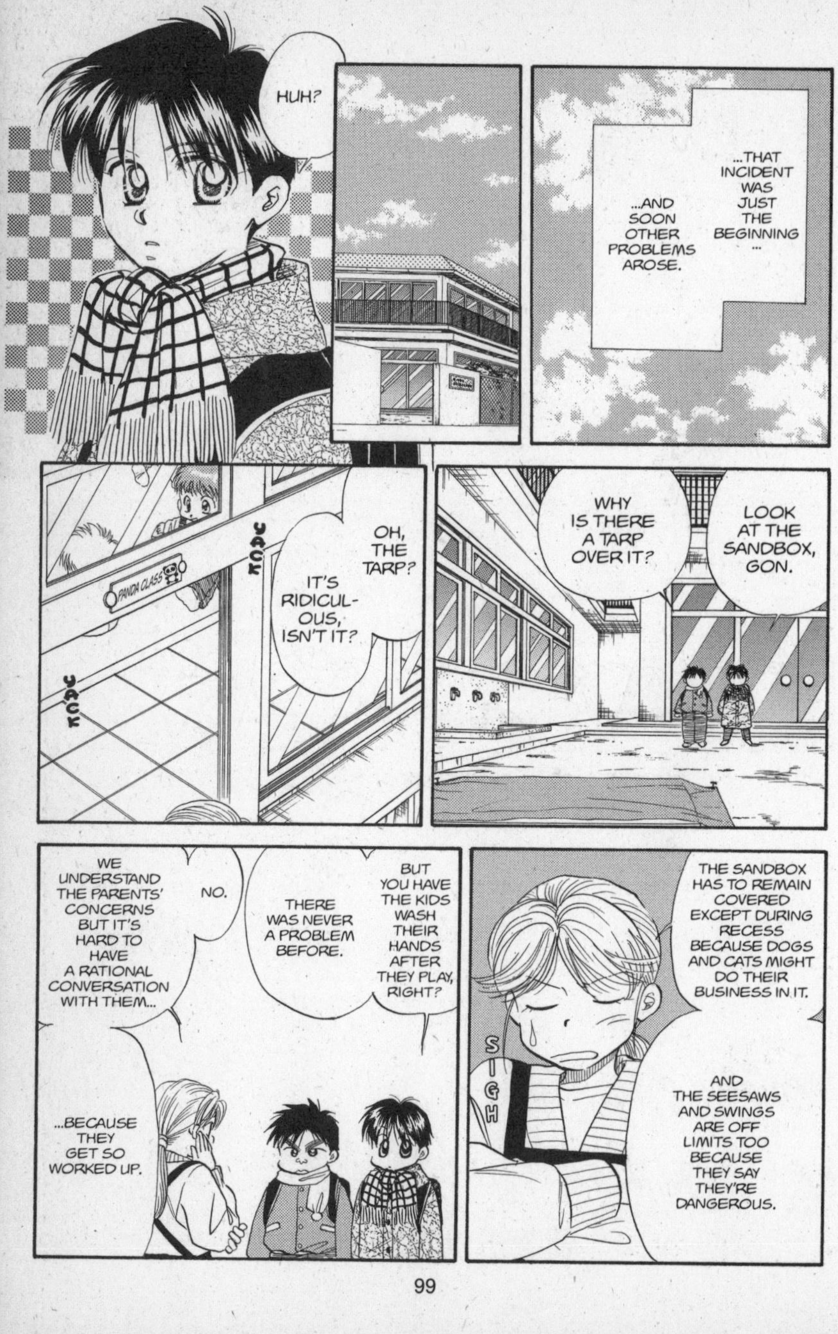
...THAT INCIDENT WAS JUST THE BEGINNING...
...AND SOON OTHER PROBLEMS AROSE.
HUH?
LOOK AT THE SANDBOX, GON.
WHY IS THERE A TARP OVER IT?
OH, THE TARP?
IT'S RIDICULOUS, ISN'T IT?
YACK
YACK
THE SANDBOX HAS TO REMAIN COVERED EXCEPT DURING RECESS BECAUSE DOGS AND CATS MIGHT DO THEIR BUSINESS IN IT.
SIGH
AND THE SEESAWS AND SWINGS ARE OFF LIMITS TOO BECAUSE THEY SAY THEY'RE DANGEROUS.
BUT YOU HAVE THE KIDS WASH THEIR HANDS AFTER THEY PLAY, RIGHT?
THERE WAS NEVER A PROBLEM BEFORE.
NO.
WE UNDERSTAND THE PARENTS' CONCERNS BUT IT'S HARD TO HAVE A RATIONAL CONVERSATION WITH THEM...
...BECAUSE THEY GET SO WORKED UP.

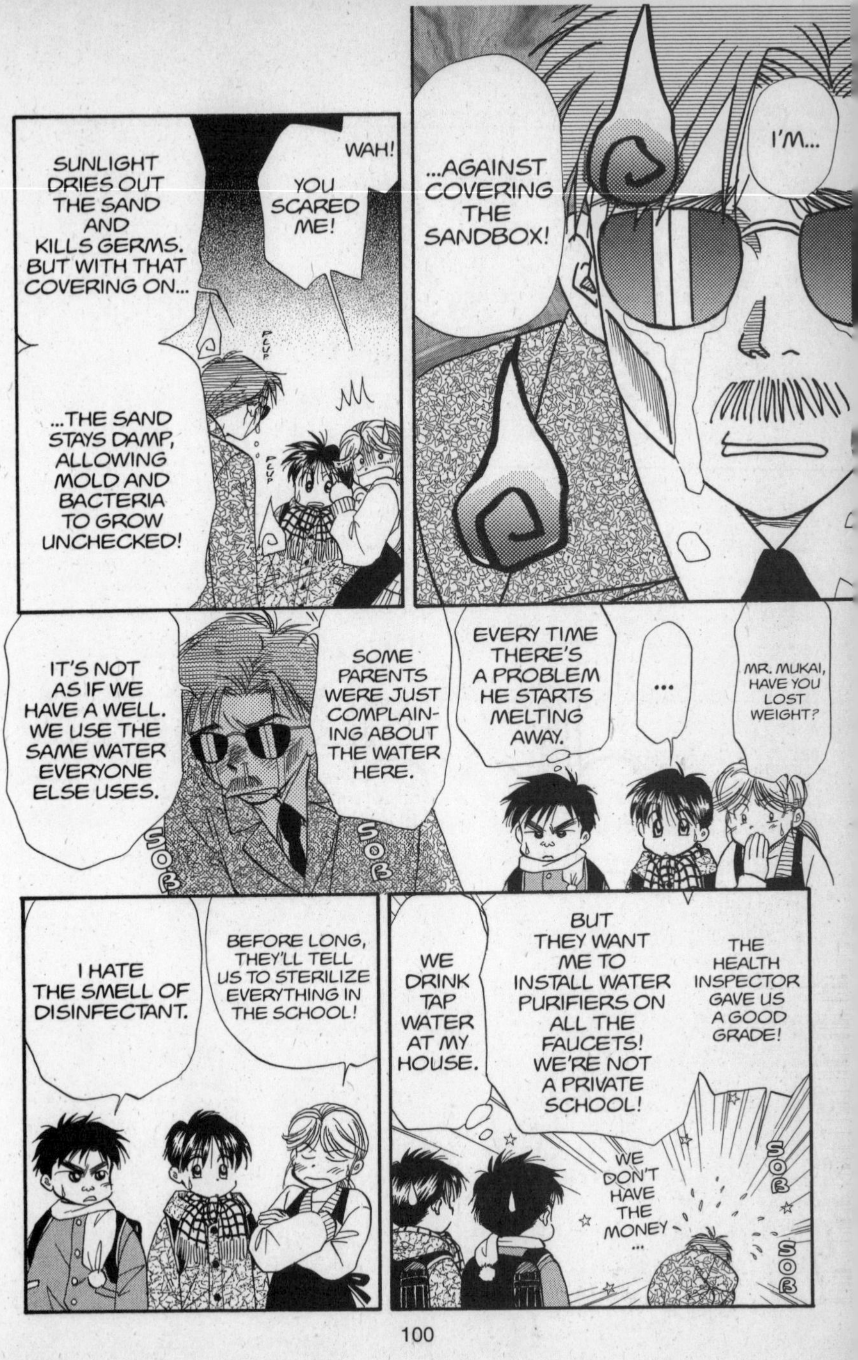
I'M...
...AGAINST COVERING THE SANDBOX!
WAH!
YOU SCARED ME!
SUNLIGHT DRIES OUT THE SAND AND KILLS GERMS. BUT WITH THAT COVERING ON...
PLUP
PLUP
...THE SAND STAYS DAMP, ALLOWING MOLD AND BACTERIA TO GROW UNCHECKED!
MR. MUKAI, HAVE YOU LOST WEIGHT?
...
EVERY TIME THERE'S A PROBLEM HE STARTS MELTING AWAY.
SOME PARENTS WERE JUST COMPLAIN-ING ABOUT THE WATER HERE.
IT'S NOT AS IF WE HAVE A WELL. WE USE THE SAME WATER EVERYONE ELSE USES.
SOB
SOB
THE HEALTH INSPECTOR GAVE US A GOOD GRADE!
BUT THEY WANT ME TO INSTALL WATER PURIFIERS ON ALL THE FAUCETS! WE'RE NOT A PRIVATE SCHOOL!
WE DRINK TAP WATER AT MY HOUSE.
SOB
SOB
WE DON'T HAVE THE MONEY...
BEFORE LONG, THEY'LL TELL US TO STERILIZE EVERYTHING IN THE SCHOOL!
I HATE THE SMELL OF DISINFECTANT.

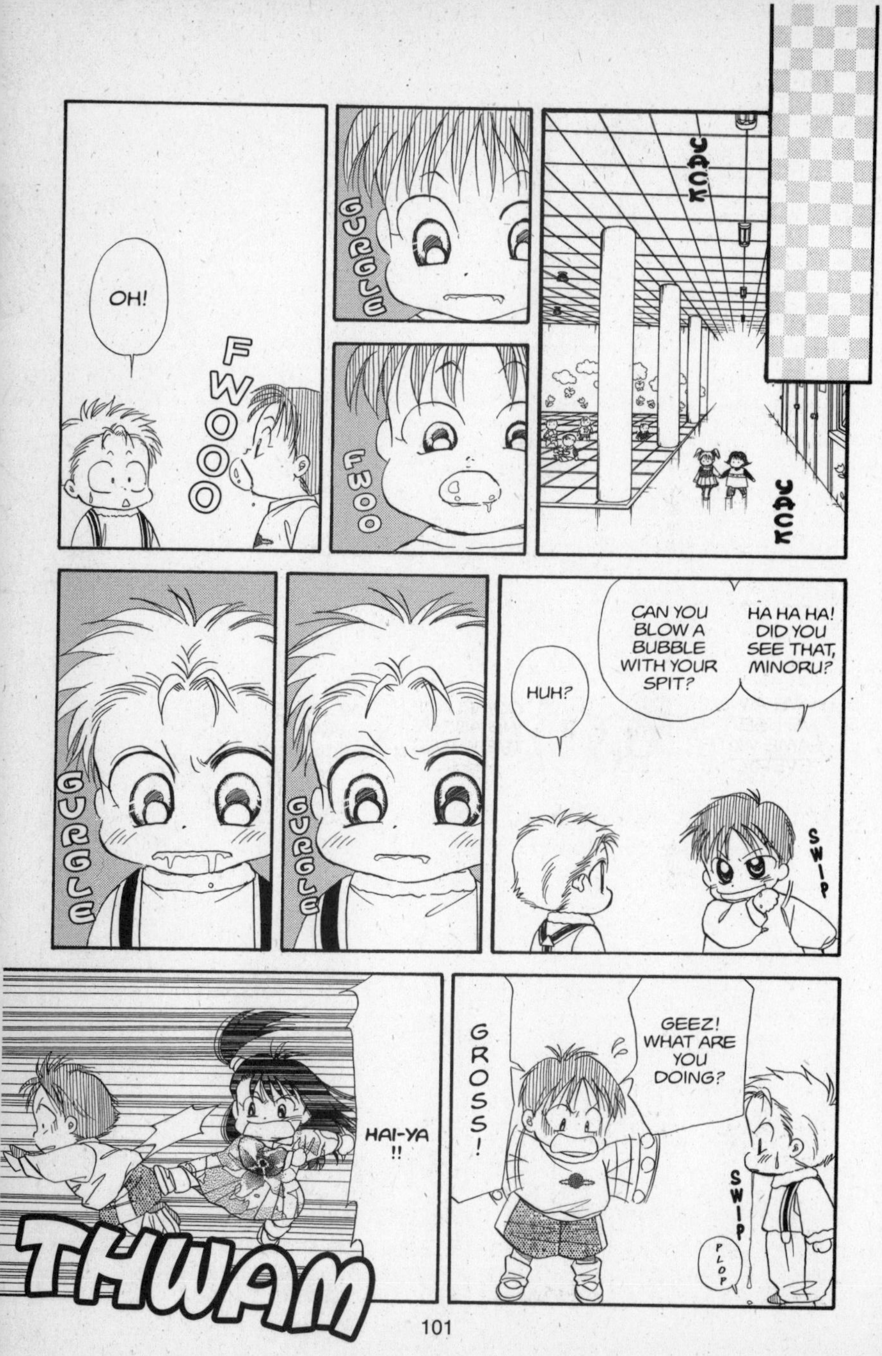
YACK
YACK
GURGLE
FWOO
OH!
FWOOO
HA HA HA! DID YOU SEE THAT, MINORU?
CAN YOU BLOW A BUBBLE WITH YOUR SPIT?
HUH?
SWIP
GURGLE
GURGLE
GEEZ! WHAT ARE YOU DOING?
GROSS!
SWIP
PLOP
HAI-YA!!
THWAM

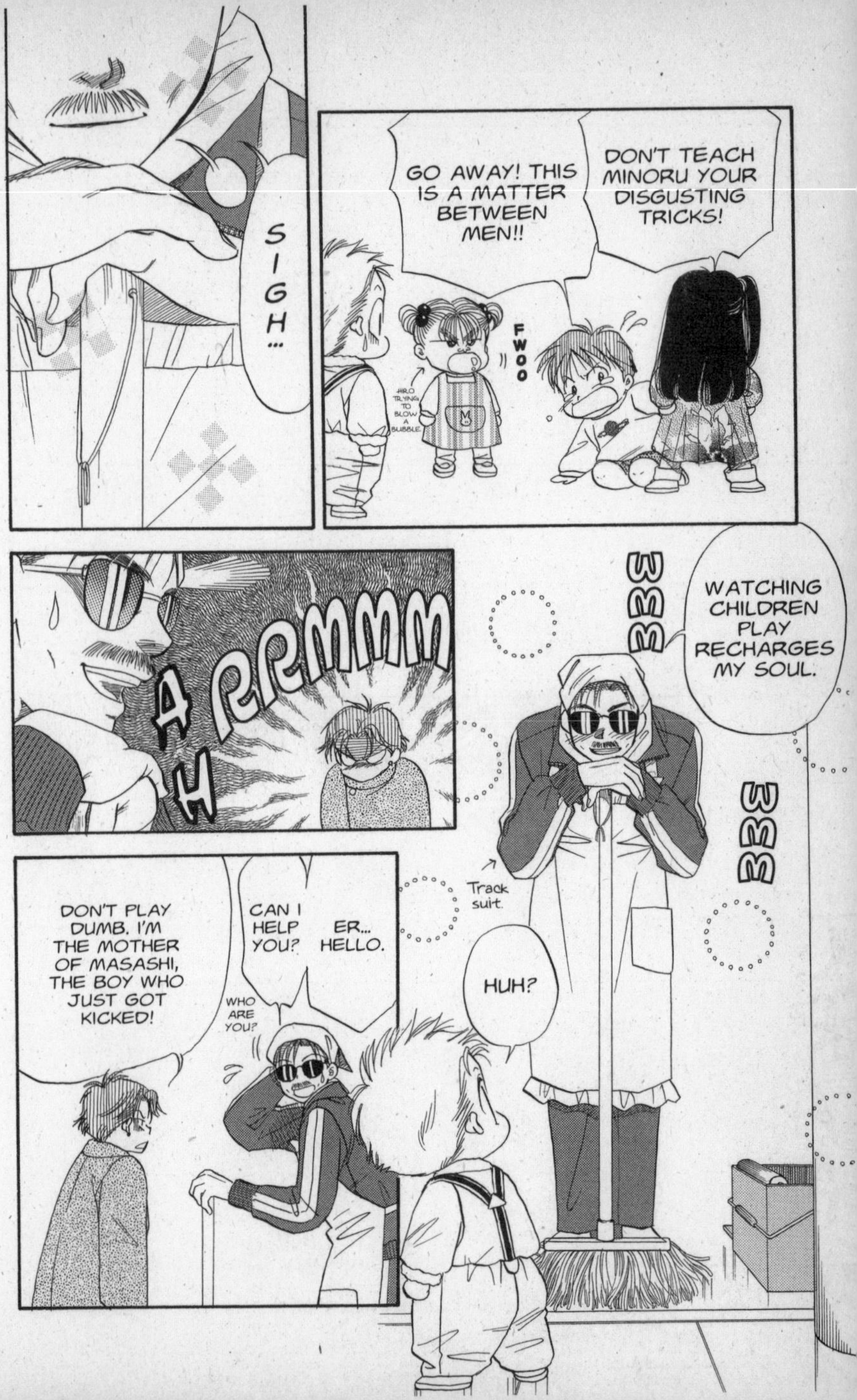
DON'T TEACH MINORU YOUR DISGUSTING TRICKS!
GO AWAY! THIS IS A MATTER BETWEEN MEN!!
FWOO
HIRO TRYING TO BLOW A BUBBLE.
SIGH...
WATCHING CHILDREN PLAY RECHARGES MY SOUL.
Track suit.
HUH?
AHRRMMM
ER... HELLO.
CAN I HELP YOU?
WHO ARE YOU?
DON'T PLAY DUMB. I'M THE MOTHER OF MASASHI, THE BOY WHO JUST GOT KICKED!

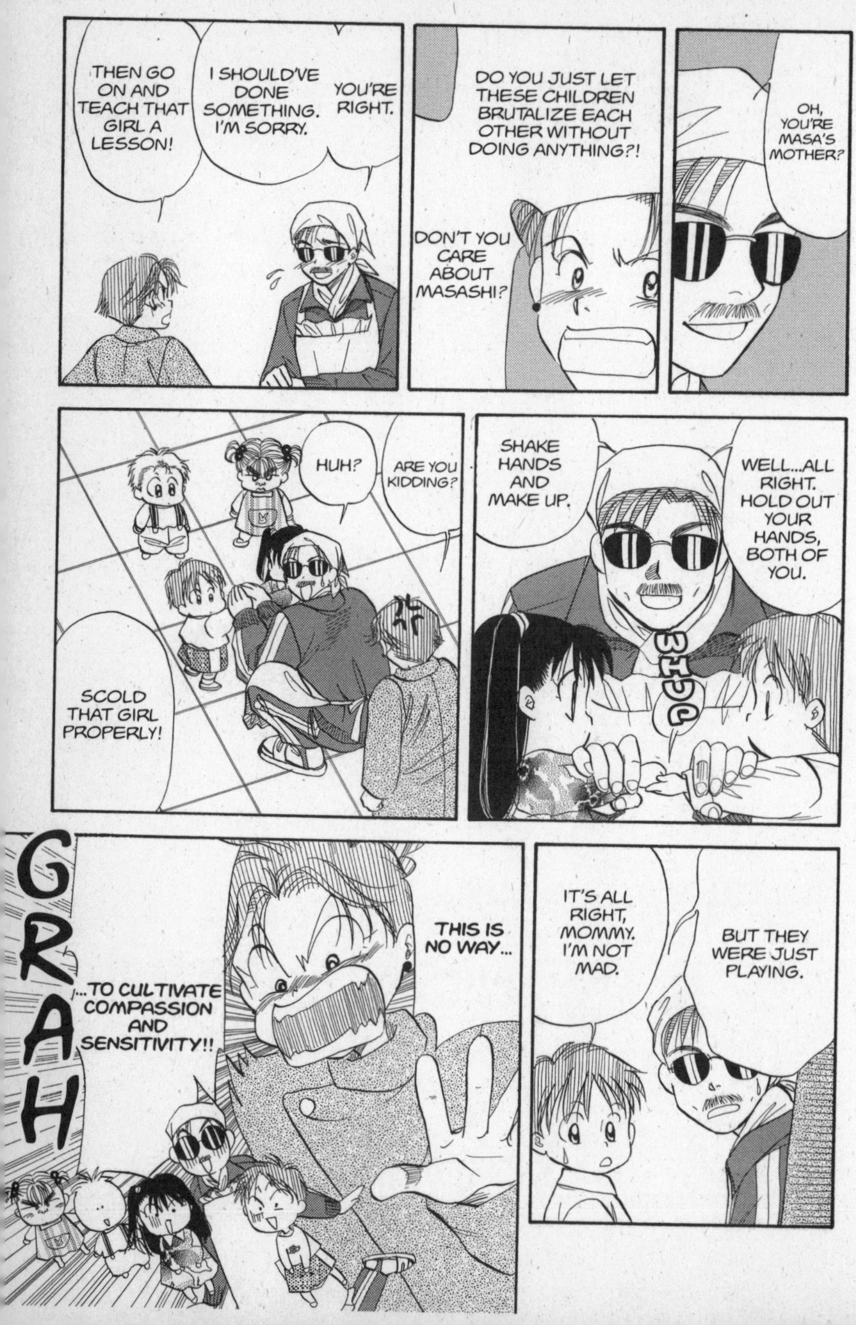
OH, YOU'RE MASA'S MOTHER?
DO YOU JUST LET THESE CHILDREN BRUTALIZE EACH OTHER WITHOUT DOING ANYTHING?!
DON'T YOU CARE ABOUT MASASHI?
YOU'RE RIGHT.
I SHOULD'VE DONE SOMETHING. I'M SORRY.
THEN GO ON AND TEACH THAT GIRL A LESSON!
WELL...ALL RIGHT. HOLD OUT YOUR HANDS, BOTH OF YOU.
SHAKE HANDS AND MAKE UP.
WHUG
ARE YOU KIDDING?
HUH?
SCOLD THAT GIRL PROPERLY!
BUT THEY WERE JUST PLAYING.
IT'S ALL RIGHT, MOMMY. I'M NOT MAD.
THIS IS NO WAY...
...TO CULTIVATE COMPASSION AND SENSITIVITY!!
GRAH

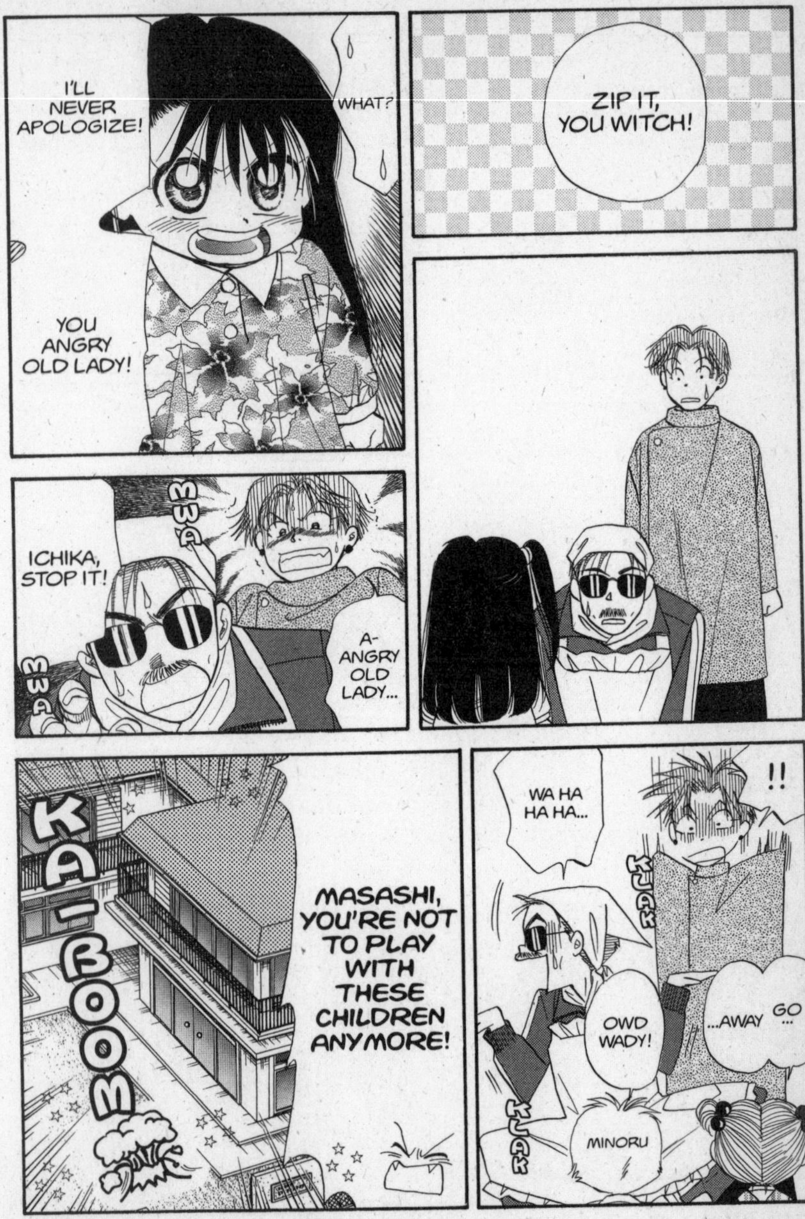
ZIP IT, YOU WITCH!
WHAT?
I'LL NEVER APOLOGIZE!
YOU ANGRY OLD LADY!
MWA
A-ANGRY OLD LADY...
ICHIKA, STOP IT!
MWA
!!
WA HA HA HA...
KJAK
GO...
...AWAY
OWD WADY!
KJAK
MINORU
MASASHI, YOU'RE NOT TO PLAY WITH THESE CHILDREN ANYMORE!
KA-BOOM

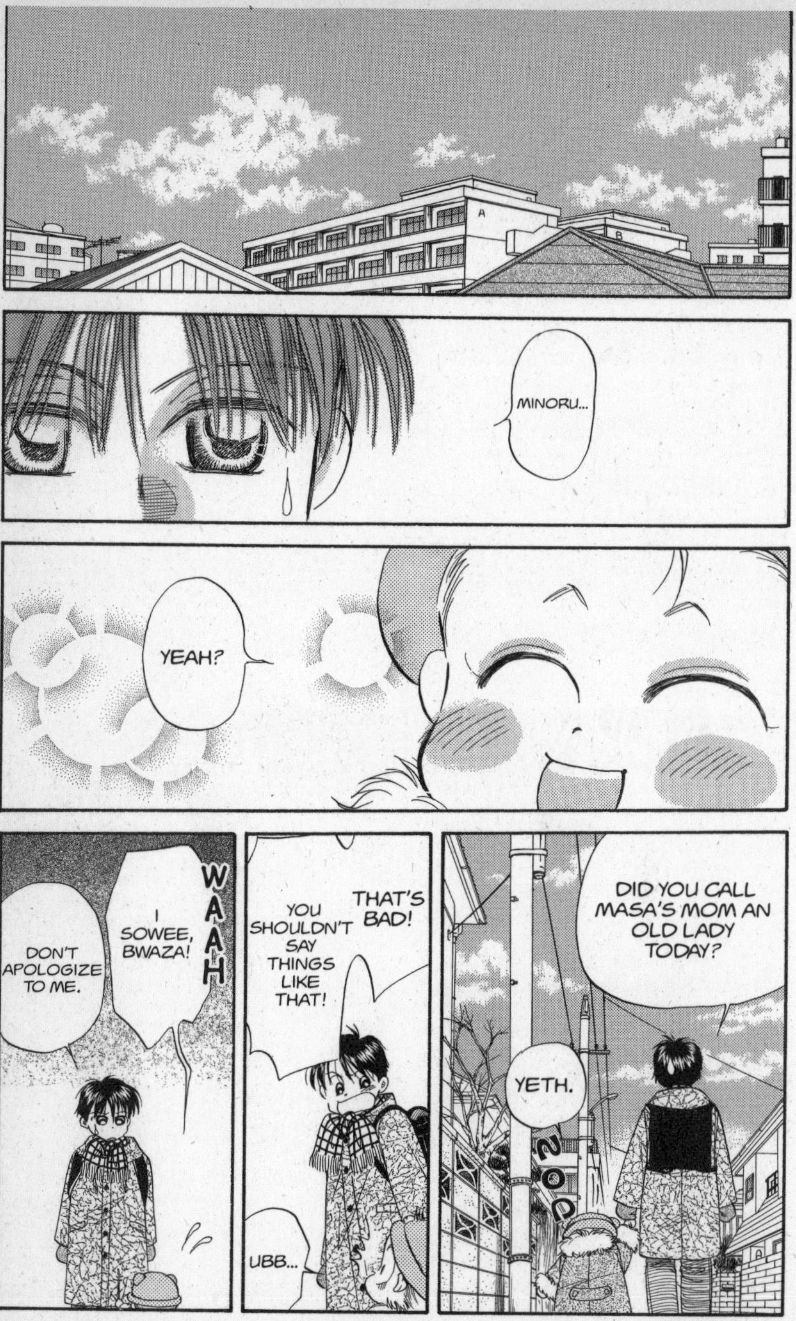
MINORU...
YEAH?
DID YOU CALL MASA'S MOM AN OLD LADY TODAY?
YETH.
THAT'S BAD!
YOU SHOULDN'T SAY THINGS LIKE THAT!
UBB...
WAAH
I SOWEE, BWAZA!
DON'T APOLOGIZE TO ME.

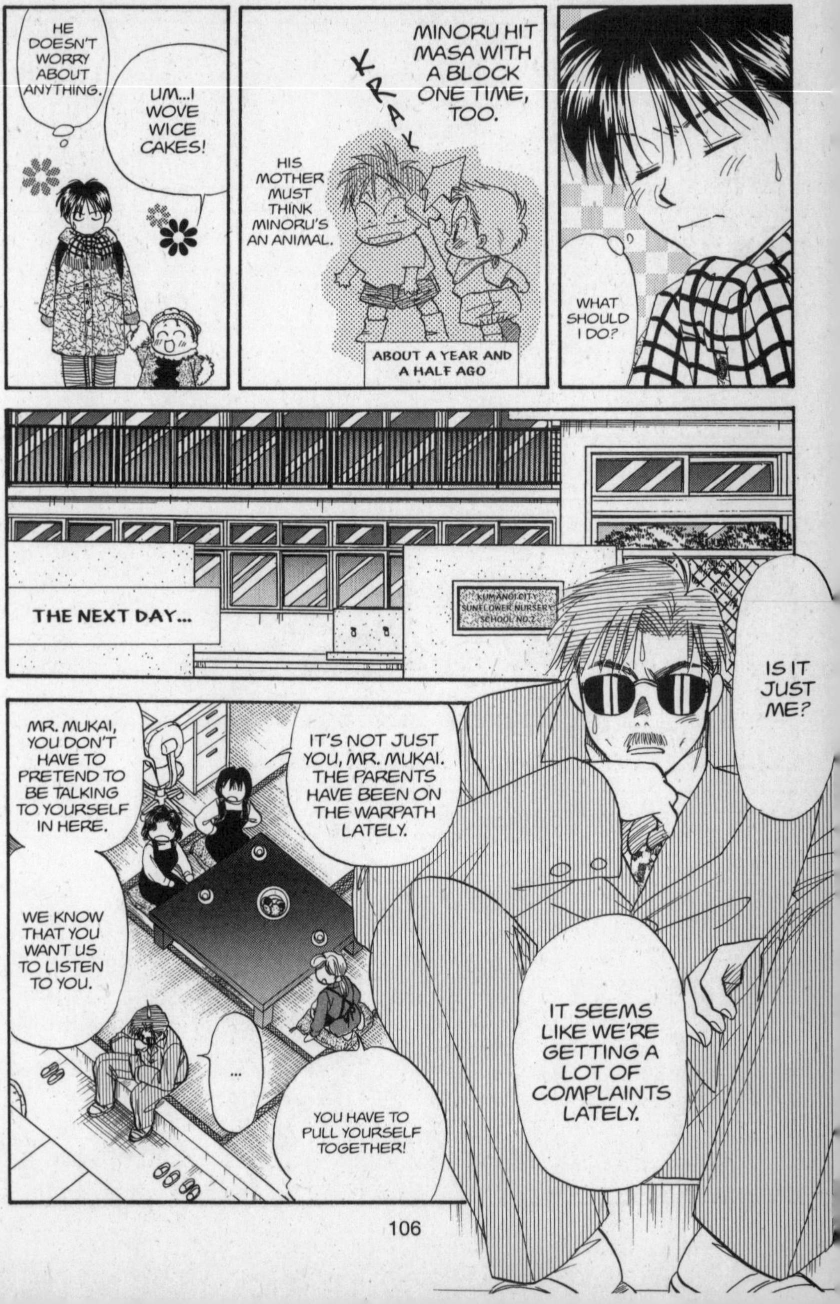
WHAT SHOULD I DO?
MINORU HIT MASA WITH A BLOCK ONE TIME, TOO.
KRAK
HIS MOTHER MUST THINK MINORU'S AN ANIMAL.
ABOUT A YEAR AND A HALF AGO
UM...I WOVE WICE CAKES!
HE DOESN'T WORRY ABOUT ANYTHING.
THE NEXT DAY...
KUMANOI CITY SUNFLOWER NURSERY SCHOOL NO.2
IS IT JUST ME?
IT SEEMS LIKE WE'RE GETTING A LOT OF COMPLAINTS LATELY.
IT'S NOT JUST YOU, MR. MUKAI. THE PARENTS HAVE BEEN ON THE WARPATH LATELY.
MR. MUKAI, YOU DON'T HAVE TO PRETEND TO BE TALKING TO YOURSELF IN HERE.
WE KNOW THAT YOU WANT US TO LISTEN TO YOU.
...
YOU HAVE TO PULL YOURSELF TOGETHER!

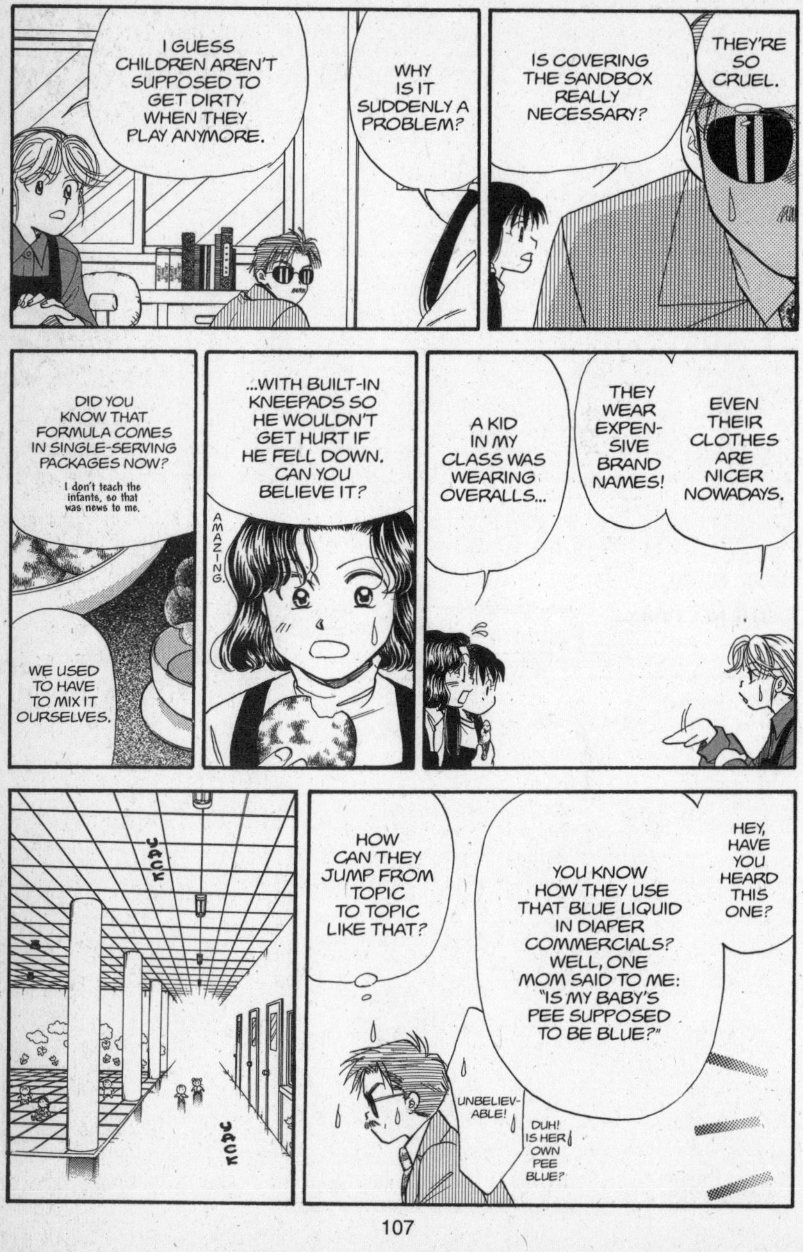
THEY'RE SO CRUEL.
IS COVERING THE SANDBOX REALLY NECESSARY?
WHY IS IT SUDDENLY A PROBLEM?
I GUESS CHILDREN AREN'T SUPPOSED TO GET DIRTY WHEN THEY PLAY ANYMORE.
EVEN THEIR CLOTHES ARE NICER NOWADAYS.
THEY WEAR EXPEN-SIVE BRAND NAMES!
A KID IN MY CLASS WAS WEARING OVERALLS...
...WITH BUILT-IN KNEEPADS SO HE WOULDN'T GET HURT IF HE FELL DOWN. CAN YOU BELIEVE IT?
AMAZING.
DID YOU KNOW THAT FORMULA COMES IN SINGLE-SERVING PACKAGES NOW?
I don't teach the infants, so that was news to me.
WE USED TO HAVE TO MIX IT OURSELVES.
HEY, HAVE YOU HEARD THIS ONE?
YOU KNOW HOW THEY USE THAT BLUE LIQUID IN DIAPER COMMERCIALS? WELL, ONE MOM SAID TO ME: "IS MY BABY'S PEE SUPPOSED TO BE BLUE?"
HOW CAN THEY JUMP FROM TOPIC TO TOPIC LIKE THAT?
UNBELIEV-ABLE!
DUH! IS HER OWN PEE BLUE?
YACK
YACK

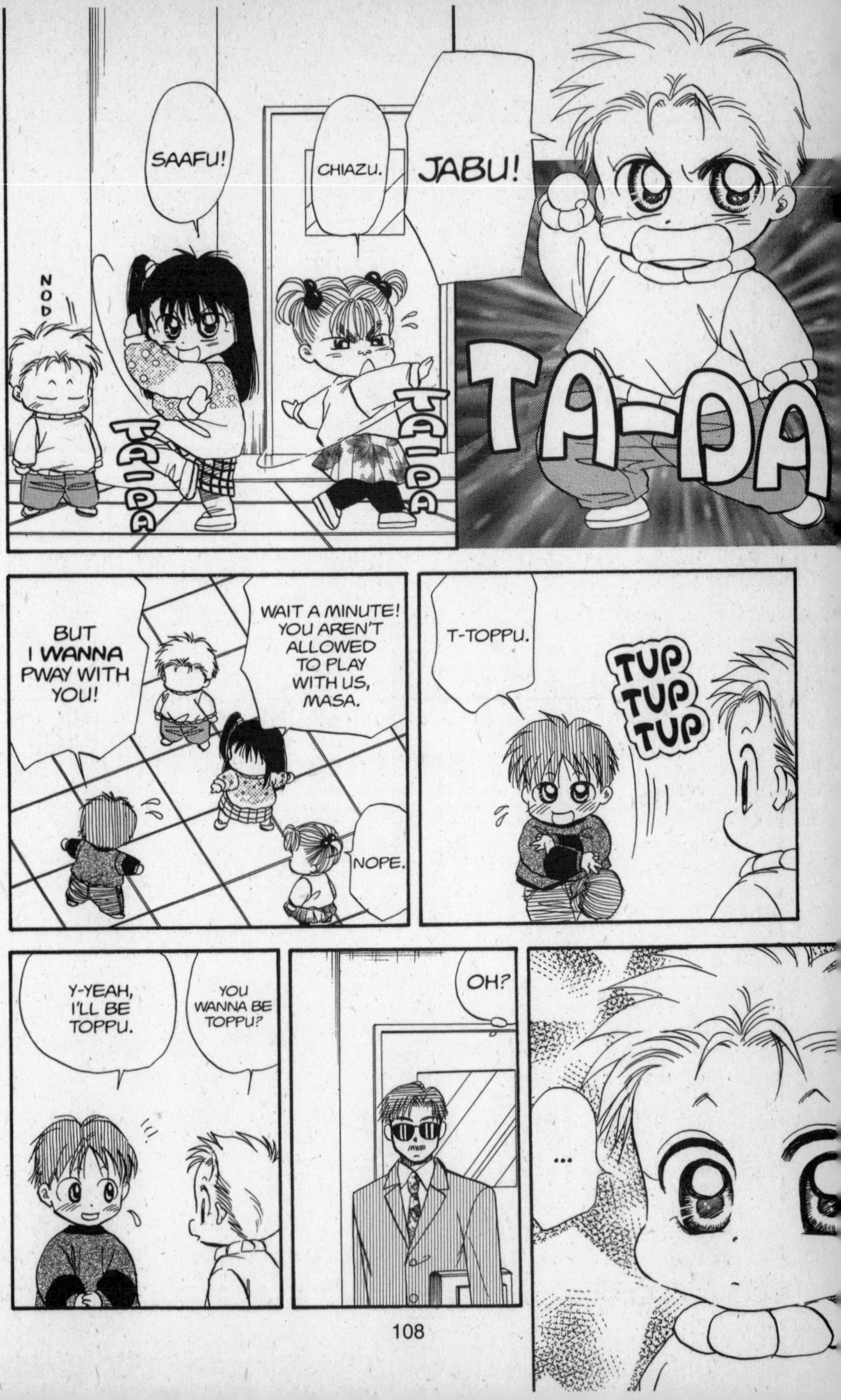
JABU!
TA-DA
CHIAZU.
SAAFU!
TA-PA
NOD
TA-PA
T-TOPPU.
TUP TUP TUP
WAIT A MINUTE! YOU AREN'T ALLOWED TO PLAY WITH US, MASA.
NOPE.
BUT I WANNA PWAY WITH YOU!
...
OH?
YOU WANNA BE TOPPU?
Y-YEAH, I'LL BE TOPPU.

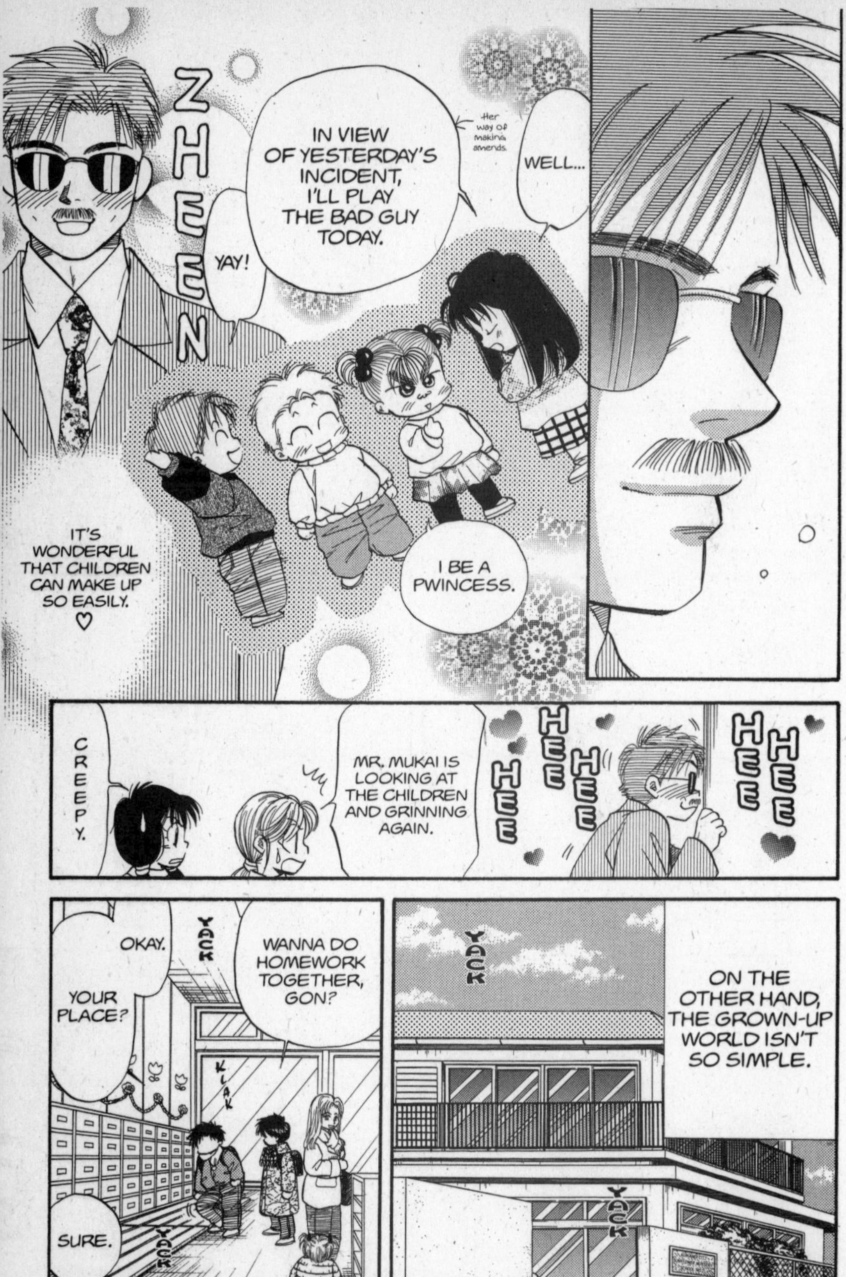
Her way of making amends.
WELL...
IN VIEW OF YESTERDAY'S INCIDENT, I'LL PLAY THE BAD GUY TODAY.
ZHEEN
YAY!
I BE A PWINCESS.
IT'S WONDERFUL THAT CHILDREN CAN MAKE UP SO EASILY. ♡
HEE HEE
HEE HEE HEE
MR. MUKAI IS LOOKING AT THE CHILDREN AND GRINNING AGAIN.
CREEPY.
YACK
ON THE OTHER HAND, THE GROWN-UP WORLD ISN'T SO SIMPLE.
YACK
WANNA DO HOMEWORK TOGETHER, GON?
YACK
OKAY.
YOUR PLACE?
KLAK
SURE.
YACK

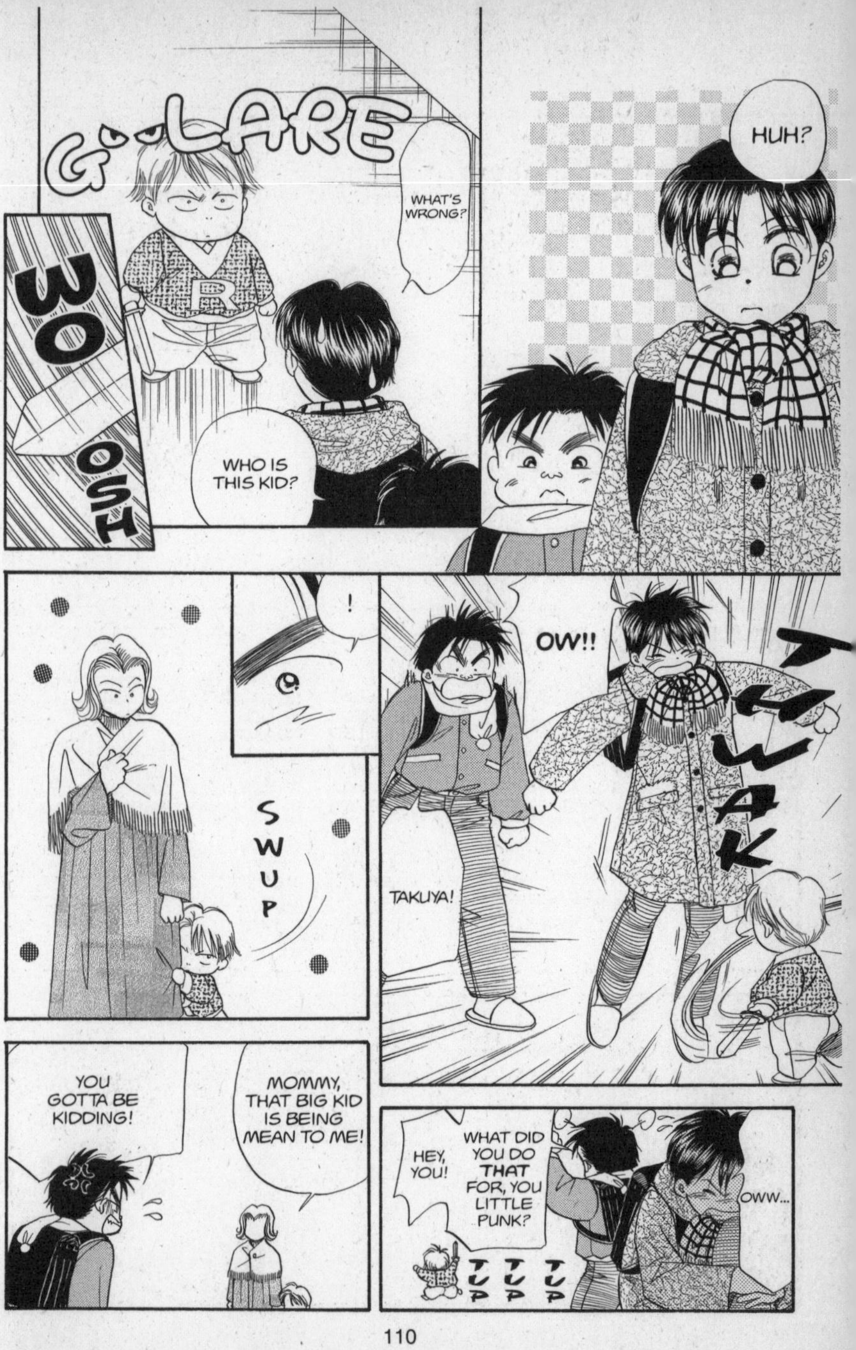
HUH?
GLARE
WHAT'S WRONG?
WHO IS THIS KID?
WOOSH
THWAK
OW!!
TAKUYA!
!
SWUP
HEY, YOU!
WHAT DID YOU DO **THAT** FOR, YOU LITTLE PUNK?
OWW...
TUP TUP TUP
MOMMY, THAT BIG KID IS BEING MEAN TO ME!
YOU GOTTA BE KIDDING!

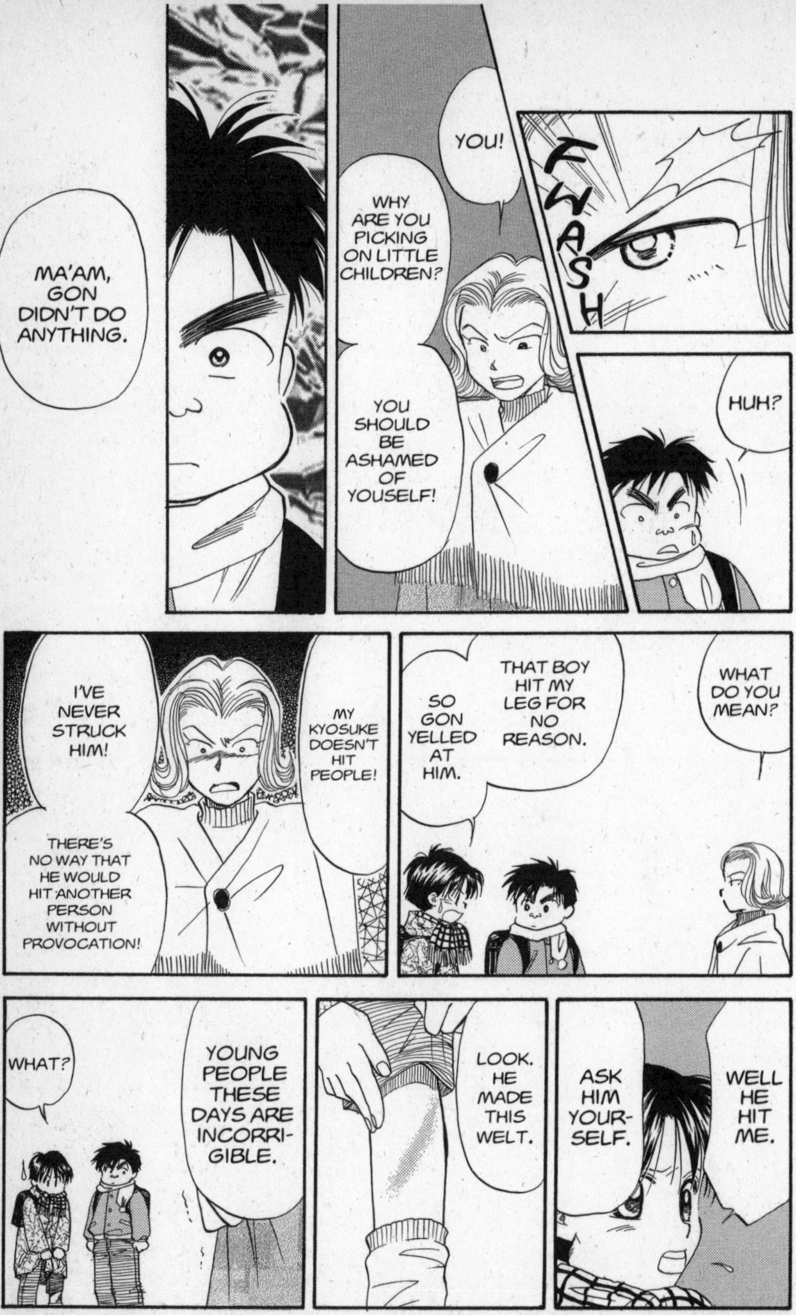
FWASH
HUH?
YOU!
WHY ARE YOU PICKING ON LITTLE CHILDREN?
YOU SHOULD BE ASHAMED OF YOUSELF!
MA'AM, GON DIDN'T DO ANYTHING.
WHAT DO YOU MEAN?
THAT BOY HIT MY LEG FOR NO REASON.
SO GON YELLED AT HIM.
MY KYOSUKE DOESN'T HIT PEOPLE!
I'VE NEVER STRUCK HIM!
THERE'S NO WAY THAT HE WOULD HIT ANOTHER PERSON WITHOUT PROVOCATION!
WELL HE HIT ME.
ASK HIM YOURSELF.
LOOK. HE MADE THIS WELT.
YOUNG PEOPLE THESE DAYS ARE INCORRIGIBLE.
WHAT?

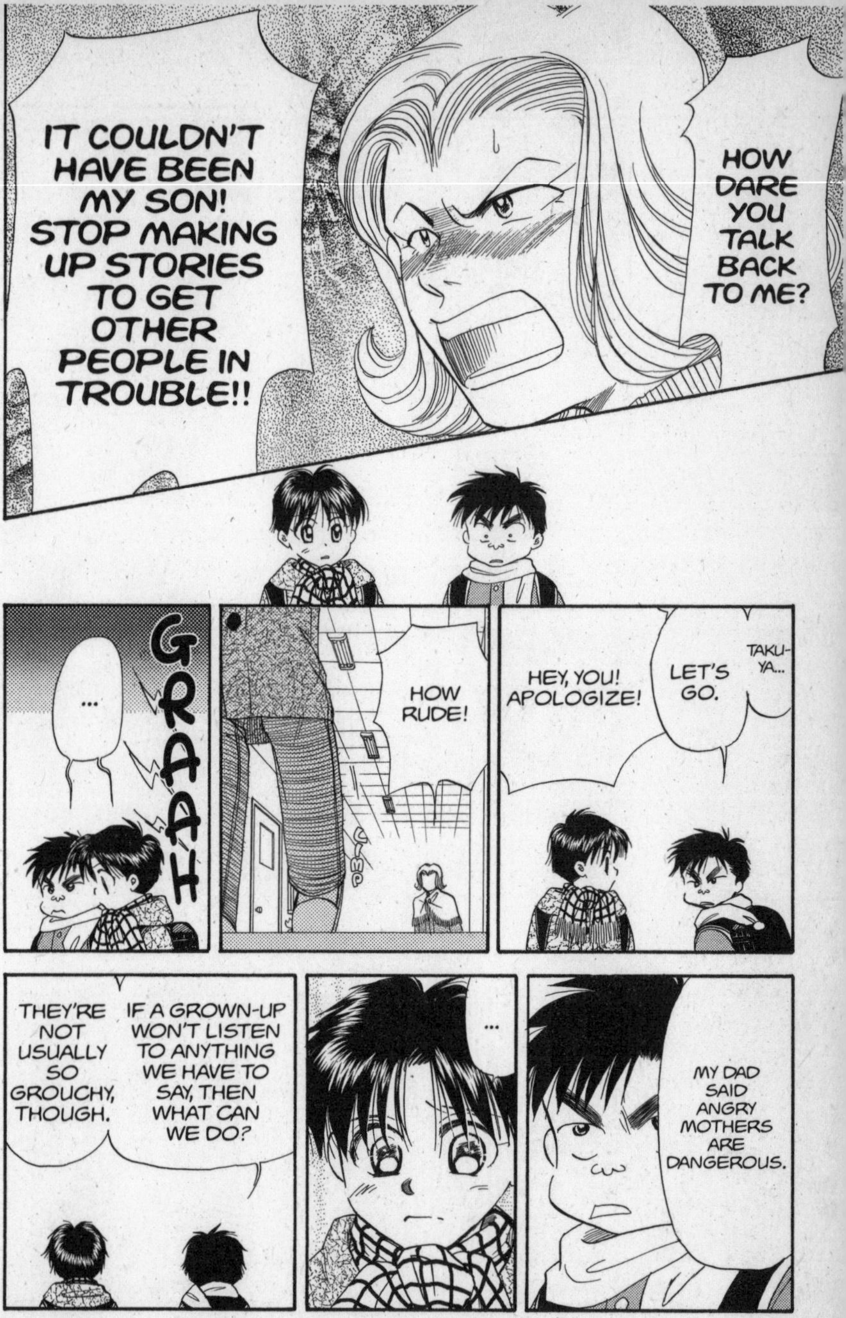
HOW DARE YOU TALK BACK TO ME?
IT COULDN'T HAVE BEEN MY SON! STOP MAKING UP STORIES TO GET OTHER PEOPLE IN TROUBLE!!
TAKU-YA...
LET'S GO.
HEY, YOU! APOLOGIZE!
HOW RUDE!
LIMP
GRAAH
...
MY DAD SAID ANGRY MOTHERS ARE DANGEROUS.
...
IF A GROWN-UP WON'T LISTEN TO ANYTHING WE HAVE TO SAY, THEN WHAT CAN WE DO?
THEY'RE NOT USUALLY SO GROUCHY, THOUGH.

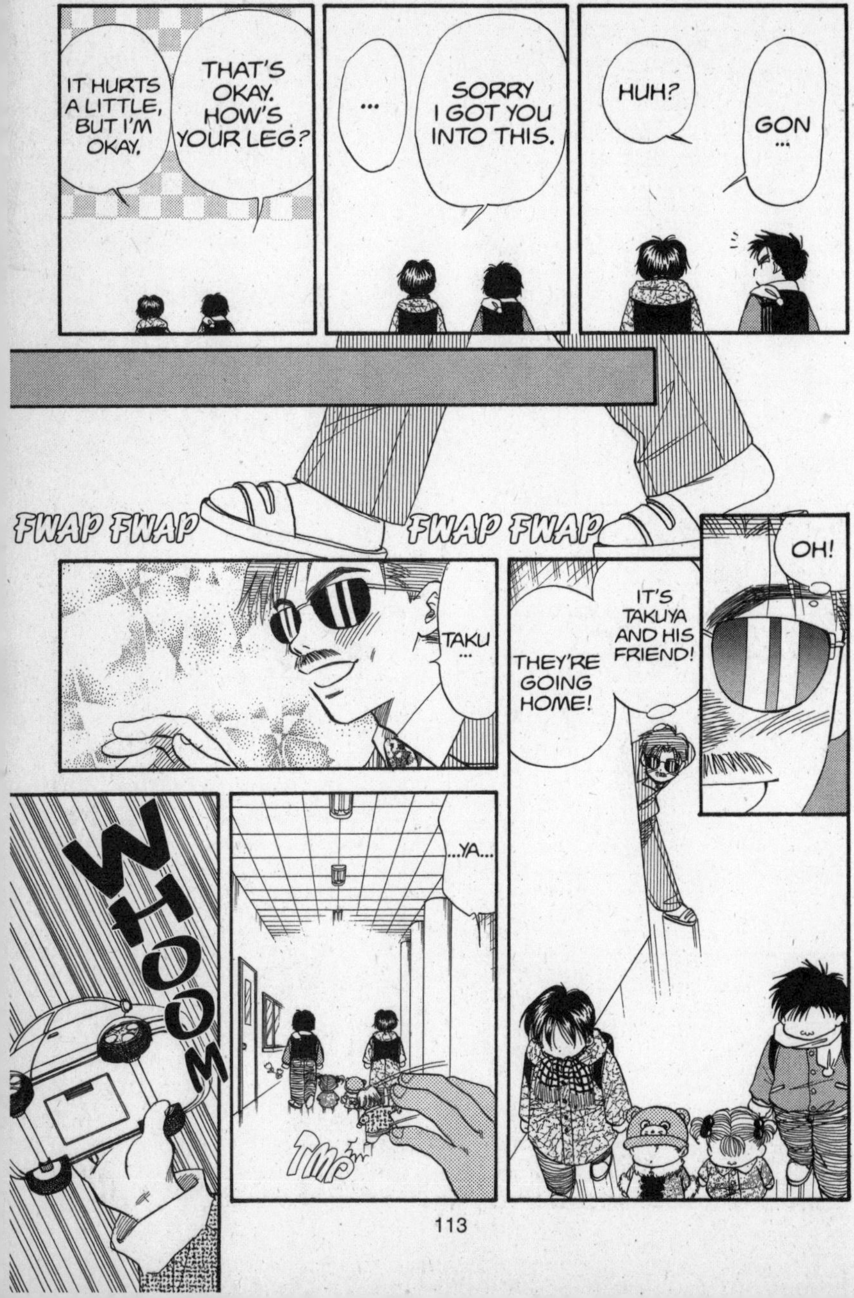
GON ...
HUH?
SORRY I GOT YOU INTO THIS.
...
THAT'S OKAY. HOW'S YOUR LEG?
IT HURTS A LITTLE, BUT I'M OKAY.
FWAP FWAP
FWAP FWAP
OH!
IT'S TAKUYA AND HIS FRIEND!
THEY'RE GOING HOME!
TAKU ...
...YA...
TMP
WHOOM

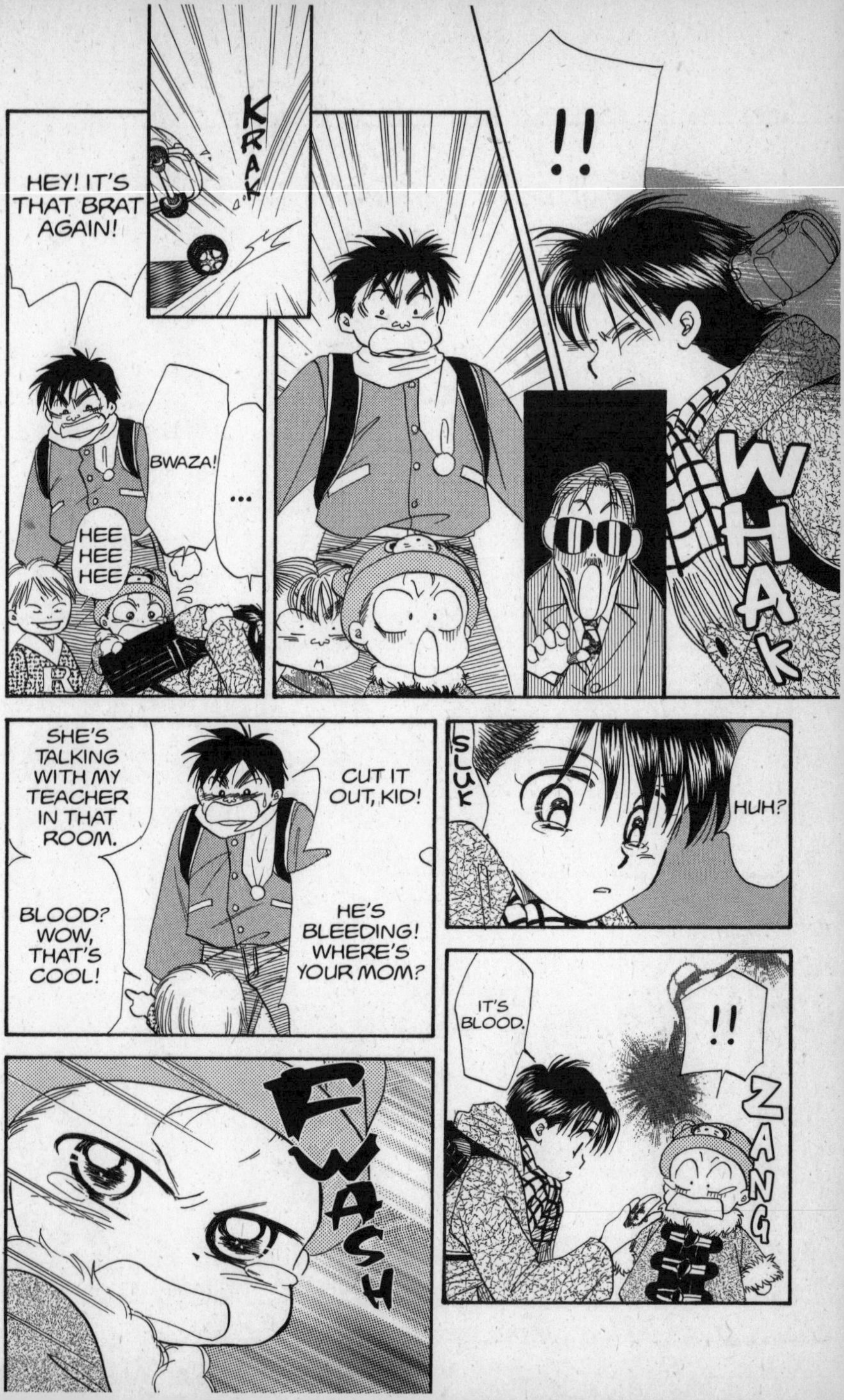
!!
WHAK
KRAK
HEY! IT'S THAT BRAT AGAIN!
...
BWAZA!
HEE HEE HEE
SLUK
HUH?
CUT IT OUT, KID!
HE'S BLEEDING! WHERE'S YOUR MOM?
SHE'S TALKING WITH MY TEACHER IN THAT ROOM.
BLOOD? WOW, THAT'S COOL!
!!
IT'S BLOOD.
ZANG
FWASH

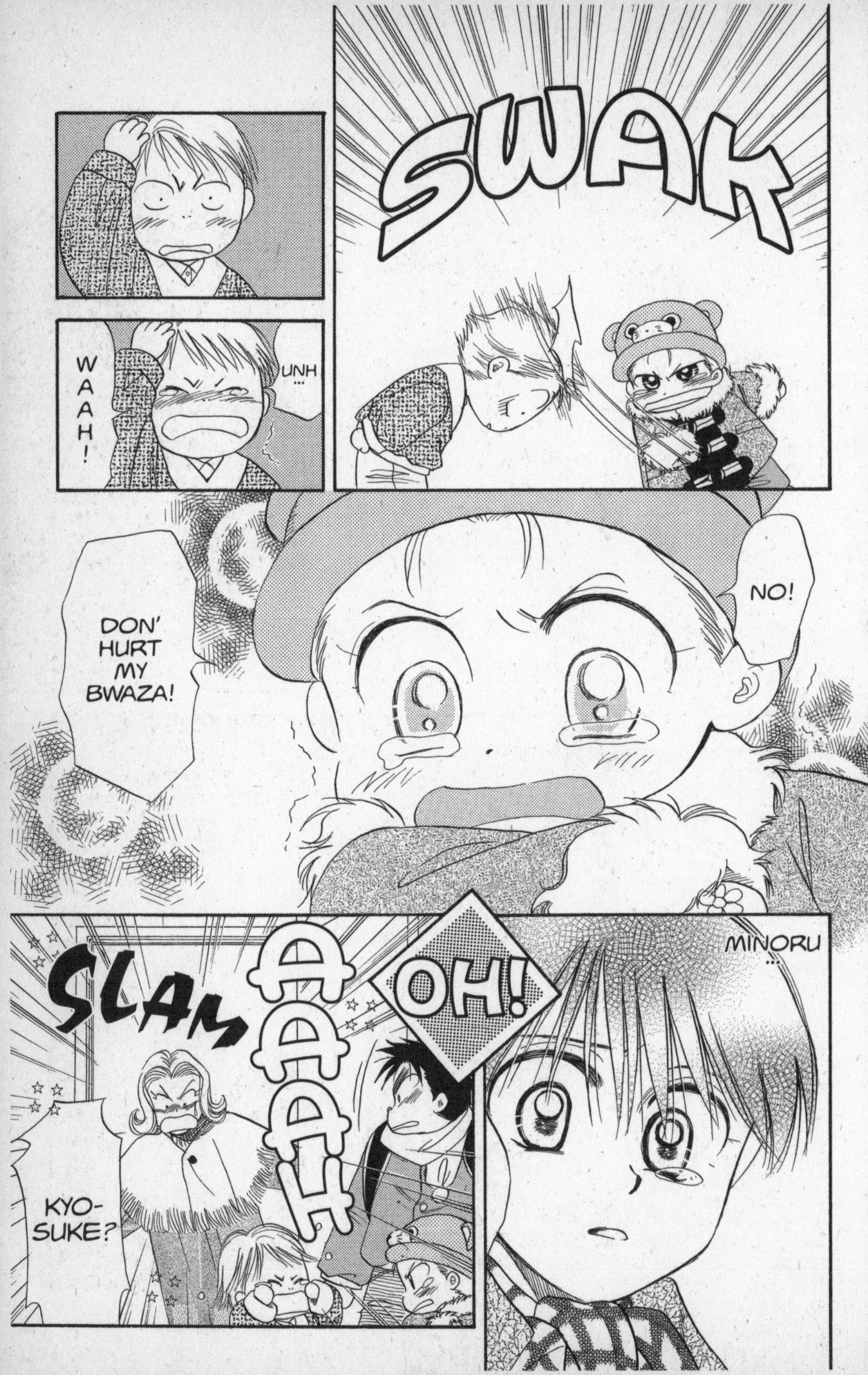
SWAK
UNH ...
WAAAH!
NO!
DON' HURT MY BWAZA!
MINORU ...
OH!
AAAAH
SLAM
KYO-SUKE?

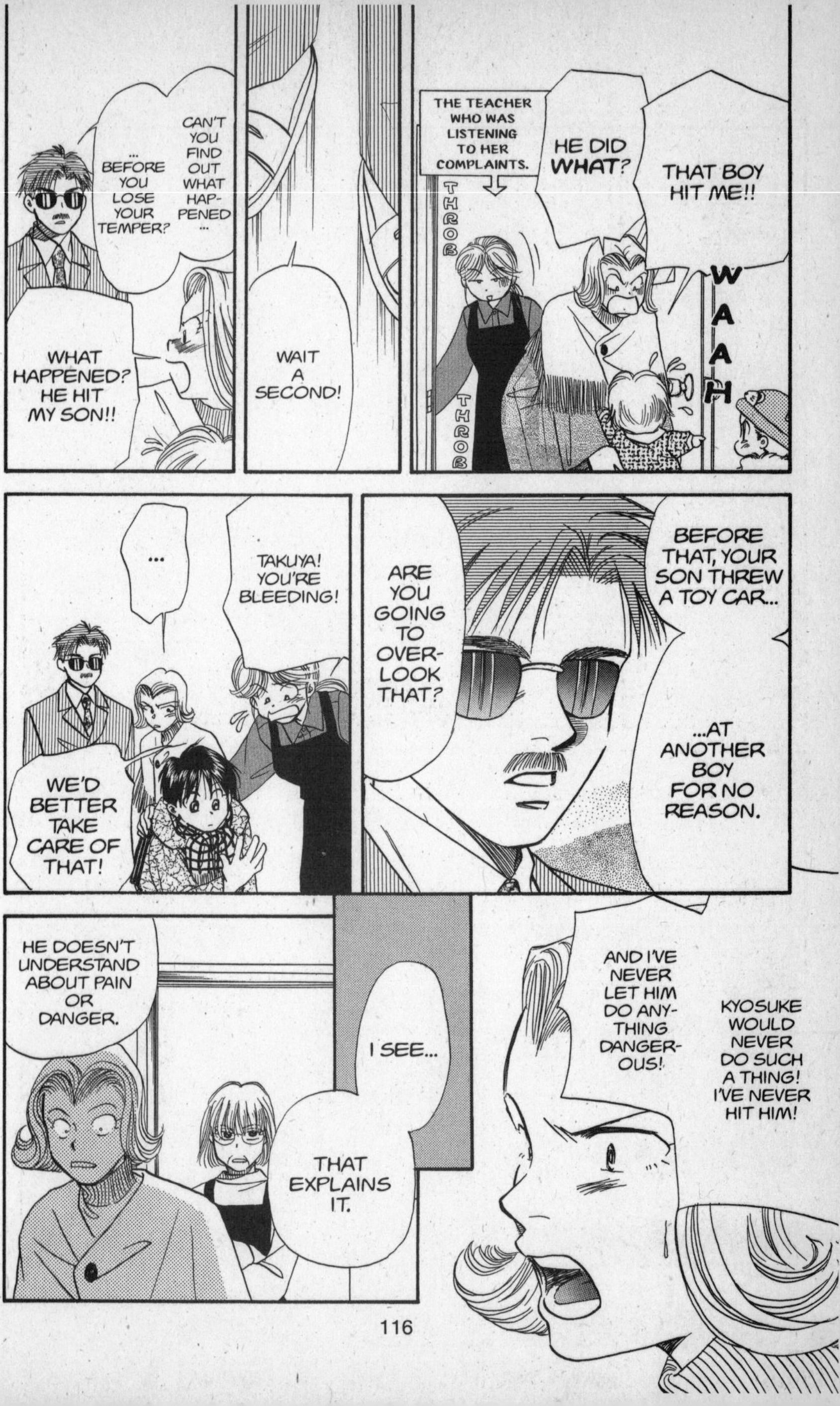
THAT BOY HIT ME!!
HE DID WHAT?
THE TEACHER WHO WAS LISTENING TO HER COMPLAINTS.
WAAH
THROB THROB
WAIT A SECOND!
CAN'T YOU FIND OUT WHAT HAPPENED ...
... BEFORE YOU LOSE YOUR TEMPER?
WHAT HAPPENED? HE HIT MY SON!!
BEFORE THAT, YOUR SON THREW A TOY CAR...
...AT ANOTHER BOY FOR NO REASON.
ARE YOU GOING TO OVERLOOK THAT?
TAKUYA! YOU'RE BLEEDING!
...
WE'D BETTER TAKE CARE OF THAT!
KYOSUKE WOULD NEVER DO SUCH A THING! I'VE NEVER HIT HIM!
AND I'VE NEVER LET HIM DO ANYTHING DANGEROUS!
I SEE...
THAT EXPLAINS IT.
HE DOESN'T UNDERSTAND ABOUT PAIN OR DANGER.

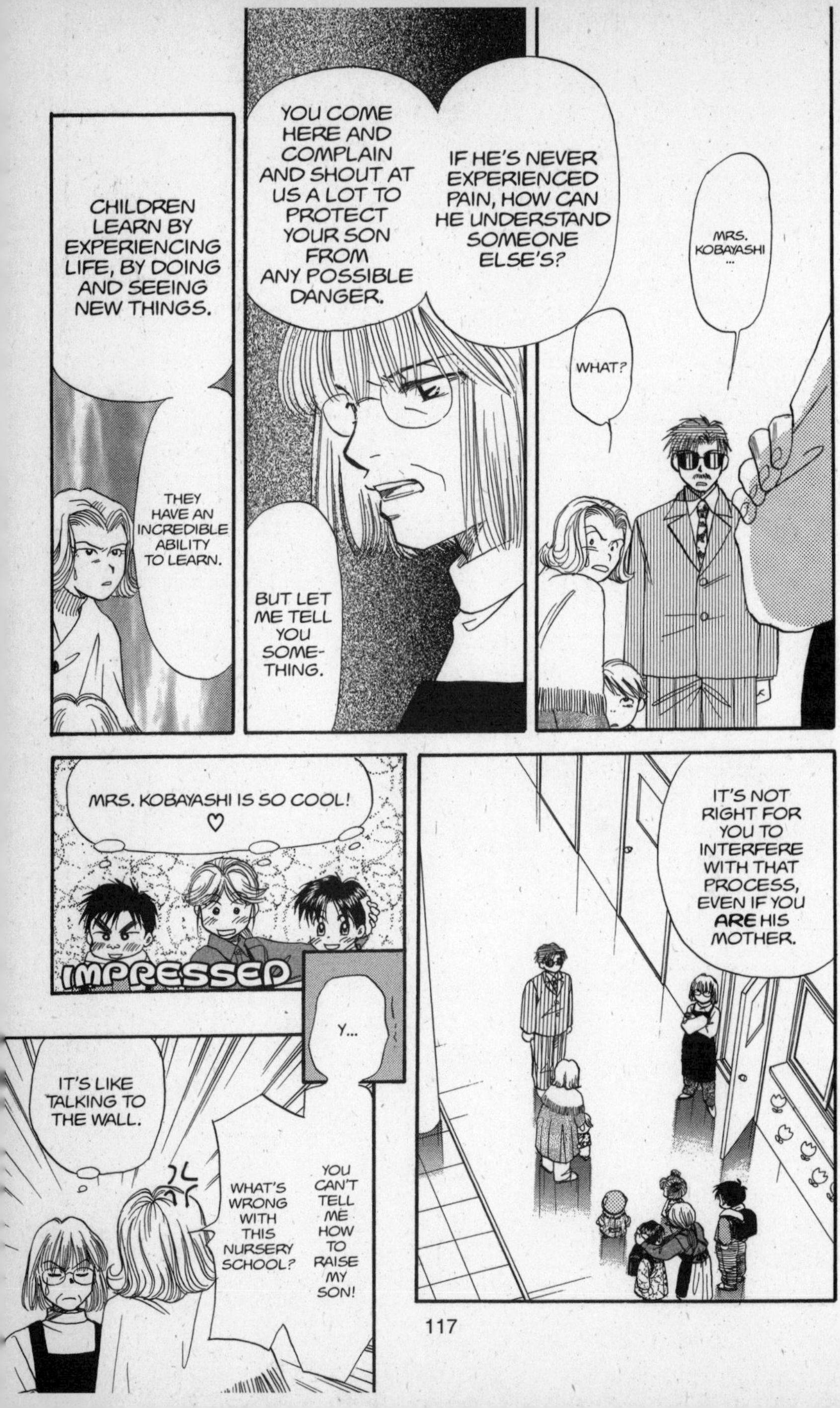
MRS. KOBAYASHI ...
WHAT?
YOU COME HERE AND COMPLAIN AND SHOUT AT US A LOT TO PROTECT YOUR SON FROM ANY POSSIBLE DANGER.
IF HE'S NEVER EXPERIENCED PAIN, HOW CAN HE UNDERSTAND SOMEONE ELSE'S?
BUT LET ME TELL YOU SOME-THING.
CHILDREN LEARN BY EXPERIENCING LIFE, BY DOING AND SEEING NEW THINGS.
THEY HAVE AN INCREDIBLE ABILITY TO LEARN.
IT'S NOT RIGHT FOR YOU TO INTERFERE WITH THAT PROCESS, EVEN IF YOU ARE HIS MOTHER.
MRS. KOBAYASHI IS SO COOL! ♡
IMPRESSED
Y...
YOU CAN'T TELL ME HOW TO RAISE MY SON!
WHAT'S WRONG WITH THIS NURSERY SCHOOL?
IT'S LIKE TALKING TO THE WALL.

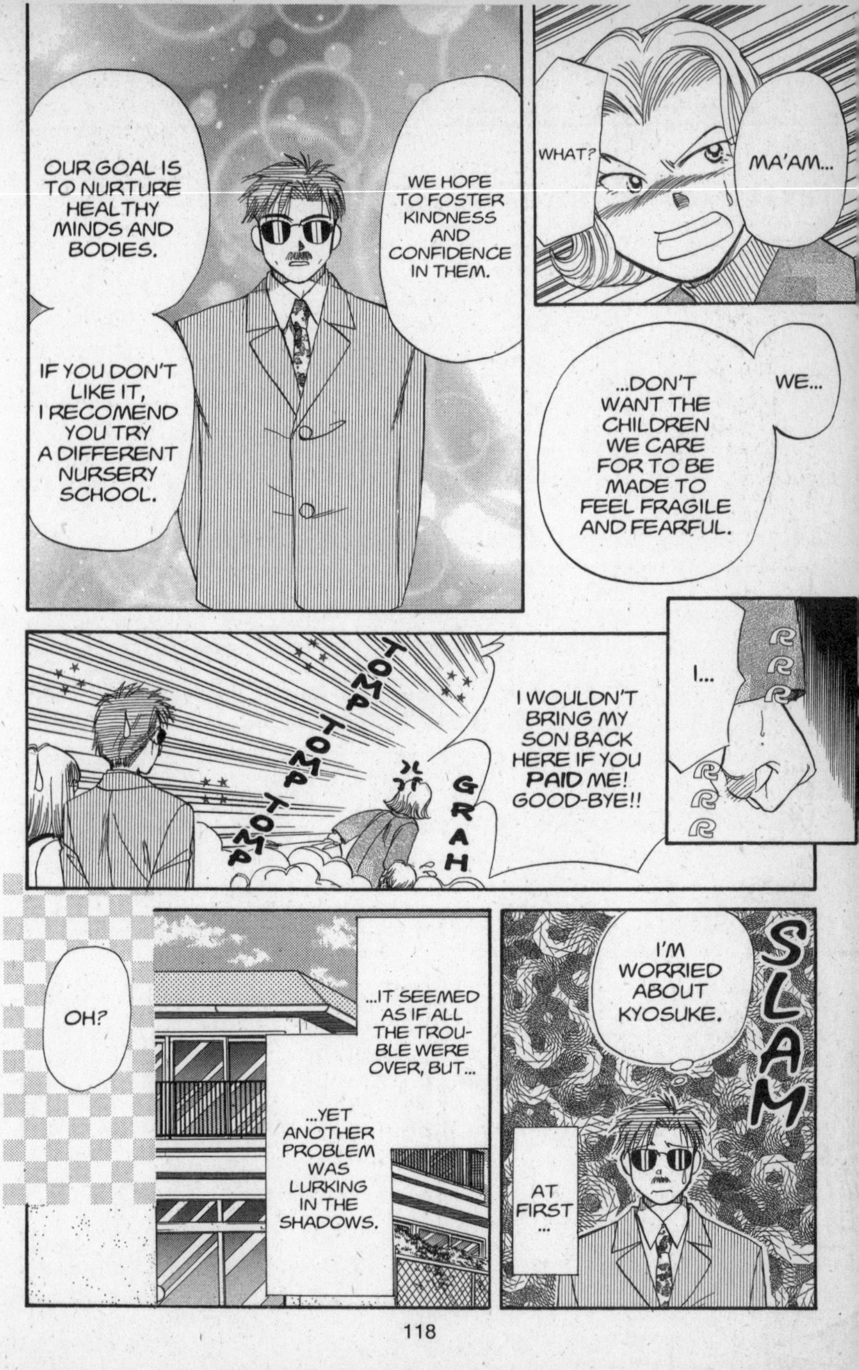
MA'AM...
WHAT?
WE...
...DON'T WANT THE CHILDREN WE CARE FOR TO BE MADE TO FEEL FRAGILE AND FEARFUL.
WE HOPE TO FOSTER KINDNESS AND CONFIDENCE IN THEM.
OUR GOAL IS TO NURTURE HEALTHY MINDS AND BODIES.
IF YOU DON'T LIKE IT, I RECOMEND YOU TRY A DIFFERENT NURSERY SCHOOL.
RRR
I...
RRR
I WOULDN'T BRING MY SON BACK HERE IF YOU PAID ME! GOOD-BYE!!
GRAH
TOMP TOMP TOMP TOMP
SLAM
I'M WORRIED ABOUT KYOSUKE.
AT FIRST ...
...IT SEEMED AS IF ALL THE TROUBLE WERE OVER, BUT...
...YET ANOTHER PROBLEM WAS LURKING IN THE SHADOWS.
OH?

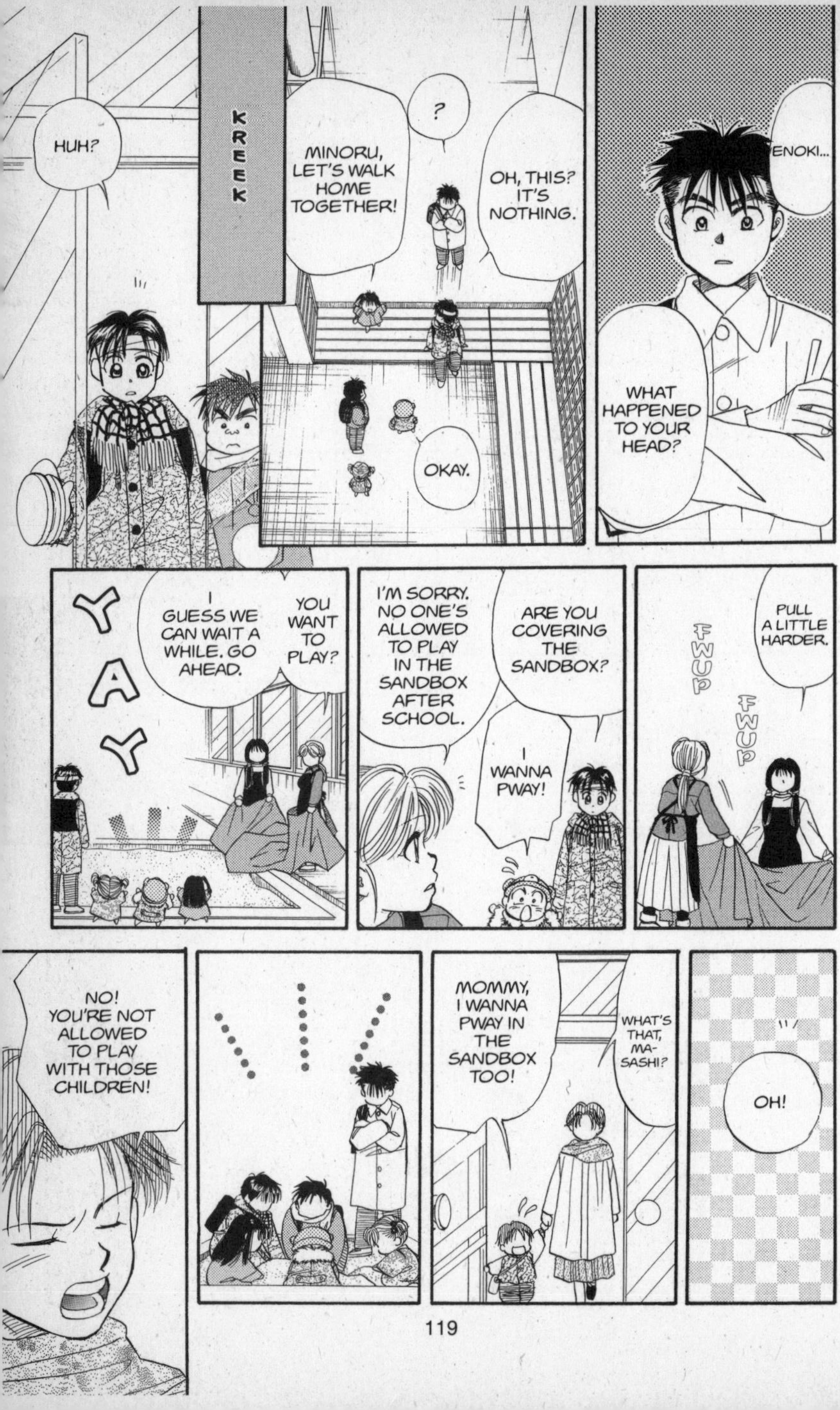
ENOKI...
WHAT HAPPENED TO YOUR HEAD?
OH, THIS? IT'S NOTHING.
?
MINORU, LET'S WALK HOME TOGETHER!
OKAY.
KREEK
HUH?
PULL A LITTLE HARDER.
FWUP
FWUP
ARE YOU COVERING THE SANDBOX?
I'M SORRY. NO ONE'S ALLOWED TO PLAY IN THE SANDBOX AFTER SCHOOL.
I WANNA PWAY!
YOU WANT TO PLAY?
I GUESS WE CAN WAIT A WHILE. GO AHEAD.
YAY
OH!
WHAT'S THAT, MA-SASHI?
MOMMY, I WANNA PWAY IN THE SANDBOX TOO!
NO! YOU'RE NOT ALLOWED TO PLAY WITH THOSE CHILDREN!

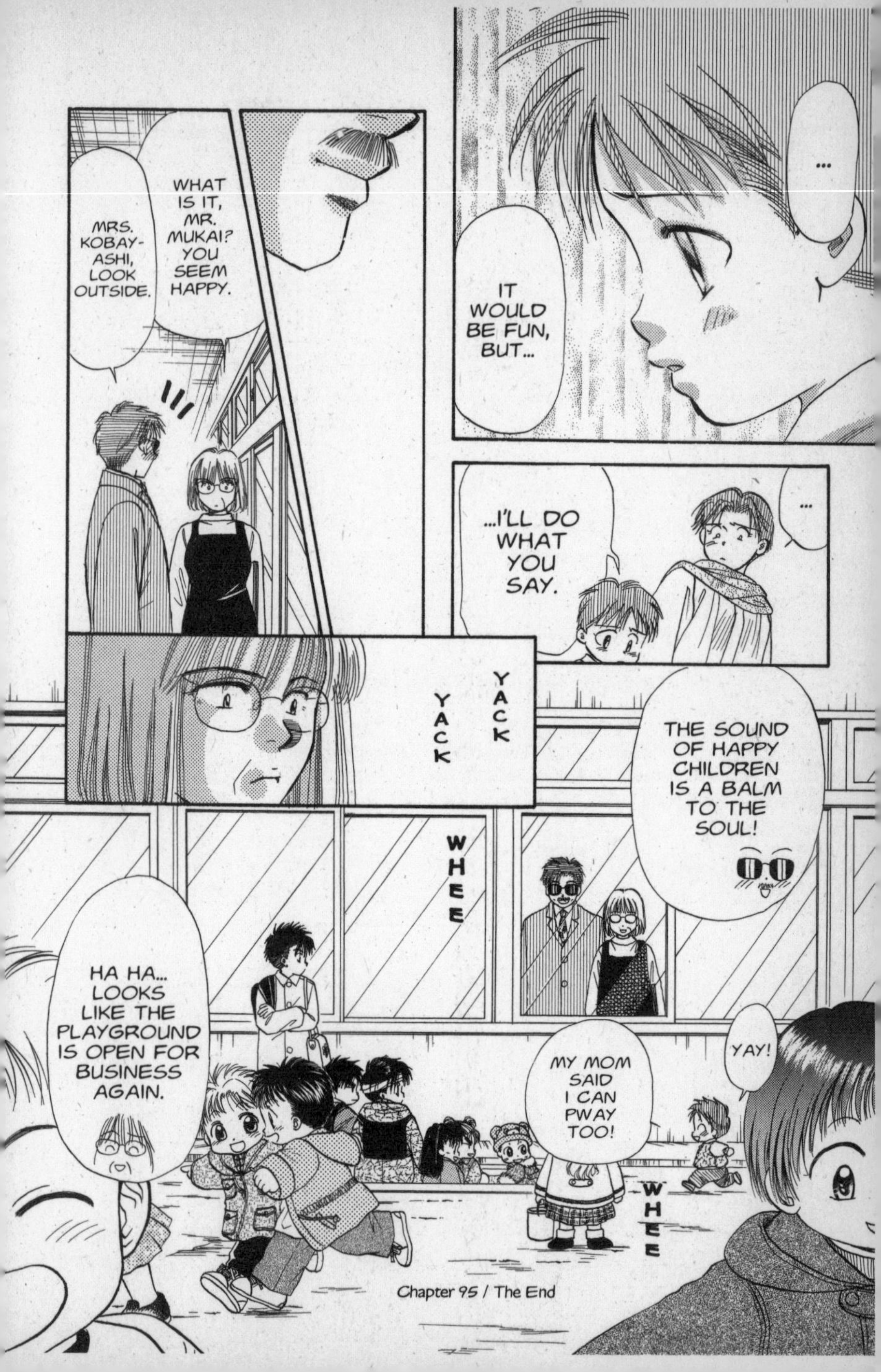
...
IT WOULD BE FUN, BUT...
...
...I'LL DO WHAT YOU SAY.
WHAT IS IT, MR. MUKAI? YOU SEEM HAPPY.
MRS. KOBAY-ASHI, LOOK OUTSIDE.
YACK YACK
THE SOUND OF HAPPY CHILDREN IS A BALM TO THE SOUL!
WHEE
YAY!
MY MOM SAID I CAN PWAY TOO!
WHEE
HA HA... LOOKS LIKE THE PLAYGROUND IS OPEN FOR BUSINESS AGAIN.
Chapter 95 / The End

Chapter 96

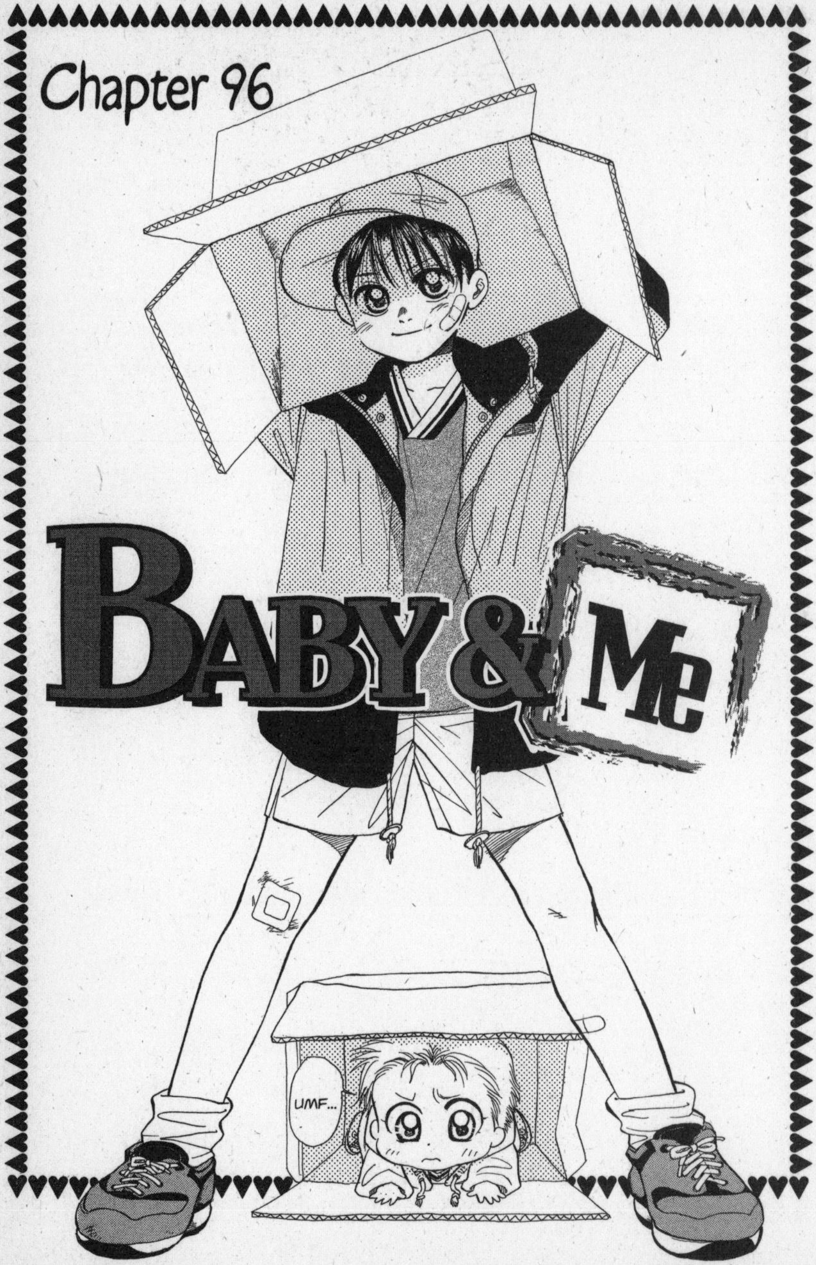
BABY & Me
UMF...

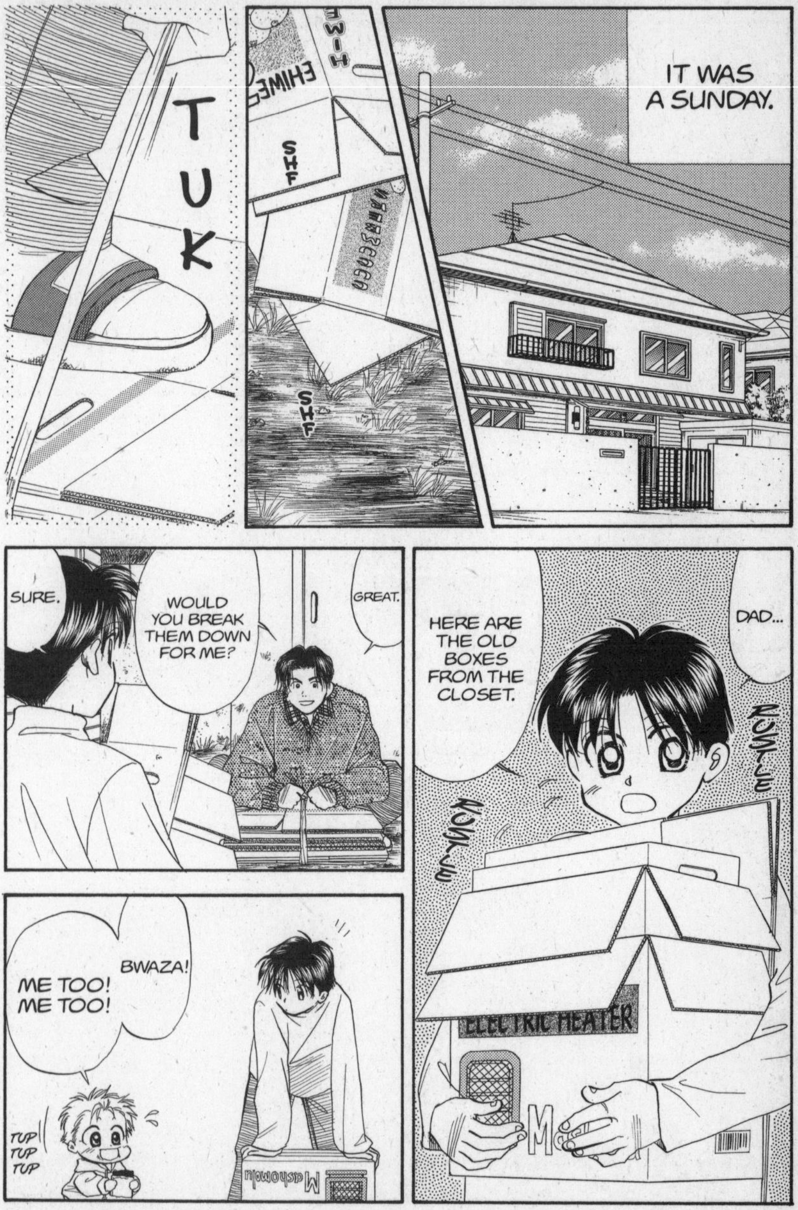
IT WAS A SUNDAY.
SHF
SHF
TUK
DAD...
HERE ARE THE OLD BOXES FROM THE CLOSET.
RUSTLE
RUSTLE
ELECTRIC HEATER
GREAT.
WOULD YOU BREAK THEM DOWN FOR ME?
SURE.
BWAZA!
ME TOO! ME TOO!
TUP TUP TUP

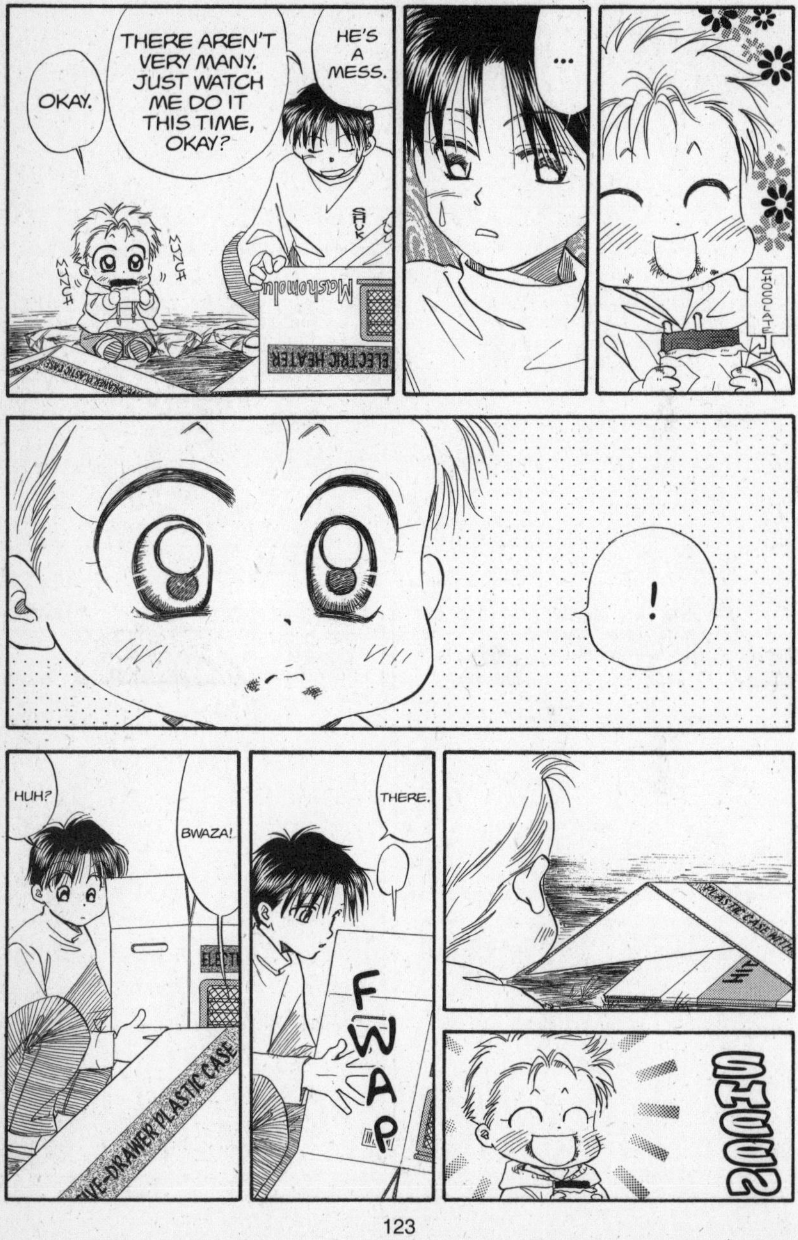
CHOCOLATE
...
HE'S A MESS.
THERE AREN'T VERY MANY. JUST WATCH ME DO IT THIS TIME, OKAY?
SHUK
OKAY.
MUNCH MUNCH
ELECTRIC HEATER
!
THERE.
FWAP
HUH?
BWAZA!

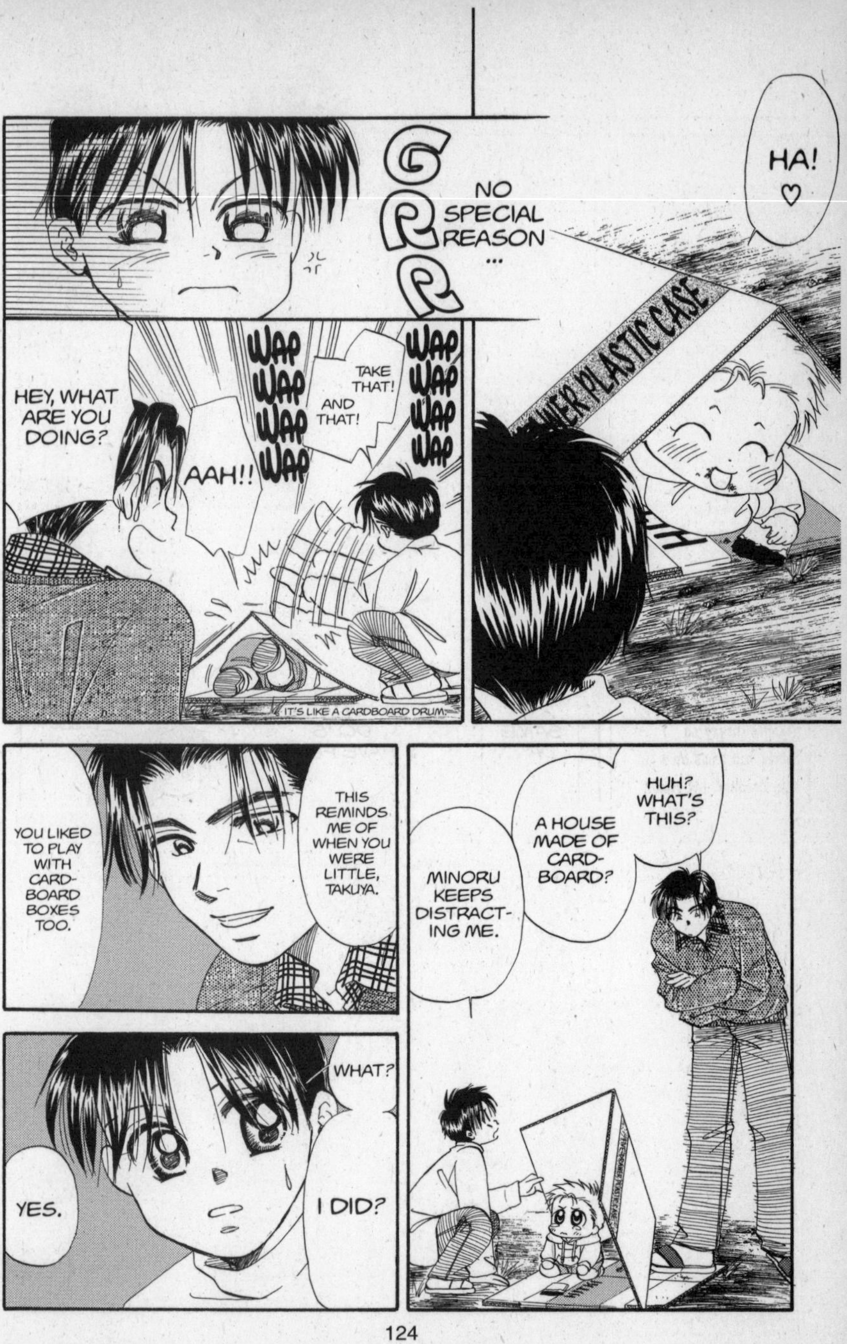
HA! ♡
GRR
NO SPECIAL REASON ...
WAP WAP WAP WAP
TAKE THAT!
AND THAT!
WAP WAP WAP WAP
AAH!!
HEY, WHAT ARE YOU DOING?
IT'S LIKE A CARDBOARD DRUM.
HUH? WHAT'S THIS?
A HOUSE MADE OF CARD-BOARD?
MINORU KEEPS DISTRACT-ING ME.
THIS REMINDS ME OF WHEN YOU WERE LITTLE, TAKUYA.
YOU LIKED TO PLAY WITH CARD-BOARD BOXES TOO.
WHAT?
I DID?
YES.

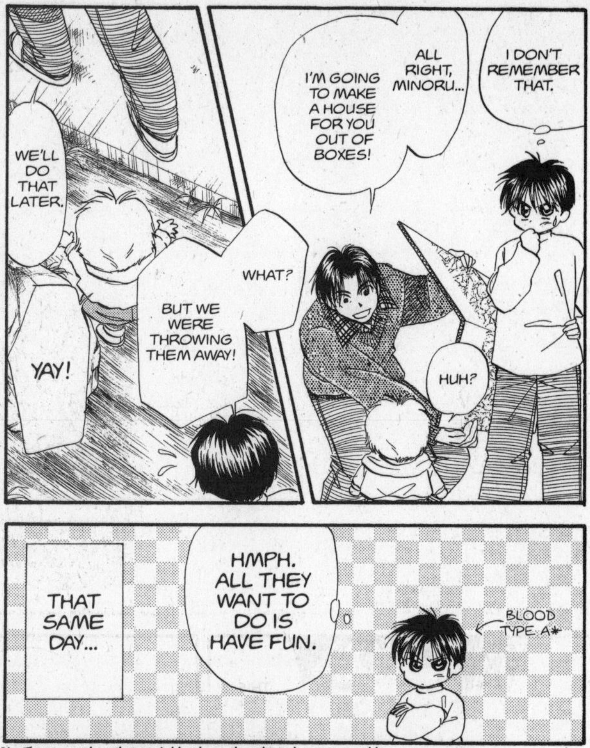
I DON'T REMEMBER THAT.
ALL RIGHT, MINORU...
I'M GOING TO MAKE A HOUSE FOR YOU OUT OF BOXES!
HUH?
WHAT?
BUT WE WERE THROWING THEM AWAY!
WE'LL DO THAT LATER.
YAY!
BLOOD TYPE A*
HMPH. ALL THEY WANT TO DO IS HAVE FUN.
THAT SAME DAY...

*In Japan, people with type A blood are thought to be very sensible.

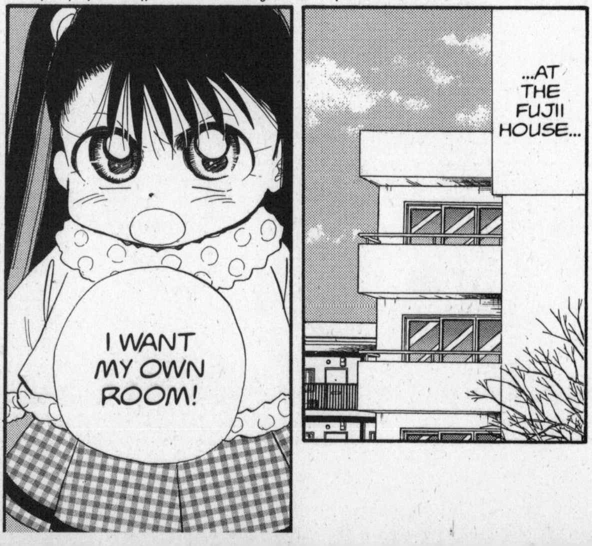
...AT THE FUJII HOUSE...
I WANT MY OWN ROOM!

Author's Note Part 6

I worked on Chapter 94 during the special year-end schedule.
At the end of the year, we have to finish our manuscripts earlier than usual before the presses and editorial departments close for New Year's.
This puts a lot of pressure on us manga artists.
There are special schedules for Golden Week and Obon as well.*
The hardest thing about Chapter 94 was drawing the costumes that appear in Takuya's dream. People don't think my drawings are very hard to do because they're so simple, but I was on a tight deadline. My editor was hovering over me, waiting for the manuscript to be finished. So I just didn't have time to research costumes.
I hope you understand.
Waah!
Anyway, I hate these special holiday schedules!
Manga artists need breaks too! At least for New Year's, please!

*New Year's, Golden Week and Obon are Japan's three biggest holiday seasons, during which businesses close for a full week.

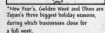

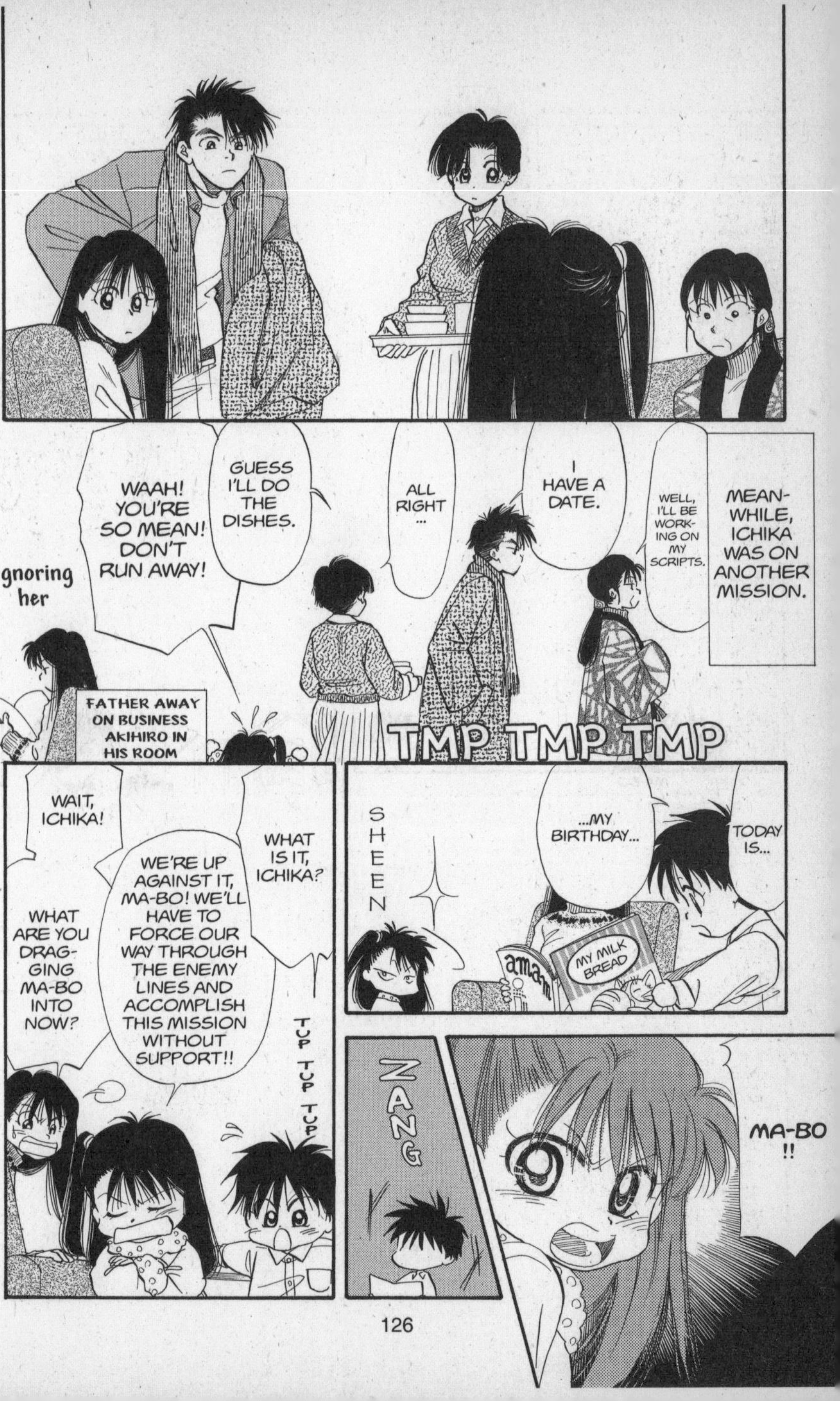
MEAN-WHILE, ICHIKA WAS ON ANOTHER MISSION.
WELL, I'LL BE WORK-ING ON MY SCRIPTS.
I HAVE A DATE.
ALL RIGHT ...
GUESS I'LL DO THE DISHES.
WAAH! YOU'RE SO MEAN! DON'T RUN AWAY!
Ignoring her
FATHER AWAY ON BUSINESS AKIHIRO IN HIS ROOM
TMP TMP TMP
TODAY IS...
...MY BIRTHDAY...
SHEEN
MY MILK BREAD
MA-BO !!
ZANG
WAIT, ICHIKA!
WHAT IS IT, ICHIKA?
WE'RE UP AGAINST IT, MA-BO! WE'LL HAVE TO FORCE OUR WAY THROUGH THE ENEMY LINES AND ACCOMPLISH THIS MISSION WITHOUT SUPPORT!!
WHAT ARE YOU DRAG-GING MA-BO INTO NOW?
TUP TUP TUP

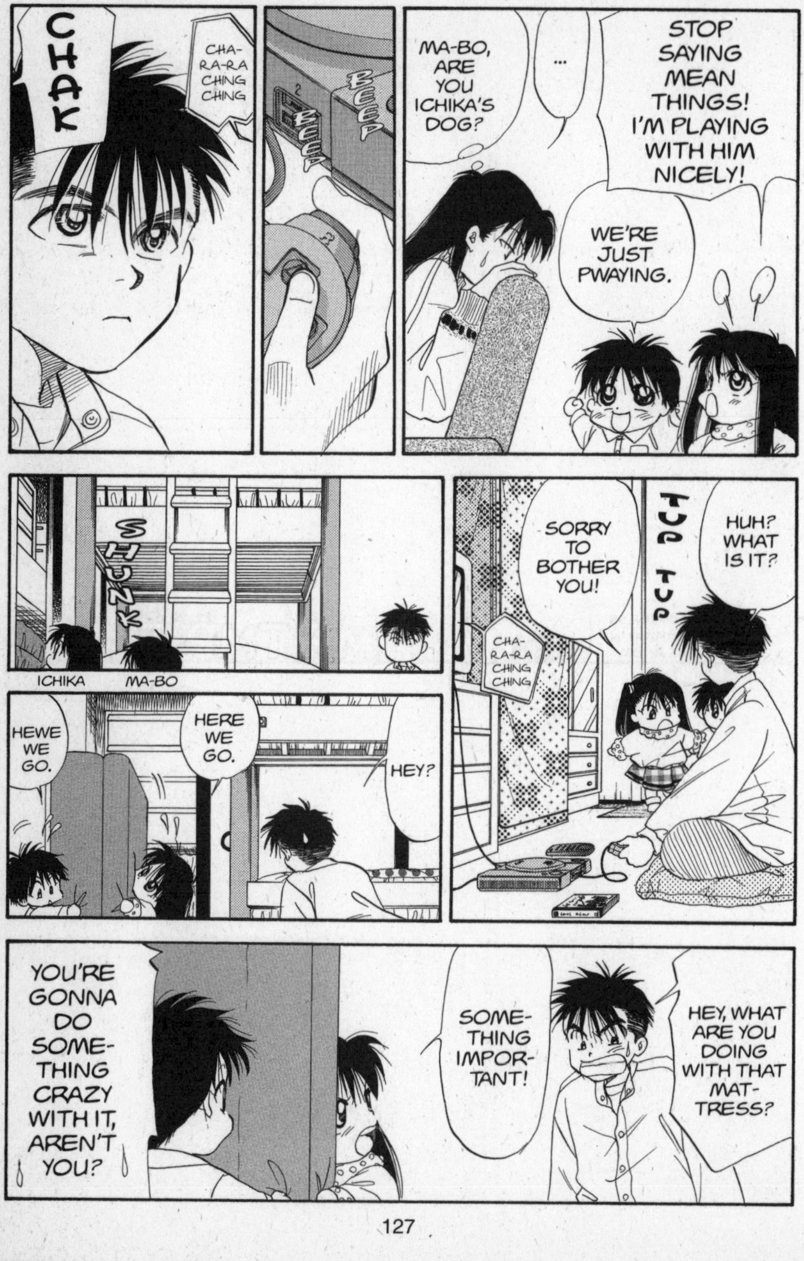
STOP SAYING MEAN THINGS! I'M PLAYING WITH HIM NICELY!
...
MA-BO, ARE YOU ICHIKA'S DOG?
WE'RE JUST PWAYING.
BEEP
BEEP
CHA-RA-RA CHING CHING
CHAK
HUH? WHAT IS IT?
TUP TUP
SORRY TO BOTHER YOU!
CHA-RA-RA CHING CHING
SHUNK
ICHIKA
MA-BO
HEY?
HERE WE GO.
HEWE WE GO.
HEY, WHAT ARE YOU DOING WITH THAT MAT-TRESS?
SOME-THING IMPOR-TANT!
YOU'RE GONNA DO SOME-THING CRAZY WITH IT, AREN'T YOU?

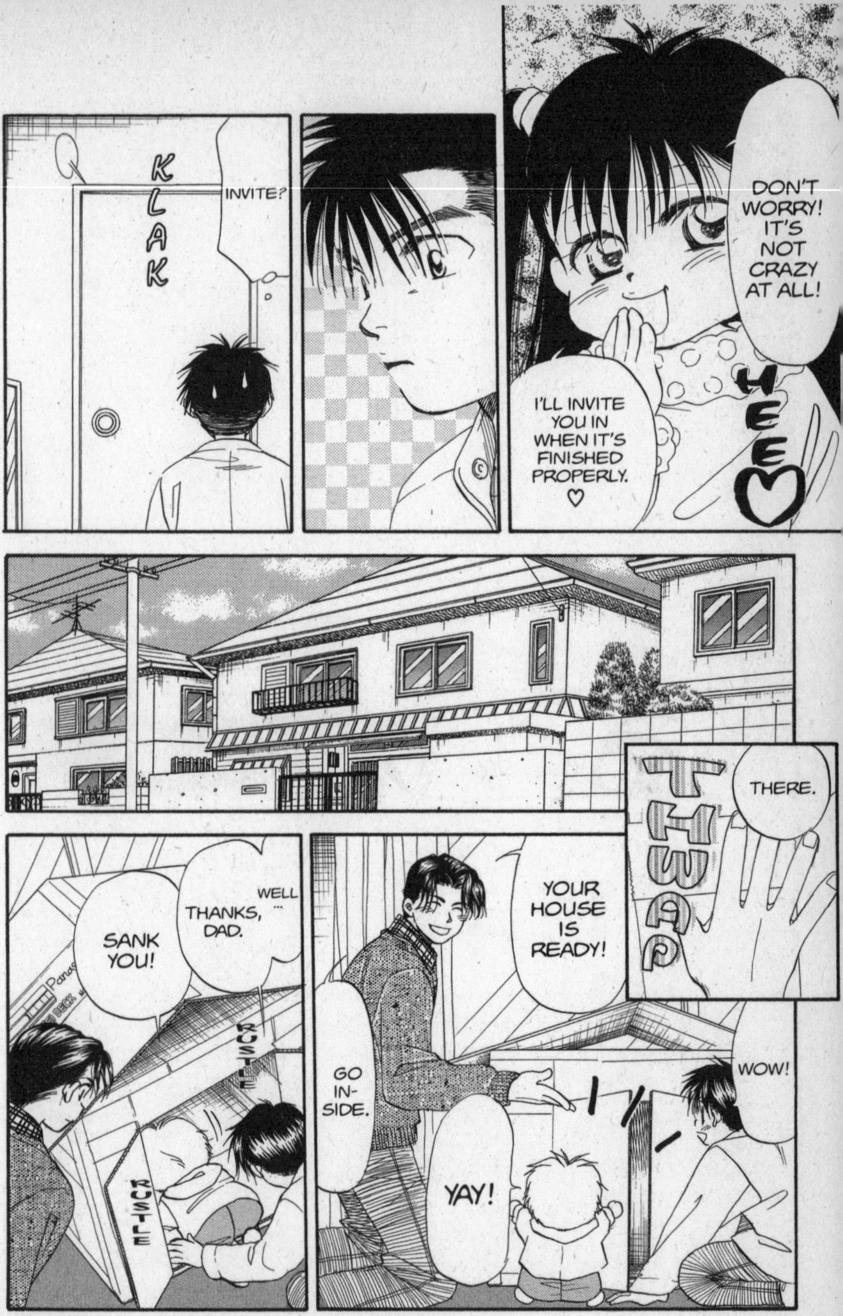
DON'T WORRY! IT'S NOT CRAZY AT ALL!
HEE♥
I'LL INVITE YOU IN WHEN IT'S FINISHED PROPERLY. ♡
KLAK
INVITE?
THERE.
THWAP
YOUR HOUSE IS READY!
WOW!
GO IN-SIDE.
YAY!
WELL ...
THANKS, DAD.
SANK YOU!
RUSTLE
RUSTLE

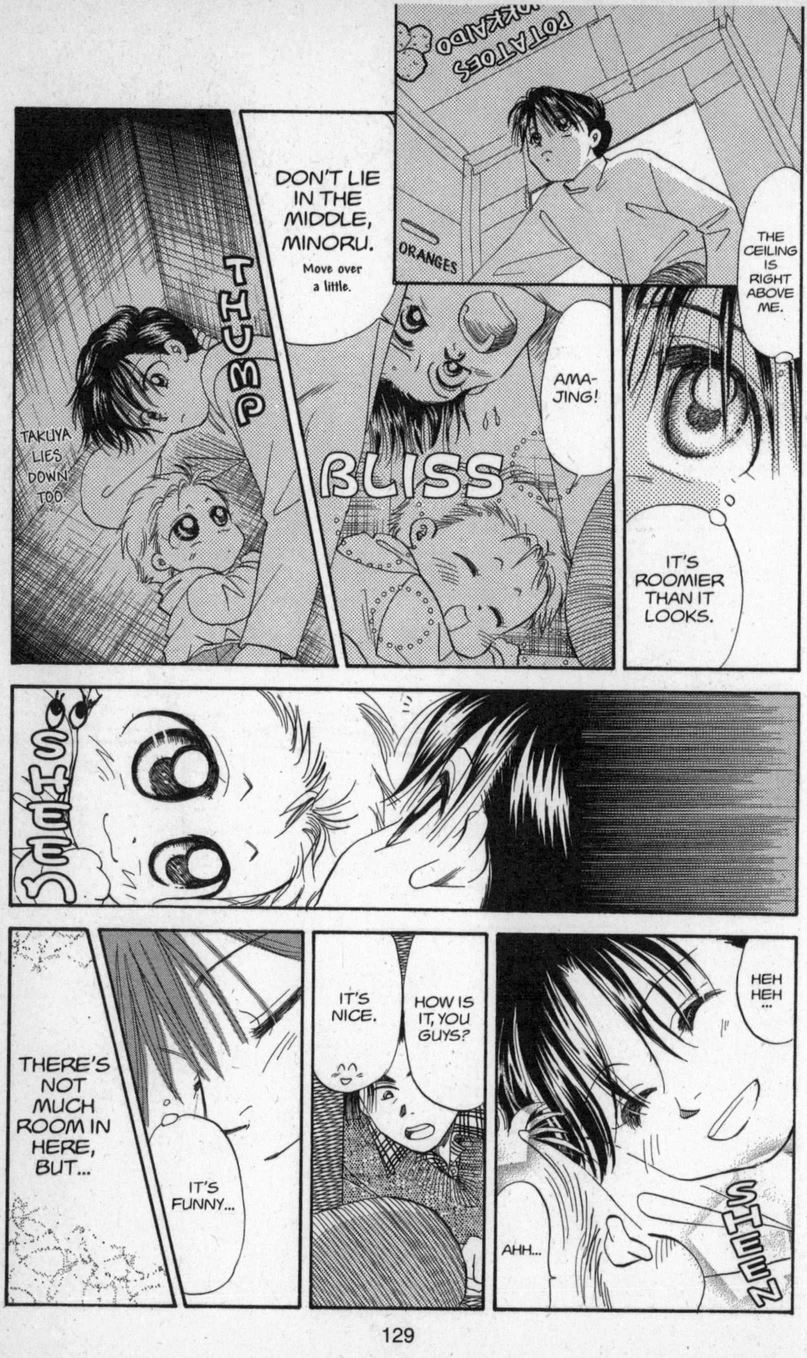
POTATOES
ORANGES
THE CEILING IS RIGHT ABOVE ME.
IT'S ROOMIER THAN IT LOOKS.
DON'T LIE IN THE MIDDLE, MINORU.
Move over a little.
AMA-JING!
BLISS
THUMP
TAKUYA LIES DOWN TOO.
SHEEN
HEH HEH...
AHH...
SHEEN
HOW IS IT, YOU GUYS?
IT'S NICE.
IT'S FUNNY...
THERE'S NOT MUCH ROOM IN HERE, BUT...

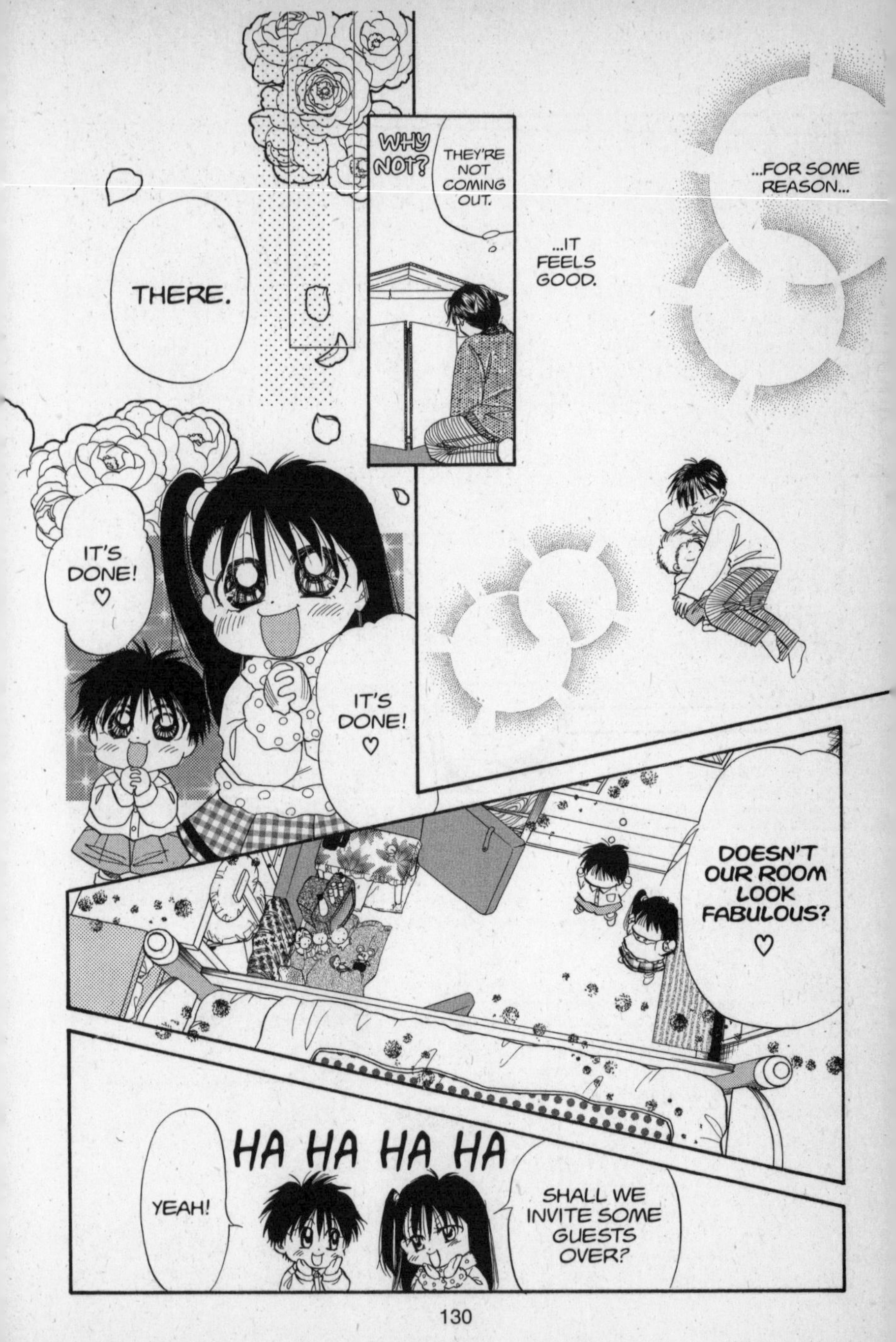

...FOR SOME REASON...
...IT FEELS GOOD.
THEY'RE NOT COMING OUT.
WHY NOT?
THERE.
IT'S DONE! ♡
IT'S DONE! ♡
DOESN'T OUR ROOM LOOK FABULOUS? ♡
SHALL WE INVITE SOME GUESTS OVER?
HA HA HA HA
YEAH!

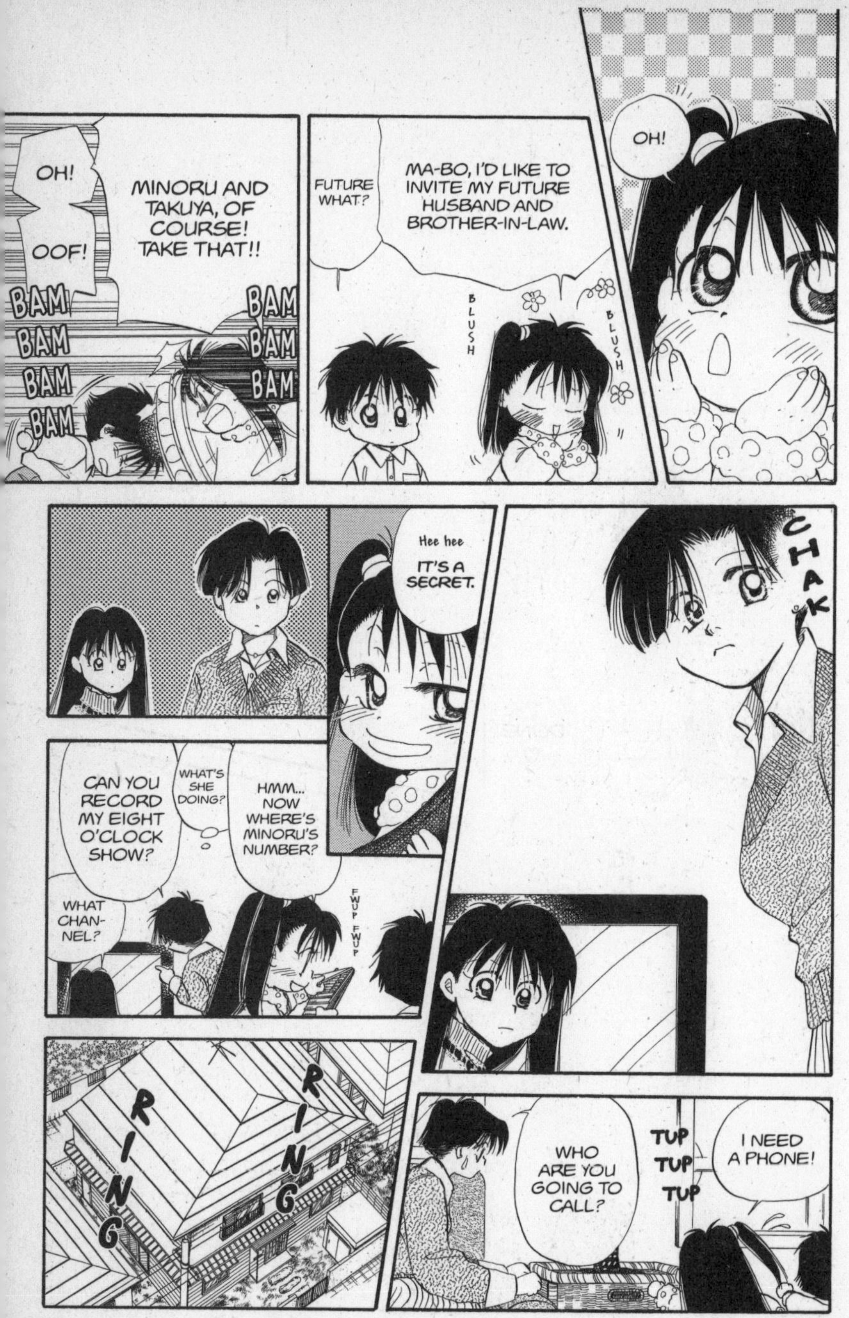
OH!
FUTURE WHAT?
MA-BO, I'D LIKE TO INVITE MY FUTURE HUSBAND AND BROTHER-IN-LAW.
BLUSH
BLUSH
BAM BAM BAM
MINORU AND TAKUYA, OF COURSE! TAKE THAT!!
OH!
OOF!
BAM BAM BAM BAM
CHAK
Hee hee
IT'S A SECRET.
HMM... NOW WHERE'S MINORU'S NUMBER?
FWUP FWUP
WHAT'S SHE DOING?
CAN YOU RECORD MY EIGHT O'CLOCK SHOW?
WHAT CHAN-NEL?
I NEED A PHONE!
TUP TUP TUP
WHO ARE YOU GOING TO CALL?
RING
RING

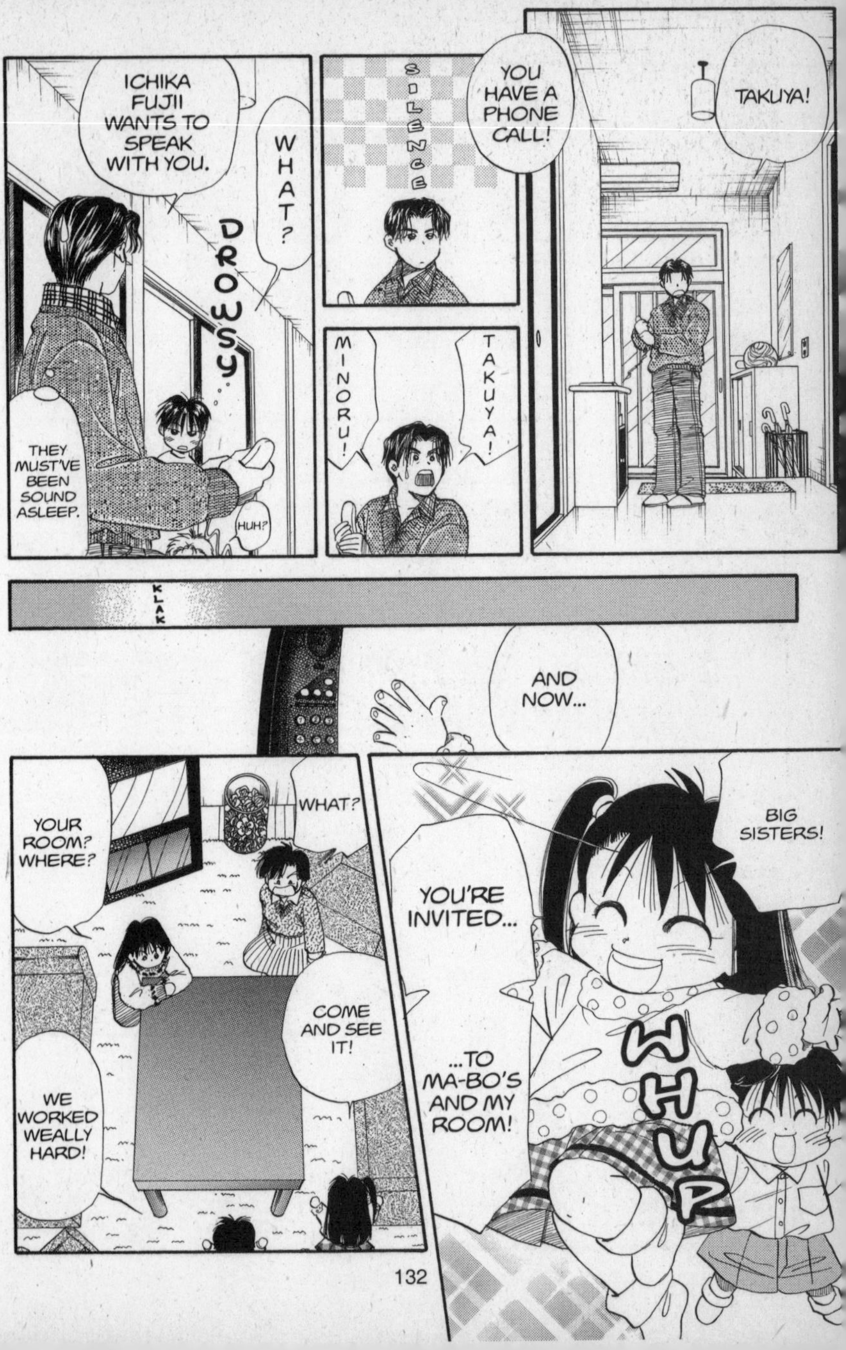
TAKUYA!
YOU HAVE A PHONE CALL!
SILENCE
TAKUYA!
MINORU!
ICHIKA FUJII WANTS TO SPEAK WITH YOU.
WHAT?
DROWSY
THEY MUST'VE BEEN SOUND ASLEEP.
HUH?
KLAK
AND NOW...
BIG SISTERS!
YOU'RE INVITED...
...TO MA-BO'S AND MY ROOM!
WHUP
WHAT?
YOUR ROOM? WHERE?
COME AND SEE IT!
WE WORKED WEALLY HARD!

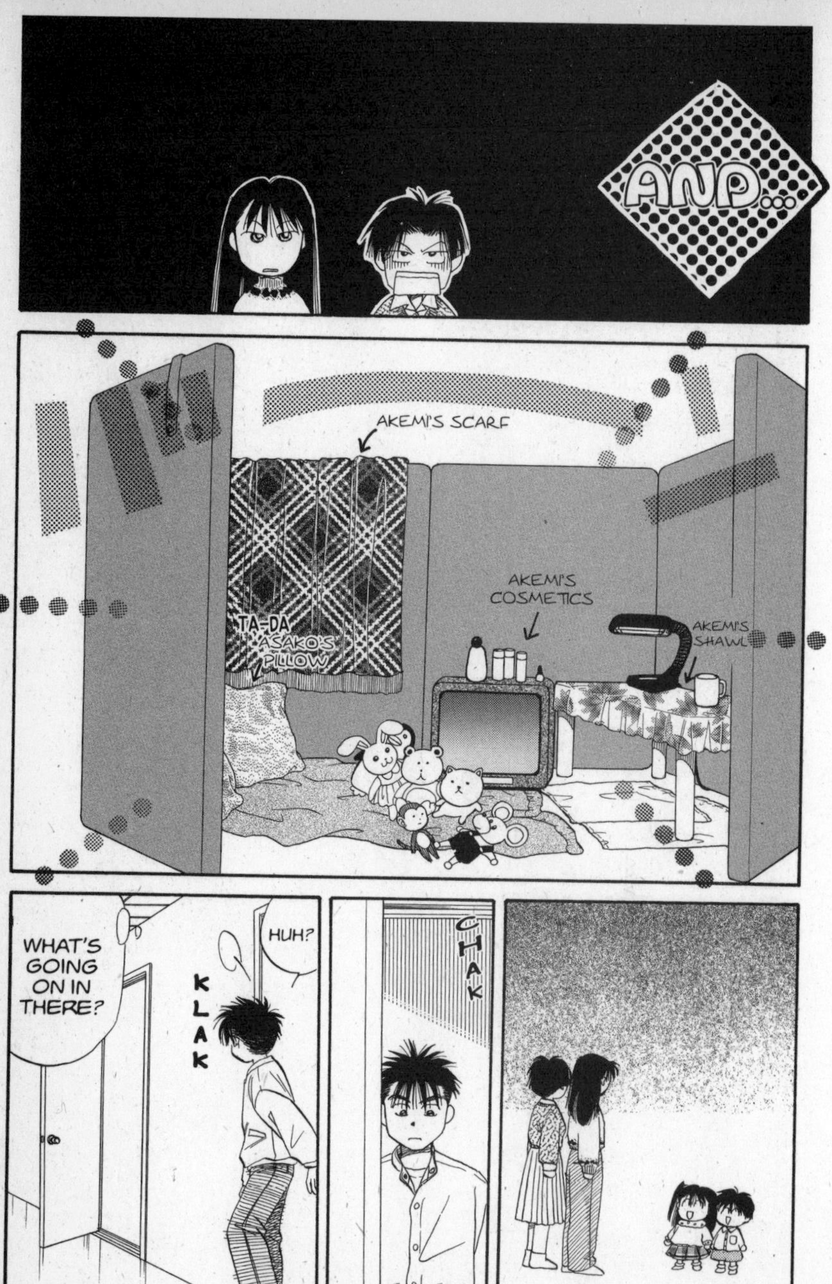
AND...
AKEMI'S SCARF
AKEMI'S SHAWL
AKEMI'S COSMETICS
TA-DA
ASAKO'S PILLOW
CHAK
HUH?
WHAT'S GOING ON IN THERE?
KLAK

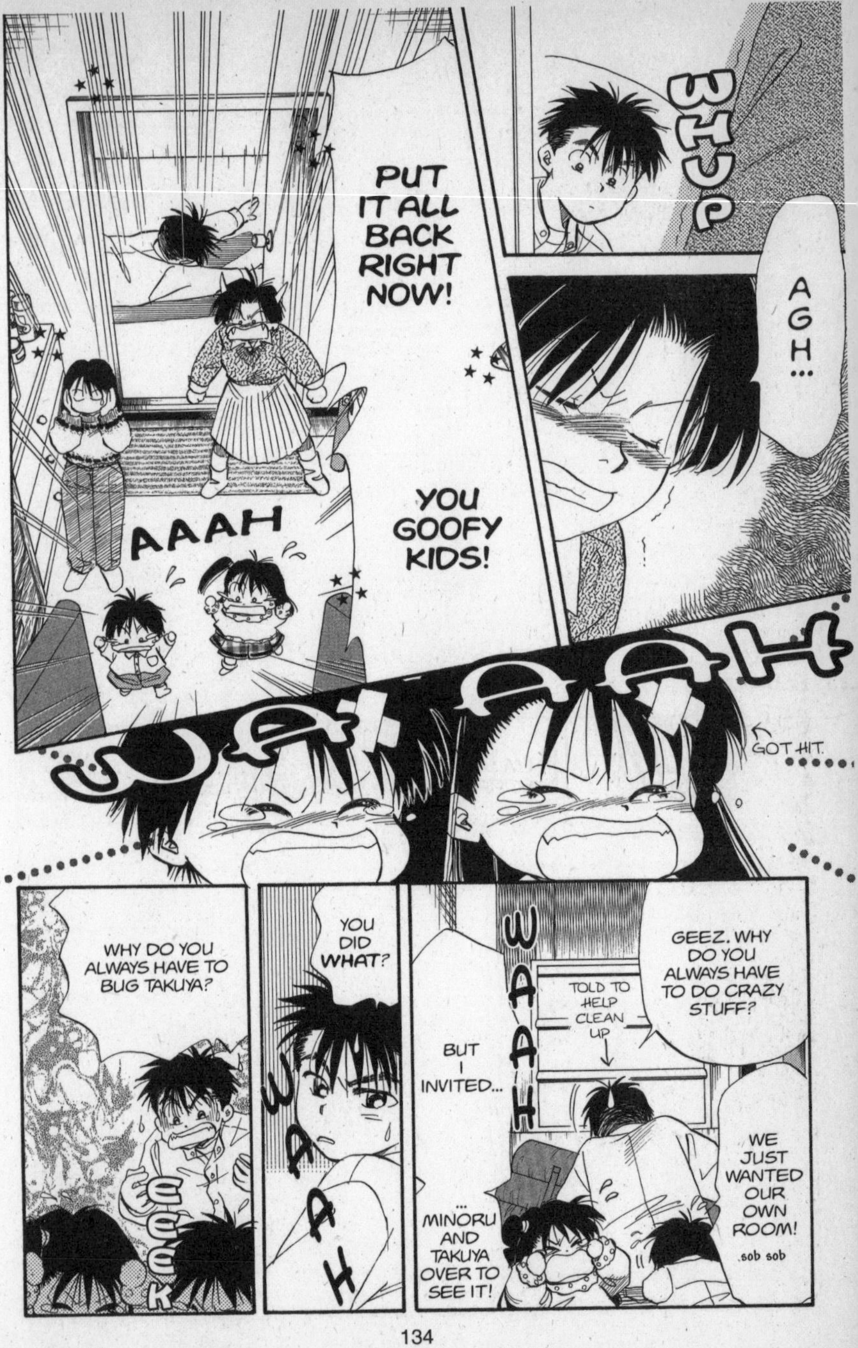
WHUP
AGH...
PUT IT ALL BACK RIGHT NOW!
YOU GOOFY KIDS!
AAAH
WAAAAH
GOT HIT.
GEEZ. WHY DO YOU ALWAYS HAVE TO DO CRAZY STUFF?
WAAAH
TOLD TO HELP CLEAN UP
WE JUST WANTED OUR OWN ROOM!
sob sob
YOU DID WHAT?
BUT I INVITED...
...MINORU AND TAKUYA OVER TO SEE IT!
WAAH
WHY DO YOU ALWAYS HAVE TO BUG TAKUYA?
EEEK

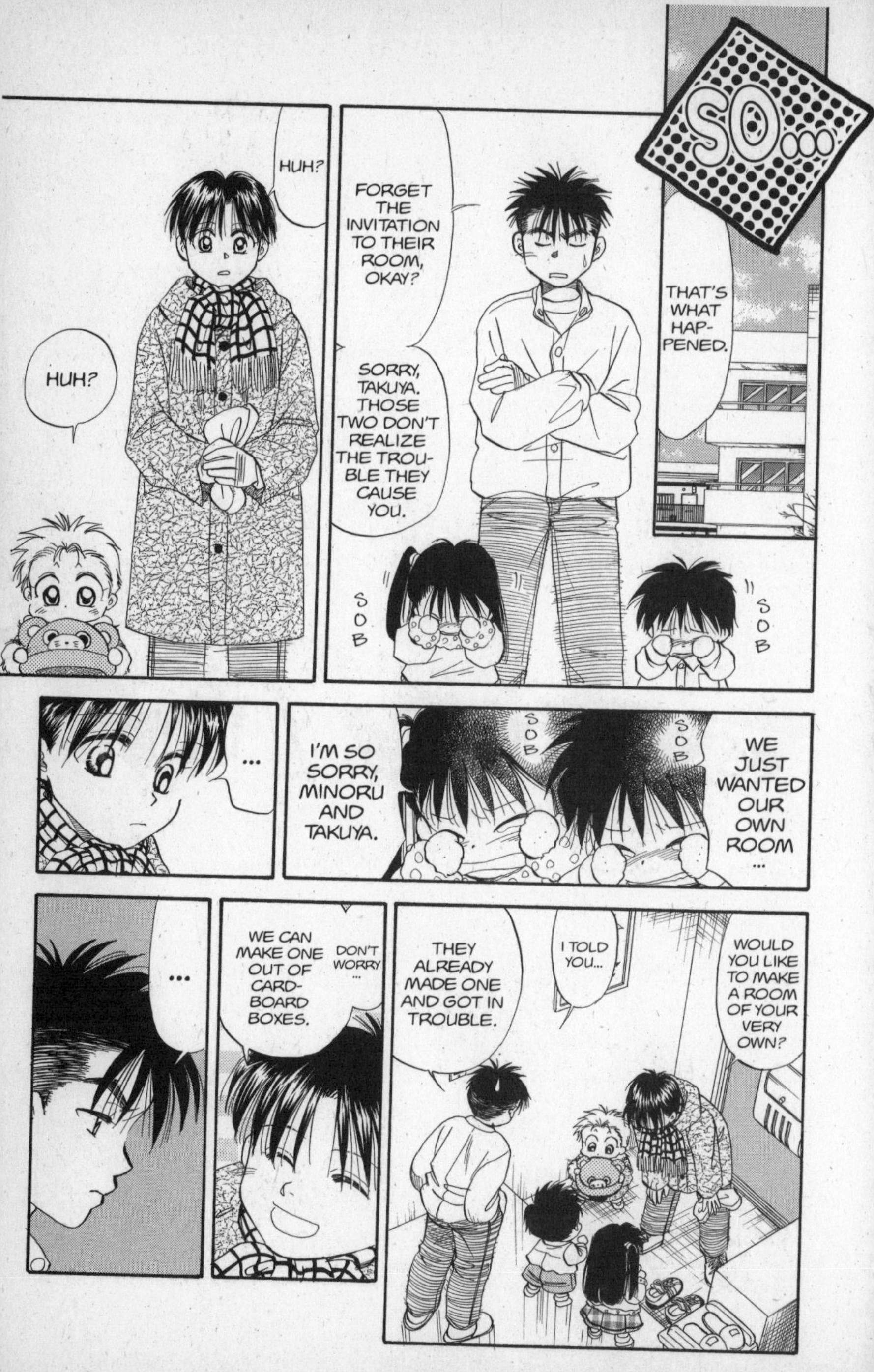
SO...
THAT'S WHAT HAPPENED.
FORGET THE INVITATION TO THEIR ROOM, OKAY?
SORRY, TAKUYA. THOSE TWO DON'T REALIZE THE TROUBLE THEY CAUSE YOU.
SOB
SOB
HUH?
HUH?
WE JUST WANTED OUR OWN ROOM...
SOB
SOB
I'M SO SORRY, MINORU AND TAKUYA.
...
WOULD YOU LIKE TO MAKE A ROOM OF YOUR VERY OWN?
I TOLD YOU...
THEY ALREADY MADE ONE AND GOT IN TROUBLE.
DON'T WORRY...
WE CAN MAKE ONE OUT OF CARDBOARD BOXES.
...

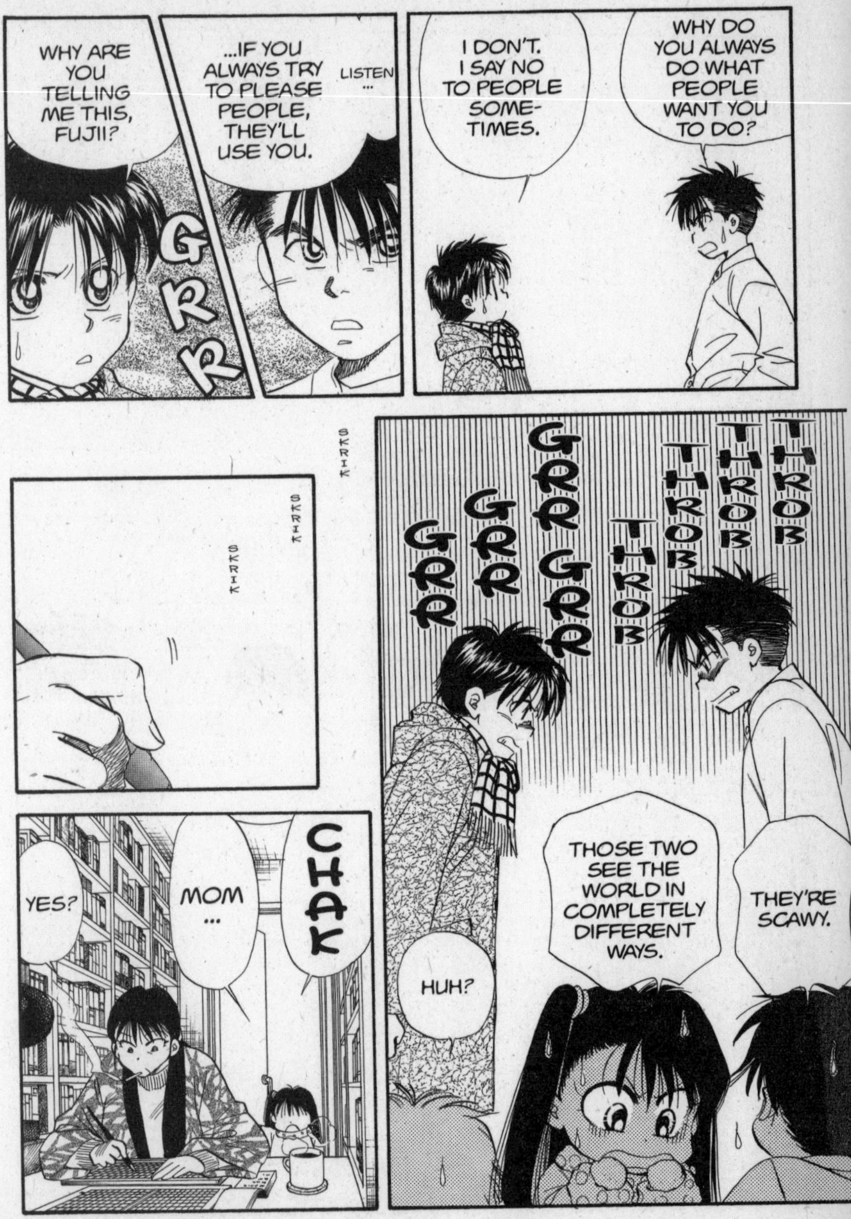
WHY DO YOU ALWAYS DO WHAT PEOPLE WANT YOU TO DO?
I DON'T. I SAY NO TO PEOPLE SOME-TIMES.
LISTEN ...
...IF YOU ALWAYS TRY TO PLEASE PEOPLE, THEY'LL USE YOU.
GRR
WHY ARE YOU TELLING ME THIS, FUJII?
THROB THROB THROB
GRR GRR GRR GRR
THEY'RE SCAWY.
THOSE TWO SEE THE WORLD IN COMPLETELY DIFFERENT WAYS.
HUH?
SKRIK SKRIK SKRIK
CHAK
MOM ...
YES?

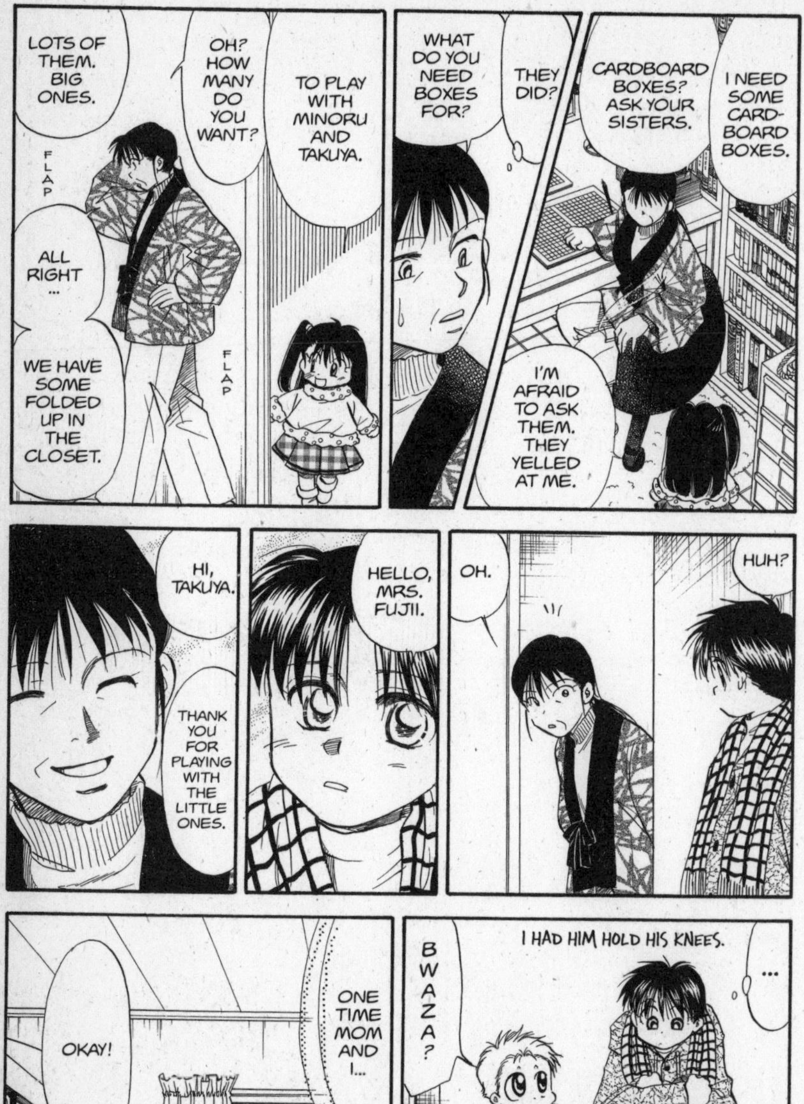
I NEED SOME CARD-BOARD BOXES.
CARDBOARD BOXES? ASK YOUR SISTERS.
I'M AFRAID TO ASK THEM. THEY YELLED AT ME.
THEY DID?
WHAT DO YOU NEED BOXES FOR?
TO PLAY WITH MINORU AND TAKUYA.
OH? HOW MANY DO YOU WANT?
FLAP
LOTS OF THEM. BIG ONES.
FLAP
ALL RIGHT ...
WE HAVE SOME FOLDED UP IN THE CLOSET.
HUH?
OH.
HELLO, MRS. FUJII.
HI, TAKUYA.
THANK YOU FOR PLAYING WITH THE LITTLE ONES.
...
I HAD HIM HOLD HIS KNEES.
BWAZA?
ONE TIME MOM AND I...
OKAY!

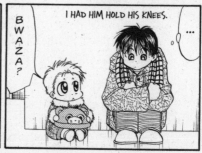

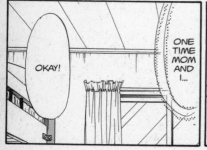

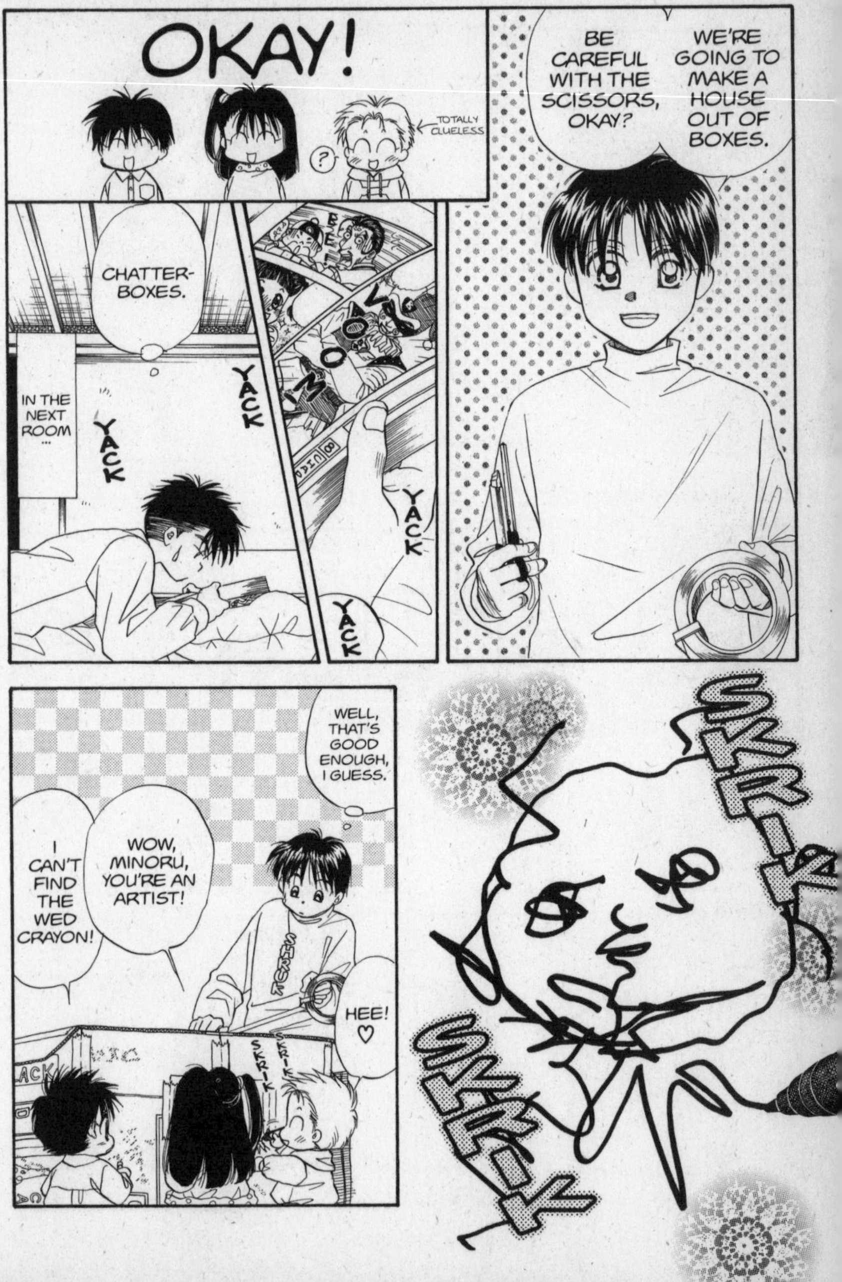
WE'RE GOING TO MAKE A HOUSE OUT OF BOXES.
BE CAREFUL WITH THE SCISSORS, OKAY?
OKAY!
TOTALLY CLUELESS
?
YACK
YACK
YACK
CHATTER-BOXES.
IN THE NEXT ROOM...
YACK
SKRIK
SKRIK
WELL, THAT'S GOOD ENOUGH, I GUESS.
WOW, MINORU, YOU'RE AN ARTIST!
I CAN'T FIND THE WED CRAYON!
HEE! ♡
SKRIK
SKRIK

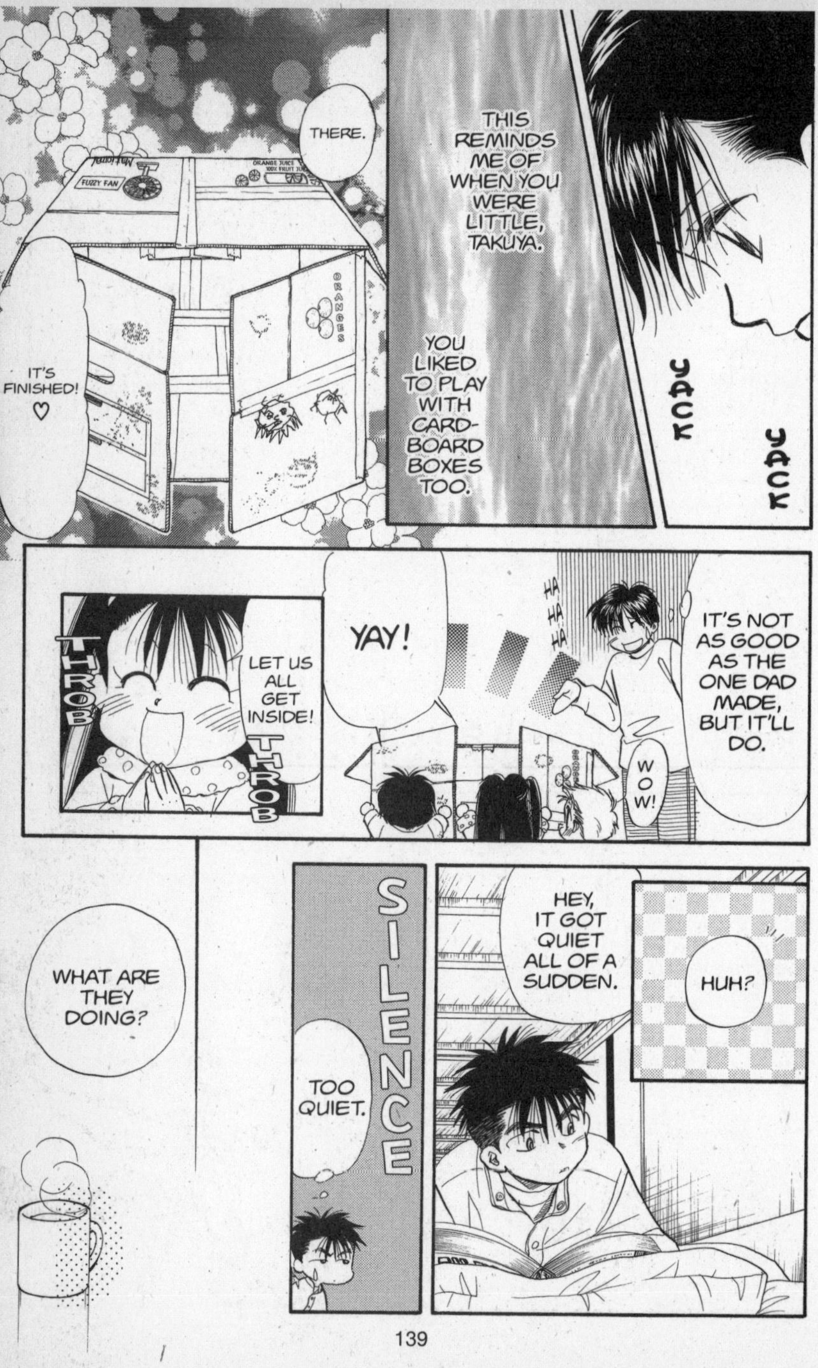
YACK
YACK
THIS REMINDS ME OF WHEN YOU WERE LITTLE, TAKUYA.
YOU LIKED TO PLAY WITH CARD-BOARD BOXES TOO.
THERE.
FUZZY FAN
ORANGES
IT'S FINISHED! ♡
IT'S NOT AS GOOD AS THE ONE DAD MADE, BUT IT'LL DO.
HA HA HA
WOW!
YAY!
LET US ALL GET INSIDE!
THROB
THROB
HUH?
HEY, IT GOT QUIET ALL OF A SUDDEN.
SILENCE
TOO QUIET.
WHAT ARE THEY DOING?

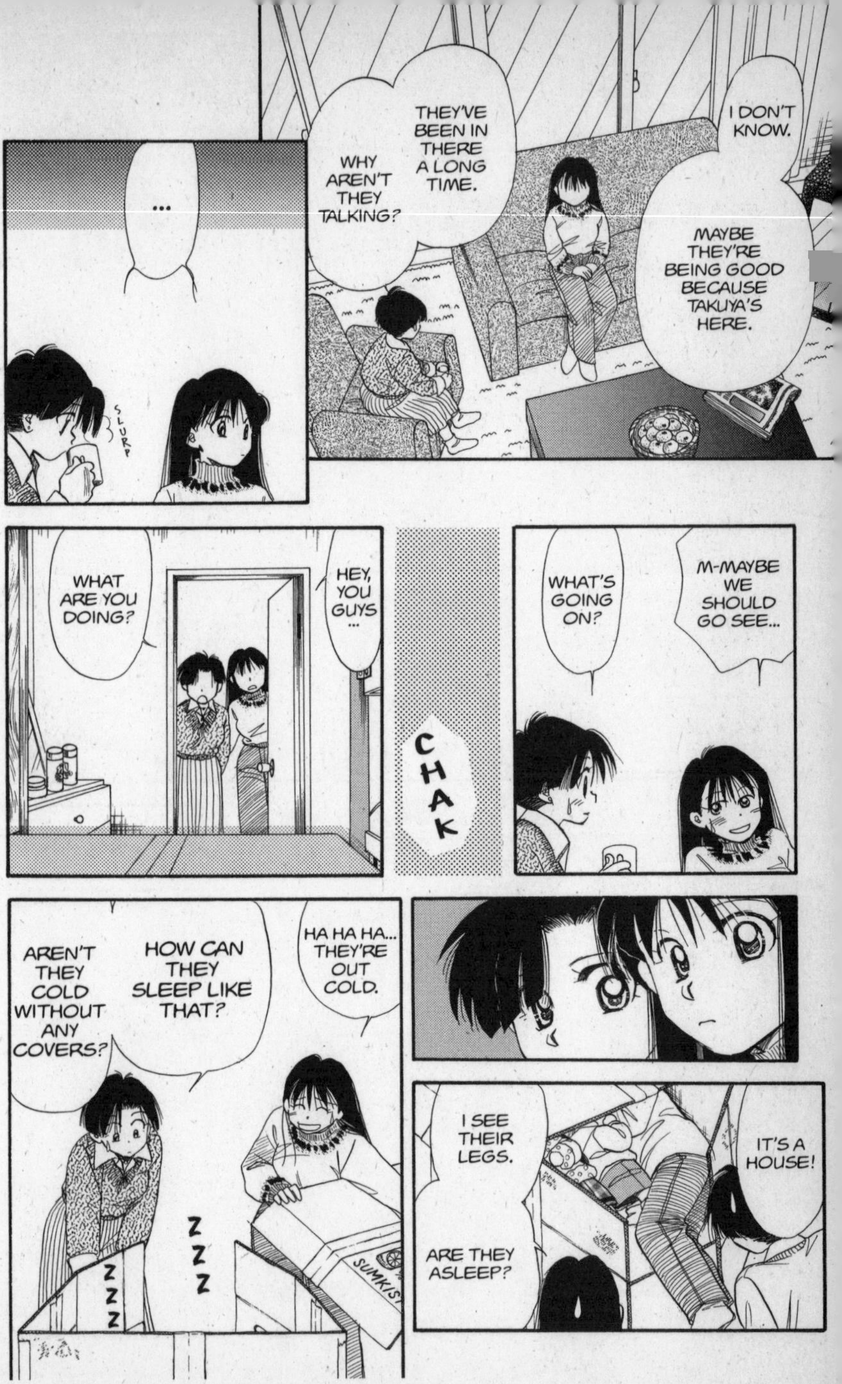
THEY'VE BEEN IN THERE A LONG TIME.
WHY AREN'T THEY TALKING?
I DON'T KNOW.
MAYBE THEY'RE BEING GOOD BECAUSE TAKUYA'S HERE.
...
SLURP
M-MAYBE WE SHOULD GO SEE...
WHAT'S GOING ON?
CHAK
HEY, YOU GUYS...
WHAT ARE YOU DOING?
IT'S A HOUSE!
I SEE THEIR LEGS.
ARE THEY ASLEEP?
HA HA HA... THEY'RE OUT COLD.
HOW CAN THEY SLEEP LIKE THAT?
AREN'T THEY COLD WITHOUT ANY COVERS?
ZZZ
ZZZ
SUMKIST

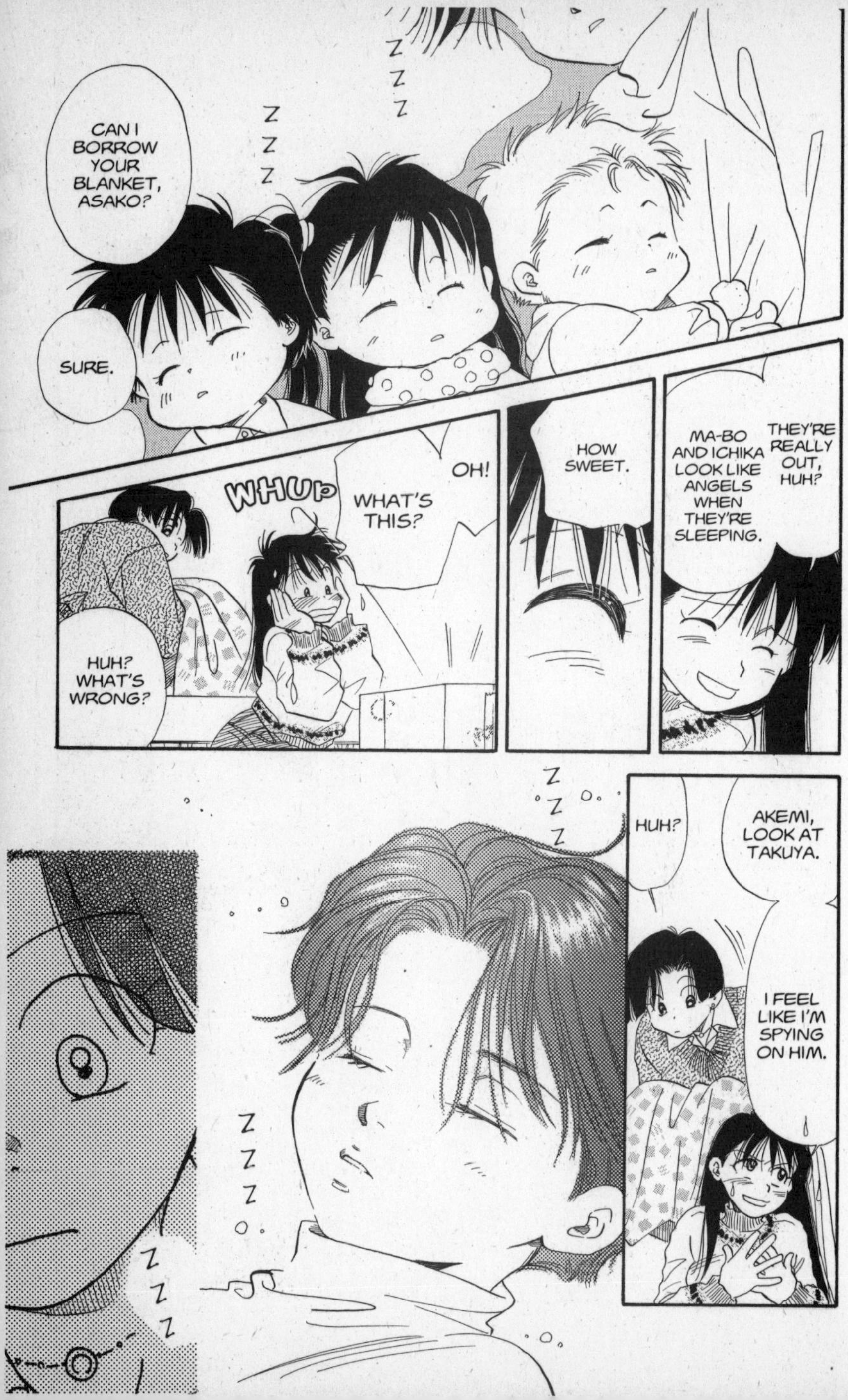
Z Z Z
Z Z Z
CAN I BORROW YOUR BLANKET, ASAKO?
SURE.
THEY'RE REALLY OUT, HUH?
MA-BO AND ICHIKA LOOK LIKE ANGELS WHEN THEY'RE SLEEPING.
HOW SWEET.
OH!
WHAT'S THIS?
WHUp
HUH? WHAT'S WRONG?
AKEMI, LOOK AT TAKUYA.
HUH?
I FEEL LIKE I'M SPYING ON HIM.
Z Z Z
Z Z Z
Z Z Z

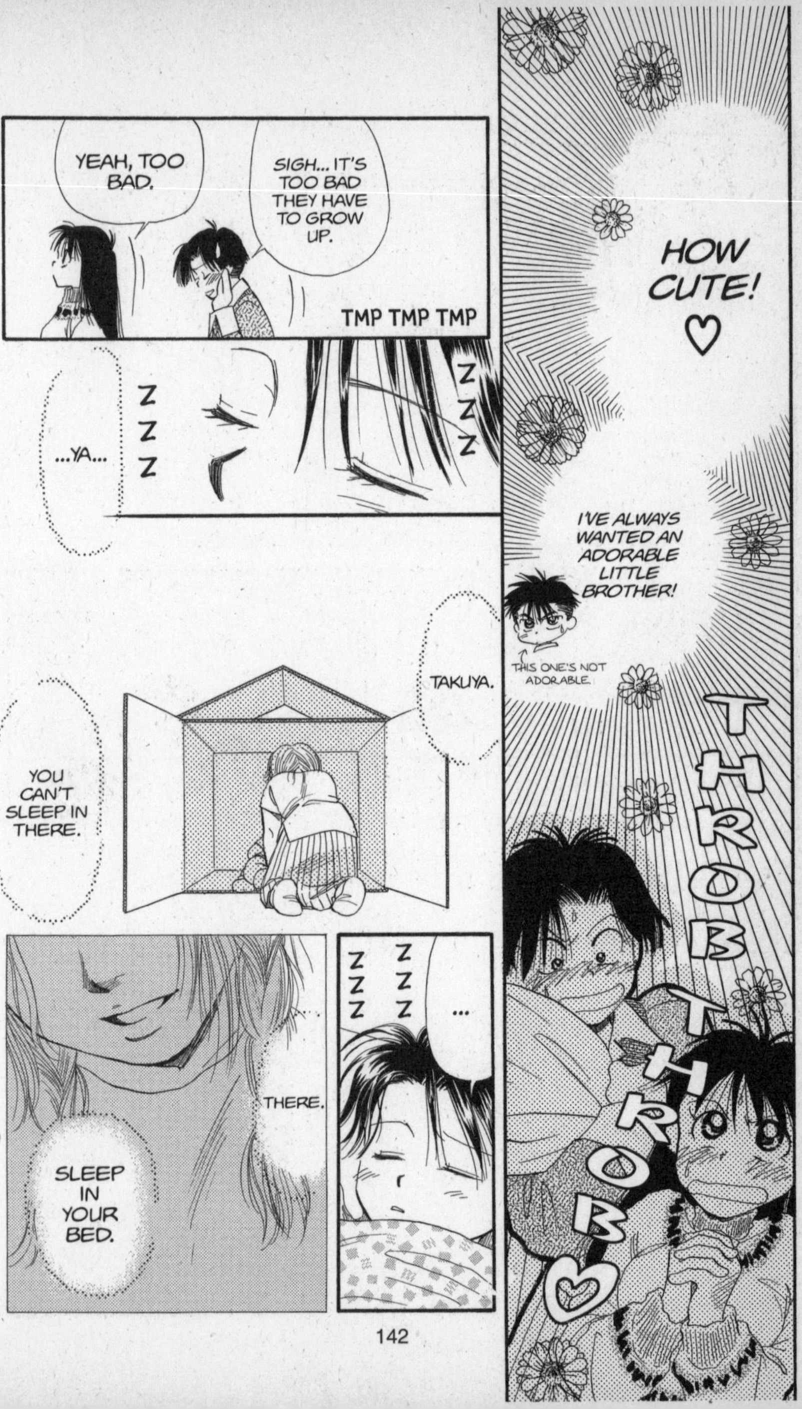
HOW CUTE! ♥
I'VE ALWAYS WANTED AN ADORABLE LITTLE BROTHER!
THIS ONE'S NOT ADORABLE.
THROB THROB ♥
THROB
SIGH... IT'S TOO BAD THEY HAVE TO GROW UP.
YEAH, TOO BAD.
TMP TMP TMP
Z Z Z
Z Z Z
...YA...
TAKUYA.
YOU CAN'T SLEEP IN THERE.
Z Z Z
Z Z Z
...
...
THERE.
SLEEP IN YOUR BED.

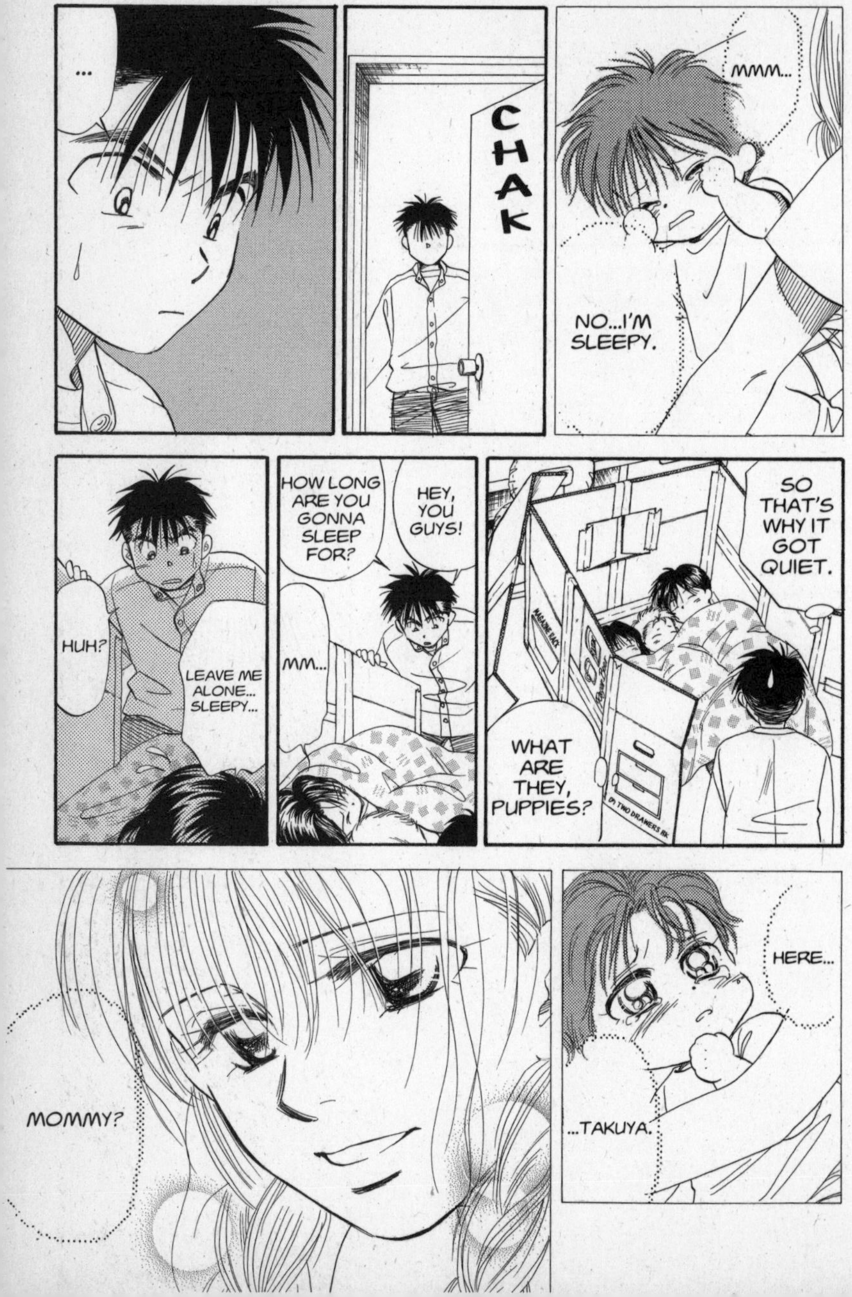
MMM...
NO...I'M SLEEPY.
CHAK
...
SO THAT'S WHY IT GOT QUIET.
WHAT ARE THEY, PUPPIES?
HEY, YOU GUYS!
HOW LONG ARE YOU GONNA SLEEP FOR?
MM...
HUH?
LEAVE ME ALONE... SLEEPY...
HERE...
...TAKUYA.
MOMMY?

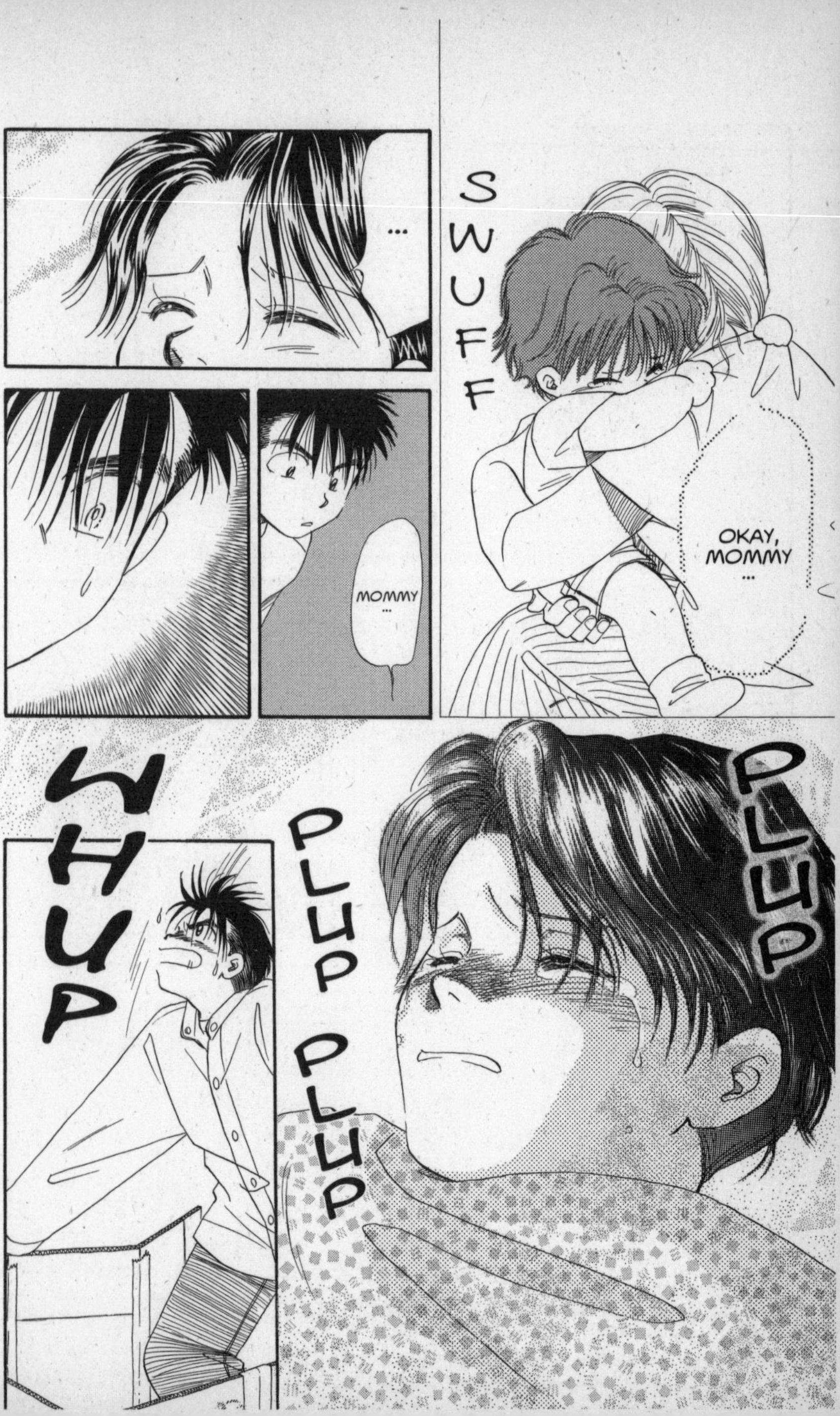
SWUFF
OKAY, MOMMY ...
...
MOMMY ...
PLUP
PLUP
PLUP
PLUP
WHUP

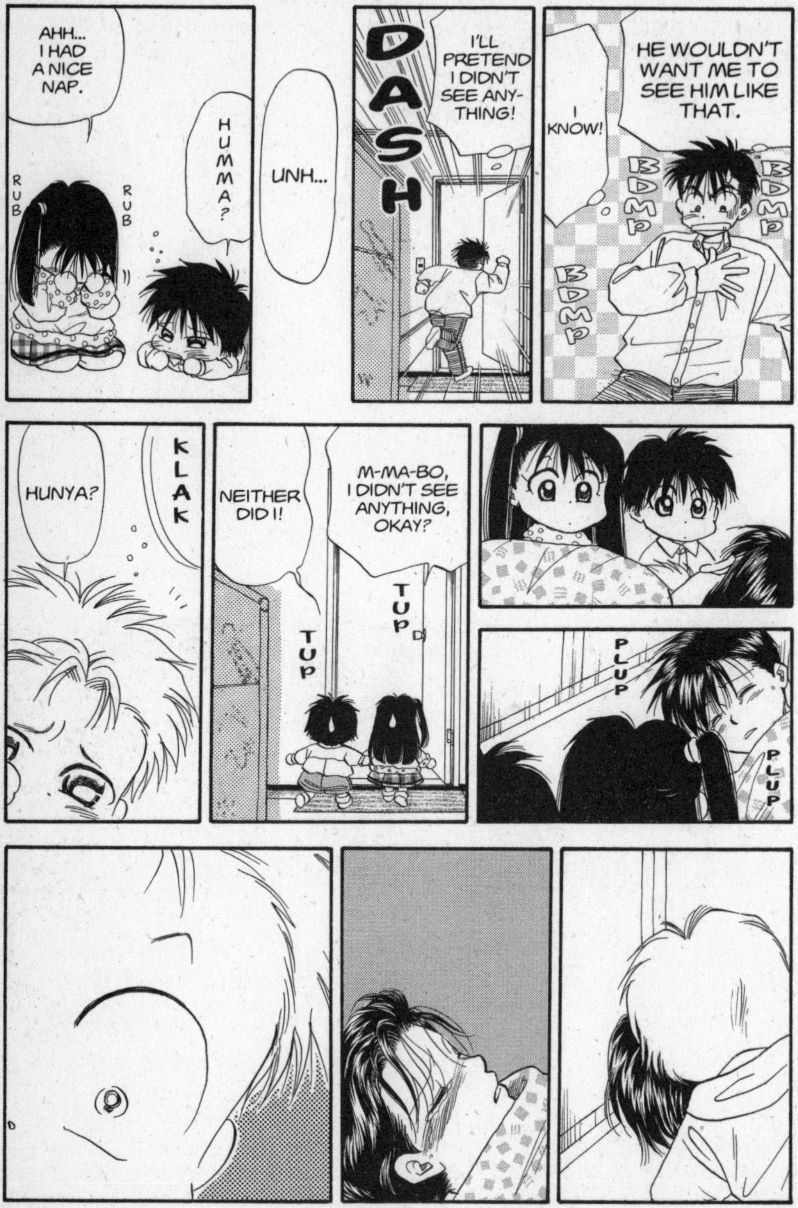
HE WOULDN'T WANT ME TO SEE HIM LIKE THAT.
I KNOW!
BDMP
BDMP
BDMP
I'LL PRETEND I DIDN'T SEE ANY-THING!
DASH
UNH...
HUMMA?
AHH... I HAD A NICE NAP.
RUB
RUB
PLUP
PLUP
M-MA-BO, I DIDN'T SEE ANYTHING, OKAY?
NEITHER DID I!
TUP
TUP
KLAK
HUNYA?

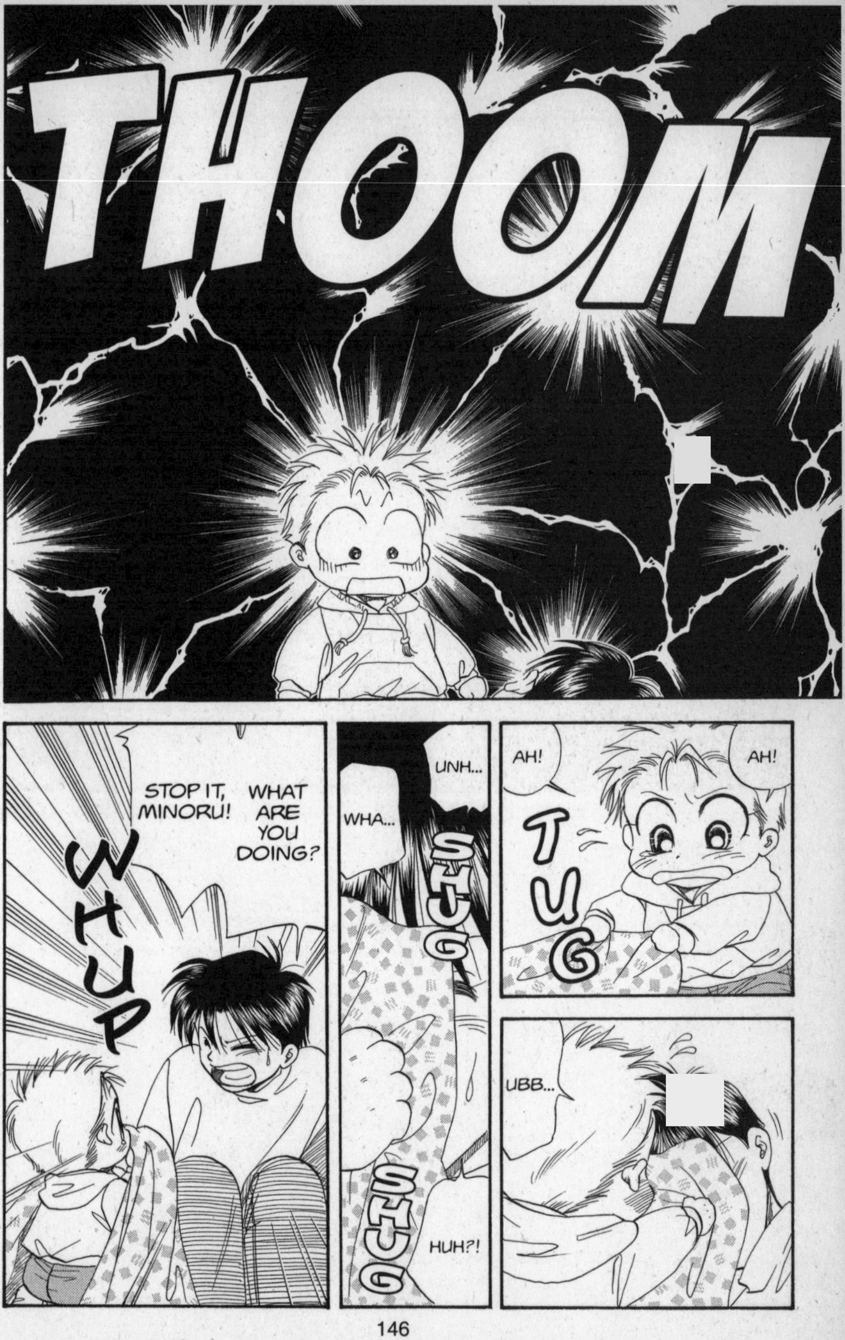
THOOM
AH!
AH!
TUG
UBB...
UNH...
WHA...
SHUG
SHUG
HUH?!
WHAT ARE YOU DOING?
STOP IT, MINORU!
WHUP

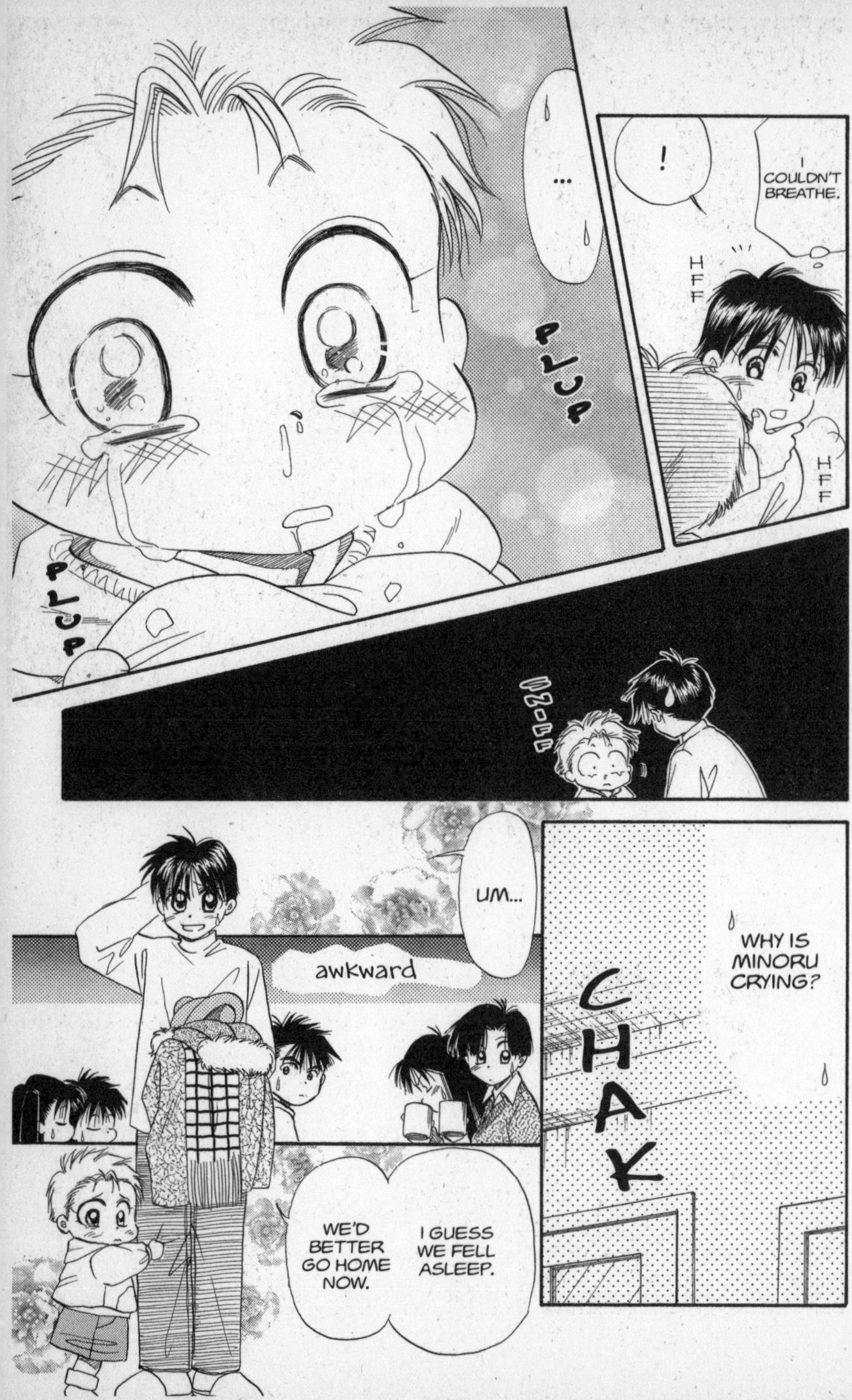
I COULDN'T BREATHE.
!
HFF
HFF
...
PLUP
PLUP
SNIFF
WHY IS MINORU CRYING?
CHAK
UM...
awkward
I GUESS WE FELL ASLEEP.
WE'D BETTER GO HOME NOW.

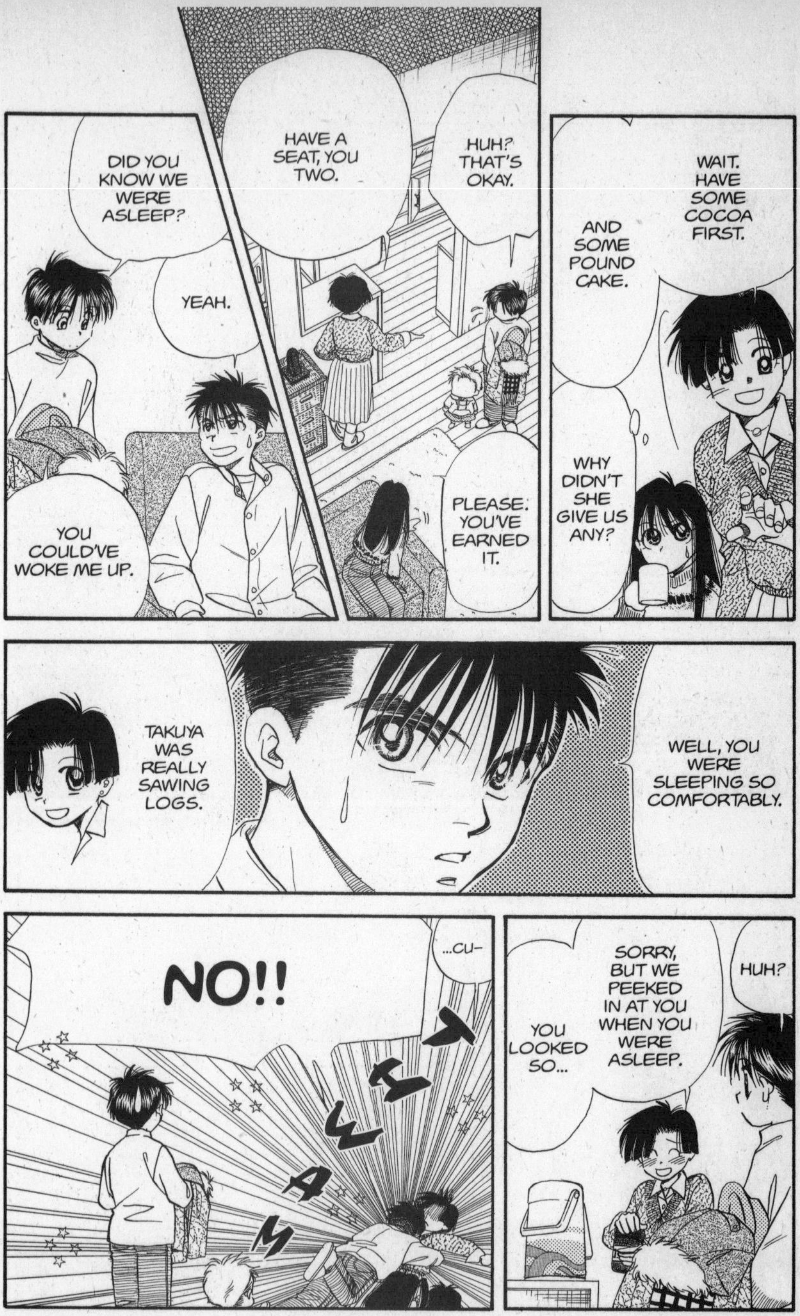
WAIT. HAVE SOME COCOA FIRST.
AND SOME POUND CAKE.
WHY DIDN'T SHE GIVE US ANY?
HUH? THAT'S OKAY.
HAVE A SEAT, YOU TWO.
PLEASE. YOU'VE EARNED IT.
DID YOU KNOW WE WERE ASLEEP?
YEAH.
YOU COULD'VE WOKE ME UP.
WELL, YOU WERE SLEEPING SO COMFORTABLY.
TAKUYA WAS REALLY SAWING LOGS.
HUH?
SORRY, BUT WE PEEKED IN AT YOU WHEN YOU WERE ASLEEP.
YOU LOOKED SO...
...CU-
NO!!
THWAM

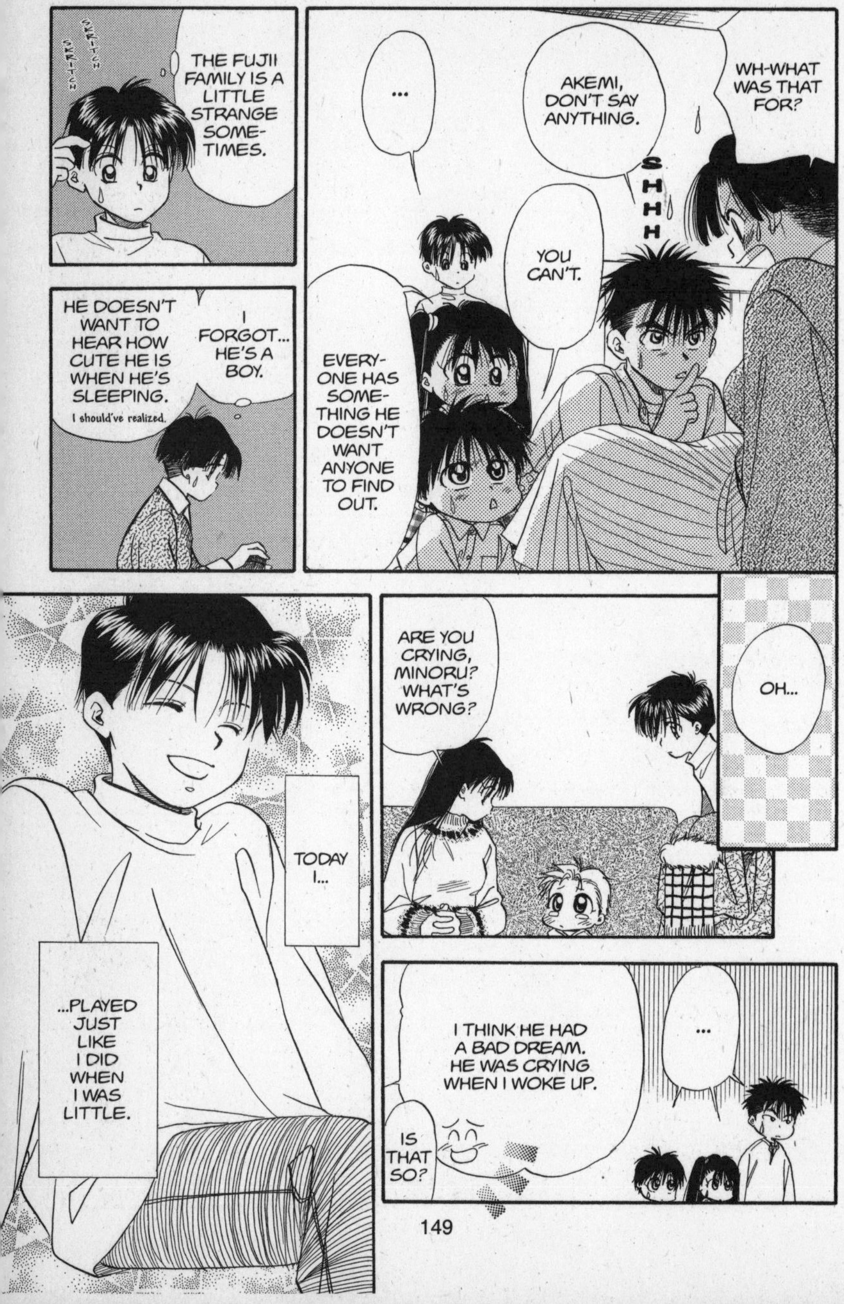
WH-WHAT WAS THAT FOR?
AKEMI, DON'T SAY ANYTHING.
SHHH
...
YOU CAN'T.
EVERYONE HAS SOMETHING HE DOESN'T WANT ANYONE TO FIND OUT.
SKRITCH SKRITCH
THE FUJII FAMILY IS A LITTLE STRANGE SOMETIMES.
I FORGOT... HE'S A BOY.
HE DOESN'T WANT TO HEAR HOW CUTE HE IS WHEN HE'S SLEEPING.
I should've realized.
ARE YOU CRYING, MINORU? WHAT'S WRONG?
OH...
...
I THINK HE HAD A BAD DREAM. HE WAS CRYING WHEN I WOKE UP.
IS THAT SO?
TODAY I...
...PLAYED JUST LIKE I DID WHEN I WAS LITTLE.

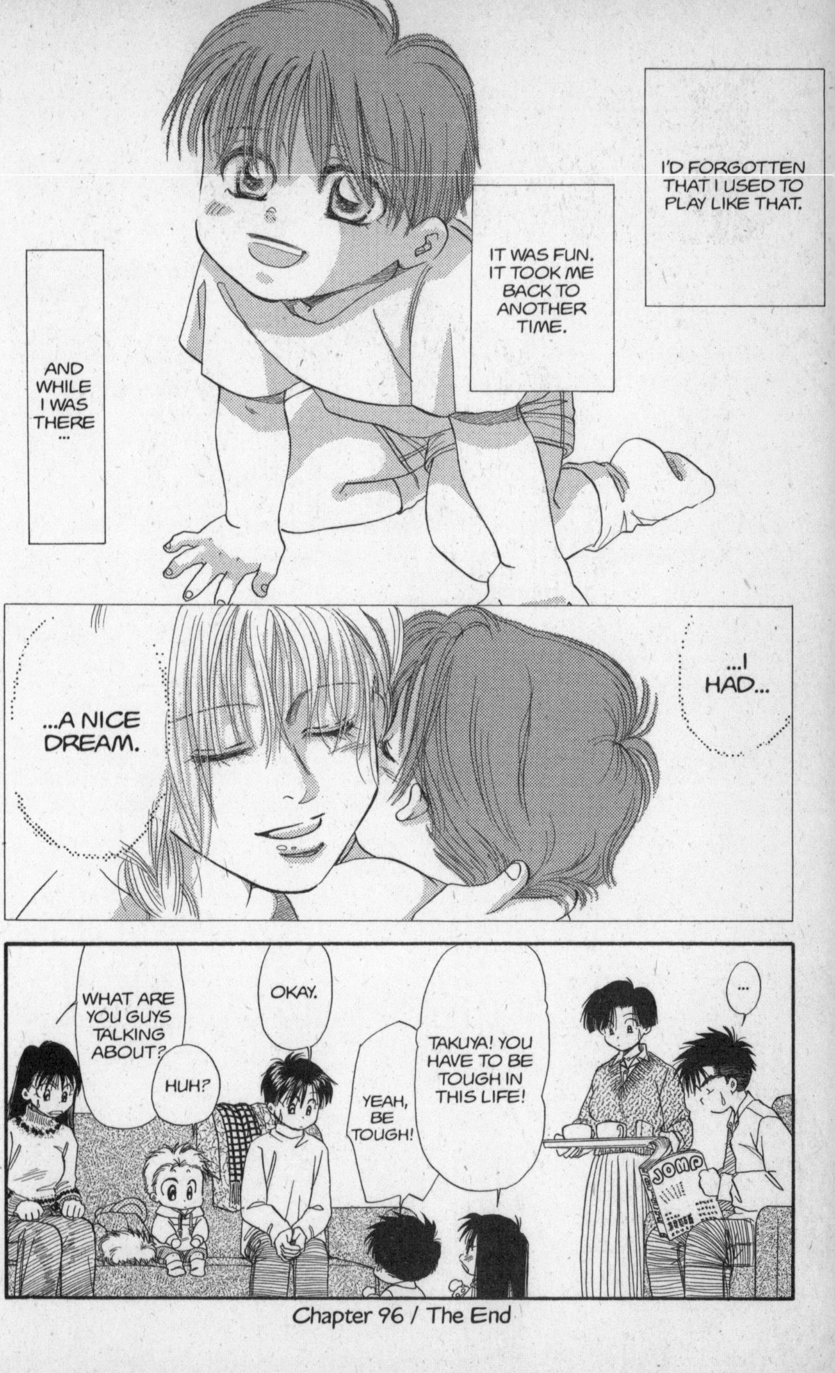
I'D FORGOTTEN THAT I USED TO PLAY LIKE THAT.
IT WAS FUN. IT TOOK ME BACK TO ANOTHER TIME.
AND WHILE I WAS THERE ...
...I HAD...
...A NICE DREAM.
...
TAKUYA! YOU HAVE TO BE TOUGH IN THIS LIFE!
YEAH, BE TOUGH!
OKAY.
HUH?
WHAT ARE YOU GUYS TALKING ABOUT?

Chapter 96 / The End

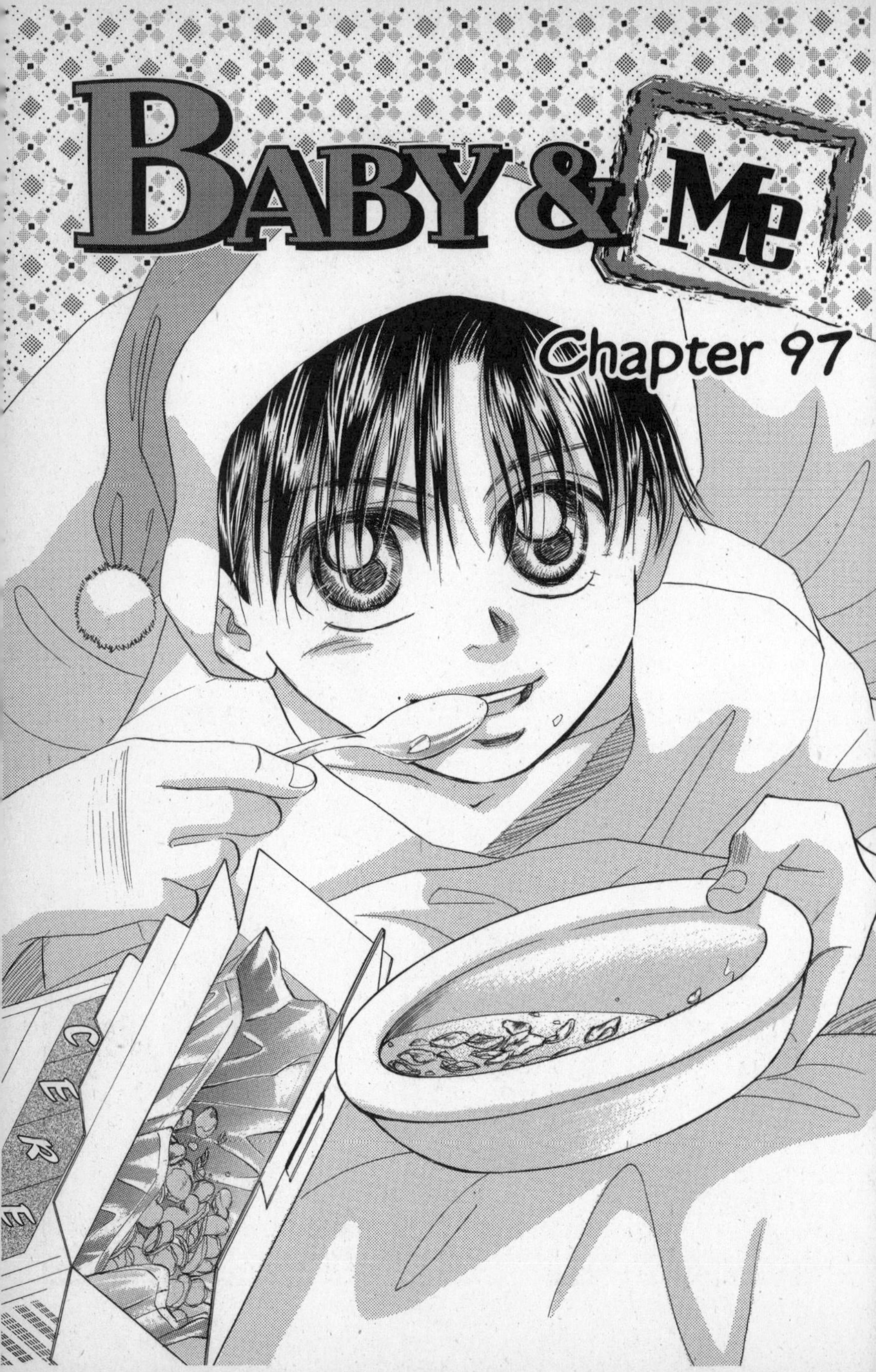
BABY & Me
Chapter 97

I'M DREADING THE SCHOOL MARATHON, AREN'T YOU?

DEFINITELY! THOSE AFTER-SCHOOL PRACTICES ARE A PAIN.

WHAT PLACE DID YOU FINISH IN LAST YEAR, TAKUYA?

I THINK I WAS IN THE TWENTIES.

YOU'RE NOT SO GOOD AT LONG-DISTANCE RACES, HUH?

I WAS IN THE FORTIES.

BUT THIS IS OUR LAST ELEMENTARY SCHOOL MARATHON, SO LET'S DO OUR BEST.

ONLY THE TOP THREE RUNNERS GET MEDALS. IF THEY GAVE OUT MEDALS FOR TWENTIETH PLACE, I'D TRY HARDER.

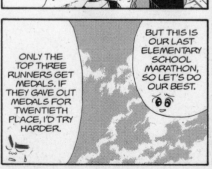

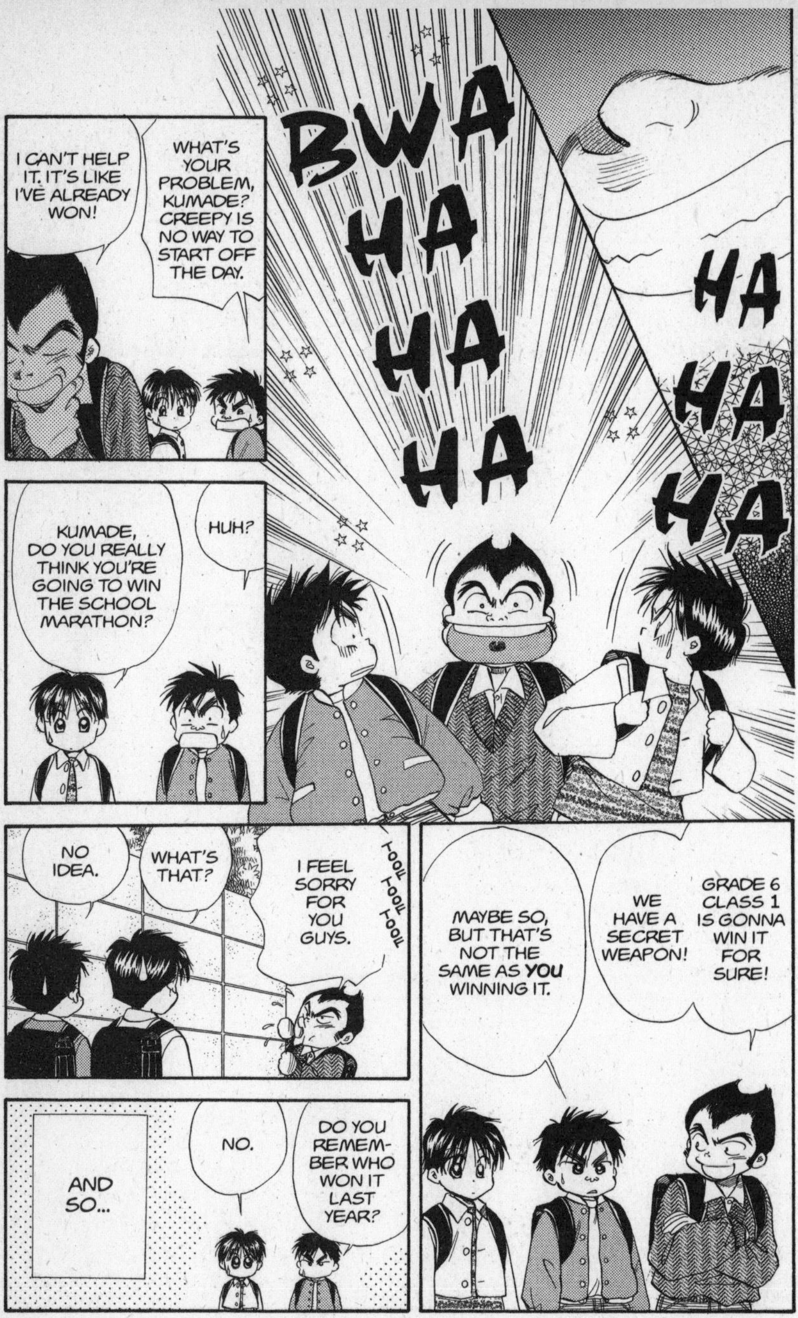
BWA HA HA HA HA
HA HA HA
WHAT'S YOUR PROBLEM, KUMADE? CREEPY IS NO WAY TO START OFF THE DAY.
I CAN'T HELP IT. IT'S LIKE I'VE ALREADY WON!
HUH?
KUMADE, DO YOU REALLY THINK YOU'RE GOING TO WIN THE SCHOOL MARATHON?
GRADE 6 CLASS 1 IS GONNA WIN IT FOR SURE!
WE HAVE A SECRET WEAPON!
MAYBE SO, BUT THAT'S NOT THE SAME AS YOU WINNING IT.
TOOL TOOL TOOL
I FEEL SORRY FOR YOU GUYS.
WHAT'S THAT?
NO IDEA.
DO YOU REMEMBER WHO WON IT LAST YEAR?
NO.
AND SO...

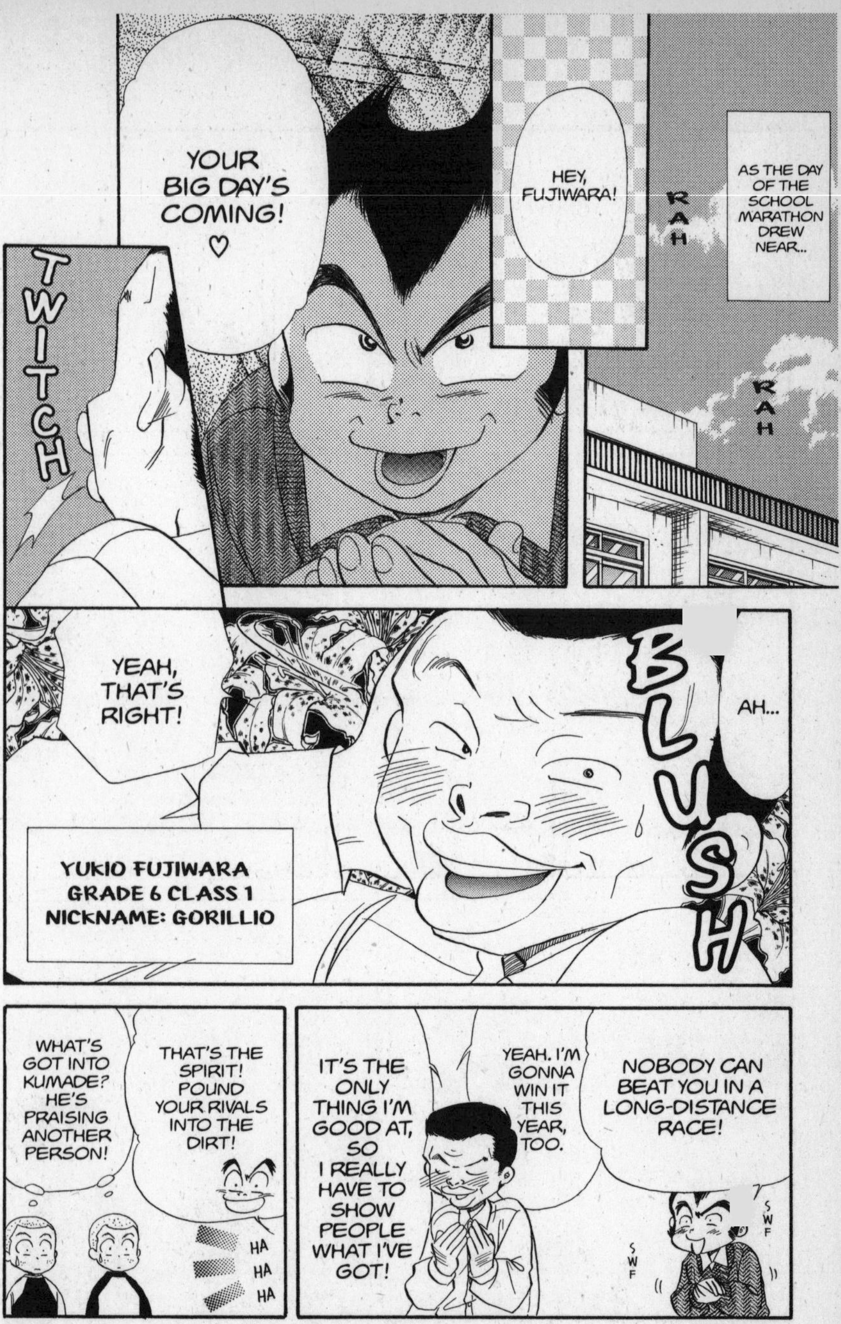
AS THE DAY OF THE SCHOOL MARATHON DREW NEAR...
RAH
RAH
HEY, FUJIWARA!
YOUR BIG DAY'S COMING! ♡
TWITCH
AH...
BLUSH
YEAH, THAT'S RIGHT!
YUKIO FUJIWARA
GRADE 6 CLASS 1
NICKNAME: GORILLIO
NOBODY CAN BEAT YOU IN A LONG-DISTANCE RACE!
SWF
SWF
YEAH. I'M GONNA WIN IT THIS YEAR, TOO.
IT'S THE ONLY THING I'M GOOD AT, SO I REALLY HAVE TO SHOW PEOPLE WHAT I'VE GOT!
THAT'S THE SPIRIT! POUND YOUR RIVALS INTO THE DIRT!
HA HA HA
WHAT'S GOT INTO KUMADE? HE'S PRAISING ANOTHER PERSON!

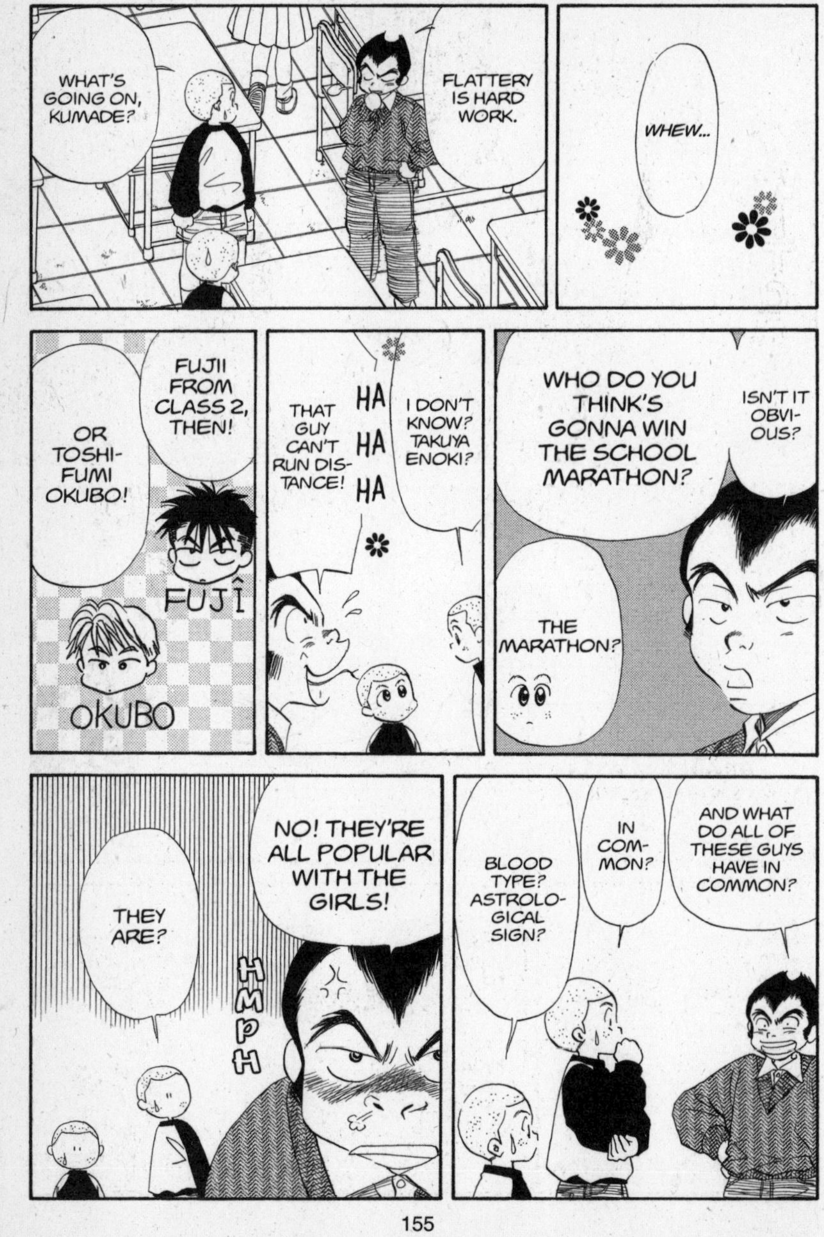
WHEW...
FLATTERY IS HARD WORK.
WHAT'S GOING ON, KUMADE?
ISN'T IT OBVIOUS?
WHO DO YOU THINK'S GONNA WIN THE SCHOOL MARATHON?
THE MARATHON?
I DON'T KNOW? TAKUYA ENOKI?
HA HA HA
THAT GUY CAN'T RUN DISTANCE!
FUJII FROM CLASS 2, THEN!
OR TOSHIFUMI OKUBO!
FUJÎ
OKUBO
AND WHAT DO ALL OF THESE GUYS HAVE IN COMMON?
IN COMMON?
BLOOD TYPE? ASTROLOGICAL SIGN?
NO! THEY'RE ALL POPULAR WITH THE GIRLS!
HMPH
THEY ARE?

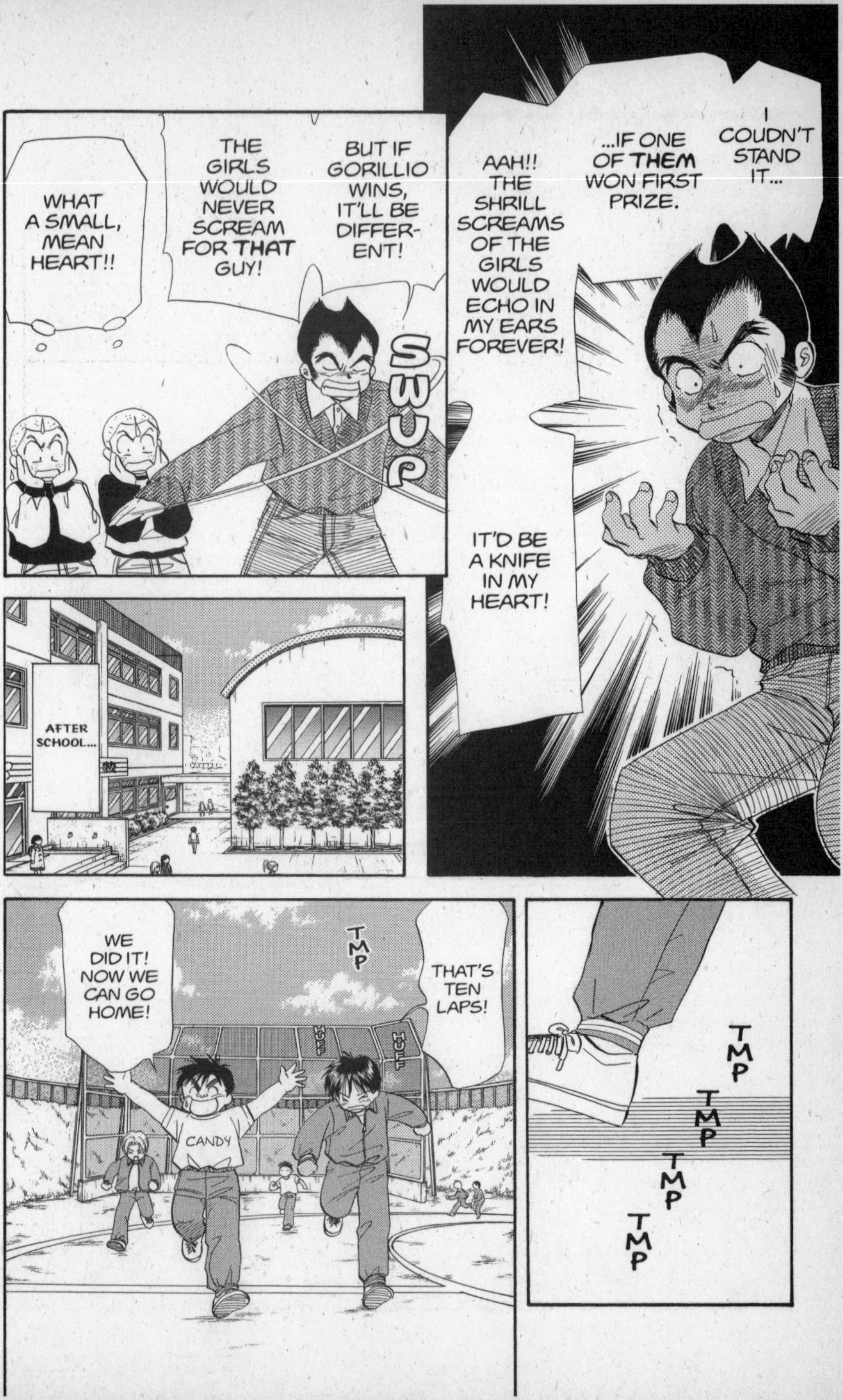
I COUDN'T STAND IT...
...IF ONE OF THEM WON FIRST PRIZE.
AAH!! THE SHRILL SCREAMS OF THE GIRLS WOULD ECHO IN MY EARS FOREVER!
IT'D BE A KNIFE IN MY HEART!
BUT IF GORILLIO WINS, IT'LL BE DIFFER-ENT!
THE GIRLS WOULD NEVER SCREAM FOR THAT GUY!
SWUP
WHAT A SMALL, MEAN HEART!!
AFTER SCHOOL...
TMP
TMP
TMP
TMP
THAT'S TEN LAPS!
TMP
HUFF
HUFF
WE DID IT! NOW WE CAN GO HOME!
CANDY

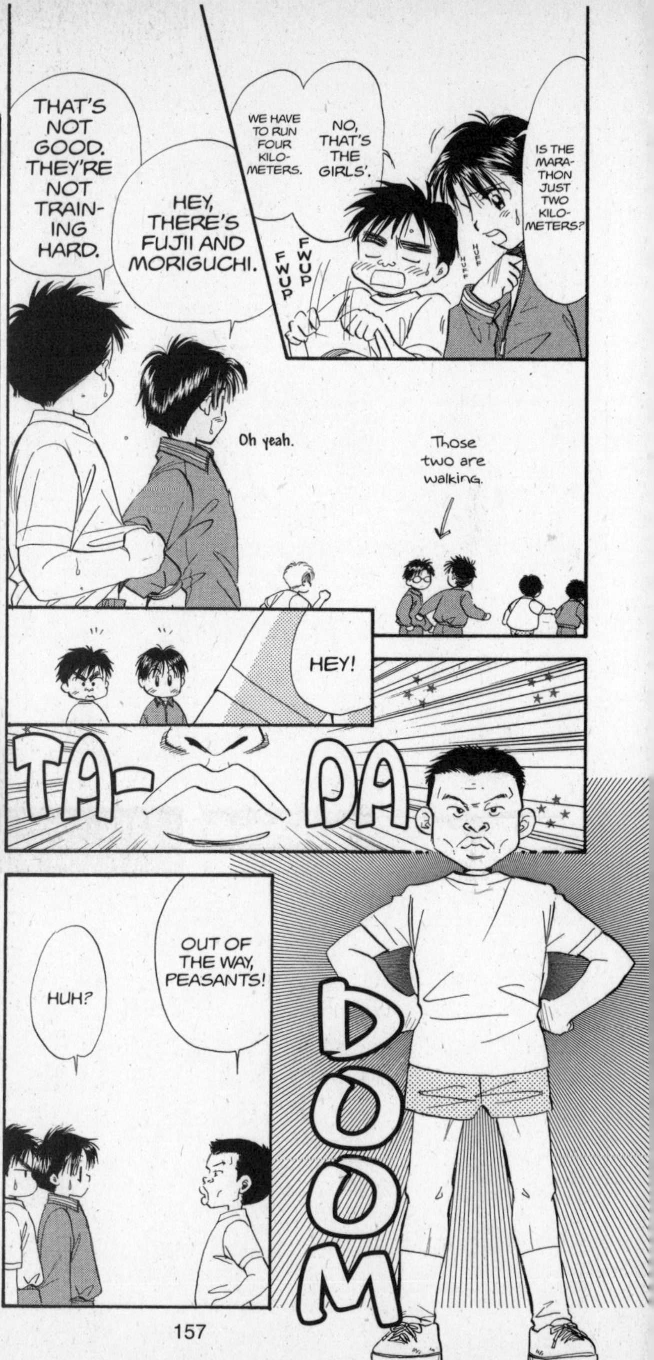
IS THE MARATHON JUST TWO KILOMETERS?
NO, THAT'S THE GIRLS'.
WE HAVE TO RUN FOUR KILOMETERS.
HUFF HUFF
FWUP FWUP
HEY, THERE'S FUJII AND MORIGUCHI.
THAT'S NOT GOOD. THEY'RE NOT TRAINING HARD.
Oh yeah.
Those two are walking.
HEY!
TA-DA
DOOM
OUT OF THE WAY, PEASANTS!
HUH?

Author's Note Part 7

This is the last column! Hooray!

To be honest, when I drew "Gorillio" Fujiwara, I felt like I wasn't doing girls' manga anymore. I'd already gone far outside the range of girls' manga by having Gon and Kumade as characters, but Gorillio was really beyond the pale! Seriously.

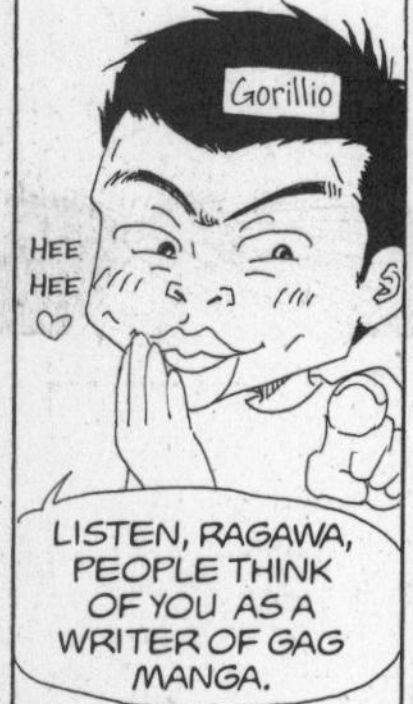
Gorillio
HEE HEE
LISTEN, RAGAWA, PEOPLE THINK OF YOU AS A WRITER OF GAG MANGA.

Well, this column is full, so this is the end. See you in volume 18! Bye for now! Marimo 5/15/97

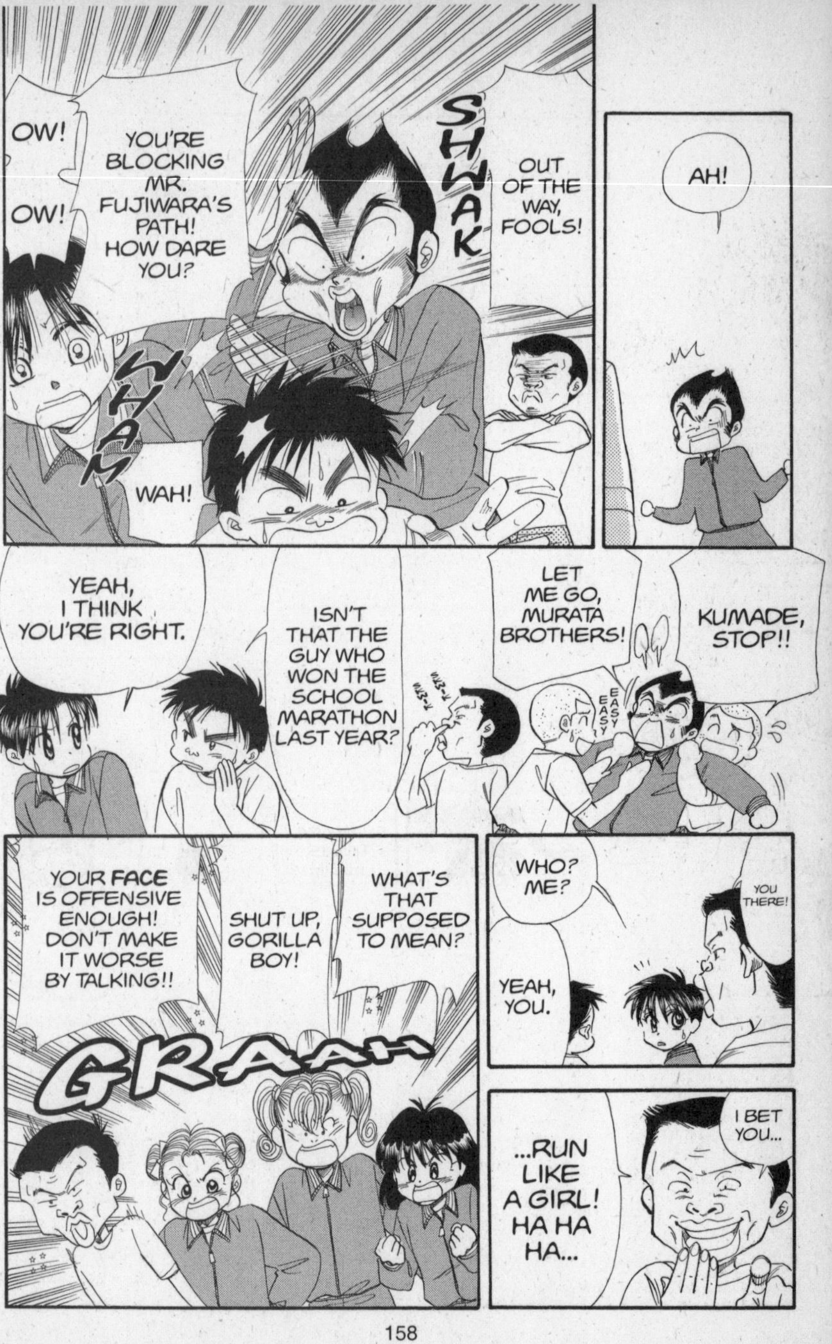
AH!
SHWAK
OUT OF THE WAY, FOOLS!
YOU'RE BLOCKING MR. FUJIWARA'S PATH! HOW DARE YOU?
OW!
OW!
WHAM
WAH!
KUMADE, STOP!!
LET ME GO, MURATA BROTHERS!
EASY EASY
ISN'T THAT THE GUY WHO WON THE SCHOOL MARATHON LAST YEAR?
YEAH, I THINK YOU'RE RIGHT.
YOU THERE!
WHO? ME?
YEAH, YOU.
I BET YOU...
...RUN LIKE A GIRL! HA HA HA...
WHAT'S THAT SUPPOSED TO MEAN?
SHUT UP, GORILLA BOY!
YOUR FACE IS OFFENSIVE ENOUGH! DON'T MAKE IT WORSE BY TALKING!!
GRAAAH

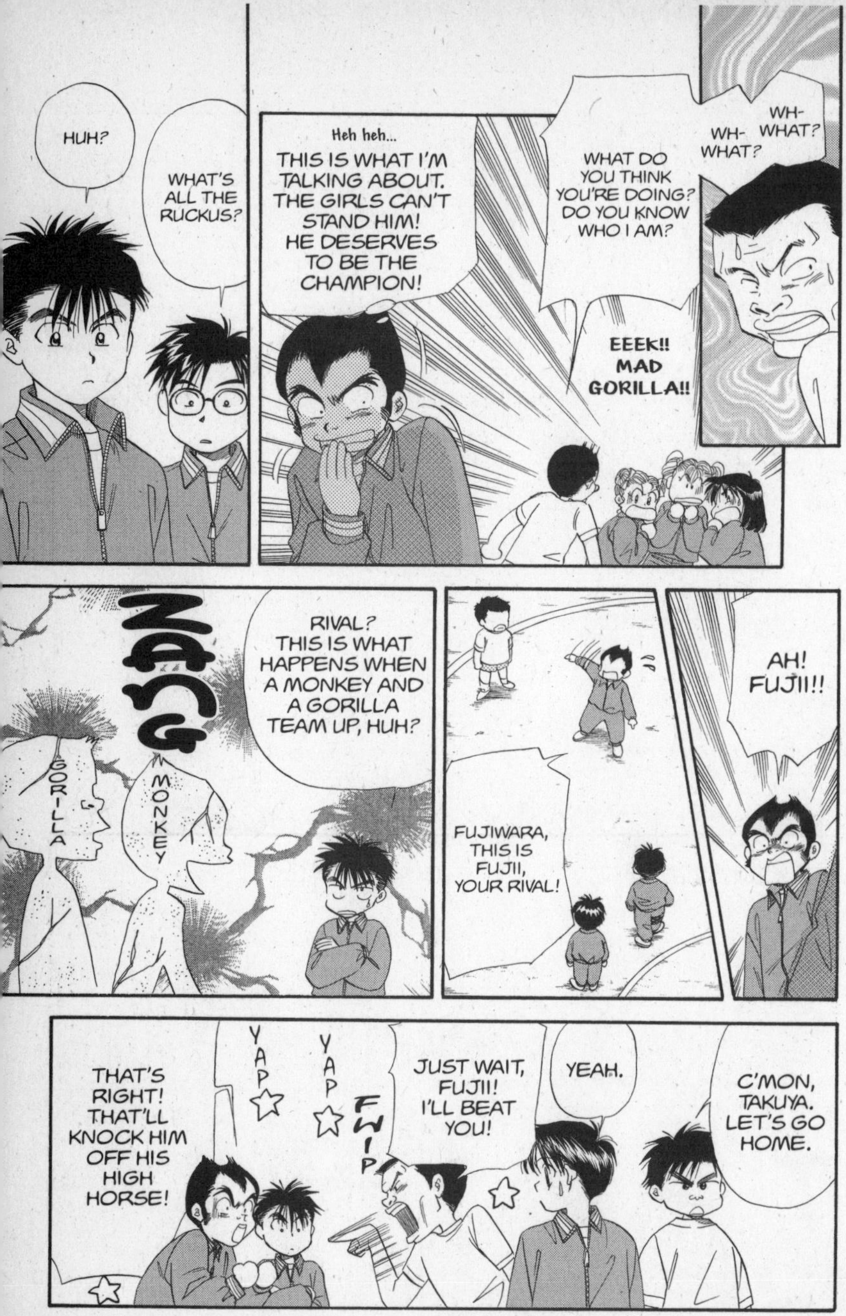
WH- WHAT?
WH- WHAT?
WHAT DO YOU THINK YOU'RE DOING? DO YOU KNOW WHO I AM?
EEEK!! MAD GORILLA!!
Heh heh...
THIS IS WHAT I'M TALKING ABOUT. THE GIRLS CAN'T STAND HIM! HE DESERVES TO BE THE CHAMPION!
HUH?
WHAT'S ALL THE RUCKUS?
AH! FUJII!!
FUJIWARA, THIS IS FUJII, YOUR RIVAL!
RIVAL? THIS IS WHAT HAPPENS WHEN A MONKEY AND A GORILLA TEAM UP, HUH?
ZANG
MONKEY
GORILLA
C'MON, TAKUYA. LET'S GO HOME.
YEAH.
JUST WAIT, FUJII! I'LL BEAT YOU!
FWIP
YAP
YAP
THAT'S RIGHT! THAT'LL KNOCK HIM OFF HIS HIGH HORSE!

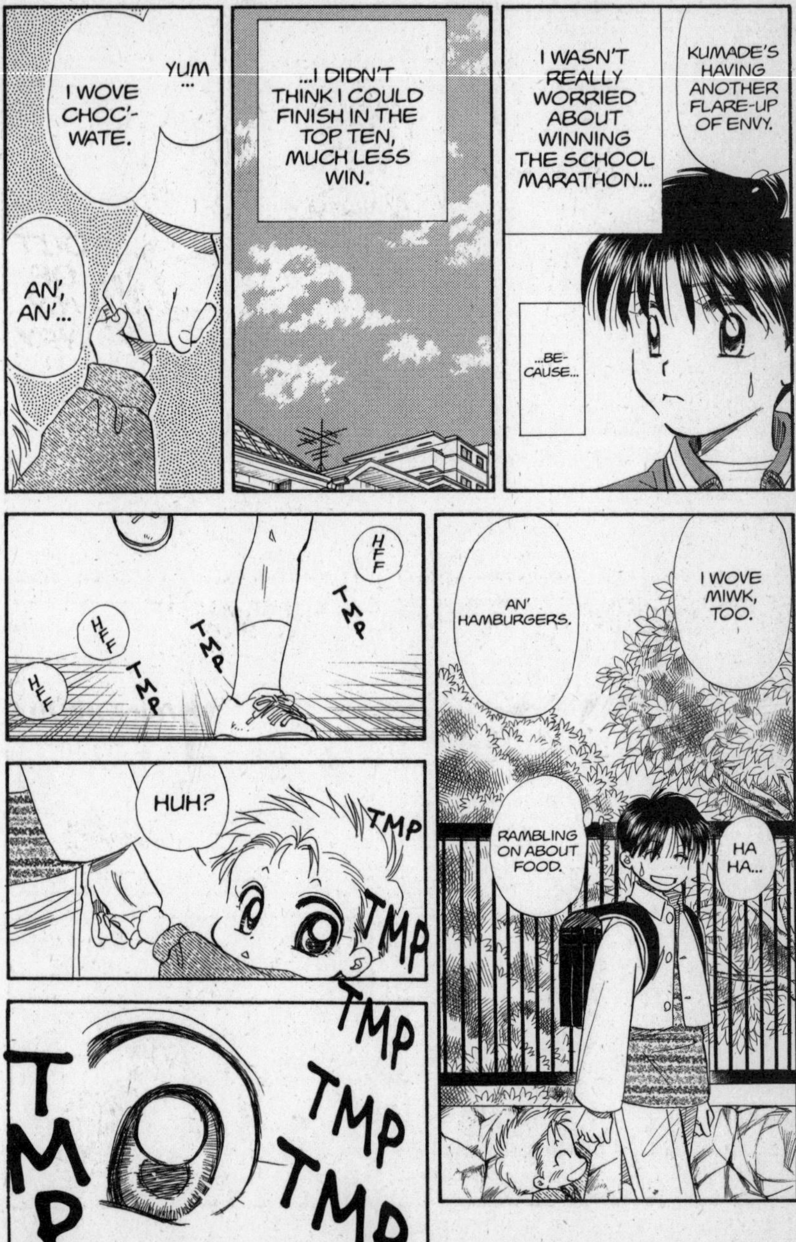
KUMADE'S HAVING ANOTHER FLARE-UP OF ENVY.
I WASN'T REALLY WORRIED ABOUT WINNING THE SCHOOL MARATHON...
...BE-CAUSE...
...I DIDN'T THINK I COULD FINISH IN THE TOP TEN, MUCH LESS WIN.
YUM...
I WOVE CHOC'-WATE.
AN', AN'...
I WOVE MIWK, TOO.
AN' HAMBURGERS.
HA HA...
RAMBLING ON ABOUT FOOD.
HFF
TMP
TMP
HFF
TMP
HFF
HUH?
TMP
TMP
TMP
TMP
TMP
TMP
TMP

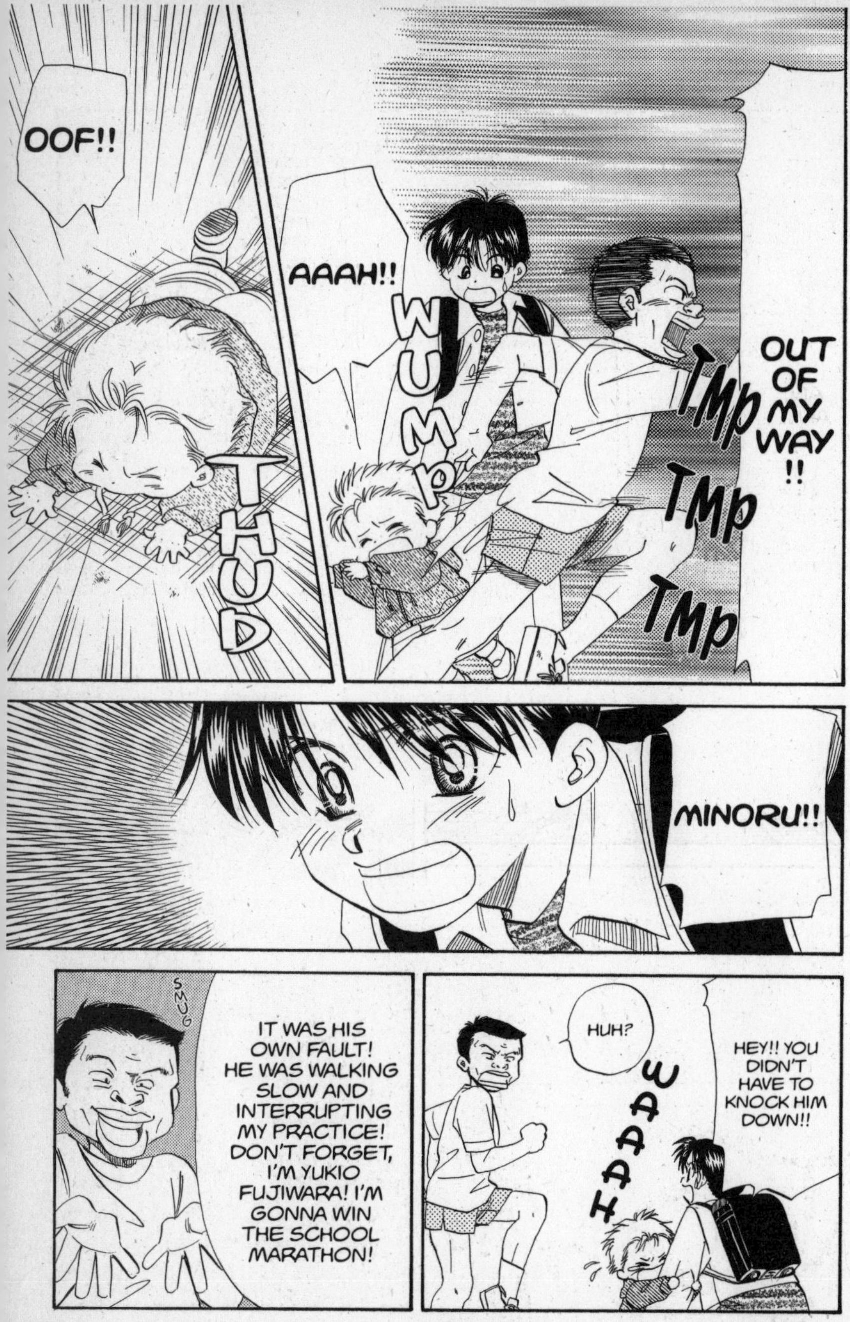
OUT OF MY WAY!!
TMp TMp TMp
AAAH!!
WUMp
THUD
OOF!!
MINORU!!
HEY!! YOU DIDN'T HAVE TO KNOCK HIM DOWN!!
WAAAAH
HUH?
SMUG
IT WAS HIS OWN FAULT! HE WAS WALKING SLOW AND INTERRUPTING MY PRACTICE! DON'T FORGET, I'M YUKIO FUJIWARA! I'M GONNA WIN THE SCHOOL MARATHON!

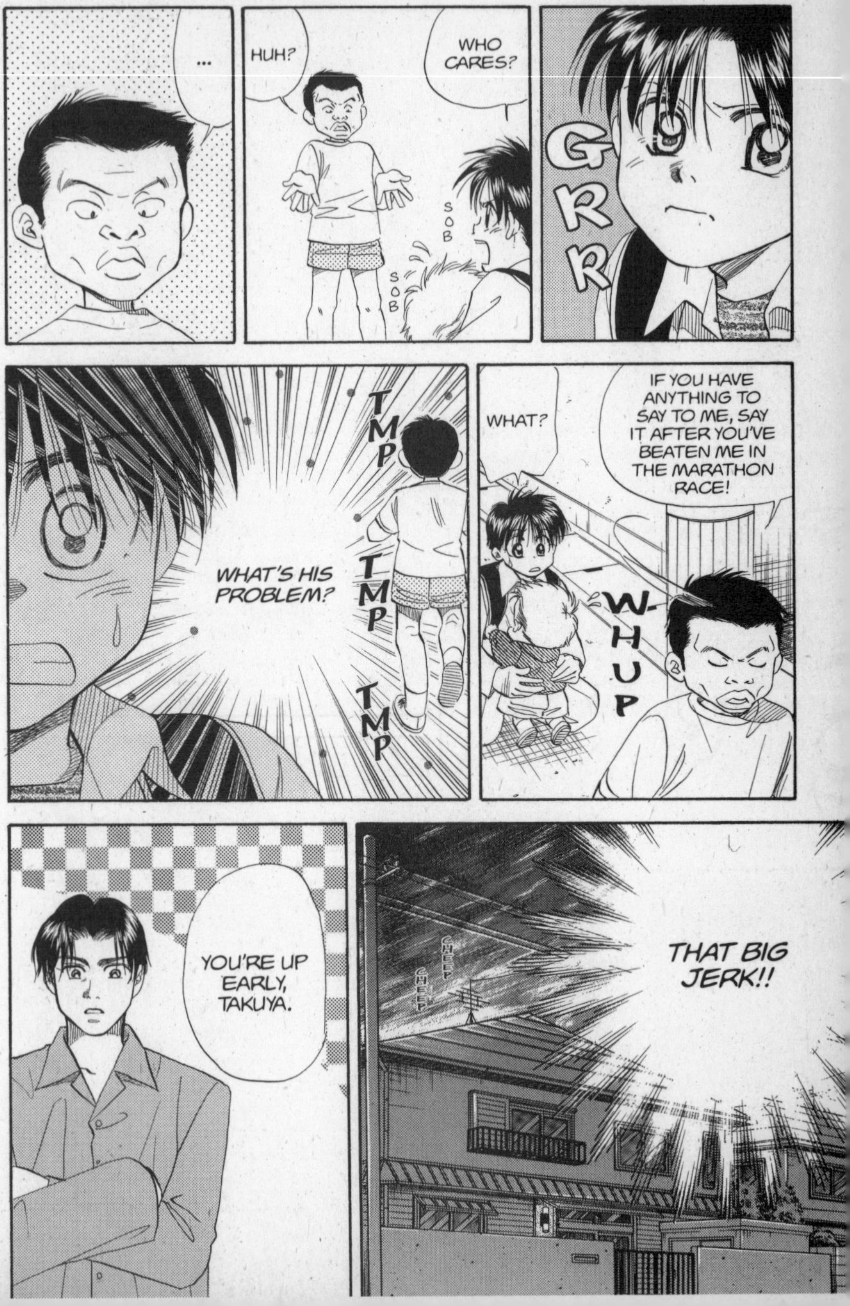
GRR
WHO CARES?
HUH?
SOB
SOB
...
IF YOU HAVE ANYTHING TO SAY TO ME, SAY IT AFTER YOU'VE BEATEN ME IN THE MARATHON RACE!
WHAT?
W-WHUP
TMP
TMP
TMP
WHAT'S HIS PROBLEM?
THAT BIG JERK!!
CHEEP
CHEEP
YOU'RE UP EARLY, TAKUYA.

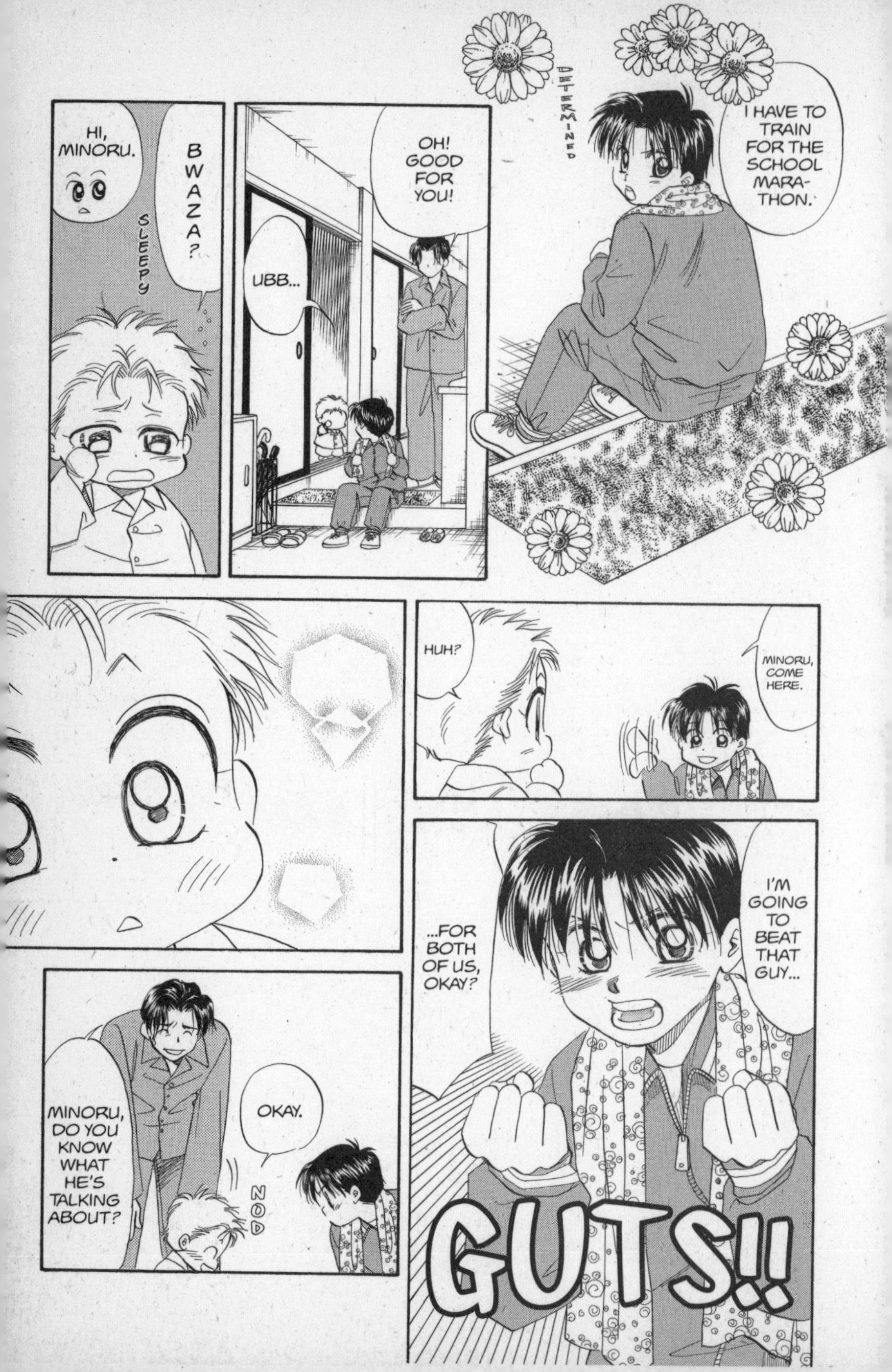
DETERMINED
I HAVE TO TRAIN FOR THE SCHOOL MARA-THON.
OH! GOOD FOR YOU!
UBB...
BWAZA?
SLEEPY
HI, MINORU.
MINORU, COME HERE.
HUH?
I'M GOING TO BEAT THAT GUY...
...FOR BOTH OF US, OKAY?
GUTS!!
OKAY.
NOD
MINORU, DO YOU KNOW WHAT HE'S TALKING ABOUT?

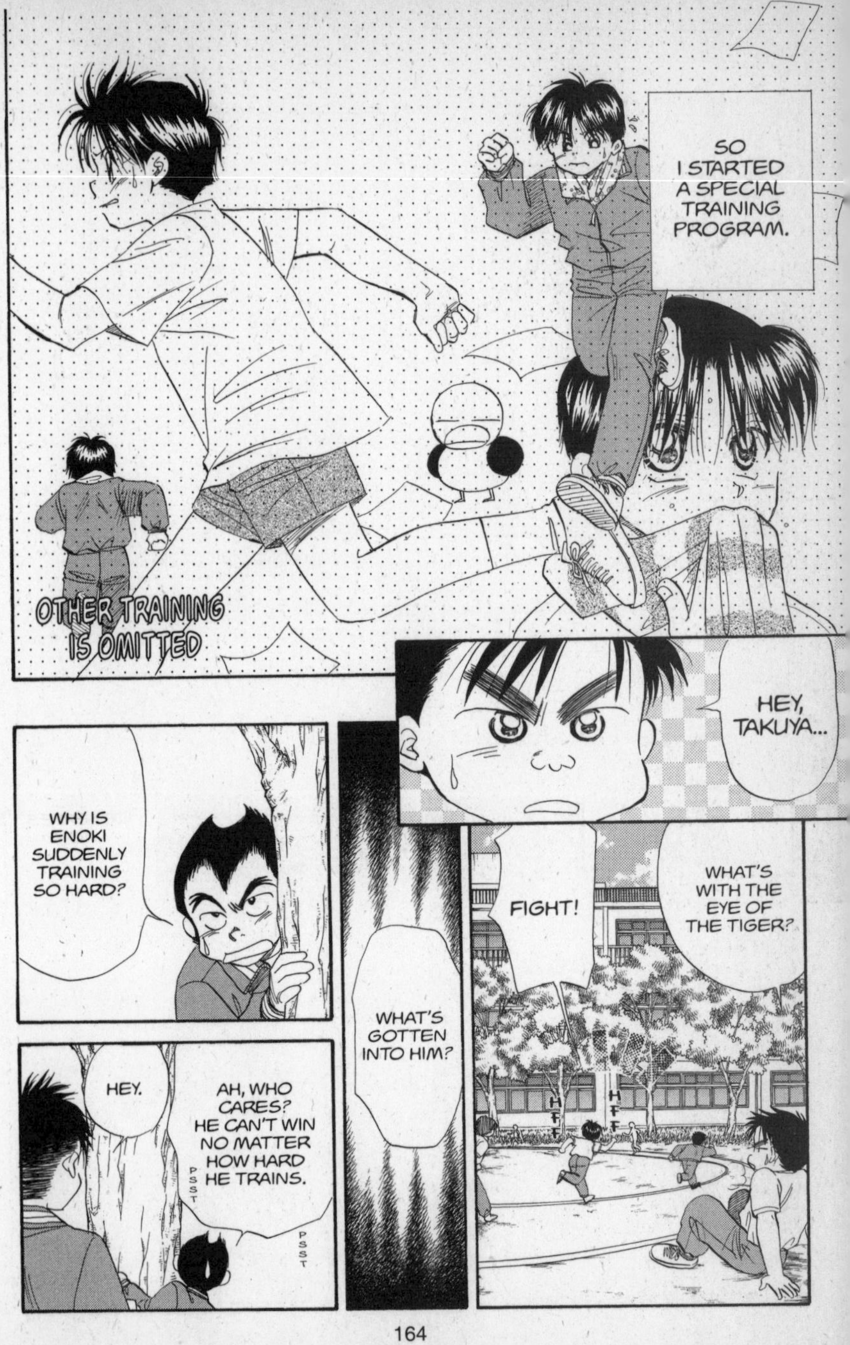
SO I STARTED A SPECIAL TRAINING PROGRAM.
OTHER TRAINING IS OMITTED
HEY, TAKUYA...
WHAT'S WITH THE EYE OF THE TIGER?
FIGHT!
HFF
HFF
WHAT'S GOTTEN INTO HIM?
WHY IS ENOKI SUDDENLY TRAINING SO HARD?
AH, WHO CARES? HE CAN'T WIN NO MATTER HOW HARD HE TRAINS.
HEY.
PSST
PSST

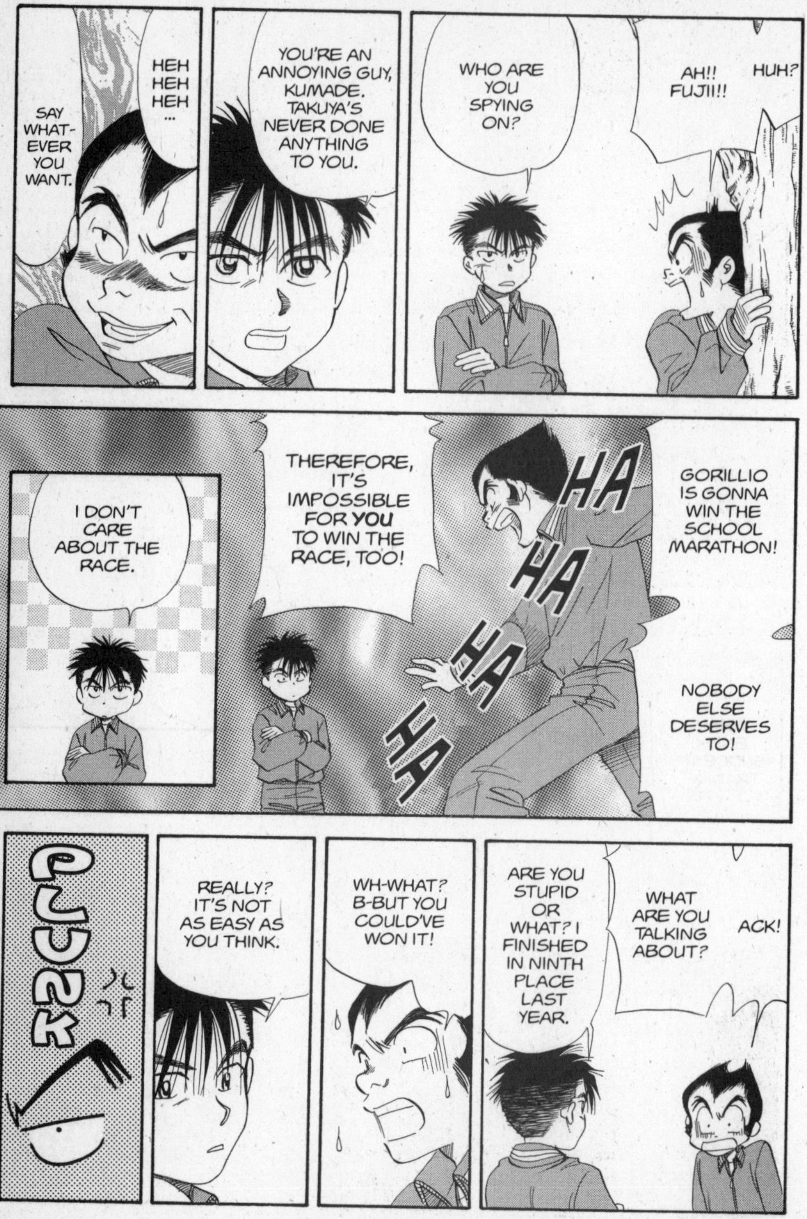
HUH?
AH!! FUJII!!
WHO ARE YOU SPYING ON?
YOU'RE AN ANNOYING GUY, KUMADE. TAKUYA'S NEVER DONE ANYTHING TO YOU.
HEH HEH HEH ...
SAY WHAT-EVER YOU WANT.
GORILLIO IS GONNA WIN THE SCHOOL MARATHON!
HA HA HA HA
NOBODY ELSE DESERVES TO!
THEREFORE, IT'S IMPOSSIBLE FOR **YOU** TO WIN THE RACE, TOO!
I DON'T CARE ABOUT THE RACE.
ACK!
WHAT ARE YOU TALKING ABOUT?
ARE YOU STUPID OR WHAT? I FINISHED IN NINTH PLACE LAST YEAR.
WH-WHAT? B-BUT YOU COULD'VE WON IT!
REALLY? IT'S NOT AS EASY AS YOU THINK.
PLUNK

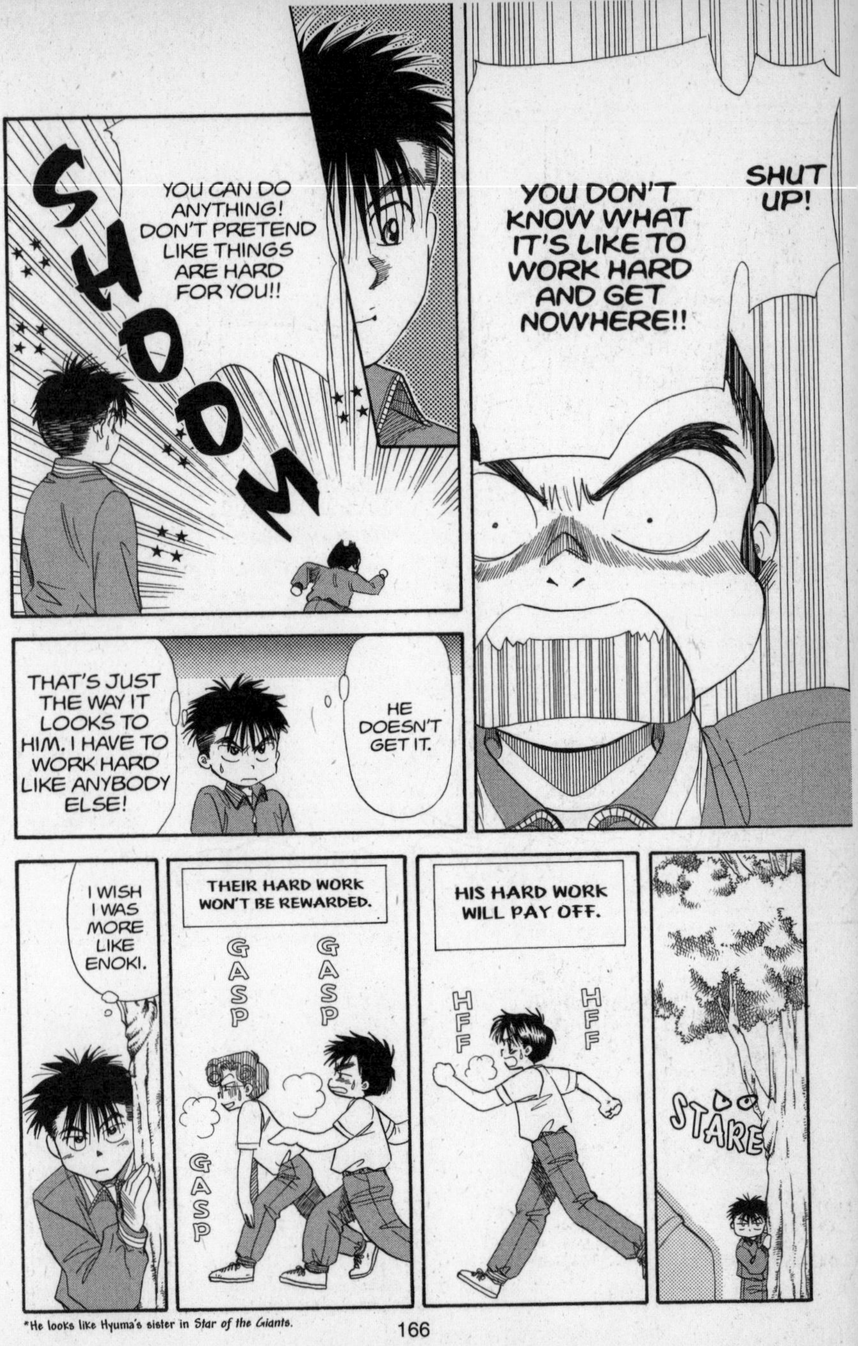
SHUT UP!
YOU DON'T KNOW WHAT IT'S LIKE TO WORK HARD AND GET NOWHERE!!
YOU CAN DO ANYTHING! DON'T PRETEND LIKE THINGS ARE HARD FOR YOU!!
SHDOM
HE DOESN'T GET IT.
THAT'S JUST THE WAY IT LOOKS TO HIM. I HAVE TO WORK HARD LIKE ANYBODY ELSE!
STARE
HIS HARD WORK WILL PAY OFF.
HFF
HFF
THEIR HARD WORK WON'T BE REWARDED.
GASP
GASP
GASP
I WISH I WAS MORE LIKE ENOKI.

*He looks like Hyuma's sister in *Star of the Giants*.

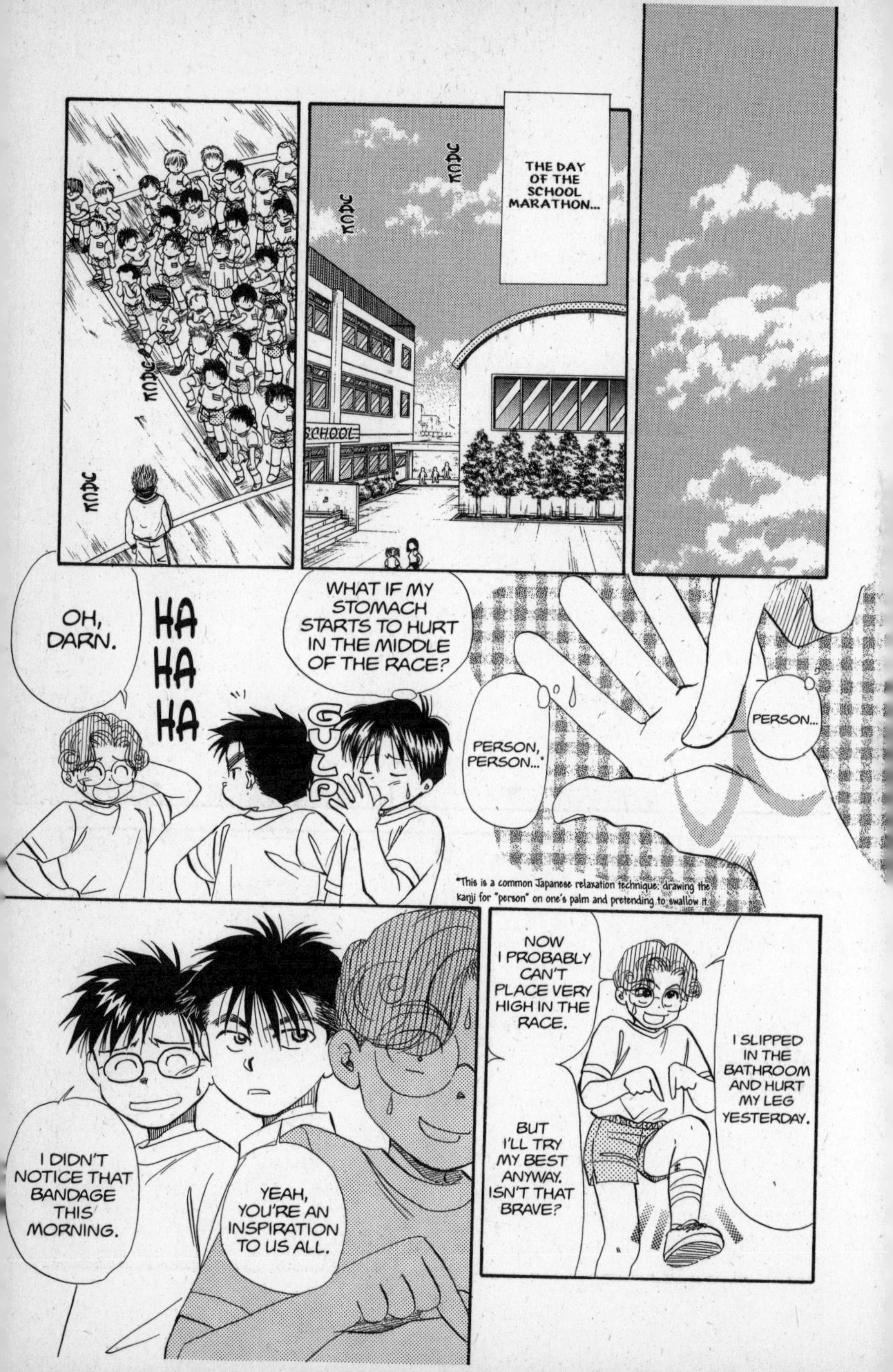
THE DAY OF THE SCHOOL MARATHON...
JACK
JACK
JACK
JACK
PERSON...
PERSON, PERSON...*
WHAT IF MY STOMACH STARTS TO HURT IN THE MIDDLE OF THE RACE?
GULP
HA HA HA
OH, DARN.
I SLIPPED IN THE BATHROOM AND HURT MY LEG YESTERDAY.
NOW I PROBABLY CAN'T PLACE VERY HIGH IN THE RACE.
BUT I'LL TRY MY BEST ANYWAY. ISN'T THAT BRAVE?
YEAH, YOU'RE AN INSPIRATION TO US ALL.
I DIDN'T NOTICE THAT BANDAGE THIS MORNING.

*This is a common Japanese relaxation technique: drawing the kanji for "person" on one's palm and pretending to swallow it.

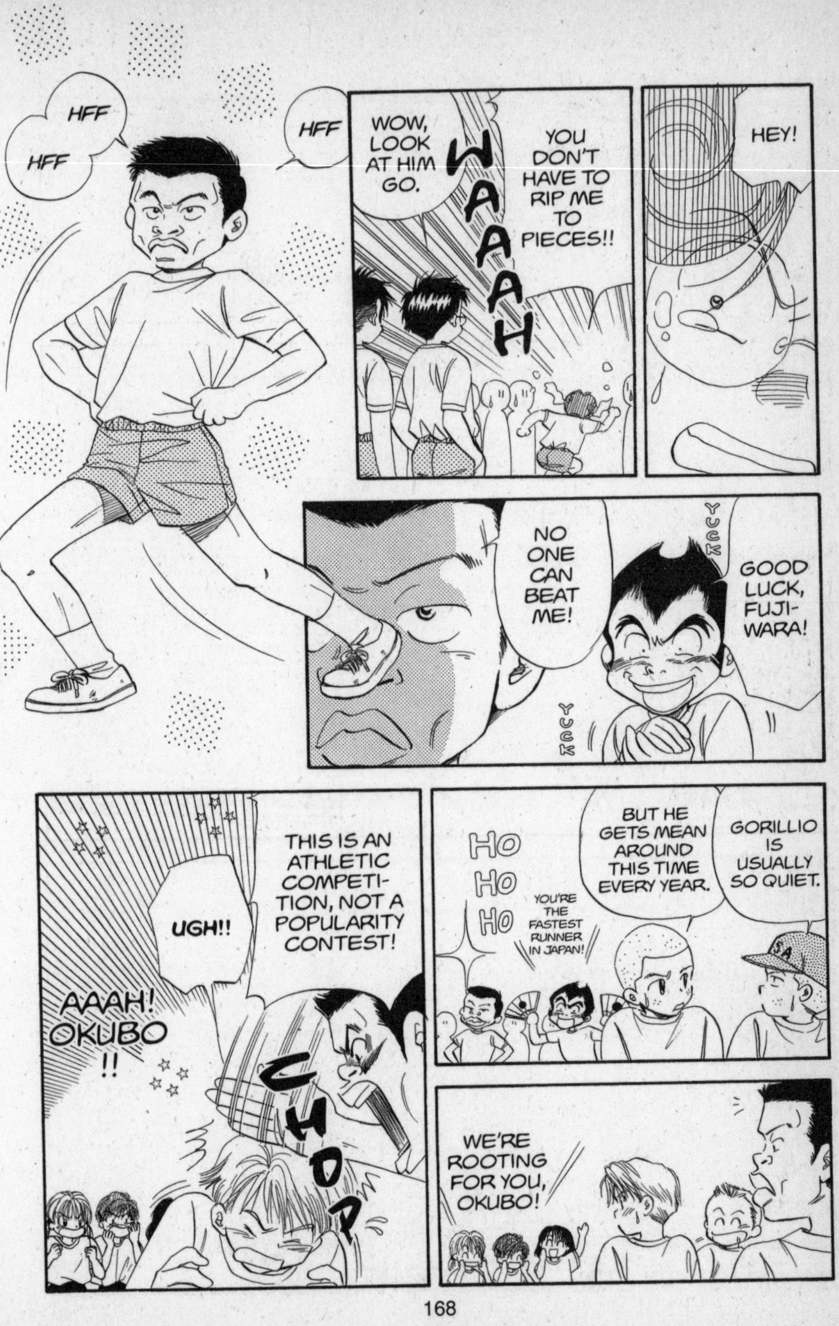
HEY!
YOU DON'T HAVE TO RIP ME TO PIECES!!
WAAAH
WOW, LOOK AT HIM GO.
GOOD LUCK, FUJIWARA!
YUCK
NO ONE CAN BEAT ME!
YUCK
HFF
HFF
HFF
GORILLIO IS USUALLY SO QUIET.
BUT HE GETS MEAN AROUND THIS TIME EVERY YEAR.
YOU'RE THE FASTEST RUNNER IN JAPAN!
HO HO HO
WE'RE ROOTING FOR YOU, OKUBO!
THIS IS AN ATHLETIC COMPETITION, NOT A POPULARITY CONTEST!
UGH!!
CHOP
AAAH! OKUBO!!

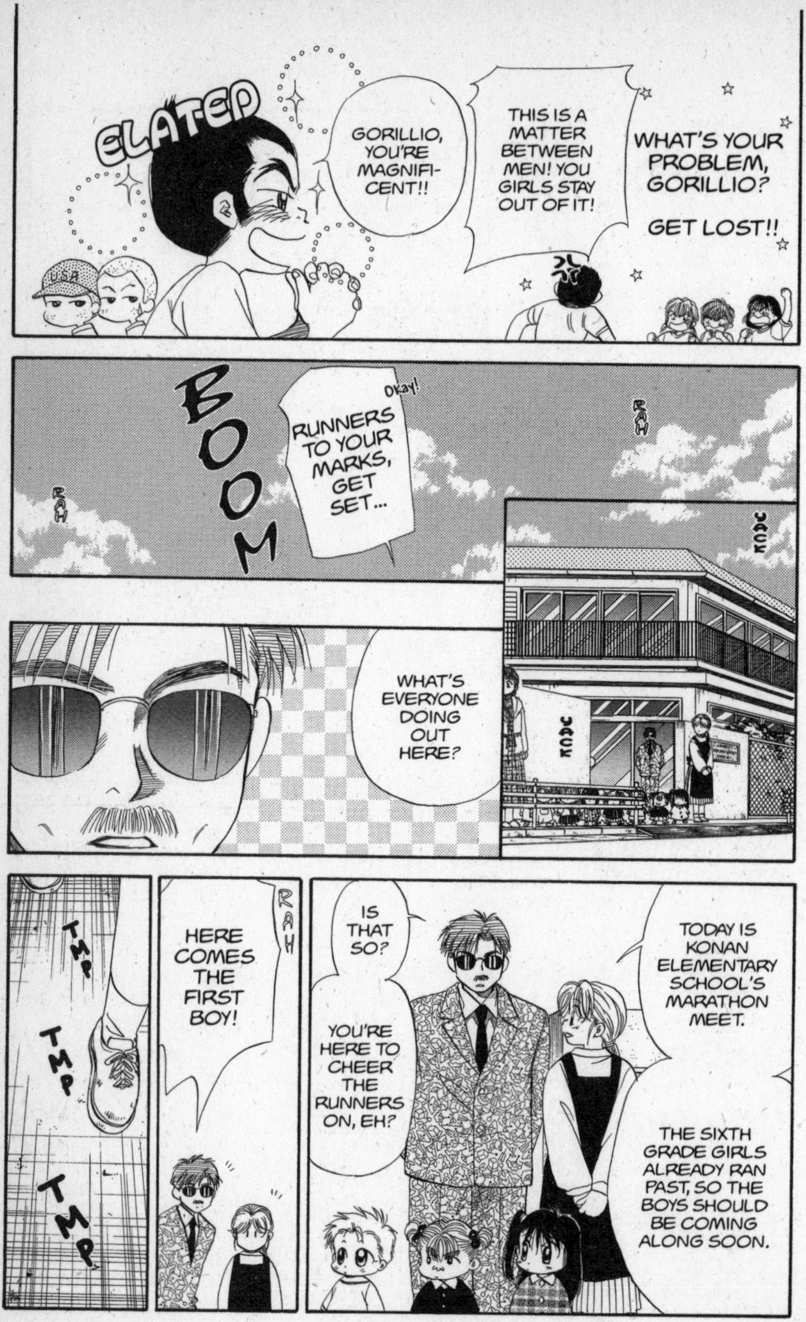
WHAT'S YOUR PROBLEM, GORILLIO?
GET LOST!!
THIS IS A MATTER BETWEEN MEN! YOU GIRLS STAY OUT OF IT!
GORILLIO, YOU'RE MAGNIFI-CENT!!
ELATED
RAH
OKAY!
RUNNERS TO YOUR MARKS, GET SET...
BOOM
RAH
YACK
YACK
WHAT'S EVERYONE DOING OUT HERE?
TODAY IS KONAN ELEMENTARY SCHOOL'S MARATHON MEET.
THE SIXTH GRADE GIRLS ALREADY RAN PAST, SO THE BOYS SHOULD BE COMING ALONG SOON.
IS THAT SO?
YOU'RE HERE TO CHEER THE RUNNERS ON, EH?
RAH
HERE COMES THE FIRST BOY!
TMP
TMP
TMP

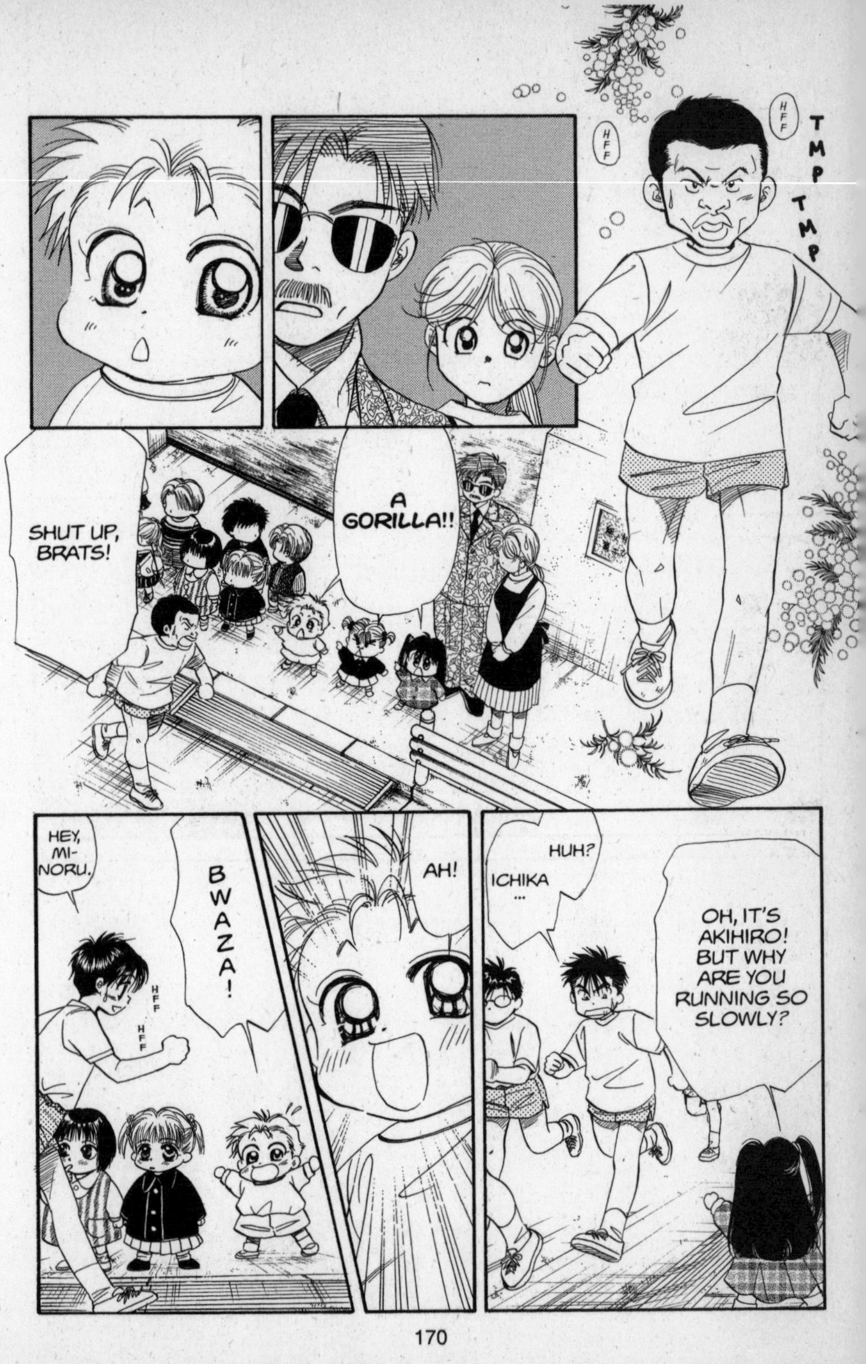
HFF
HFF
TMP TMP TMP
A GORILLA!!
SHUT UP, BRATS!
OH, IT'S AKIHIRO! BUT WHY ARE YOU RUNNING SO SLOWLY?
HUH? ICHIKA...
AH!
BWAZA!
HEY, MI-NORU.
HFF HFF

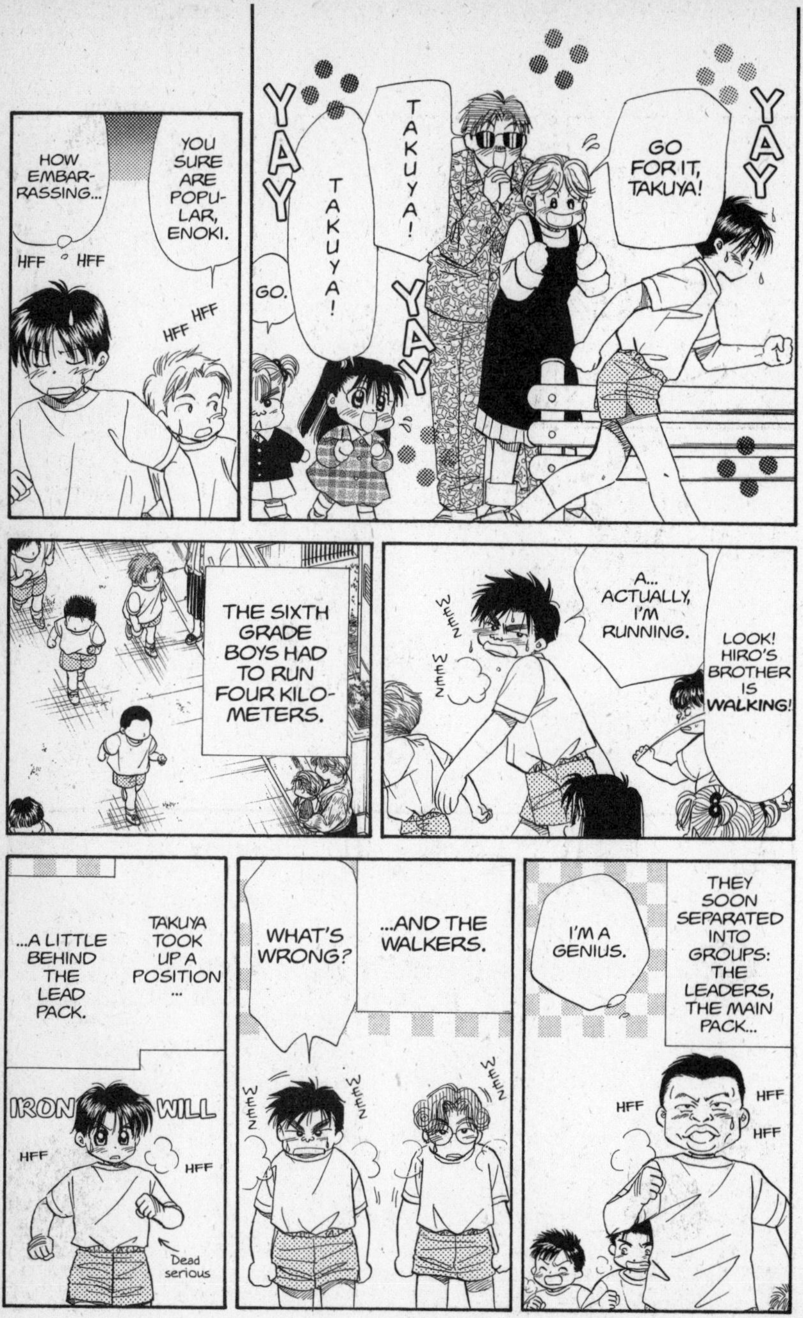
YAY
GO FOR IT, TAKUYA!
YAY
TAKUYA!
TAKUYA!
YAY
GO.
YAY
YOU SURE ARE POPULAR, ENOKI.
HOW EMBARRASSING...
HFF HFF
HFF HFF
LOOK! HIRO'S BROTHER IS WALKING!
A... ACTUALLY, I'M RUNNING.
WEEZ
WEEZ
THE SIXTH GRADE BOYS HAD TO RUN FOUR KILOMETERS.
THEY SOON SEPARATED INTO GROUPS: THE LEADERS, THE MAIN PACK...
I'M A GENIUS.
HFF
HFF
HFF
...AND THE WALKERS.
WHAT'S WRONG?
WEEZ
WEEZ
WEEZ
TAKUYA TOOK UP A POSITION ...
...A LITTLE BEHIND THE LEAD PACK.
IRON WILL
HFF
HFF
Dead serious

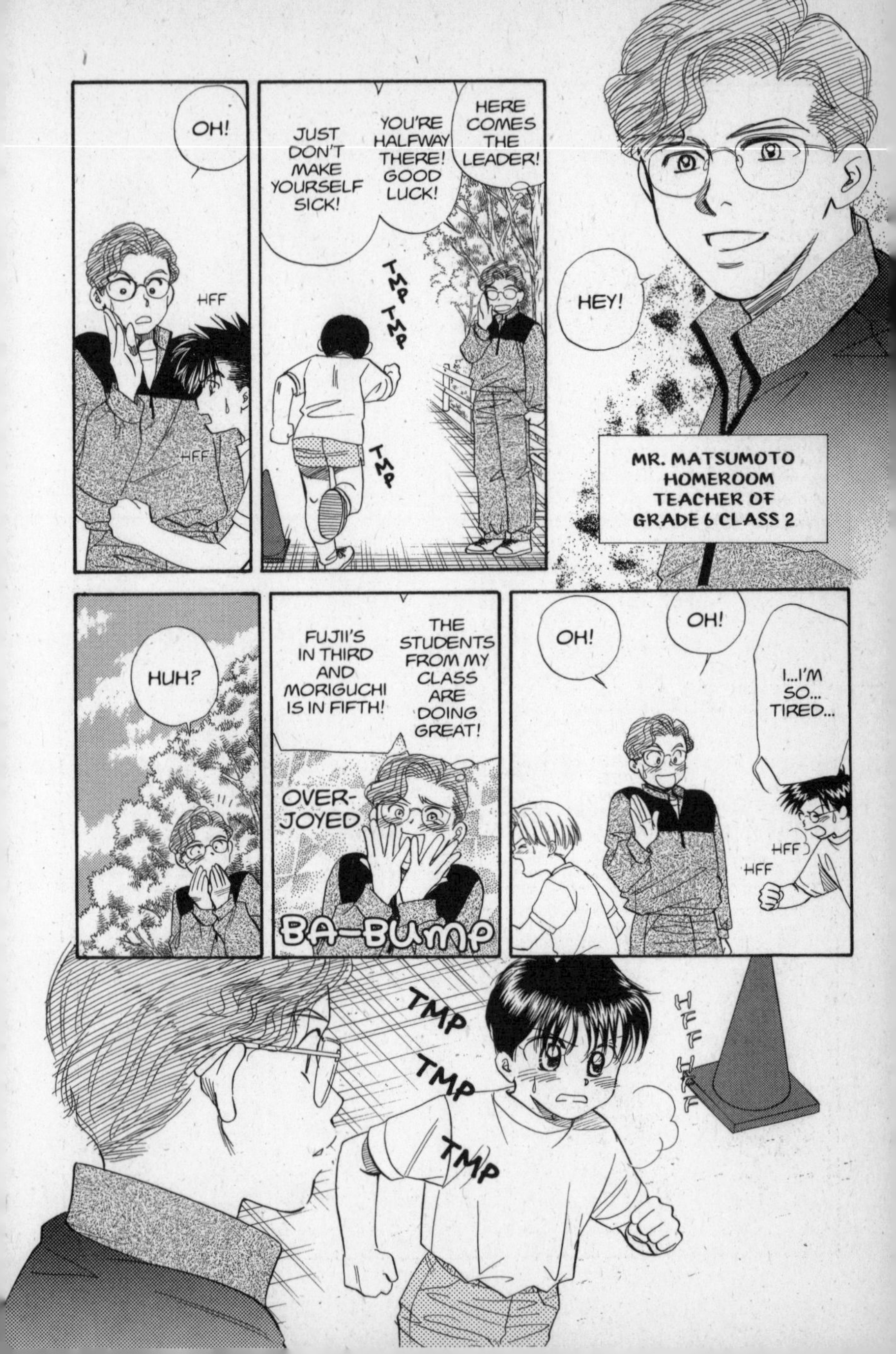
HEY!
MR. MATSUMOTO HOMEROOM TEACHER OF GRADE 6 CLASS 2
HERE COMES THE LEADER!
YOU'RE HALFWAY THERE! GOOD LUCK!
JUST DON'T MAKE YOURSELF SICK!
TMP TMP
TMP
OH!
HFF
HFF
I...I'M SO... TIRED...
OH!
OH!
HFF
HFF
THE STUDENTS FROM MY CLASS ARE DOING GREAT!
FUJII'S IN THIRD AND MORIGUCHI IS IN FIFTH!
OVER-JOYED
BA-BUMP
HUH?
HFF HFF
TMP
TMP
TMP

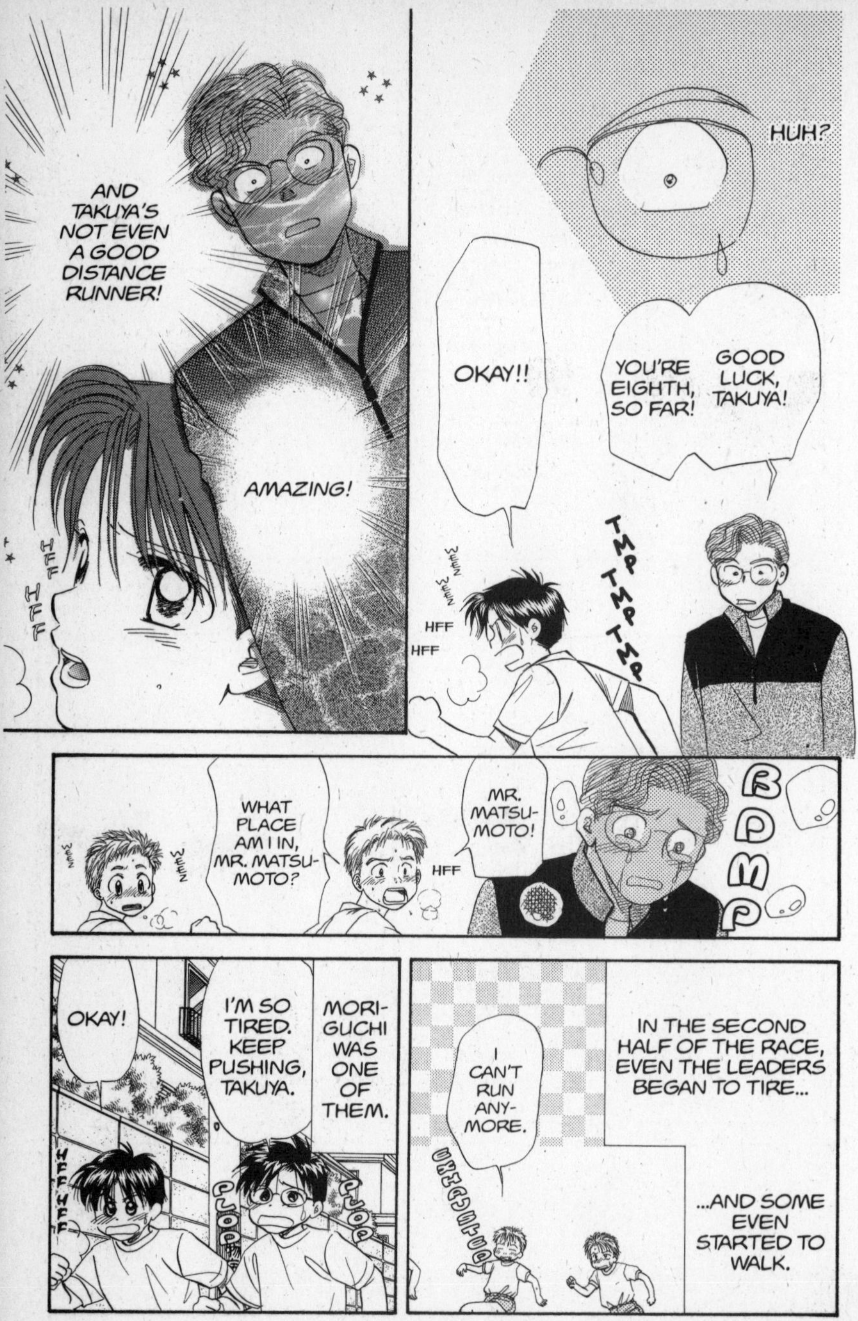

HUH?
GOOD LUCK, TAKUYA!
YOU'RE EIGHTH, SO FAR!
OKAY!!
WEEN WEEN
HFF HFF
TMP TMP TMP TMP
AND TAKUYA'S NOT EVEN A GOOD DISTANCE RUNNER!
AMAZING!
HFF HFF
MR. MATSU-MOTO!
HFF
WHAT PLACE AM I IN, MR. MATSU-MOTO?
WEEN WEEN
IN THE SECOND HALF OF THE RACE, EVEN THE LEADERS BEGAN TO TIRE...
I CAN'T RUN ANY-MORE.
...AND SOME EVEN STARTED TO WALK.
MORI-GUCHI WAS ONE OF THEM.
I'M SO TIRED. KEEP PUSHING, TAKUYA.
OKAY!
PLOP PLOP
HFF HFF

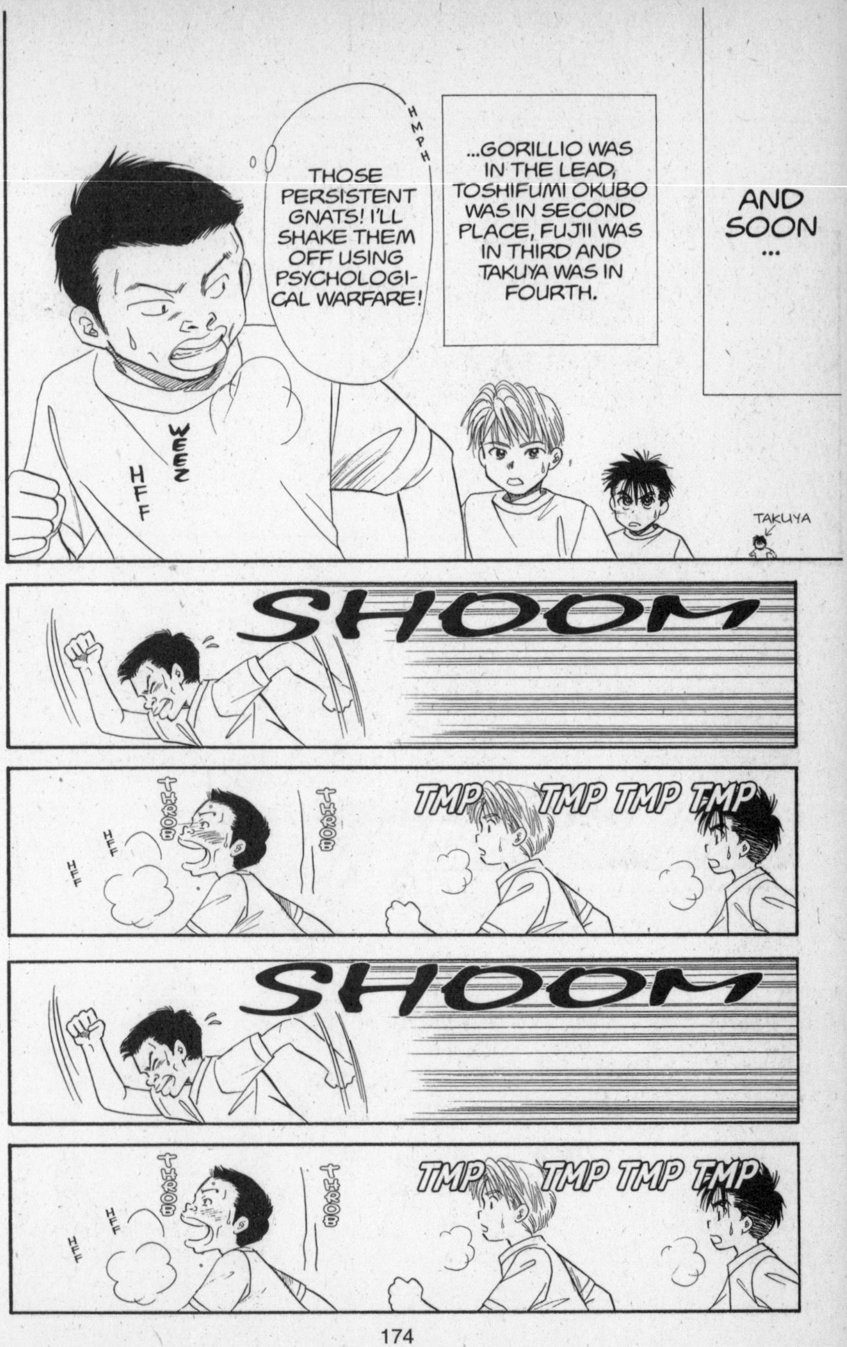
AND SOON ...
...GORILLIO WAS IN THE LEAD, TOSHIFUMI OKUBO WAS IN SECOND PLACE, FUJII WAS IN THIRD AND TAKUYA WAS IN FOURTH.
HMPH
THOSE PERSISTENT GNATS! I'LL SHAKE THEM OFF USING PSYCHOLOGICAL WARFARE!
WEEZ
HFF
TAKUYA
SHOOM
TMP TMP TMP TMP
THROB
THROB
HFF
HFF
SHOOM
TMP TMP TMP TMP
THROB
THROB
HFF
HFF

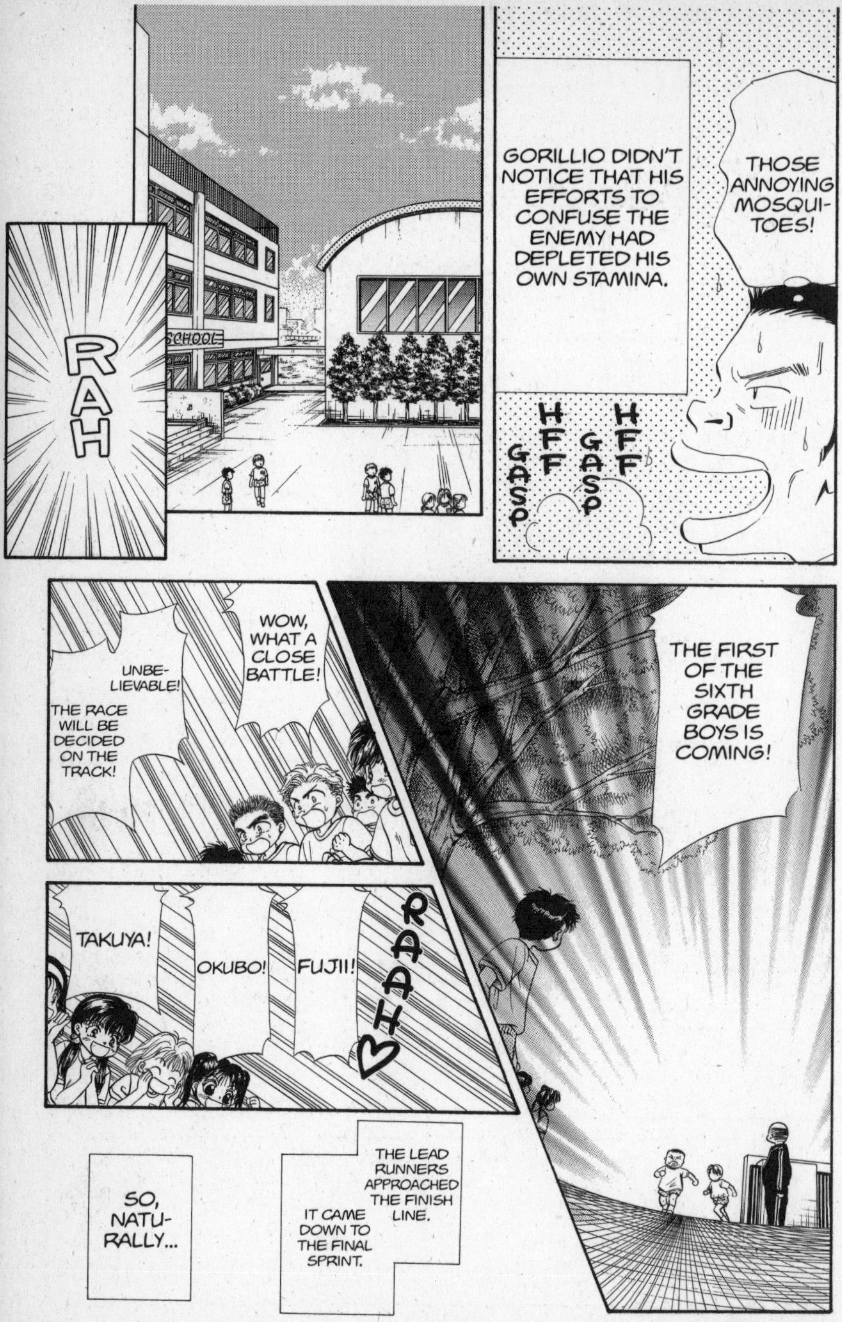
THOSE ANNOYING MOSQUI-TOES!
GORILLIO DIDN'T NOTICE THAT HIS EFFORTS TO CONFUSE THE ENEMY HAD DEPLETED HIS OWN STAMINA.
HFF HFF
GASP GASP
RAH
THE FIRST OF THE SIXTH GRADE BOYS IS COMING!
WOW, WHAT A CLOSE BATTLE!
UNBE-LIEVABLE!
THE RACE WILL BE DECIDED ON THE TRACK!
RAAH♥
FUJII!
OKUBO!
TAKUYA!
THE LEAD RUNNERS APPROACHED THE FINISH LINE.
IT CAME DOWN TO THE FINAL SPRINT.
SO, NATU-RALLY...

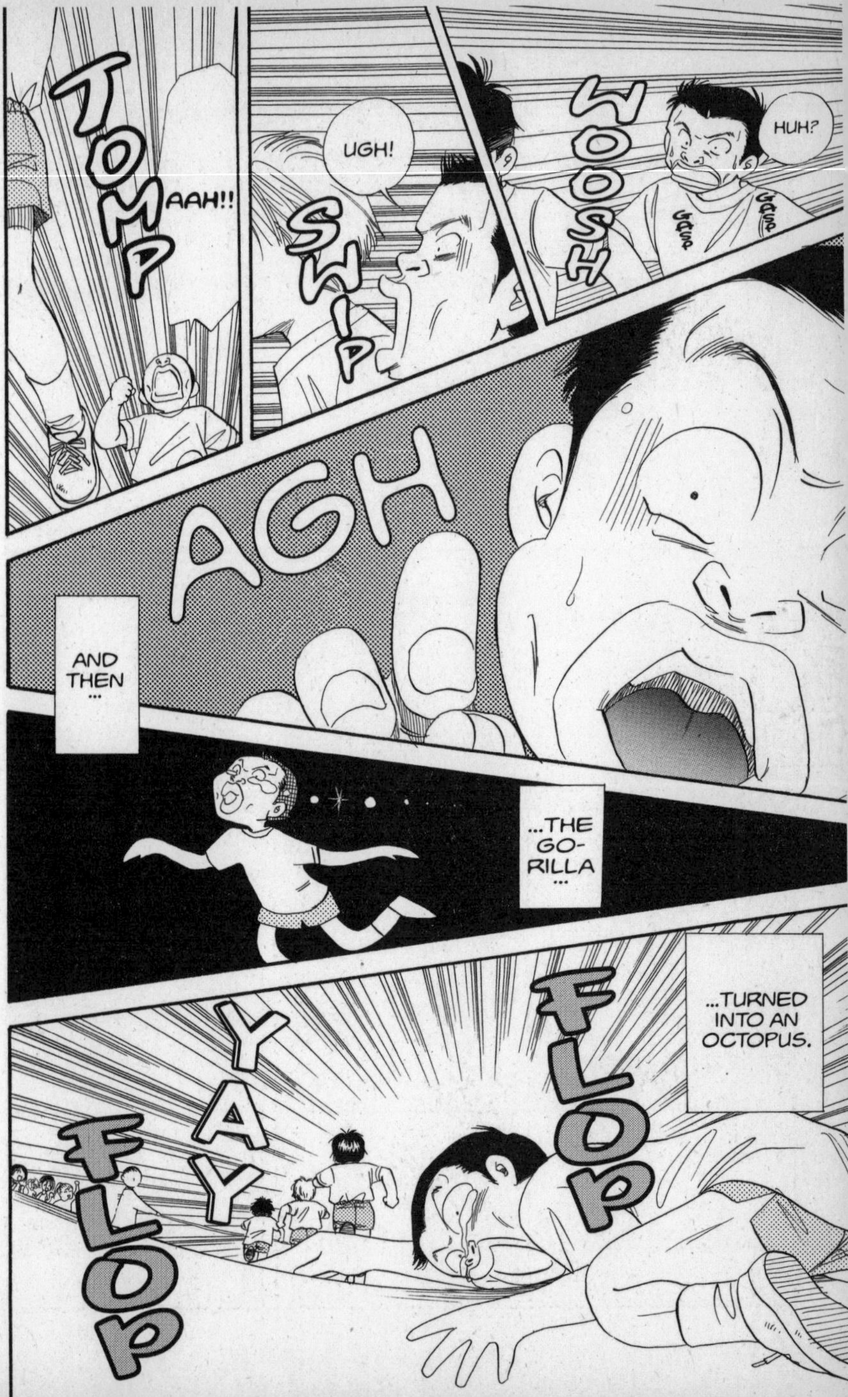
HUH?
WOOSH
GASP
GASP
UGH!
SWIP
TOMP
AAH!!
AGH
AND THEN ...
...THE GO-RILLA ...
...TURNED INTO AN OCTOPUS.
FLOP
YAY
FLOP

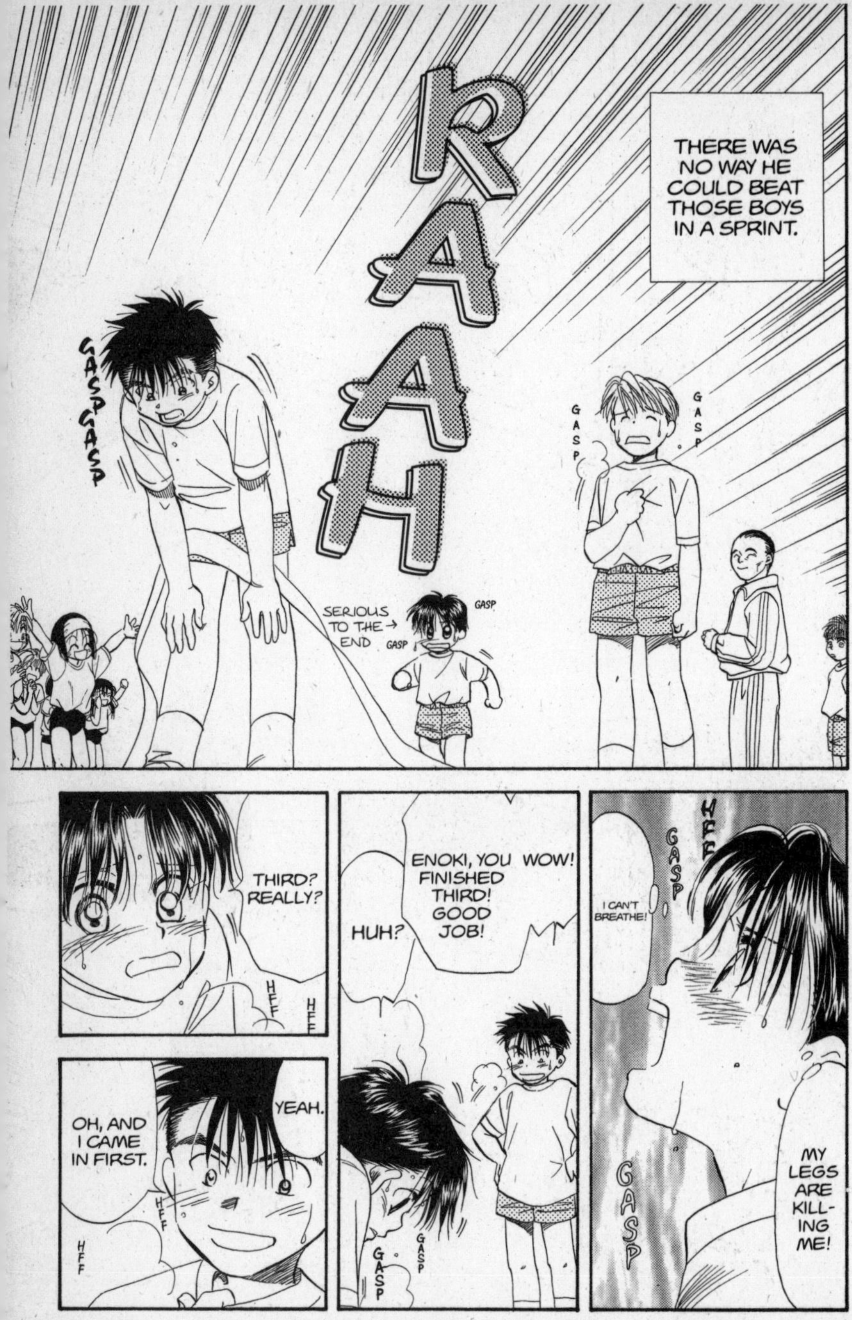
THERE WAS NO WAY HE COULD BEAT THOSE BOYS IN A SPRINT.
RAAH
GASP GASP
GASP
SERIOUS TO THE END
GASP
GASP
GASP GASP
HFF
GASP
I CAN'T BREATHE!
GASP
MY LEGS ARE KILLING ME!
WOW!
ENOKI, YOU FINISHED THIRD! GOOD JOB!
HUH?
GASP
GASP
THIRD? REALLY?
HFF
HFF
YEAH.
OH, AND I CAME IN FIRST.
HFF
HFF

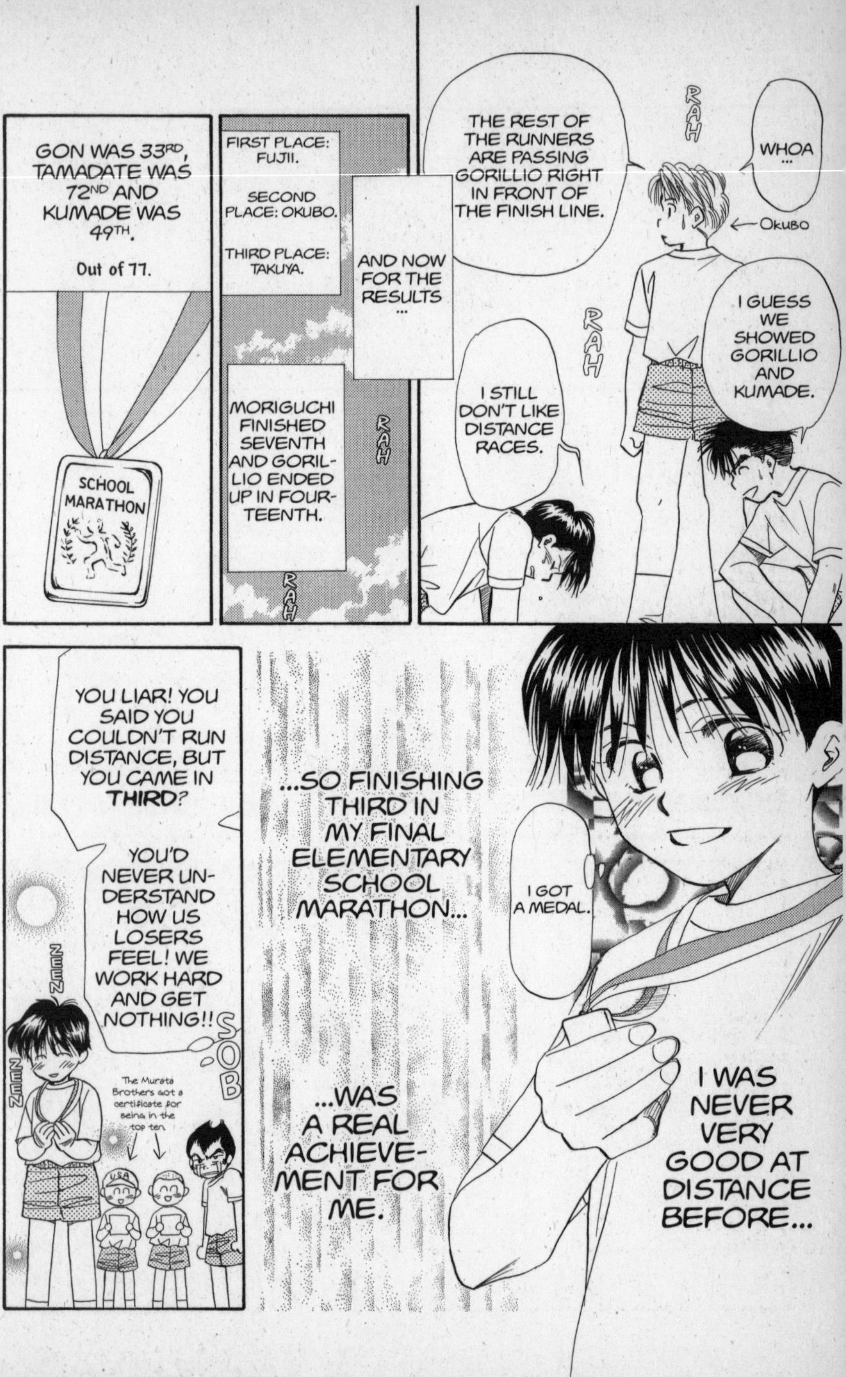
THE REST OF THE RUNNERS ARE PASSING GORILLIO RIGHT IN FRONT OF THE FINISH LINE.
RAH
WHOA...
Okubo
I GUESS WE SHOWED GORILLIO AND KUMADE.
RAH
I STILL DON'T LIKE DISTANCE RACES.
AND NOW FOR THE RESULTS...
FIRST PLACE: FUJII.
SECOND PLACE: OKUBO.
THIRD PLACE: TAKUYA.
MORIGUCHI FINISHED SEVENTH AND GORILLIO ENDED UP IN FOURTEENTH.
RAH
RAH
GON WAS 33RD, TAMADATE WAS 72ND AND KUMADE WAS 49TH.
Out of 77.
SCHOOL MARATHON
I WAS NEVER VERY GOOD AT DISTANCE BEFORE...
I GOT A MEDAL.
...SO FINISHING THIRD IN MY FINAL ELEMENTARY SCHOOL MARATHON...
...WAS A REAL ACHIEVEMENT FOR ME.
YOU LIAR! YOU SAID YOU COULDN'T RUN DISTANCE, BUT YOU CAME IN THIRD?
YOU'D NEVER UNDERSTAND HOW US LOSERS FEEL! WE WORK HARD AND GET NOTHING!!
SOB
ZEEN
ZEEN
The Murata Brothers got a certificate for being in the top ten.
USA

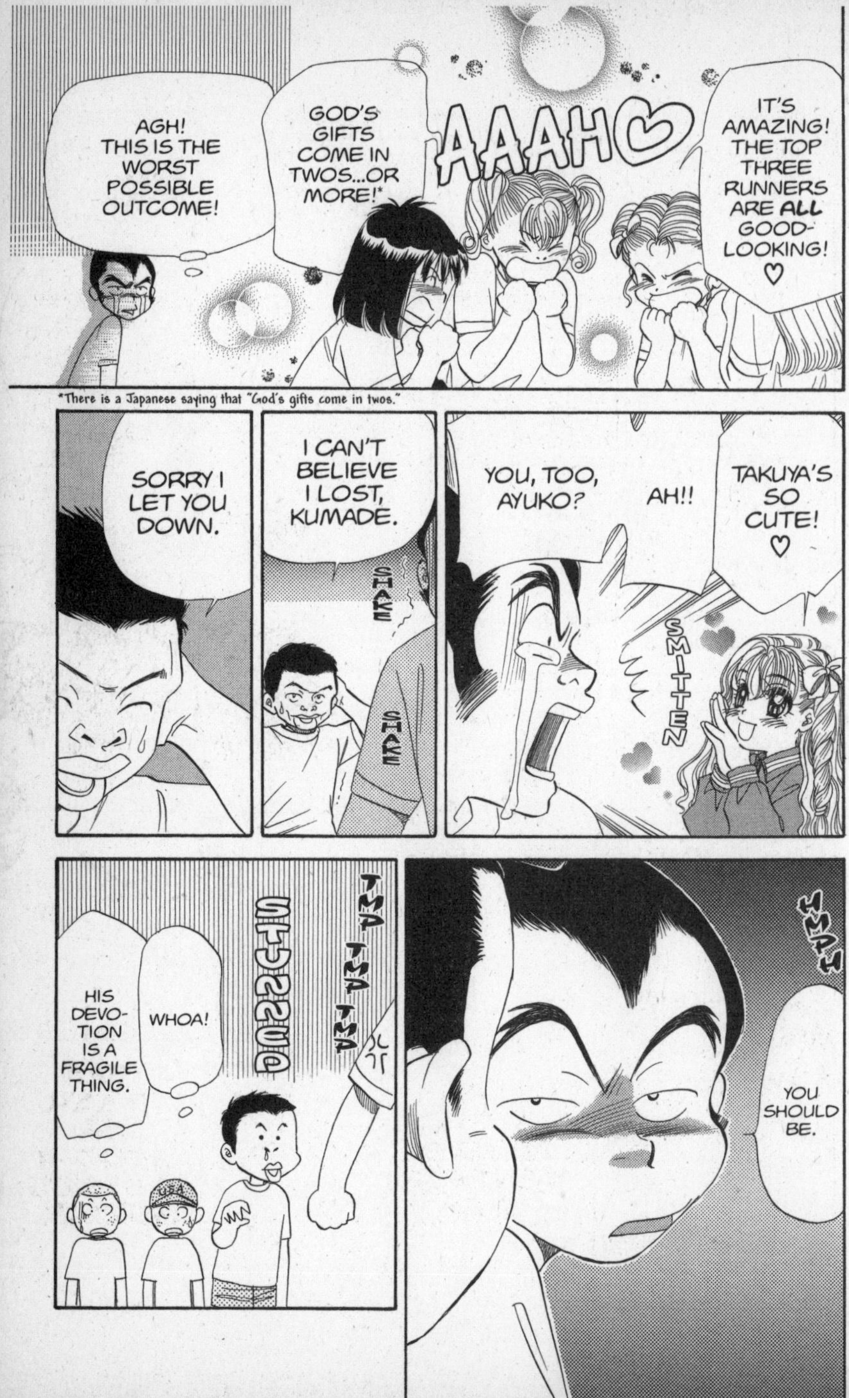
IT'S AMAZING! THE TOP THREE RUNNERS ARE **ALL** GOOD-LOOKING! ♡
AAAH♡
GOD'S GIFTS COME IN TWOS...OR MORE!*
AGH! THIS IS THE WORST POSSIBLE OUTCOME!
TAKUYA'S SO CUTE! ♡
AH!!
SMITTEN
YOU, TOO, AYUKO?
I CAN'T BELIEVE I LOST, KUMADE.
SHAKE
SHAKE
SORRY I LET YOU DOWN.
HMPH
YOU SHOULD BE.
TMP TMP TMP
STUNNED
WHOA!
HIS DEVOTION IS A FRAGILE THING.

*There is a Japanese saying that "God's gifts come in twos."

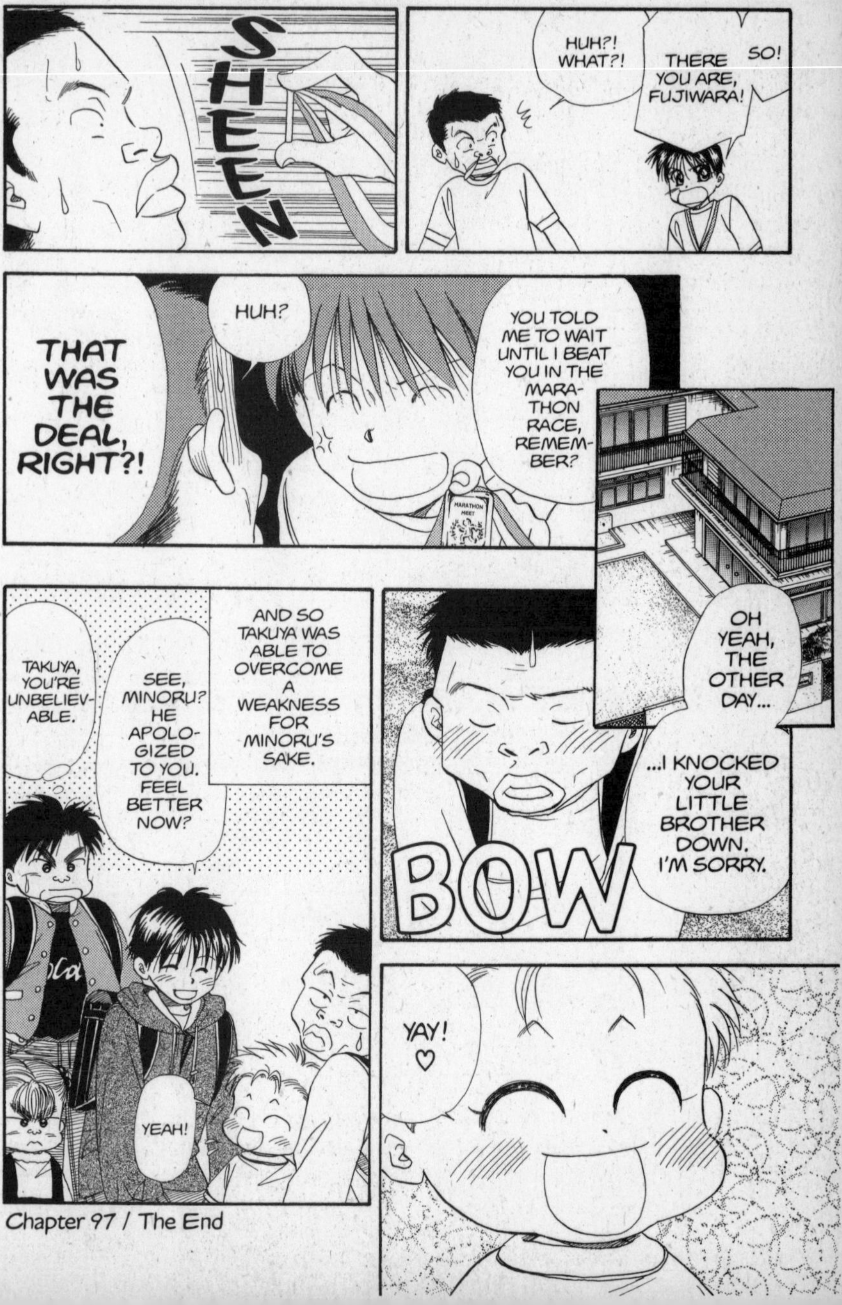
SO!
THERE YOU ARE, FUJIWARA!
HUH?! WHAT?!
SHEEN
YOU TOLD ME TO WAIT UNTIL I BEAT YOU IN THE MARATHON RACE, REMEMBER?
HUH?
THAT WAS THE DEAL, RIGHT?!
MARATHON MEET
OH YEAH, THE OTHER DAY...
...I KNOCKED YOUR LITTLE BROTHER DOWN. I'M SORRY.
BOW
YAY! ♡
AND SO TAKUYA WAS ABLE TO OVERCOME A WEAKNESS FOR MINORU'S SAKE.
SEE, MINORU? HE APOLOGIZED TO YOU. FEEL BETTER NOW?
TAKUYA, YOU'RE UNBELIEVABLE.
YEAH!

Chapter 97 / The End

Tell us what you think about Shojo Beat Manga!

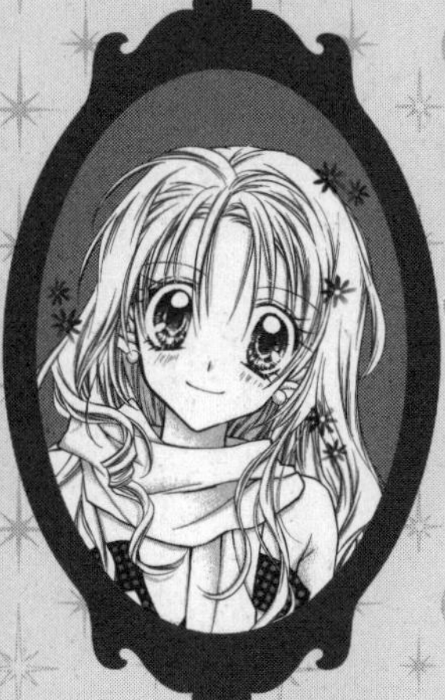

Our survey is now available online. Go to:

shojobeat.com/mangasurvey

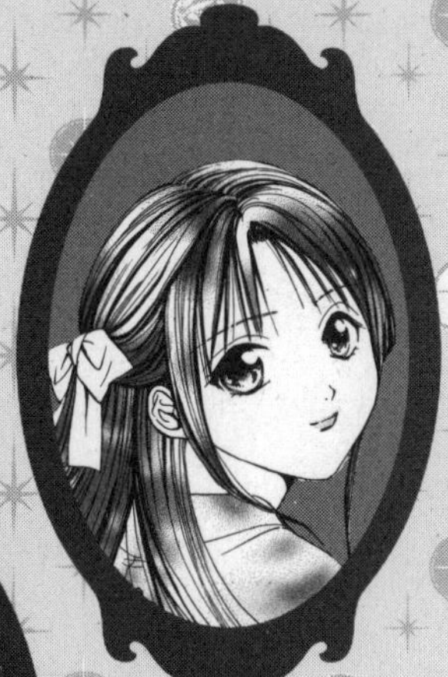

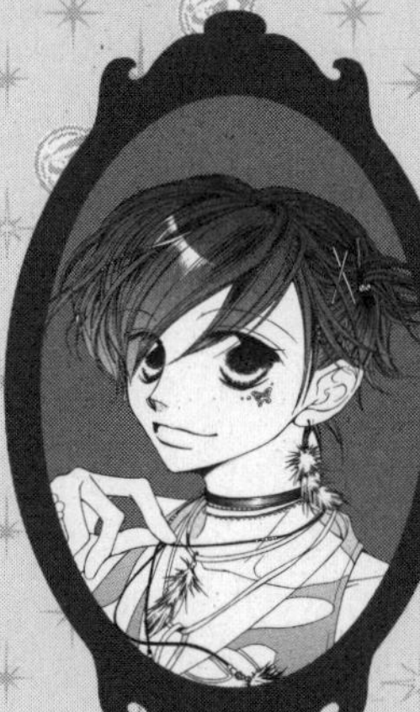

Help us make our product offerings better!

viz media

Shojo Beat MANGA from the HEART

THE REAL DRAMA BEGINS IN...

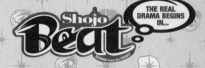